THE PLAIN VANILLA ASTROLOGER

by
Pat Geisler

ACS Publications

by Pat Geisler

Cover and book design by Maria Kay Simms

Library of Congress Control Number 2013935604

International Standard Book Number: 978-1-934976-48-7

Published by ACS Publications,
an imprint of Starcrafts LLC
334-A Calef Highway, Epping, NH 03042
http://www.acspublications.com
http://www.starcraftspublishing.com
http://www.astrocom.com

Printed in the United States of America

THE PLAIN VANILLA ASTROLOGER

by PAT GEISLER

Dedication

This book is for my family—

For my children, Deborah, Susan, Douglas and Elizabeth, who kept me going all the years I worked long hours as an astrologer and journalist and who were my first fans and biggest boosters; It's for my dad, who saved the poem "The Astrologer's Song" by Rudyard Kipling for me years before I ever thought of becoming a professional astrologer; for my sister, Judith, who kept a record of my predictions for her for nearly three decades and gave me priceless feedback.

It's for all the people in my astrological family who make me proud to be one of them. I hope this book will find a place on their shelves.

Table of Contents

List of Charts Shown in This Book

Note: Some material in this book has appeared elsewhere. The "Tale of the Dragon" is posted on the Zodiacal Zepher (*www.zodical .com*) and other articles are on various websites.

The Plain Vanilla Astrologer
Introduction

Dear reader (she said, in her old-fashioned introduction):

You must know something about astrology or
we wouldn't be meeting like this.

So, I won't bother telling you how to cast a chart or what an Ascendant is. Other people do that just fine. I don't like to teach that part of astrology anymore anyway. Thank God for those who do. Go see them. Pay them lots of money and learn what they can teach you and then we'll talk.

In fact, I will assume you know most of the basics. I'll try to remember to explain new terms as I go, but if you run into something that isn't clear, get a good astrology text and look it up. Then come on back. Don't write me and ask. I'll probably be senile by the time this is finished.

What this book is about is how I see things. I hope you'll find it useful and interesting. If it begins to bore you, for heaven's sake stop reading and go do something more amusing. We learn best what we enjoy. I've enjoyed astrology ever since I began learning it. I want to share some of my pleasure with you.

This is not intended as a book for beginners or the general public, but rather for the astrologer who wants to see how the parts fit together. The chapters are meant to illuminate a subject, rather than be exhaustive treatises. Plan to get more information from other authors. I have listed the names of several and recommended their books. This is not a complete textbook. I should probably repeat that a few more times for people who will howl when I have omitted something that interests them.

The book got written only because my friends have nagged me unmercifully for years. They all but got out of the car and pushed me to the finish line. In fact, its existence owes a great deal to Cecilia Mazzola of Houston, TX, who kept an enormous collection of material I had written in various places over the years and Chris Turner of Sydney, Australia, who managed to sort it all out for me. She spent many, many hours on the work, making me feel guilty if I lagged behind her efforts to get the job done. Without them I would cheerfully have lapsed back into a recliner with a new knitting project.

Besides, Keiko Ito of Tokyo, Japan, was sending me things to keep me on track.

There are other friends who read parts and encouraged me and some who offered experienced help along the way. My daughter Deborah helped edit the finished product. And as I say, many others just stood in the background with large forks and jabbed me when it looked like I was slowing down on the way to the finish line.

A few pieces of the material in here have seen the light of day in other places. I include them since they say what I want to say and I didn't think there was any particular merit in rewriting it to sound different.

The title to this book started out as a joke. An astrologer friend began calling me the "plain vanilla astrologer" in contrast to "fancy" astrologers with longer wind and bigger theories. It amused me. I figured fancy flavors come and go but plain vanilla lasts forever.

So, if you're in the mood for vanilla, pull up a chair and let's talk. Just don't expect me to have all the answers.

The Astrologer's Song
by Rudyard Kipling

Oh, look at the heavens above, and behold
The planets that love us, all harnessed with gold.
What chariots, what horses against us can bide,
When the stars in their courses do fight on our side?

All thoughts, all desires that are under the Sun
Are one with their fires - - and we, also, are one.
All matter, all spirit, all fashion, all frame
Receives and inherits its strength from the same.

Oh, man, who denies any power but thine own,
That power in the highest is mightily shown;
Nor yet in the lowest is that power made less clear;
Oh, man, if thou knowest, what treasure is here!

Earth quakes in her throes, and we wonder for why,
But the blind planet knows when her ruler is nigh.
Attuned since creation to perfect accord,
She sings at her station and yearns to her lord.

The waters have risen, the springs are unbound,
The floods break their prison and raven around.
No ramparts can hold them, their fury will last
'Til the sign that controls them sinks low, or swings past.

Though terror o'ertake us, we'll not be afraid,
No power can unmake us save that which has made.
Nor yet beyond reason nor hope shall we fall,
All things have their season and mercy crowns all.

Then doubt not, ye fearful, the Eternal is King!
Up, heart, and be cheerful, and lustily sing!
What chariots, what horses against us can bide
When the stars in their courses do fight on our side?

Chapter 1

East of the Sun and west of the Moon
Key Factors in Compatibility

Check Dare & Sun/moon mid point

In an old fairy tale a lovely young maiden must make a long trip to find her beloved, who is under an enchantment. She must find him in the land "east of the sun and west of the moon."

In astrology, that's the Sun/Moon midpoint, the place half way between, where the doorway to selfhood lies. In human relationships, it is one of the strongest contacts between any two people, and is particularly significant in gauging the strength of the tie between man and woman.

The Sun/Moon midpoint is like the front door to your house and anyone who has a planet that contacts it by conjunction or opposition is like a person with a key to your house. They can walk right in, look around all they wish, understand everything completely and come and go as they please. The person with such a key never misunderstands your motivations and perceives much that is not spoken between you. In short, you have few—or no— secrets from them. They know who you are.

Those who have their benefics (Jupiter or Venus) or their Sun or Moon near your Sun/Moon midpoint tend to stay in your life forever and become close friends. They are like welcome visitors whenever they come and bring cookies and birthday presents. Mercury there is like the town gossip, who knows just what you want to hear, for instance.

Because they know who you are and like you there is a great sense of security in the relationship. You can say absolutely stupid things and forget important anniversaries and they will forgive you and still be a friend. You can trust what they tell you and they will do you good wherever they can.

People who have malefics there understand you also, but have a capacity to hurt you that no one else does. They know how to "get under your skin."

A woman whose Sun/Moon midpoint is contacted by a man's Mars, for instance, may find him intensely attractive sexually but feel threatened by his temper. She is apt to get hurt in the relationship if the man is not careful or is feeling vengeful. It is not necessarily a violent contact, but it can be.

When the contacting planet is Saturn, the planet person thinks the midpoint person needs more structure or discipline in some way and the Sun/Moon midpoint person feels rejection and humiliation and often a sense of coldness from the Saturn person. This aspect is also harmful to the midpoint person. Never take advice from anyone whose Saturn falls near your Sun/Moon midpoint. They don't have your welfare in mind, just their own idea of what you **should** be.

The outer planets, when in contact with the point, have their own effects. Neptune is glamour, lack of a realistic viewpoint or outright deception. Never rely on it. Uranus brings unexpected crises and breakups. It can be exciting, but very unreliable. Pluto will plunder you of material goods, or try manipulation and coercion. It can be criminal trouble, too, or merely reflect an association that is not good for you or that takes you "down" into a lesser and more negative environment.

This midpoint only works by conjunction or opposition—I do not use any other aspect to it at all. Orb is pretty tight, too. The opposition to the midpoint is somewhat like someone at the back door. Less obvious, perhaps, than the front door, but those who come to the back door have been there before and are just as familiar with the way in. Pride is sometimes a defense against unwelcome intrusion with the conjunction. It deserts one entirely when the opposition is in force.

The reason this aspect is so strongly felt is the sense of nakedness and defenselessness the midpoint person has in the relationship. In a good relationship, there is so much trust one barely thinks about it. Not so when the malefics are involved. No one likes to feel vulnerable to someone who doesn't like them. That kind of contact is very uncomfortable and difficult.

All human relationships have pluses and minuses. Those which involve the planets of one person to the Sun/Moon midpoint of another are particularly powerful in their effects and offer absolutely reliable information to the astrologer. They are often the reason why siblings do or do not become "friends" in adulthood, for instance, and why partners do or do not ever truly get the most out of their cooperation.

In all chart comparison work, an aspect to Sun/Moon midpoint is at the top of the list. The second most sensitive point of contact between two charts is the Moon of one to the Ascendant of the other. Carl Jung, the famous psychologist who did what is generally accepted as the first true statistical study in astrology, found that the most likely contact between two people who married each other was the Moon of one to the Ascendant degree or the rising sign of the other.

The Ascendant is the outer persona of the individual, the point of entry to the world, and the keynote of each life. The Moon symbolizes all our emotional needs, our habits and lifestyle and our grounding in the world. It is also the past which has made us what we are today.

Therefore, when these two sensitive points conjoin, the emotional self of the one meets the persona of the other and sympathy occurs. This contact is another that opens the door to instant understanding between two people. When any two people have it, they leap over all the normal preliminaries and seem to start their relationship in the middle, where true accord lies. Between people of the same sex, it is instant friendship.

Between a man and a woman it is a kind of deep friendship that can lead very quickly to other kinds of intimacy if the rest of the chart agrees. If not, they will still greet each other with warmth even if years have passed since they last met.

Because the Moon is so significant in the emotional life, anyone whose Moon falls near another's Moon also has a kind of instant concord with them. It is said that contacts of the Moon to another's Sun also bring that, but I am not so sure that is as reliable an indicator. When the Moon contacts another's Sun, the Sun can tend to overwhelm the Moon and it is the Moon person who feels more vulnerable and least in charge of the development of the relationship. If there is friendship, it seems to be at the disposal of the Sun person. If there is animosity, it is the Moon person who suffers.

The opposition between a man's and a woman's Sun and Moon is quite complementary, however. I like it much better than the conjunction, since it seems to lend balance to the relationship.

But Moon to Moon is a powerful emotional contact, and between a man and a woman who are romantically inclined, it can lead to a lifelong tie of the strongest kind. Friends with this aspect are never in doubt about each other. For one thing, they both respond to the same events in the same way. They never have to wonder how the other person "feels" about anything. They know. It creates a trust in each other's responses on a profound level.

They want the same kind of home. They may have different ideas about the furnishings, but they can find a middle ground suprisingly well. What pleases one usually finds an echo in the other and compromise is so normal they hardly give it a thought. They have the same domestic habits. Two people with Scorpio Moons both want things put away when not in use, for instance. They tend to be tidy in their domestic habits and despise mess and clutter. Open cupboard doors and dirty dishes in the sink annoy them both.

Two people with Pisces Moons may like to leave things where they fall. Pisces sees mess as creative. Or at the very least, comfortable. Pisces Moon types don't get upset by a partner who leaves shoes in the kitchen or towels draped over the tub. They clean up when they get around to it and don't expect tidiness to last.

Virgo Moon people are picky and meticulous and want partners who appreciate that and spot the errors that need to be fixed.

It is extremely difficult for outsiders to intrude on a relationship between two people with their Moons conjunct unless one of the partners has become deeply unhappy. Even so, if the injured partner gets anything resembling a true apology or atonement from the other, the third party is apt to find any possibility of a relationship as ephemeral as smoke on a windy day. A married couple with this combination often has the same approach to child rearing and may even want the same size family. They adjust to the partner's desire quite readily on these issues. Both have the same kind of family loyalty and understand it in the other. They have the same emotional responses to mothering and nurture in general. This is not an intellectual thing, but an emotional one and we should be clear on this. One partner can take an entirely different approach to the notion of breast feeding an infant, for instance, based on study or research. And yet when confronted with the reality of it, both will react "in the gut" in the same way.

These three aspects, the Sun/Moon midpoint tie, the Moon/Ascendant and the Moons-conjunct are far and away the most likely to determine the strength of relationships. They are not, of course, the only ones, merely the ones I consider at the top of the heap. Chart comparison or synastry is a blend of many factors in the chart, but starting with these aspects gives any astrologer a good lead.

The question of orb arises. The answer is the same as it is to every question of orb—

the closer the aspect, the stronger it becomes.

For a simple rule of thumb, use about five degrees on either side of the Sun/Moon midpoint, and for the conjunction of two Moons. However, even Moons in the same sign are strong. The Moon/Ascendant contact has surprisingly wide latitude and seems to work somewhat even if the contact is merely in the same sign. Obviously, closer is better.

These are not exact answers, I know, but I have seen some very strong relationships at wider orbs and others with no apparent interest in each other at closer ones. You may ask if it is due to other factors in the birth patterns and we will both be quite happy when I say yes. Nothing is quite as cut-and-dried as we should like, sometimes, but these aspects are as reliable as any I have found.

They do not give duration, of course, nor describe where the relationship is headed, nor whether it is sexual or merely friendly. Those things are elsewhere in the chart. They merely establish emotional sympathy, a necessary precursor to any relationship between human beings, who are, after all, formed with emotional natures.

> ***But in the place east of the Sun and west of the Moon,
> we can all find someone to love.***

Chapter 2

Someone to love
The Partner We Seek

We are born knowing the kind of partner we want. We are also born knowing the kind of sexual relationship we will want when we grow up.

House 7 describes our partnership needs, but Venus and Mars also tell us about the sexual ones. The Mars drive is the sexual area. Venus is its emotional component. House 8 describes what we want in a physical relationship. House 2 is what we bring to it.

Our first experiences may or may not satisfy us. Some people are never satisfied by sex even if they are deeply in love with the person they are sleeping with. Others may find a dramatic awakening when they fall in love, but for others, it takes a few years and a long and steady relationship before that occurs.

One of the big reasons is that Venus is emotional satisfaction and Mars is the act. It is a big help if one partner's love-making "satisfies" the other one and vice versa. Mars may stir up the sexual drive but if there is no Venus contact, there's not likely to be the same sense of "satisfaction." Conjunctions are not necessary, sextiles and trines will do nicely.

This simple awareness is a big help for astrologers who counsel couples because some people spend a lot of time in bed without feeling "satisfied" by it. A Venus in Gemini is quite satisfied by conversation afterwards but the Venus in Cancer wants to be cuddled and if the cuddling is missing, there goes the satisfaction, no matter how great the sex act itself was.

Venus in Taurus is highly sensual and enjoys sex, but is surprisingly picky about the loving part. It loves only once or a very few times in life. Venus in Aquarius is looking for more than a body type to find completion. It wants some one to care about who shares mental interests and ethical standards. When the Mars of one person meets the Venus of another it can be deeply rewarding to both.

It's like pie and ice cream. Some people don't notice if you serve pie plain but others are downright passionate about it: pie must have ice cream with it or it just isn't pie. There are others who crave a slice of nice sharp cheese on theirs.

This works for both sexes, of course, so if there is no Venus/Mars contact between the two charts, the couple really needs to explain to each other what they need to feel satisfied and remember to give it to each other. If there's no Venus/Mars at all they probably aren't going to last long in the sexual field and perhaps the attraction is elsewhere. Venus aspects are strong in friendship as well, and this is why couples who are also friends usually find satisfaction in sex: there are Venus ties to each other's emotional needs. But when they can't keep their hands off each other, it's Mars.

One's own Venus and Mars package describes how intense the interest is in the opposite sex. Any aspect between them can keep the person sexually aware on a lifelong basis. Parents of teens who have Venus-Mars conjunctions or squares in their natal charts really need to provide some clever chaperoning or things will progress rapidly to all kinds of conclusions as soon as the opposite sex is discovered. And that may happen shortly after they leave the cradle. It's one way to insure survival of the species, of course.

Years ago I realized that there were so many techniques available to me for chart comparisons that I could spend endless hours trying to do them all. I chose to stick to the classic planetary package and have found it quite sufficient to help me see how couples relate to each other.

I don't use any composite charts (I don't know how you average out two people) and mostly don't bother with much in the way of midpoints beyond the key Sun/Moon one. Occasionally if I am bored and have extra time on my hands I might look at more things such as reflex points and declinations, but usually simple longitudinal comparison gives plenty of information. Besides, the other stuff is often merely confirmation of what you already see.

Once in a while a Mars/Venus or Mars/Uranus or Venus/Uranus midpoint will stand up and demand to be noticed in a romantic relationship and I am not averse to using them. I tend to use whatever is at hand and some people can be terribly involved with someone in a midpoint contact. But usually it's also shown several other ways.

I take each chart and put the other person's planets around on the outside. That way I can see how A affects B and how B affects A. The angles and the Moon's nodes offer vital information about the strength and longevity of the contact, regardless of the type of relationship. This works for college roommates of the same sex, or business partners as well. Even your favorite tennis partner will compare well with this technique.

If you are doing charts where you don't find much in the way of natal contacts, look to progressions. There are relationships started under progressions that lose all impact once the progressions wear off. I have seen this in two marriages hastily entered under potent progressions. In both cases the couple simply lost all interest in each other. No fighting, they just became strangers asking themselves "How did we end up here?" One marriage ended quickly, the other lingered but became a "brother-sister" set-up for a few years first.

When such things occur, study Mars and Venus. They really do tell the tale. If the natal package is lacking, the progressions that heighten their importance can fool both people. One man was studying astrology and was completely bewildered that his intense romance went kaflooey in less than a year after the marriage. After I showed him what happened in his chart by progression he lost his guilt over the divorce.

My mother said the old timers always believed in long engagements, because, she said, "You gotta summer with 'em and winter with 'em first." Oddly enough, a year's time is a good way to use up the power of progressions and make sure the fundamental attraction of two natal charts remains. When one person meets another, there are usually progressions that draw them together in the first place. The old timers were right.

One long-time client and her fiancee came for a chart comparison. Their on and off romance had lasted for several years. They had a most unique set-up in their patterns. Their natal contacts were weak but their progressions fluctuated. The couple would have a very intense sexual relationship for a few months and then break up for a year or longer before coming together again for another intense few months.

They weren't happy when I explained how this worked and told them I thought the progressions would fade again and again and eventually simply wear off, leaving them with the natal contacts which were pretty weak to support a long-term marriage. I never heard from either of them again, so I don't know what they did, but they weren't really pleased with their reading at the time. I could only hope they would remember it if they married because they really weren't as compatible as they wanted to be.

As a rule, I rarely do so much on progressions for a chart comparison, but when the natal charts do not show any strong attraction and marriage is being contemplated, it's worth it to check. Whenever you expect to see something and it isn't there, look for the reason. It's usually a progression. One you may see a lot is when one person has a progressed planet moving toward a contact with a planet in the other person's chart. The one whose planet is moving usually initiates contact.

In one case, a woman's progressed Mars, located in Leo in her natal 7th, applied to conjunct the position of the man's Sun in Leo. Now granted, her Mars in his Sun sign showed a likelihood of pretty strong attraction to begin with but it was several degrees from exact. By progression it moved to complete the aspect and that's when she met him. I must say he was very happy about it, too. They had a pretty intense love affair and married promptly. Mars always symbolizes what a woman wants in a man, and hers showed she wanted exactly what he had to offer. Venus is what a man wants in a woman. The man's Venus was in her Sun sign—a classic case of congenial contacts.

We should all be so lucky as to find exactly what we want in a partner. A lot of air sign men can't handle Scorpio intensity. But a lot of Scorpios can't deal with air sign people's emotional detachment either. What happens when they marry each other? They take on the need to learn how to do exactly that. Karma? Who knows, but astrologers see such blendings often enough to wonder. It's worth repeating here that we are not attracted solely by Sun sign but by the totality of the pattern another person has.

What Mars in Libra says is that a woman likes the Libra qualities of thoughtfulness, emotions that are firmly under control, and the way Libras pay attention to one. But you don't have to choose a Libra Sun sign (though that's pretty pizzazzy sometimes) to get the Libra qualities. How about a Libra Ascendant or a Libra Moon? Or a Taurus, who also has all the Venus qualities of sweetness and is bound to charm, too?

Libras and Aries, Taureans and Scorpios are always dealing with the fundamental Venus/Mars attraction and such Sun signs are natural partners in a way. Cancer always looks for the stability that Capricorn represents and Capricorn likes the Cancerian sensitivity and its way of making a good place to come home to. Our Sun signs do give us some basic needs.

But the Moon plays a big role, too. We all marry for some of the emotional satisfaction our mothers gave us and we choose partners that reflect that. True partnership is simply not based solely on physical equipment—but compatibility of heart and mind as well. We all have a partnership "image" we are seeking and that's a topic I sometimes lecture on. Our natal 7th house provides the template. It's really interesting how that built-in template does not necessarily imply a specific sex or romance at all. Partnerships such as college room-mates, or business associates also fit into the 7th house "template."

It's more that we seek someone who fills in our missing spaces. The Mars/Venus part of it is necessary in any full romantic relationship but most of us meet a lot of people in our lives that we will never consider as partnership material. But business partners need compatibility to work together for years and roommates also need a certain sympathy to tolerate each other at close quarters. Such relationships may be vital but not at all romantic. For these and other such pairings, the Venus/Mars component is not the same.

Two gay men who came to me at different times several years apart and who both wanted to discuss partnerships, had entirely different needs. One man was all earth and water. No fire and air planets in his chart at all. He needed somebody in his life who was going to stir up the energy field and stimulate his mind and sociability. The other man, oddly enough (and by the way, I don't believe they knew each other at all) was all air and fire. He needed somebody who was going to gentle him down and provide some stability and empathy for all that flash and dash.

Those descriptions could fit women or heterosexuals just as easily as gay men, obviously. We are all so many things and have so much to give that finding a perfect relationship is a whippoorwill dream. Won't happen. But if we can get some—or most— of our needs met in a partnership, it isn't written in stone that only one sex can always fit the bill.

If either Mars or Venus is heavily involved with Uranus and/or Neptune—particularly with Houses 5 and 8 involved—the individual could swing both ways or only be interested in their own sex. If they don't, then the involvement with those planets shows up in different areas of their lives. The spouse or a partner is not the only 7th house person we meet. In a general sense all strangers fit into the 7th.

All relationships which are sexual but not marital belong to the 5th. A relationship with a lover changes if they marry. Then it gracefully shifts into a true partnership and becomes a 7th house matter. A friendship which may become a sexual affair does not remain an 11th house matter, but becomes a 5th house one.

Some of the very oldest of writers used to use the 3rd house of neighbors for a man's mistress. They apparently distinguished a mistress (a semi-permanent non-marital sexual relationship) from a casual sexual one. Of course, they didn't say what house the woman would use. Now I am not sure why they used that house, except maybe they thought the man would see the mistress when he was "in the neighborhood." Since I have never counseled a man with a true permanent "mistress" whom he actually supported and then visited at regular intervals, I have not had occasion to test that one. Perhaps it's because few men find any need for that in these days when most women support themselves anyway. In which case, the "mistress" is really a "sexual relationship outside of marriage " and would be a 5th house person.

I try to avoid using the outer planets as significators in such matters since the classic rulers give quite adequate information. Use the ruler of the 5th or a planet there unless this is an arrangement where the man supports her completely and keeps a separate establishment for her. Then I think I would go back and look at the ancient rule of the 3rd house. Mistresses were pretty common in earlier times and I should think astrologers then knew what they were doing. Their world was just vastly different from ours.

Look first at the 7th house to see what is happening with any current marital relationship. If that is going sour, hanky panky can show up in the 11th (the spouse's 5th if the partner is suspect) or in the 12th of the other spouse's chart. If it gets that far, many people just separate and get a good lawyer. Not every marriage endures. Many celebrity marriages end up in the courts and the entertainment industry seems to thrive on illicit relationships. Some of them—such as the world-famous Elizabeth Taylor-Richard Burton affair of the late 20th century—begin when the two actors are working together, particularly in the role of lovers. Those two were pretty compatible, or might have been, had it not been for the heavy drinking which marred their relationship possibilities. Still, they chased each other around the world and married each other twice.

The nodes are involved whenever a significant person enters our lives, since the nodes seem to deal with all the relationships we have. I talk more about the nodes in another chapter. But since our children are significant in our lives, it's no surprise to me that they are also usually involved in nodal ties. Some are closely tied to their parents, or one of them perhaps but that's true of any family, especially with more than one child. The "Daddy's girl" or the "Mother's Boy" have been around for millennia.

Some people marry those who were born on the same day or very close to it. I think of such close temporal contacts as verging on the inevitable. Those people have nodes which link up. Sometimes you will find key planets conjunct one of the nodes, which ze-roes in on that of the other person. Say one party has a Saturn/South Node package. The other will also have the same package, so that each has Saturn on the other's South Node. Those are enormously powerful ties and show enduring relationships with lessons to be learned on both sides. If it were the North Node and Saturn it would be equally enduring but each would help the other to grow in some key way. The powerful compulsion is less evident in this one. It all goes back to the natal pattern. Some natal patterns attract each other and some don't. It's as simple as that.

There is an old idea that circulates periodically about "soul mates." I have been asked about it by a great many romantic clients at various times over the years. I am not sure what the true meaning is but here is some material I have read from older authors.

Madame Blavatsky's book, *The Secret Doctrine* contains information on the idea and so does *The Light of Egypt* by Thomas Burgoyne. Both of these books were published in the 19th century but both are still around for those interested in the idea. I'll just talk about Burgoyne's notion, since it was the clearest explanation I ever read.

Burgoyne said that the spiritual entity—the soul— that was given individual form by the creator was too pure and lofty a being to experience earthly incarnation very easily. In order for the soul to become incarnated, it had to be somehow weakened, or toned down, so it was split into two parts, in which each got the same qualities but in different proportions, he said. The male would have less of the female qualities and the female would have less of the male qualities. The male would function as positive on the physical and mental planes (more) but negative (less) on the emotional and spiritual ones. The female would get less of physical and mental planes and more of the positive emotional and spiritual ones, his book explains. Both would experience many lives as they grew and only when the earthly plane had been left far behind and some of the higher planes had been passed through as well would the twin souls re-combine in order to complete the return journey back to the creator. Meanwhile, it would be best if they did not meet while incarnated as it would merely slow them down, he wrote.

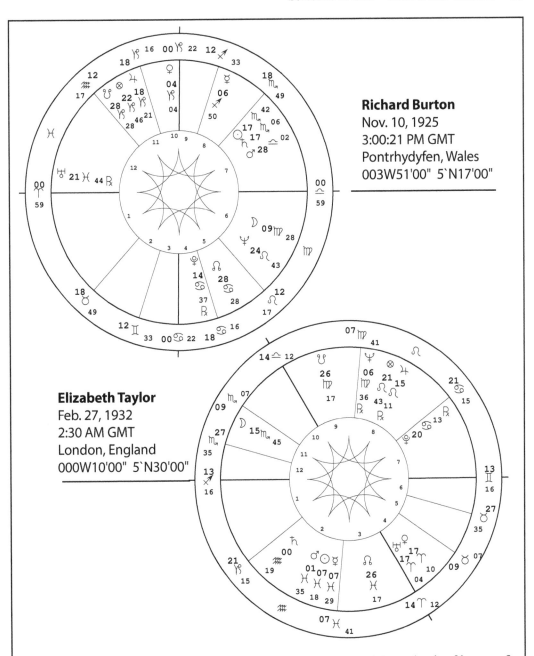

Richard Burton
Nov. 10, 1925
3:00:21 PM GMT
Pontrhydyfen, Wales
003W51'00" 5`N17'00"

Elizabeth Taylor
Feb. 27, 1932
2:30 AM GMT
London, England
000W10'00" 5`N30'00"

Richard Burton and Elizabeth Taylor were one of the most celebrated pair of lovers of the 20th Century. Both were incredibly talented. Burton, a Welchman, was nominated for an Oscar seven times, but never won. Taylor had two and was nominated for four others. Their destinies make fascinating reading for the astrologer who looks at these charts. They were married to each other twice, both times unsuccessfully. Burton's heavy drinking and their constant fighting ended the relationship, but their romance made headlines all across the globe and the fabulous jewels he gave to her were some of the greatest in the world. Both had multiple marrriages before and after the end of their years together.

Burgoyne, writing in a Victorian, paternalistic era, said the problem was that society in his time put far too much emphasis on the male qualities and undervalued the female ones, preventing the female half of the soul from developing fully, and thus limiting the progress of the whole spirit. Because if either half got to the "rejoining" level, it would still have to wait for the other half to get there in order to go on. That meant that both needed to be fostered and encouraged, not merely members of one sex. As I recall he deplored societies in which women were prevented from participating fully. Those were interesting concepts in his day and far ahead of his time.

Anyway, if there is such a thing as "soul mates," it may be this or something entirely different. I leave it up to the reader to explore. It was not something I pursued. Burgoyne was what we today would perhaps call a psychic or mystic and he is long dead so there is no way to ask him where he got the idea. Blavatsky and Alice Bailey were two other authors of this type who may have things to say about it.

Study the seventh house. It is always who we hunt for to love, just as the first house is who we are and what we offer in love. It's all about "you" and "me."

Chapter 3

A light to see by
The Sun

Nobody says much about the Sun other than it's your Sun sign. It's as if it were just some bright lamp off in the distance while the real action is elsewhere. Not so. Its influence is so pervasive that it's understandable we take it for granted. And yet, transits and progressions to our Sun provide us with some of the most simple and revealing analyses and forecasts. The solar return, solar arc and the secondary system of progressions are all based on the Sun's motion. Of course, the motion is really the earth's, but like all astrological expressions, this one is buried in the depths of antiquity where "apparent motion" became the standard for astrologers.

Indeed, our entire notion of time is based on our planet's movement relative to the Sun. At some times during the year it appears to move faster or slower relative to the earth. And it is said to move more slowly near the summer solstice and more quickly near the winter solstice.

Finding the speed of the Sun or any planet is very easy. Look in the ephemeris and see where it is when you were born. See where it will be 24 hours later. Measure the distance. That is how fast it is traveling. Most computer programs do the work for you, of course. Subtract the little number from the big number. Presto: your answer.

So what is fast and what is slow? Fast is somewhat more than average motion and slow is somewhat less. Simple. The Sun moves a little less than one degree when it is near the summer solstice (0 Cancer). It moves a little more than one degree when it is near the winter solstice (0 Capricorn). Look in any ephemeris and watch the movement change. However, its "average" motion during the year is one degree per day. It moves at exactly that speed when it is near the spring and fall equinoxes. (0 Aries and 0 Libra.)

The old Chaldean order of the planets was based on their perceived speed, slow to fast— Saturn, Jupiter, Mars, Sun, Venus, Mercury, Moon. This is a handy way to remember "average" speeds. The Moon, of course, is the fastest because it can shift up to 15 degrees per day. Saturn and Jupiter move bare minutes per day.

Are you a morning person, fit as a fiddle at 6 am or does it take you until 9 at night to really get into gear? Or maybe you're just an afternoon person who does your best before the dinner hour and loves to socialize after work. Could be you were born 12 hours earlier and reach your peak then,

Are you constantly half sick around the December holidays? Your birthday is probably in June. Do you get your annual cold in March? You were probably born in September. When the Sun reaches its farthest point from the birthday location 6 months out of every year we all feel at a low ebb, physically. This is one of those overlooked and very regular occurrences for most of us. Capricorns may get their dose when the Sun is in Cancer, and otherwise healthy Aries types can come down with a dandy sinus infection when the Sun hits Libra.

Many people in the final stages of their lives die around the time the Sun returns to its birth position. Often a few days before, when the Sun's power to aid is "worn out" for the year. The solar return revitalizes us but sometimes not fast enough and death may come a few days after the birthday. It's one of those curious things one notices in life.

A well-aspected Sun at birth gives more vitality than a Sun with many squares or oppositions. Again, it is so obvious we may pass right on by when seeking explanations for behavior and health patterns, especially involving the outer planets, Uranus, Neptune and Pluto. The outer planets are, in comparison, the Johnny-come-latelys of the Zodiac.

The angular Sun has a very wide orb. Some writers give it up to 12 or 13 degrees, as large as the orb of Jupiter, which is also nearly 13 degrees, particularly when it occupies an angle. This lends power to planets in the Sun's general vicinity, which is not true of any other planet or position in the chart. The Moon's orb is also wide, but the Sun and Jupiter are wider. Even when cadent, the Sun's orb is never less than 8 degrees on either side.

The ancients claimed Jupiter (Roman name) or Zeus (Greek name) was chief of the gods, probably because the planet was so big. Jupiter gives off its own energy just as the Sun does. However, the Sun far and away wins that race. It is always the key factor in the natal chart. All of us seek to express the Sun's qualities in our lives. When we are children and live at home, we respond most quickly to the Moon position that was in effect when we were born. But the process of becoming a strong and self-sufficient individual is the path we take to the Sun qualities. The Sun describes the physical characteristics we were born with. The Moon is how well they work. If Sun occupies a weak place in the chart, it tends to make followers, not leaders. For those with cardinal Suns who instinctively seek leadership roles it can mean serious frustration unless they move to an area where their Sun becomes angular when the chart is relocated.

Planets that occupy the angular houses always manifest strength and if Sun is the only angular placement in the chart it has a lot of power to help the individual reach goals. It is stronger than any other placement that could be there.

In every birth chart, Sun also represents male energy or a man. It can be father, husband, employer, President or male stranger. In a man's chart it is additionally his very persona, his health, his career and his ability to influence events around him. It is the ego and the power or weakness of his place in society. There is only one zodiac sign ruled by Sun, Leo. In a woman's chart, Sun is all those things as well, particularly if she has a career of her own, but women's health patterns are more strongly keyed to her Moon. Additionally, Sun is the husband, if she has no employment outside the home.

When Sun is in the masculine signs of air and fire, the men born then are more secure in their own masculinity, all things being equal. They simply know who they are and if they don't have a woman in their life they can function quite well all by themselves. Women have more strength in the earth and water signs and they, too, are more comfortable there. They are much more independent and self-sufficient. As a general rule, women born under air and fire signs are more needful of masculine input and approval in their lives, just as men born under earth and water signs need the feminine influence and respond readily to it.

These simple facts can often account for the stresses in some marriages, when air or fire men and earth or water women wed and both have their own ideas about things and insist on them. They need to learn to accommodate each other, rather than compete. Women from fire and air signs are less inclined to compete with men, while water and earth men are more inclined to find the independent women easy to deal with. These are small things many astrologers overlook and can be quite revealing when one is doing a chart comparison.

Our Sun symbolizes the best in our natures—the high ideals, the moral virtues and the sense that the strong should help the weak, not take advantage of them. It makes us open, lacking in deceitfulness and honest in our dealings with others. It improves the function of any planet that aspects it favorably.

As the slower moving planets transit across the natal position our Sun had, it can bring important events into our lives. A Jupiter transit can bring honors and opportunity, travel and social pleasures. Saturn forces us to slow down, accept limitations and responsibilities and deal with what "is" rather than what we wish life offered us. Mars stirs the libido and assertiveness can prompt arguments and stress as well as sexual activity. Venus brings women to men as Mars brings men to women. Uranus is always about important change. Neptune can be illness, divorce or simply self-delusion. Pluto shows it is time to clean out the psyche and find out who we are.

It's always a major mistake to ignore a transit to one's Sun position.

Chapter 4

The Sun shall not smite thee by day, nor the Moon by night

Eclipses

The problem of eclipses is positively ancient. The title to this chapter comes from one of the Psalms written by King David, which is sometimes called the "astrologer's psalm" because it promises protection so that "the sun shall not smite thee by day nor the moon by night."

Ancient astrologers were well aware of the life-changing events which eclipses of Sun or Moon could bring. Eclipses are big traffic signs warning us of road changes ahead. Many are feared, and rightly so. But others should be greeted with glad cries and are not.

Let's see if we can sort them out.

One of astrology's most basic lessons is that the natal chart is the root out of which the tree grows. Every successful forecast depends on how well you have studied it.

Before it's possible to estimate the impact of a transit of any sort—and an eclipse is a transit—one absolutely must understand the relative strength and weakness of the planets and angles within the birth pattern. Some charts have planets that are angular. These occupy the power zones of the chart, which are, in order of power, Houses 1, 10, 7 and 4.

Some planets rule those key signs on the angular houses and swing a lot of clout, too. An example is a chart with Capricorn rising and Saturn as the ruler. Saturn has a lot of power in that particular chart no matter what else is going on simply because it rules the first house of "self."

The Sun and the Moon of every chart are crucial positions. Other planets in the natal may be part of specific structural patterns such as T-squares, or grand trines or yods. Some have only good aspects. Some planets seem to have only bad aspects. Some rare few seem to have no aspects at all. The vast majority of charts have some good, some bad aspects. Each of these conditions will cause an eclipse to behave in a particular way when it makes contact with a planet.

Eclipses have a ranking of power. All Solar Eclipses are innately more powerful than Lunar Eclipses. Their effects last longer and are stronger in the changes they create. Astronomically, the Sun is the source of its own energy, after all, while the Moon is merely its reflected light. The most powerful solar eclipse is a total eclipse visible in your location. That means you are "under the path of totality." That's as potent as it gets.

Second most powerful is a total eclipse that is not visible where you are. Then come the annular and finally the partial eclipses. Of those two, the annular is considered stronger than the partial because it is closer to totality. We rank the lunar eclipses by the same method: Strongest is a total eclipse visible overhead. Second is a total eclipse not visible in your area. Weakest of all is a partial lunar eclipse.

I have been asked many times about the tendency of people to travel to an eclipse site of totality in order to see the show. In my opinion it is the height of foolishness to intensify the eclipse's ability to injure you if it strikes any important point in your chart. If it doesn't, then you are probably OK, but I still wouldn't do it.

The next question of course is orb—how close does the eclipse have to come to something in a chart to be effective? Well, it depends. What does it depend on? How powerful the eclipse is and what it aspects in your chart, of course.

The most powerful aspect is the conjunction. Next is the opposition, followed by the square, although sometimes the square works more powerfully than the opposition. As in all transit work, the so-called "stress" aspects produce stronger effects than the easier trines and sextiles. Aspects of trines and sextiles tend to protect one from difficulties that may be indicated. But even these statements are not always completely borne out by subsequent events. Sometimes the trines and sextiles just bring the effect faster and if it's not a good effect, they weren't a lot of help. However, one must start somewhere so start with these rules and experience will help you modify your judgment.

As a general rule, eclipses lose their potency beyond 5 degrees of contact. Most astrologers use 3 degrees as the allowable orb. Major impact is one degree or less. The power diminishes rapidly with each additional degree of distance.

A total solar eclipse visible overhead, however, will affect all the matters of the natal house in which it occurs, even if it doesn't specifically contact a planet. It is like the ten-ton gorilla—it sits wherever it wants to and affects everything wherever it is.

First you judge how powerful an eclipse you have to work with and how close it comes to a position and then you decide how powerful the contact point is in the scheme of things in the chart.

Which Aspects Work?

As with all transits, as I said, hard aspects to the natal chart are the most effective. A transit, by its very nature, is a sometime thing and the sometime is pretty short. You need the hard aspects to launch any real action.

Soft aspects can hardly be noticed sometimes, but they may bleed off the trouble of a hard aspect elsewhere, "softening" the impact.

Contacts to unaspected planets in one's natal chart can be dynamite. Truly unaspected planets can be unbelievably potent in the natal pattern and an eclipse on such a position brings strong action. But truly unaspected planets are hard to come by. Very few of us get them. Most of them turn out to have a minor aspect, such as a semi-square from another planet, or a sesqui-square, that limits their scope. Occasionally the unnoticed aspect is a septile (51 5/8 degrees) or quintile (72 degrees), or even a bi-quintile (144 degrees). And we must not forget the parallel of declination, which can link two planets very strongly.

However, when in doubt, stick to classic Ptolemaic aspects (conjunction, square, trine, sextile and opposition) and you'll be fine. Just don't put too much stock in sextiles and trines.

Generally speaking, the strongest eclipse impact comes from hits to the Sun, Moon or angles of the chart. Next are eclipses on planets ruling the Sun sign or the rising sign, or the angular houses. Then contacts to other planets.

There is room for some dispute over which can be more powerful, the square or opposition aspect. As I have said, we can rank the square as somewhat stronger because the opposition tends to involve other people in the situation while the square is an in-your-face problem that you, yourself, can't avoid dealing with.

One important thing to remember about an eclipse near Sun or Moon is the potential to affect the eyesight. Get an eye exam promptly and also check with the doctor any symptoms which can be related to the back or the heart (solar organs) if there are other indicators of health effects. For instance, it may be time for blood pressure medication, or cataract surgery. Both Sun and Moon rule the eyes, so pay attention.

One of my clients had a torn retina after such an aspect. Others just need stronger glasses. Of course you want to know which is good and which is bad, right? Elementary, my dear Watson.

Eclipses on natal planets with no bad aspects or on the two benefics, Jupiter and Venus, can often be good. Sometimes very, very good. An eclipse on a well-aspected part of fortune is not to be sneezed at, either. The latter can bring money, as can an eclipse on Venus. Venus will also produce marriage, and I have seen eclipses on Venus precede marriage by two weeks or less. Occasionally—as happened to Prince Charles of England—Venus eclipses came practically on top of his two wedding dates.

Eclipses on Jupiter can bring career advancement or honors as well as opportunity for travel or social improvement. In the natal 10th it could bring a promotion or a big prize or honor for one's work.

An eclipse on a man's well-aspected Sun will likely relate to career and health change but good aspects to the natal position are protective, shielding him from the worst when the situation around him is falling apart.

For a woman, it will also mean meetings with men or men who will be important in her life. The same can be true of a man, of course. If the eclipse hits the Moon and a woman has a career for which she has had specific training, (as opposed to a "job" anyone can fill and which may be temporary) a solar eclipse will affect that as well. Factory work is in the "job" category, although the work of a tool and die maker or a pharmacist, which require specialized training and skills, are "careers."

I specify some differences between men and women in the work world because it is pretty generally accepted that men have lifelong working careers (even though some work at "jobs") while women may sometimes move in and out of the work force, depending on whether they have children or not. They, too, can have both "jobs" and interrupted "careers." How we might interpret for a woman could relate to her career or the career of the man in her life. If she is unemployed and relies on her spouse for support, her eclipse could relate to her husband. Or, for a "house husband" who relies on his wife., his eclipse could relate to her work.

Suppose she's independently wealthy and unmarried? The Sun refers to her status and importance as a factor in society. Perhaps she is a force for good in the arts world, or the leading light in a charitable endeavor. Nevertheless, because it is the Sun that is eclipsed there is a masculine flavor to the aspect. If not her work, then, it may mean an important man comes into her life.

A special exception exists for royalty or heads of state. The queen of England is a solar figure despite the fact that she is married. She has a career as royalty, which is never interrupted. Her power comes innately from who she is. At lower levels of power—the mayor of a community comes to mind—the position may be temporary or part of a longer "career" in politics. Nevertheless, while the position is occupied, it is solar. In both cases the Sun is the indicator.

An eclipse on a well favored Moon is apt to result in attention—sometimes a great deal of public attention, as well as meetings with important women. An eclipse on a stressed Moon can be serious problems ahead. They may involve health, family affairs or property.

It is not particularly favorable for a woman's health in the short term. A harsh eclipse on a rising Moon can result in a serious finding about one's health. But it highlights a problem that needs resolution, which has the long-term effect of improving one's health once it is dealt with.

Because the Moon also deals with home and family, an eclipse on a well-aspected Moon can mark the time of a home purchase, or important work to renovate or improve the home as well as changes for the women in one's life. It can bring favorable changes into the family circle, altering the direction of the lives of children, perhaps, or signaling a change in their status. Maybe it will be the year they become independent, or go away to college. But even when the outcome is good, an eclipse may mean trauma. All change is traumatic, by its very nature, so we shouldn't expect an easy ride with a major eclipse.

If the natal Moon has harsh aspects, such as oppositions or squares, particularly to malefics, all the areas of the chart which are ruled by the Moon and the aspecting planets can suffer. The eclipse on the natal Moon will affect all the things the Moon naturally rules as well as the area specific to each chart. If Cancer is on the cusp of the second, it will be hard on income, for instance. If Cancer is on the 8th, the issue of debt, inheritance or perhaps a legal settlement will be hit. If Cancer is on the 9th it could also be an in-law matter, or one involving grandchildren. Should the natal Moon be in House 6 and ruling House 8, it might mean surgery.

Now obviously our judgment of any prediction depends on the natal chart. I can't say this too often since it's the rule people tend to forget. If the natal contact point in question is not well aspected, you can be sure trouble will follow. If there are both good and bad aspects, the results will be mixed and will depend on which aspects are the stronger. All applying aspects are automatically stronger than all separating ones, you know. That's because they are increasing in strength as they near perfection.

Once perfection has been reached, it's like getting to the top of the hill for a child with a sled: after that it's all downhill. (For most of us, perfection was when we were 16 and knew everything there was to know. Now that we are older, we look back fondly on those years, even as we realize how little we can be sure of, and that perfection is permanently out of reach.) Anyway, that's why separating aspects are weaker. The term "perfection" is used astrologically to mean "exactitude."

So, back to my point. If an eclipse hits Mars, for instance and Mars has two natal aspects—a nice applying trine to Jupiter and a harsh but separating square to Saturn—the separating square may mean problems, but it is the weaker aspect of the two and the trouble won't last. The applying trine to Jupiter is the stronger, so it can haul you out of the trouble, wipe your nose and get you back in business. In this example, the bad is weaker and the good is stronger.

It is exactly the reverse if there is a separating trine to Jupiter and an applying square to Saturn. Optimism won't help—in the end, trouble will come and you will have to deal with it. The trine to Jupiter won't be as useful. It may only give you the hanky and tell you to go wipe your own nose.

The principles are pretty simple. The difficulties come when things get mixed. One of the problems a lot of inexperienced astrologers have is thinking that all natal aspects to the benefics are good. Wrong. A natal square to Jupiter can bring trouble just as readily as a square to Saturn. It's only the kind of trouble that is different. But a square is a square is a square. This is why it is so important to examine the natal chart. A strong natal chart with a good aspect between planets struck by an eclipse does fine. A weak chart or a planet which gets bad aspects natally is a different kettle of fish when it is struck by a powerful eclipse.

There are also difficulties in estimating the impact of an eclipse over a point which is part of a "formation." Such a formation may be a T-square, a grand trine or even a grand cross in the natal chart. An eclipse which strikes a stellium of planets can have a domino effect on all of them. The effect will work in terms of the kind of formation it hits. It sets off the natal package—it does not create a new one, or contradict the natal.

If the eclipse transit is to one of the points in a grand trine, obviously the individual has plenty of talent and resources to deal with whatever the eclipse brings. It may be tough, but it's workable. If it is to a well-aspected point of a difficult package, it will be just like the mixed good/bad combination I just mentioned above.

A T-square has built-in stresses and power that an eclipse can unlock but unless the individual has some nice aspects somewhere else in the chart to some arm of the T-square (which can act to soften the impact), it can bring some very tough times. It's very like a rambunctious horse that needs an experienced rider who will insist on sticking to the road instead of allowing the horse to go galley-west over the hills and far away.

There are many ways we judge how well situated a planet is in the birth pattern. The angles contain their own inherent areas of influence.

Any eclipse on the Ascendant or to a planet in the first house tends to show a change in the way the body functions. Some people redecorate themselves, others have babies or lose pregnancies or get involved in accidents which put them on crutches. Some have major health problems. Perhaps it comes the year before a woman has her first child. Or the year after a man learns he has a heart blockage. In either case, a physical trauma changes their lives, or it may signal discovery of a serious problem.

We should not underestimate the power that her first childbirth has on a woman. It is THE major physical trauma of her life, no matter how easy or difficult subsequent deliveries may be. In my opinion it ranks well above a middle-aged heart attack for this reason: The heart attack usually offers a chance for recovery and a return to an earlier (reasonably good) physical condition; it may mean increasing physical activity and improving the diet and taking medicine to get there but it does not always redirect the entire course of the life.

Parenting, however, goes on forever, and changes a woman's entire self-image, sense of duty and responsibility and rearranges her priorities forever. It also alters a woman's body permanently. Don't believe me? Ask a doctor. The very bones shift after childbirth.

Now obviously some heart attacks are more serious than others and I don't in any way intend to minimize their import or danger. I merely mean that childbirth almost always comes early in life and redirects all subsequent events. The heart attack usually comes much later and may not mean a major redirection, particularly if there is full recovery.

Eclipses to rising planets also—by the very nature of rising planets—affect he physical body. If there are any stresses on such planets, expect trouble, ill health and disease to manifest or require treatment after being neglected in the past. If the planets contacted are cardinal, trouble blows up quickly and can be resolved quickly, such as by strong medicine or surgery. If the planets are mutable, it can indicate a long period of chronic difficulty that takes continuing treatment. If the planets are fixed, the damage may be heavy and permanent and take far more treatment and medication to fix. Even so, a lifelong effect may be felt.

Eclipses on the 7th cusp show something related to partners and all partnership matters. They can also signal law suits or the ending of partnerships or changes in the health of partners. Sometimes it points to a change of residence. (The 4th house is where you live now—the 7th is the residence to which you move later.)

Eclipses on the MC are indicative of changes in the company you work for and may affect your status along with it. If you own a house, you'd do well to have the roof inspected.

Eclipses on the 4th cusp affect home and family. They can refer to your house and its very foundation. Be sure to keep an eye on problems in the basement. The MC/IC axis also has impact on your parents' lives or your relationship with them. It can relate to property matters in general, particularly any land or real estate which one may own. This can be a tricky eclipse to analyze in the chart of a client with more than one piece of property, especially multiple investment properties. As a general rule, I give the current residence to the 4th house cusp and other property to the ruler of the fourth. Sometimes it works pretty well. It's not a perfect choice and some charts refuse to be organized tidily in this way. In those cases, one is forced to use the derived house technique of skipping a house and using the next one in line to judge matters of several properties. The fourth is always where one lives, but the 6th could be the first investment in real estate, the 8th the second investment and so on, around the chart.

By the way, I mentioned that the MC refers to the company you work for. Your immediate supervisor is the ruler of that house, and your position and reputation are indicated by any planet in that house, when there is difficulty deciding which is being affected. If you are self-employed, the rulerships shift a bit, but the MC is always "the venture," the ruler is always "the one in charge" and the planet in the house is "who is affected."

In judging eclipse power on a planet, it is absolutely mandatory to go back to the basics of chart analysis and see what house the planet rules and what house it is in and what planets aspect it and from which houses.

An angular Moon belonging to a Cancer Sun person or someone with Cancer rising is going to have a far greater sensitivity than a cadent Moon belonging to an Aries Sun or ascendant type, for instance. Why? Obviously because a Cancer Sun person is automatically affected heavily by the Moon and the Aries is more affected by Mars. Additionally, simple angularity is always a strong indicator of power.

Of course, having said that, I must now backtrack and remind you that I am speaking in generalities that can easily be altered by the setup of a particular chart. Take a Leo Sun person for instance. Ordinarily Sun, particularly in Leo, is the most dominant factor. Maybe this Sun is succeeded, though, and making only one or two minor aspects. But, the chart has a potent Moon ruling one of the angles and sitting on the 4th cusp (providing accidental dignity) and making good aspects to everything else in the chart. Wham! We have major impact whenever Moon is struck by anything and the Sun, particularly early in the life, may then be less significant in the forecast.

As is true for all of us, the Moon's influence is stronger in childhood when we live in the parental home and the Sun is stronger in significance later in life when we become independent. Many of these "rules" are self-evident but are sometimes overlooked or forgotten by astrologers who may seek more complicated and convoluted methods to get answers as their skills increase. Occasionally it pays to go back to simple basic rules to keep the analyses from running away with you.

Another such rule is the importance of the afflictions to the chart in youth. All young people respond more dramatically when their hard aspects are hit than do older people. Older people have been there before and learned how to handle the stresses over a lifetime. As they age, the energy begins to shift if it has been wisely confronted in the past and eclipses on squares can even bring benefit. To the young, an eclipse always seems to mean trouble. It's just the way it works.

Major eclipses—such as the Millennium eclipse of Aug. 11, 1999, that involved all the fixed signs—was related to a great many areas of life. (See chart on page 27.)

Another consideration about an eclipse is the sign in which it occurs. In health matters, for example, eclipses in Leo target the back and spine, rather than the arms or the big toe, which come under other signs.

As another possible example, it's easy to say of an eclipse, "Oh, but it's hitting my natal Venus and Uranus in Leo and I think it means a love affair or a job change." It may indeed, but be aware of other meanings of Leo, such as a child. So it could be a warning to use care to avoid pregnancy if you are not ready to raise a child. If you want a child of course, it would point to a good time to launch a pregnancy or perhaps see a physician if there is a problem in achieving one. Or, if you already have a child, the problem may be related to the child—school, or health and the like. Again, judgment means going back to the natal pattern. How does the natal position work, what stresses does it contain, and how will a nudge from an eclipse affect it?

It pays to keep basic house and sign meanings in mind. A Taurus eclipse is going to have a financial effect. Period. No matter what else it does, it does that simply by coming under the Taurus umbrella. This is true for all of the signs and whatever they rule. That Taurus eclipse in the third house probably means car trouble and/or a sibling who borrows from one or who needs financial help. In the fourth house it will mean spending on home or family. Write down your expectations in advance. Look back on your notes after the eclipse has come and gone. It's a good way to improve your judgment.

Now the vital question becomes: When does the eclipse activate? When do the events it foretells occur? The general rules are that the most powerful effects are felt when the Sun or Mars squares, conjuncts or opposes the eclipse point. Next in powerful activation come contacts involving the Moon or other planets. If Mercury or Venus is prominent in the chart under study, then transits by those planets can set off the eclipse effect.

How long do eclipses last? Generally speaking, a solar eclipse is said to last at least a year and a lunar one, 6 months. However, I find that a powerful solar eclipse on Sun, Moon, angles or angular planets "sensitizes" that point for some time, perhaps three years or more, and the effects of contacts by other planets will be felt in a gradually weakening way. I don't see the same strength from the lunar eclipses. One old rule says a solar eclipse theme lasts in years as long as the totality did in minutes. A three minute totality works out to three years of time for the eclipse theme to be in effect Since an eclipse can last up to 7.5 minutes, it limits an eclipse's viability to 7 years and six months.

And let's not overlook another factor. Eclipses in cardinal signs bring dramatic events that may be one-of-a-kind things. Eclipses in mutable signs bring situations that can become chronic or show up in many varied ways. Eclipses in fixed signs bring harsher situations that can last a very long, long time.

Now that we've covered that material, there is a final consideration to talk about. The eclipse pattern can involve a transiting planet and that dramatically alters its potency. An eclipse conjunct transiting Saturn is quite different from one that is conjunct transiting Jupiter or Venus. The malefics are trouble, pure and simple, when connected to eclipses. Don't get all psychological on me about eclipses. We aren't talking psychology here. We are talking blunt astrology. Saturn can be a cold, harsh influence on the world, bringing expansions sharply to heel and imposing discipline and restriction. The one at 19 degrees of Gemini conjunct Saturn in June of 2002 launched a huge plunge in the stock markets during the summer that followed. It particularly hit stocks with a Gemini influence—telecoms and transports.

Many years before it occurred I noticed the dire import of the eclipse of Aug. 11, 1999. That eclipse, sometimes called the "Millennium Eclipse," (see page 27) was part of a very nasty fixed grand cross with Uranus, Mars and Saturn. It was a total eclipse as well, with a path of totality which cut a wide swath of darkness from the Mediterranean across the Middle East and well into Asia.If you are not familiar with it, take a good look at the pattern because it is one of the harshest I can imagine and you won't likely see another this bad very soon. From a mundane perspective (mundane astrology deals with the world events and destiny of nations) it signaled enormous historical impact. It will well repay some study.

The attacks on the World Trade Center twin towers in New York City occurred when Venus came to that millennium eclipse degree on Sept. 11, 2001. This was just past two years after the eclipse. Before that, earthquakes and volcanic action had also been triggered by transits to the 18 Leo degree of the eclipse. Its force was felt around the world by nations with planets at 18-20 degrees of the fixed signs which were put under such stress by the eclipse.

Contrast that with an eclipse conjunct Jupiter which has the exact opposite theme, fostering expansion, good feelings and opportunities for beneficial developments.

Before you even consider what an eclipse might mean in a particular chart, you must say to yourself, "Ah, but what KIND of an eclipse is this?" Listen carefully to the answer because it will affect the way it works in an individual horoscope pattern.

In 2000 a new Moon was square the previous December's Solar Eclipse in 4 Capricorn. Whatever the eclipse meant would likely manifest then. Strong lunar aspects can trigger eclipse effects. Capricorn eclipses show geophysical matters, business and entrenched authorities anywhere. In the Capricorn city of Cleveland there are two Ford plants in Brookpark, a Cleveland suburb, which shut down over Legionnaire's disease— the first the day before the new Moon and the second a few days later. Was that a business effect? Of course. Also, as the Sun neared the point of the square to the eclipse there was a big earthquake in Japan.

I had a client with this eclipse conjunct his Moon, ruler of his MC. His job was affected when a woman was named his boss shortly after the eclipse. The square from the Sun at the new Moon meant further changes. He did not consider her a very good boss and she was not a fan of his either, but a second eclipse brought him an assignment under another executive, so he was able to largely sidestep the woman who disliked him. He had some other things happening in his chart which softened the effect on his career, but the woman did become his boss for a while.

A 0 degree Cancer eclipse coming in June, 2001 was activated by a Mars station in May at 29 Sagittarius. (Opposing), and a Mercury station later in the year, also at 29 degrees of a mutable sign. There is not a lot of spread between the 4 Capricorn eclipse of December with the stations near 0 cardinal and the 0 Cancer eclipse ahead. All this obviously put a lot of pressure on any entity who had a chart with an early and important cardinal placement as the executive did. And before you ask, yes, eclipses can be triggered in advance, sometimes up to a month in advance.

As I mentioned, Lunar Eclipses are slightly different to interpret and weaker than Solar Eclipses. Because the Moon implies a feminine energy, a Lunar Eclipse on the Sun can refer to an important woman in the life, or perhaps to to health, home and children. The health issues are for the women, but the home and children possibilities should not be overlooked in lunar eclipses for men. If one has a house being built or a child with a health problem, the Lunar Eclipse can seem just as important as a Solar Eclipse for a while. Lunar Eclipses don't last as long as solar, so the events they anticipate usually show up promptly. Events associated with them are over and done within 6 months. The orb is even tighter than with a solar eclipse, because the lunar is weaker in the first place.

Almost everyone seems to think all eclipses are always bad. **Not so.** Even eclipses on Saturn can bring benefit if Saturn is well aspected at birth. The benefit seems to follow a problem which has to be solved first—or even a seeming catastrophe. It's sort of like an "all's well that ends better." I'll give you a personal example. A tree fell on my house one September, following a solar eclipse in Leo opposed my Saturn in Aquarius by one degree. A second eclipse a few months later was exactly on my Saturn, and it took nearly that long for me to finish putting my library back in order.

The tree that came down was at least 200 years old—probably a lot more—(very Saturnian, eh?) but had been rotting out in the trunk for a long time before a huge storm. It came down while I was in bed about 6:30 a.m. and when I heard the crack I knew what it was. It felt like somebody threw a couple of cars at the house. I ran down stairs and flipped on the lights over the patio to see this monster lying there like a weary Godzilla. Did I mention the oak was about 28-30 feet around? One of the big branches had struck the roof, going into the ceiling of my computer/library room and going through the roof of my garage. The claims adjuster later told me that if my walls had not been brick the tree would have torn the back of the house off because only brick was strong enough to take all that weight. The main part of the tree missed the house by about —oh, 5 or 6 feet. That would have wiped me out and the house, too.

Anyway, to make a very long, involved story shorter: The repairs ended up getting me an entirely new roof on house and garage, all new gutters, which fixed a big drainage problem I had had for some years, repairs of three windows which I couldn't open before (Old crank mechanisms were jammed too badly) can now be opened and I got a room completely redecorated, new ceilings, walls repaired, ceiling painted, new wallpaper etc.

It forced me to do the agonizing work of actually reducing my library by about a third by getting rid of books I really didn't like anyway. This was not my astrological library, you understand. Just my sci-fi fiction. I have the room lined in bookshelves pretty much all the way around. I know, I know—I am a nut. My family has been telling me this for years.

My daughter helped me with the redecorating and it was absolutely wonderful. It was a pleasure every time I walked in to get on the computer. It was a mess for a while, of course, but luckily occurred under a cardinal Moon. Repairs went very quickly. I shudder to think how long repairs would have taken had the catastrophe happened under a fixed Moon. It

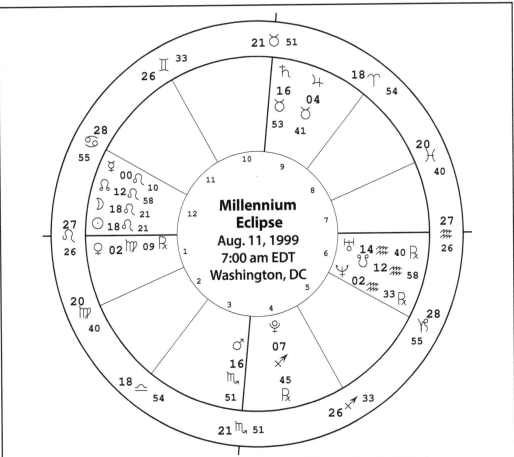

One of the most severe eclipses in modern time was followed by the fall of governments, economic disaster and earthquakes along the path of totality. Two years later, the bombing of the World Trade Center in New York City happened when Venus was exactly on the degree of the eclipse at 18 Leo. This is often referred to as the Millennium Eclipse.

would still be going on and I would be in a padded room. The damaging storm occurred with Moon in Aries and the entire repair task went exceedingly fast. My insurance company was wonderful. The amount of damage was very little compared to what it could have been.

So there you are, the tale of two eclipses, both within one degree of Saturn, which brought good things in the wake of the problem. The tree stump ground down into astonishingly wonderful mulch. The patio suddenly had Sunshine and things in the yard began growing as they hadn't in years. The old oak had smothered everything with too much shade.

A carver took some of the logs, turning them into memorial bowls for my children who had once played on a swing on one arm of the old tree. It took two commercial grinder trucks, two dump trucks, two flat bed trailers and 13 pickup truckloads to cart away all the wood. Much of the wood went to people who needed it for heating their homes. I filled up my wood racks with about a cord and gave the rest away. I was the "wood fairy" of the neighborhood for a while there.

So unless you have a really afflicted position getting hit within a degree or two of an eclipse, you can probably relax—catastrophe will pass you by. Eclipses are dramatic transits, but they are still just transits and sometimes when we get too excited over them it pays to remember there are about 4 per year—sometimes five—and we have lived through a great many and often without any disaster at all showing up in our lives.

Nevertheless, the old timers who wrote the psalms thought a little prayer before the eclipses was in order so that "the Sun may not smite thee by day nor the Moon by night."

Occultations

Occultations are mini-eclipses. An occultation of Jupiter is when the Moon passes between it and the earth and hides it. It is a Jupiter eclipse, basically. Ditto with any other planet. When the Moon's declination and that of the planet are the same, the occultation occurs with every conjunction. It can last for months, if the planet is very slow moving.

Suppose you have transiting Uranus on your natal Moon and for several months in a particular year there is an occultation of Uranus every time the transiting Moon gets near it. Since it is so close to the natal Moon, it would hit a woman's children and her health affairs, of course. If you happen to have a natal Uranus/Moon square or opposition, the power jumps exponentially. Every month some new catastrophe can occur like clockwork. Sickness, accidents, trouble at school— you should keep a record for posterity, but once it's over all you may want to do is forget it.

Most people won't even notice it, of course. If they don't have any natal pattern to vibrate to it, it passes them by. And that's the big key with occultations or eclipses of any sort, for that matter. If they echo or reinforce a natal set-up, they are trouble. Otherwise, you get no action at all. But be sure to notice them.

Other Eclipses

The solar eclipse before birth is sometimes considered important by some astrologers. The lunar one doesn't count. When the degree on which it occurs is later aspected or transited, it may coincide with strong events in the life. Everyone should locate the one before their birth and keep the degree in mind. It is effective for the entire lifetime.

A **progressed eclipse** is something else entirely. Not everyone gets one. Here's how to have a progressed solar or lunar eclipse. The natal lunar nodes must be within about 90 degrees after the degree of your natal Sun (that measures to 90 years in a progressed chart). For example, suppose you have the Sun at 0 Libra and the south node at 2 Scorpio. In approximately 32 days after birth, which measures to the 32nd year of life, the Sun will reach 2 Scorpio by progression. If the progressed Moon is in Taurus at that time, for instance, and fairly close to the North Node, it will form a progressed lunar eclipse. If it is in Scorpio and reaches the progressed Sun close enough to the South Node, it will be a progressed solar eclipse.

One of the problems of the progressed eclipse that folks overlook is the health implications. In House 12, I would expect that there may be hospitalization ahead or perhaps a family member whose health problems will keep one running in and out of the hospital. Check House 6 very carefully, and the ruler of the Ascendant, to see which is implied. Such progressed eclipses often relate to the eyes, so it's time for a thorough eye exam. If you wear glasses, they will probably need changing. If not, you may find you need glasses now. If you already have eye problems, be sure you have a good physician and in case of doubt, get a second opinion, particularly before approving any surgery on the eyes. Should the eclipse come in an area of the zodiac known for eye problems—between 5-8 degrees of Leo, for instance—it means super care should be taken.

Don't overlook the back problems often associated with eclipses on the Sun—even the progressed Sun. If the Sun is well aspected at birth, such problems probably won't be permanent, but muscle strain and complaints of pain may be annoying. In a fixed sign they can be severe. Avoid starting any program of heavy exercise that can affect the back. In other words, you don't lift weights now—wait a few months before learning to do so and then do it under careful supervision.

Look to the natal house in which the progressed eclipse occurs. Some houses are trouble, plain and simple. The 8th with its financial and medical implication is one. The 12th house is still the house of "chickens coming home to roost," so those are places to study carefully. In any 12th house progression be careful about the feet. Make sure your shoes fit so you don't start a problem and avoid wearing shoes that hurt or make you walk funny. That can have ramifications for a long time.

Born under an eclipse

It makes a difference as to WHEN the birth occurs. If the birth occurs immediately just before the solar eclipse, it means the child may likely face a major health problem of some sort in the first year. It was considered most dangerous for the health of a female child since the influence of the Sun "overpowered" that of the Moon. "Just before" means within orb of it but not exact. Like all aspects closer is stronger.

Any new Moon birth diminishes the Moon's influence, and since it deals with female health and the reproductive function in general, it tends to give a nervous constitution and female difficulties. Not good for having children later on. Men born during this time either don't understand or sympathize with women or may have difficulties with them later in life. Birth after the eclipse is easier and less dangerous, particularly if the eclipse is not total. But for a man it may mean a wife with a health problem or one who has few children, and those with difficulty. For a woman, again it's an aspect of difficulty having children.

Babies born exactly under a solar eclipse have been said not to survive long. This means exact, not just "within orb." Especially if there are afflictions to that eclipse point, survival is unlikely.

Lunar eclipses are quite different. The lunar eclipse, unlike the solar, emphasizes the Moon since it occurs at the full Moon. The Full Moon child always needs the spotlight and it's amazing how many of them end up on stage. Even if it's not a career, many will gravitate toward the theater in school. If it's not an actual stage, they still want attention and have emotional intensity front and center in their lives. They need huge gobs of approval and can produce a lot of emotional fireworks or waterworks, if they don't get it. You'll find the sign of the Moon much more influential than normal in their lives.

Unlike the solar eclipse which squelches the Moon, the lunar eclipse gives it top billing, and there is plenty of female influence in the life. It may bring strong female relationships, or strong women generally into the life.

Child bearing is a big deal even if the number of children is not large. In a way, it almost seems like a Cancer influence because of the lunar prominence.

Eclipses warn that these can be problems. So can parental issues, or family matters. Those are the first things to look at when you have a lunar eclipse at birth.

Chapter 5

Our daily bread
The Moon

The Moon is the lens through which we express who we are to the world. People with mild signs for the Moon—Cancer, Pisces, Gemini and Libra—present themselves as much more passive, congenial and non-threatening than those with the Moon in more aggressive signs.

People with harsher Aries, Leo, Capricorn and Scorpio Moons often seem more like people we don't want to argue with or aggravate. They often get credit for being stronger characters than they are, particularly if the Sun sign doesn't back up the first impression.

Here's an amusing way to spend a dull party with people whose charts you know. Watch how others react to the Leo with a soft Pisces Moon.

I once had a friend with that particular combination who seemed to be the meekest, mildest character in town. She would never stand up for herself and she had a difficult marriage to an overbearing man that she didn't know how to deal with. Then, an excessively strict teacher at school frightened one of her children. That Leo mom sat up and snarled in true Leo fashion. The teacher was one accustomed to being the dominator in any interaction with parents. She got an education from that mother. The moral of the story? Never try to push around the children of Leo or Cancer Sun sign mothers. They cornered the market on protective instincts.

The Moon has so much influence over us all that it can be said to be the major daily power directing our activities. It governs the sheets on the bed that we get out of in the morning, the food we eat for breakfast, the kitchen where we eat it and the wife/mother/cook/woman who may fix it for us. It rules silverware (the real kind as well as other types of tableware), dishes, all the furniture in the house and the kind of home we make. It's our pots and pans and the goldfish bowl, which after all is water and the "home" of the gold fish.

One of the interesting things to do is use the Moon to forecast one's activities a month in advance. Write the ideas in a small notebook and at the end of each day write down what actually occurred. It's an eye opener.

Maybe the phone rings off the hook with the Moon in Gemini. You go to the grocery store with the Moon in Cancer and do the laundry with the Moon in Virgo. In Taurus the Moon prompts you to sit down and write checks for bills and in Leo one has the urge to sleep late and have a drink before dinner.

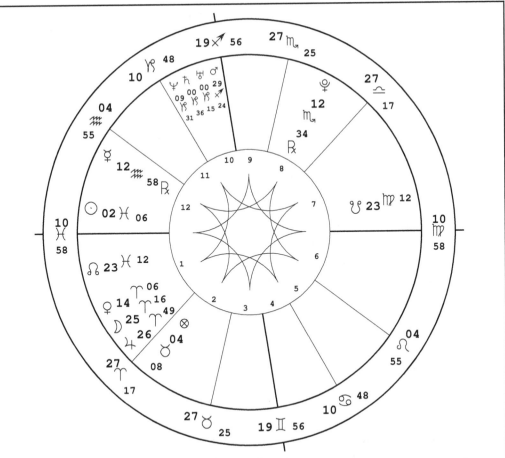

This man trained as a chef. The angular Moon between the two benefics in the first house describes his dream of owning his own restaurant. The conjunction to Jupiter shows him, likely to achieve his goal, and also to teach cooking at some point in his future. Venus is an excellent indicator of business acument, Jupiter trines to his MC, Mars and the Saturn//Uranus conjunction out of sign are also promising AA Rodden rating for birth chart.

Each person may respond differently as the Moon changes signs. One common denominator is often the Moon's monthly transit of the natal Saturn sign. Some people simply feel "down" but others get bad news then. It may be a time when one's projects don't seem to go right.

When the daily Moon crosses one's natal Jupiter, there is an urge to plan travel or buy imported items or blow up balloons for the children. Watch your activities and see what correspondences occur. Because people are so individual many activities recur month after month in a different way for you than for someone else.

The Moon cannot be over-estimated in life. It rules the entire process of child bearing and rearing, from the start of the mother's puberty to the moment she conceives her first child and far, far beyond as it covers the years of family growth and development. It is the broad family life and the home one lives in. It affects the habits we develop to shape the way we live. It deals with our health and our relationships to the female half of humanity.

Moon is the light by night and the source of romantic inspiration in all ages and time periods. Its influence stretches from a silly mood to a serial killing. Its power in the birth chart is simply enormous. For a man, it embraces all the women in his life and the contributions they make to it. For a woman, it's all that and more. It is her own life. It is the major indicator in all reproductive issues as well as the entire emotional and sympathetic side of existence.

In a broad sense every woman expresses in her life the maiden, mother and crone, the old wise woman of ancient legend, symbolized by the waning Moon. The Moon's phases of new, full and dark were said to correlate with that development. Unless death comes first, all women progress through those stages. There was no comparable development of quite this kind invented for men. They simply aged. True, one can see signs of similar growth in men, from youth to maturity to old age but the changes, by tradition, were not ruled by the Moon. In earlier times, the menstrual cycle, which matches the lunar cycle, was seen as heavenly confirmation of the Moon's link to womanhood.

In a birth chart, the Moon always reflects how mother dealt with one during childhood, and in the child's chart, it shows how the child "sees" her. Its aspects show whether the mother's health may have been stressed by the birth, as well as how she was doing at the time.

A square to Saturn from the Moon in the child's chart shows the birth came at a difficult time for the parents for some reason. It may have been that money was tight, or the father's job was at risk, or some other problem was weighing on the family. In any case, the child tends to absorb some degree of feeling not "wanted" and experiences a sense of uncertainty about life. Later on, that aspect often leads the individual to work hard to establish his or her own security, and such individuals often become quite successful, thus proving that there is no bad aspect without its compensations.

Aspects always modify the way the Moon or any planet functions, and the late Grant Lewi wrote about such aspects in a modern way that illuminated the issues, and his book, *Heaven Knows What,* contains much about aspects that will help any astrologer.

In the mother's chart, the Moon shows when and how many children she will have as well as her desire for them. For example a Moon conjunct Saturn in Gemini in the 8th house showed a mother barely a week shy of 40 when she chose to have her first baby. In past eras, 40 was considered very old for a mother and dangerous to her health. Now it isn't as devastating as it was then but times have changed and medicine has vastly improved.

There is still a higher likelihood of birth defects and more stress on the mother's health at that age. Babies are simply healthier if mom is in her 20s, and mom recovers faster. A great many women who know this have nevertheless delayed child bearing for a number of reasons but later decide to have children anyway. The Moon's conjunction to Saturn can show delay. It can also show difficulties in delivery when tied to other troublesome planets.

Generally speaking, miscarriages show in the 5th, which has overall rulership of one's children. Mars or any malefic in House 5 in a woman's chart may show that she doesn't want children for any number of reasons, and may decide not to have any, or it may indicate that she suffers a miscarriage or has an abortion. However this is not absolute—at another time, she may bear a healthy child. If she does want children, good prenatal care is especially important.

A series of miscarriages is difficult for many women. Today's in vitro fertilization is just one technique which may help overcome infertility problems and as a modern "technical" avenue may be chosen by someone with a good aspect of Uranus or the benefics to her Moon. The inability to carry a pregnancy to term, or sometimes even to become pregnant, can be seen through the lunar position and its aspects. The fire Moons need good aspects because fire in itself is not a fertile element. Afflicted air may also be barren. Earth and water, however, get pregnant easily and tend to carry to term.

However, for the Moon to simply be in air or fire is not a sufficient indicator of trouble. Aspects from malefics can be an indicator of problems. Any Moon sign can be fertile if unafflicted, receiving aspects from benefics or simply being in the 5th house. I have the chart of a mother with a full family. She has the Moon in House 5 in Gemini. The Moon also receives a nice sextile from Mercury, the co-ruler of children. She had seven children. Her chart is elsewhere in this book. (See page 283.)

Another woman's chart with the Moon in Libra had four children of her own and one adopted. She has Cancer rising and Moon in House 4 square Pluto and opposing Uranus. The stress to her Moon was a primary indicator that all of them were born by Caesarean section, but with no affliction of of Saturn or Mars to her Moon, she did have her children.

The Moon in the 8th or 12th in the mother's chart can sometimes mean the loss of a child. Sometimes it can show the loss of the mother when young in a child's chart, or the loss of a caretaking female. It might be the grandmother who has been the "babysitter" for the child, or even a beloved nanny. It's not a position I like to see, particularly.

I use the fourth house in the mother's chart for her first child, the 6th for her second and so on in the derived house system. I only use the 5th for the first child in the father's chart. The 5th house is always "all" of one's children, of course, but looking at the derived houses enables one to pinpoint the affairs of a specific child. The first child alters a woman's entire life, physically and every other way and sets it on new "ground" so to speak. It isn't the same for a man, hence the choice of houses.

I do not count children who never lived and never took a single independent breath. Unless there was a live birth, the house does not reflect the pregnancy, in my opinion. A live child is not the same as an aborted fetus. The key thing is that the child lived—however briefly—after its separation from the mother. Then a house reflects it.

One of the most helpful things you can do as a parent is to learn about your child's Moon. The Moon deals with how a child sees its mother and what elements of her personality the child responds to most readily. Any parent with several children knows that each child will respond differently to the same treatment.

A child with a Virgo Moon sees mother as a hard worker with rules about cleanliness and tidiness and wants them followed. In Pisces, mom is much more casual about disorder and more openly affectionate. The late Evangeline Adams, the "mother" of American astrology, wrote quite a bit about this issue and it is worth getting her book and reading her analyses. They were a big help to me early in my career and explained why certain behaviors were more effective with one child than with another. Saturn and the Sun in the child's chart show the relationship to the father, of course. It is usually less intimate than the relationship to the mother, but there are exceptions to every rule.

Once you know how your child sees you, then it's time to respond in ways that will best get your message across. The Libra Moon child responds well to logic. All the air Moons like explanations. Give them plenty of it. Handle water Moons gently. The Pisces Moon child needs lots of positive emotional feedback before ever hinting there is something that needs improvement. They are too vulnerable to criticism. A Virgo Moon child wants to do better anyway and can tolerate a lot more of it. A Cancer Moon child may simply wilt without mother's attention, to say nothing of criticism. Pushing too hard against a Scorpio Moon child on discipline issues develops resentment and anger, but they like rules and structure to their day.

The earth Moon children are very amenable to whatever Mom wants and will try hard to please. All children need emotional warmth and cuddling, even though some will not seek it out like the water Moon child will. It's not a good idea to give all the good stuff to one child just because the other didn't "ask" for it.

Children born with fire Moons appear more independent than they truly are. They need approval badly but given even a dab of it, will cope quite well. Learning these things can really boost parenting skills. I strongly recommend it.

To read about children from the mother's chart requires a look at the planets in those houses or that rule those houses and the aspects they make. It really takes the whole chart to do that.

Major transits to the Moon may trigger menopause if the woman is in her late 40s to mid 50s. Often the chart will show Uranus conjunct Moon, or Saturn conjunct or aspecting Neptune or Pluto. Some of this is part of the natural cycle in the natal pattern. Someone born with a lunar opposition to Uranus will get the conjunction in her mid 40s when transiting Uranus gets there. Neptune takes roughly 14 years per sign—somebody with a natal square of Neptune to the Moon has 3 signs (42 years) to live through before it conjuncts or opposes the Moon's birth position.

A woman born with Saturn opposition Moon will have Saturn conjunct Moon at 14, obviously too early for menopause. But 29 years later, when she is about 43, a second Saturn transit to Moon is likely to trigger it. Some women have patterns that show Moon will get a late contact at age 50 or so. Most women have menopause begin somewhere in the 40s.

Shutdown of the reproductive function starts slowly and takes 2-5 years. It's an individual thing, I find. Some women may feel the need to replace the hormones in the effort to stay youthful and more attractive. I don't argue with them, but I didn't think it was a good thing for me to tamper too much with natural cycles. Personal choice. Nowadays some women are finding that it is not the wonderful idea they thought it was in the beginning and has effects that weren't known earlier.

I sometimes think we are all spoiled by modern medicine, which makes us expect to feel at optimum levels of comfort in all conceivable situations. Doesn't happen. In fact, I always remember something I read years ago. It was this: Most of the world's important work is done by people who feel rotten that day. It always amused me and when I thought about it, inspired me to do better.

Menopause is not debilitating. It's a nuisance and annoying. But it is not nearly as likely to get you in trouble as puberty was, and it doesn't cripple your ability to function. Just get through it and you're done. Sooner or later you have to anyway unless you die while you're on estrogen. And that's a much bigger problem.

A key thing to consider in charts for children is their Moon, which tells you how they "see" their mother and what qualities they most respond to. A daughter's Moon in Aquarius says she responds most to communication, and needs that most from her mother The mother with a Gemini Moon instinctively mothers from the mental point of view and the daughter, especially a Gemini Sun child with an Aquarius Moon, responds to the air-ness.

If the mother has an Aquarian Sun or Moon, she has to be careful to provide emotional warmth and affection as well as mental stimulus. It is the "coldest" mother, in one sense, meaning a child will often set aside the emotional needs in favor of responding to the social and intellectual ones. Children try to live up to what they think their parents want of them. In a family with a lot of air, it is less distressing and if the child's Moon is well aspected, the negative sides are not as pronounced. In a different kind of chart, an Aquarian Moon is harsher.

The Libra and Capricorn Moon children absorb courtesy rules, diplomacy and tact easily. The Taurus and Pisces Moons tend to get spoiled because of their sweet dispositions.

Evangeline Adams also had some interesting things to say about Venus in Aquarius. She said that in mothers, it gives a keen awareness of what is truly good for their children. Not what they want to give them or what the child wants, but what is truly good. The result is that sometimes they seem cold or detached, but their judgments are often astoundingly perceptive.

Capricorn and Scorpio Moons can show the child sees mother as controlling, dominant and powerful (Capricorn). Scorpio can show the child sees mother as possessive, excessively emotional and not necessarily in a good way. One child with the Moon in Capricorn unusually well aspected thought his mother could move mountains. He had a brilliant and capable older sister and also calmly expected her to "move mountains." So a negative position is not always negative any more than a good position, like the Moon in Taurus, is always good. Sometimes Moon in Taurus can be greedy and rigid and a Cancer Moon can become weak and wishy-washy.

One of the things an angular natal Moon does is prompt the child to leave home and find its own destiny fairly early in life. This is particularly obvious with the fire Moons. An Aries Moon doesn't give it a second thought. The Sagittarius Moon usually manages to start traveling before it is much more than 18 anyway and even the Leo Moon, despite its ties to family, will make its own home elsewhere promptly. The Moon in the various houses gives a lot of tendency for change in those areas of life. All by itself, it is one of the strongest indicators that things will change when it is angular in a solar return or hits the natal angles in a progressed chart. It is a key factor in electional and horary work.

All angular Moons are more "domestic" than cadent Moons. Those who have them usually cook and keep a home quite comfortably, the men as well as women. Cadent Moons may not even notice there is a kitchen in the house. The chart accompanying this chapter shows how one man focused his rising Moon on a career as a chef. (See chart on page 31.)

In House 1, the person is excessively sensitive to Moon's phases. Opinions and emotional responses can be a constant roller coaster unless there are good, stabilizing aspects. In the second house, money comes and goes, but seldom stays. These are people who are sometimes comfortable in jobs with commissions that come at irregular times. The Moon here also describes something about the work choices, as any planet in a house does.

A third house Moon gives an itchy foot for traveling and siblings who come and go in the adult life. Sometimes there is a very close, emotional tie with at least one. In the fourth house the broader family is an overriding concern. Since this is the area where Moon "belongs" it has particular power and if it rules an angular house, can determine success or failure in those areas of life.

In the fifth, children are pleasureful and romances readily produce young. This can shock teenagers interested in sexual experimentation. Moon in the 6th is a touchy stomach and afflictions can bring constant health concerns. In the 7th, the partner will be sensitive and restless. It always describes the marriage, so it's worth examining the aspects.

Moon in the 8th house can mean inheritance, particularly from the mother or her side of the family, and a struggle to invest for old age. There are always too many reasons to take money out of the savings account for these people. Harshly aspected it's a warning of taking on too much debt and going under as a result.

In House 9 there is a love of learning and home-loving in-laws and grandchildren. House 10 produces those with strong domestic interests and sometimes skills. It's a great position for chefs as any angular Moon is. One woman I know was an executive in high tech with her Moon in Aquarius near the MC. She worked in several innovative high tech ventures. A truck driver had his Moon in Gemini in 10. Gemini likes to drive almost anything.

In House 11: A great many acquaintances and a high turnover in the social life. People with 11th house Moons know a lot of women but unless the Moon is fixed or well aspected, they tend to come and go in the life.

Moon also rules the public and that means public attention. Those with prominent Moons positively adore being noticed in public or by the public. Public notice will sometimes come through being spokesman for an organization they belong to, or work for. They can be joiners at various times in their lives, but seldom consistently.

In 11, it is also good for dealing with other people's children, even if they don't particularly like any children but their own. Other people's children tend to see the Moon in 11 person as somebody they can talk to, and do. Sometimes the youngsters are related to them—nieces, nephews and so forth, but it doesn't matter to the kids.

In House 12, the emotional nature is carefully guarded, and the individual has difficulty expressing feelings. When he or she does, they see it as risky and not always profitable. A well-aspected Moon there gives many quiet benefits through women all during life. Poorly aspected, women behind the scenes can be harmful. It will pay to treat women with extreme care.

The cyclic nature of Moon is quite pronounced in any area of the chart. It's always feast or famine, no matter where it falls. Because it deals with the emotional side of our natures, our Moon heavily affects our normal personalities and how we deal with others in many ways. Fire Moons, particularly when well aspected, are quick to express positive feelings and avoid dealing with negative ones. The Aries and Leo Moons will deal better with confrontation and negativity than the Sagittarean one. Leo is one of the signs that gives management skills. Aries tends to get bossy under stress and may have a hot temper if the Moon is afflicted, but Sagittarius just leaves if things look dicey.

Earth Moons are less volatile and seldom aggressive with others. They can be quite stubborn, however, and intent on getting their own way when pushed. They may do it in a diplomatic way, but they will persist until they accomplish what they want to do. They will fight back strongly if abused.

Air signs can often talk people into anything. Sometimes they talk so long people will throw up their hands and give them whatever they want just to get some peace. Air Moons are very good at complicating issues or sorting them out, depending on which side they're on. Their judgment is clear. They are also highly logical and can make very cold-blooded decisions. Emotional appeals are less successful with them than with any other Moon position.

The water Moons are totally engaged with others and highly vulnerable to any emotional appeal. It gives them insight into the feelings of others and increases the ability to respond. You will find them in the fields of acting, literature and caring for the needs of others. If there is any Saturn aspect these people can suffer a great deal of unjustified guilt over the problems of others.

Moon's sensitivity to aspects shows sharply in domestic arrangements. It deals with all the normal home and family issues everyone has and rules the habits we form in childhood. Cardinal Moons change readily, fixed Moons rarely and mutable Moons prefer small increments to avoid the trauma of bigger change. Mutable signs hate change. The fixed signs will do it if they have to but they like operating in a "rut" and will make a new one if forced out of the old one.

A good example of that is dieting. Cardinal signs charge in and try to do it all yesterday. They are suckers for the ads that say one can lose ten pounds in ten days. Fixed signs don't believe the ads and just try to eat sensibly until the ten pounds are gone, no matter how long it takes. Mutable signs have another approach. One woman I knew once informed me that she lost 20 pounds one year by eliminating one slice of bread daily. She was a Virgo. Another just gave up butter for life. She had a Gemini Moon.

The Moon really does affect our daily life more than we think. One should always be aware of what it is up to each day. Life will then have a few less surprises.

Making a home

Sometimes basic astrology techniques can help us do something as simple as making a home for ourselves. Home is ruled by the Moon so here are some tips on how to be at home where you are.

Cancer rules food, right? So start cooking, baking, filling your spot with good smells. Buy and use a bread machine (man, does that smell like "home"). If you aren't a baker, spend some of every week's grocery dollar on stuff for soup. (There are directions on packages. If you can read, you can make soup.) Then cook the soup. There are directions on bread machines. Running a washing machine is tougher.

If you have fresh bread and homemade soup in your kitchen once a week, you will feel happy, safe and pampered, I guarantee you. Chocolate chip cookies you make are a bonus. And most grocery stores will sell you the dough all ready to pop in the oven.

Second, the Moon rules growing things, such as gardens. Plant chives, lettuce, tomatoes, anything. If you don't have an outdoors, plant them indoors or on your balcony. Mix in a few flowers. Grow something. If it's a canary, or goldfish, that also qualifies. Cats are good. So are dogs. Cancer rules nurturing.

Third, the sign Cancer deals with containers of all kinds—bags, baskets, bowls, buckets, bottles and the like. Put them around. All kinds. Fill some with candles, some with soap in the bathroom, some with reading material in the living room, with pillows or slippers in the bedroom, with things of whatever sort you have. Make sure every room has a visible container in it. At least one. The laundry room should have a basket for clean clothes or a hamper for dirty ones or both.

That's inside. Now go outside and look at what you have that is yours. Your spot, if you like. Put your name somewhere, even if it's only on the mailbox. Find a place for a chair to watch the Sunset. Put a chair there. Figure out where you want to put your car. Put it there every day.

Next examine the neighborhood. Now obviously people aren't going to bombard you with presents and attention just because you're there, but they will be curious about you. It's human nature. Talk to them. Try to make a few friends. Find out who needs help. Offer to help, even if it's just picking up a loaf of bread for old Mrs. Whosit on the corner when you shop for those soup ingredients. Share some of the soup with her. Better yet, invite her over, put your plant (you do have one by now) on the table and serve the bread in a basket. Put a bit of yourself into the neighborhood and before you know it, it will be your neighborhood.

Check out the town. Find a place that needs you. Give of yourself. If you put a little love into a place, love comes back and that makes it "home."

Sure it takes a little time and effort. But less than you think. Follow the Cancer rules and the Moon side of yourself responds and provides instincts that make you feel this is "home." It is the Moon that is our emotions and happy, warm, safe comforted emotions are what we need to give ourselves.

By the way, it's not enough just to think about doing this. You actually have to do it. When you pamper yourself, the child in you responds. It's really a lot simpler than we think.

Childbirth

I have found Pluto involvement important—anytime you see progressions and transits involving that planet in the chart of a young woman it can trigger a fertile time.

However, for conception, a good Mars transit of any of the four angles is helpful. Mars, after all, is cellular activity—and also the planet which symbolizes both sex and the start of anything. The Moon is too obvious an egg symbolism for words. So we have both Moon activity and that of Mars needed. Luckily, Mars is also sexual activity so that works out pretty well.

The key things to predicting when a child will arrive is the mother's Moon and her angles. The actual birth often comes when Mars activates her Moon, one of her angles or its ruler when she is nearing term. Some women have Mars aspecting the MC or its ruler at the time of child birth. You'd think it would be the Ascendant, but that simply doesn't hold true all the time. Any aspect will do to set things off—even a semi-sextile to the ruler of one of the angles. Watch also for Mars aspecting anything in the mother's 6th. If it's close to the full Moon and Mars is nearing an aspect to an angle you are definitely in the ball park. Full Moons can often set off labor. Watch all lunar aspects and aspects to the woman's solar sixth house.

The sex of the baby is based on her Moon sign's gender and the baby's ruler. This is another time the derived house system helps out. If it is the 4th or the 6th child you can often see quickly which one it will be. Heavy earth and water show feminine births. Air and fire produces boys. Whichever is stronger gets the call.

Most women have a 5th house general indication of sex of the children. One woman with Jupiter in Gemini had only boys. Another with the Moon there in a water sign produced only girls The indications are likely to be mixed however, and that's when you have to do some careful checking of the houses to see if the particular child coming next gets a male or female indication.

Some careful thinkers may remind me that it is the father's sperm contribution which determines sex, but this is not as reliable as one would think. The woman's body tends to be more acidic or alkaline at the time of conception and often "favors" male or female children. Among the old wives' tales I heard when young was that there were things women could do to encourage boys, such as vinegar douches, which would alter the PE in the vagina. Oddly enough I never heard of any way to encourage girls. It was an interesting commentary on the times.

There are women with harsh planets in House 5 who never produce children at all, despite all the equipment being perfectly acceptable. Astrologically speaking, perhaps their systems may be so extremely inhospitable to the arriving sperm that conception simply can't occur.

Saturn or Uranus in House 5 can bring problems in conception. A bit of medical assistance is of great value in cases like this. Nowadays that can range from "accumulating" sperm in the low-sperm-count cases to actual "in vitro" fertilization.

But generally speaking, Mars and the Moon, of course, are the most help in achieving conception. One woman with Mars in the 5th in Taurus had no difficulty becoming pregnant but miscarried several times or chose abortion since she didn't want children.

The Moon's nodes are involved whenever a significant person enters our lives, since the nodes deal with all the relationships we have. Since our children are significant in our lives, it's no surprise to me that they are active. Some are very involved and others are less, but that's true of any family with more than one child.

If those with multiple children check the Mars positions at the time their various children were born they might be surprised to see the ties. Perhaps this also accounts for the "irritation" factor in child-rearing, since Mars is the planet of the irritating and of annoyances.

The late Comedian W.C. Fields said the best way to raise children was to keep them in a barrel with a bung hole until they were 16 and then seal up the bung hole. Great joke but there are times every mother can agree with him.

At any rate, I found a book on Astro Conception very helpful. There is another one I haven't seen in a while, "Lady, I Have Your Number," which includes some of the same material.

I haven't found any sure-fire way to pinpoint adoption. It shows in the charts of those who are adopted but the most I can see in the charts of those who choose the child in the first place comes from the 11th house indicators. Those can be hard to judge.

Chapter 6

Gardening by the Moon

As the Moon changes its appearance gradually during the lunar month, so, too, the energy fields around the earth change, offering good times and bad for things to be accomplished.

Planting by the Moon is one of the oldest astrological skills, still practiced by a surprising number around the world who know that it can give them stronger plants and richer yielding crops. The rules for using the phases of the Moon are fairly simple. Here are the ones I use for gardening by the Moon. When I stir myself to actually do it, that is.

Plants whose fruits, stems or edible portions come above the ground—such as beans, celery, peas, tomatoes and lettuce—should be planted after the new Moon and before the Full Moon. This is the waxing phase.

Plants whose roots are eaten—carrots, potatoes, turnips and yams—should be planted after the full Moon before the next new Moon. This is the waning phase. A good Saturn aspect is excellent for stability and sturdy growth. It also improves "keeping" quality.

Nothing should be done under the Full Moon. It kills transplants and isn't helpful to seeds. Wait a day Nothing should be planted with the Sun in Leo. It's too strong an influence. In the northern hemisphere it's too late in the growing season anyway.

Farm almanacs still give the times each month when the Moon is new and full. These can guide the home gardener as well. Flowers, shrubs and trees have slightly different rules.

Plant perennials, trees and shrubs, where good root development is desired, during the waning phase. Bulb flowers, or those that arise from corms—daffodils and irises—should be planted in the waning phase.

The zodiac signs give additional help. Use a water sign when a juicy fruit or vegetable is desired. The water signs are Cancer, Scorpio and Pisces. This improves melons and grapes. To avoid onions and peppers with too much heat, do not use the fire signs for planting. Fire signs are Aries, Leo and Sagittarius. As a general rule, they aren't the best for food. On the other hand, if you want super hot jalapenos, use the Aries Moon for planting. They'll be as spicy as you could wish. If you want mild sweet peppers, use Taurus. Be careful with onions. If you like a hot onion, go for a fire sign, but if you like the Vidalia type sweeter one, use earth or water Moons. Earth signs are good for increasing fiber and helping fruits and vegetables keep well in storage. The earth signs are Taurus, Virgo and Capricorn. They also help with berries grown on perennial bushes and improve yield. Air signs are good for weeding, particularly in the waning phase of the Moon. Aquarius is the best of the three. Air signs are Gemini, Aquarius and Libra. The best weeding is done under Leo or Aquarius—they don't come back. Never weed under Taurus or Scorpio. The weeds get stubborn and persist.

Plant flowers under Taurus and Libra. Roses do best under Taurus for scent but Libra is also favored by a lot of people.

Get a good Venus aspect for sweetness in berries and peas and melons. It is also a good planet for improving general flavor. Mercury is helpful with ornamentals like those colorful cabbages. When you plant things you want to cross-fertilize, use Mars, it also gives tang (but as I told you, makes hot peppers hotter). Want a very BIG pumpkin? Plant with a strong aspect to Jupiter. Don't put your zucchinis in then unless you like a lot of surplus and zucchinis tend to give it anyway. With any encouragement they will take over the neighborhood. Jupiter gives abundance.

Things planted for their seeds should go into the ground during the Scorpio Moon. Flowers are prettiest when planted under Taurus and Libra. Virgo is best for herbs and dye plants. Capricorn is what you want for trees and shrubs, though flowering shrubs do very well under Taurus or Libra, too. Pisces is particularly good for vines of all kinds, especially grapes intended for wine, Cancer gives the tastiest vegetables and salad greens. If you like multiple blossoms use Pisces.

Air signs rule things that grow high off the ground—apples and cherries and other things that grow in trees. Fire signs rule berries that grow low on bushes like blueberries and elderberries and the type of sericulture for desert plants. Earth signs rule things that grow on the ground or nearly touching it—like strawberries or tomatoes... and water signs rule things low to the ground or that lay on it and need lots of moisture—cucumbers, for instance or melons. Hay would be another.

Marigolds planted under Moon in Leo are excellent at repelling harmful insects. Sunflowers also do especially well with this sign. However, the time when Sun is in Leo is not very good for planting anything—from July 22 to Aug. 21. If you need to weed and the Moon is in Leo or Aquarius, the weeds will be slow to return. Don't bother weeding before Full Moon. Do it afterwards. The dark phase of the Moon, when it can't be seen in the sky at all, is the best.

For pruning to encourage growth, use an earth or water sign before the full Moon. For pruning to discourage regrowth, use an air sign after the full Moon.

The native American Indians used to plant things together in threes—a corn stalk, a pumpkin or squash vine and beans. That's when you use Pisces, which rules threes. It sounds odd but turns out to be an exceptionally intelligent way of keeping and restoring soil fertility. If you plan such companion planting, use Gemini for twos, or Virgo. Virgo is great for organic planting and grains of all kinds.

Night flowering plants are for Cancer. So are most white flowers like lilies of the valley or gardenias etc.

All the earth and water Moons are good for food. All the air and fire Moons are good for weeding. For weeding success, just use one of the barren Moon signs and don't worry about the aspects. You'd spend more time on the astrology of the thing than on the weeding and there would just be more weeds the next day. And besides, sometimes the only time we have to weed is when the Moon is in Cancer or Pisces or Taurus. Well, like a lot of things in life, just do it. So, they come back...you knew they would.

Use the waning Moon in Cancer for the moving of plants. If you want the pruning to limit size and shape, use Leo. Otherwise use Taurus to encourage better growth.

The overall rule is: waxing Moon for annuals, waning Moon for perennials, Taurus for pretty, Pisces for juicy, Cancer for taste, and Scorpio for seed. The rest is variable.

A void of course Moon does not affect routine jobs that are done over and over. It's something to watch out for when you are doing the initial launch of a new garden, however.

Each of the signs has its value and each phase of the Moon can enhance the effectiveness of the gardener's labor. It would be a shame to ignore the advantage this oldest of astrological knowledge can give. Using it rewards the wise gardener.

Chapter 7

Jack be nimble
Mercury

The childhood nursery rhyme about Jack who jumped over a candlestick is a Mercury tale. Mercury energy is quick, slick and hard to catch and Mercury people all have a bit of the trickster about them. Mercury energy is how we get information. The idea of switching identities, particularly gender identities (Shakespeare loved that one) is very Mercurial. Mercury is neither male nor female but "other," which can mean "both" because information comes from a point of view and many of us tend to have primarily male or female points of view. It is eye-opening to trade views or roles.

The Kokopelli of the Southwestern U.S. Indian tradition, or the Coyote of the plains Indians are all ancient Mercury figures of fun which can occasionally turn sinister or cruel, playing tricks and being amused by the problems of others. There is also a whimsicality here which is definitely Mercury. Remember, Mercury is cold-blooded and not very sympathetic in many cases.

Sexual identity is something we see changing in the modern world with actual surgery being chosen to somehow overcome or alter the original androgynous pattern. Any time there seems to be a look that is less clearly male or female there may be a Mercury action worth examining in the natal pattern.

There is a problem many of us have today with the outer planets. We forget how important the inner planets are and what they really deal with. Mercury is far more than just a telephone call or a messenger. Mercury is part of our very nature and allows to express many more qualities than we realize. It is the planet closest to the Sun and often hidden by its rays and is how we hide ourselves and our privacy as well.

In my experience, people who have Mercury retrograde at birth can just ignore all the rules the rest of us use when Mercury goes retrograde three times a year. It seems to be a favorable time for them and things they start at that time do fine. They also talk a great deal during these phases, opening up and feeling more comfortable doing so in ways they don't at other times of the year. It's almost as if they've been waiting for "their turn." It's the very best time to get information out of them because when Mercury is direct they may avoid giving answers to questions. Mercury ℞ is the "ill wind" that blows some good for those born with it.

The late Evangeline Adams said that the Moon ruled the sense impressions and that Mercury ruled what the mind did with them—in other words, how it processed the information it received from the receptors. I paid a lot of attention to this early on because the other texts I learned from did not explain some sharp divergences I found. It may sound like nit picking, but I think it is the reason that Mercury functions are not always what we expect. I think it also accounts for a great deal of the misunderstanding on how to read intelligence in the chart.

A friend of mine is always giving me the business because I once called Mercury in Taurus "slow" when she knows she is quite intelligent and has rapid responses to many things. But I think in Taurus Mercury IS slow—slow to process all it takes in because as it processes the information, it embeds it in stone. Once learned, it's there forever.

Some of us process instantly but the information can be gone rather quickly, too. It's terribly frustrating, for instance, to teach the same things to people repeatedly because information doesn't seem to "stick" in their brains even when they are trying hard to learn. The key seems to be a combination of Moon/Mercury function in the chart. This is what Evangeline Adams believed, at least.

The brightest minds I know tend to have one of two combinations: a fast Moon (daily speed faster than average) AND slow Mercury (especially near a station) OR a slow Moon (speed below average) and a fast Mercury (nearing 2 degrees daily motion or more). One of the best indicators, of course, is Mercury at or near station, such as the chart above. This idea may also account for the apparent problems in dignity/debility assignments. You have a lot of very bright people with Mercury in signs of its fall, for instance. But if it was moving slowly at birth while the Moon was fast OR fast while the Moon was slow, or was at or near a station (either retrograde or direct) it beefs up the intelligence considerably.

Here's a tip on Mercury retrograde that I have found invaluable. If you make an appointment with someone under a retrograde period, never make the appointment for a time after Mercury goes direct. You or the other person never show up. I've seen this one over and over. Move heaven and earth to fit things in or do it at an ungodly hour while Mercury is still retrograde. If you make an appointment with someone before the retrograde phase for a time during it, they change the appointment. Never fails. The rule is: **See people during the same phase as when the appointment was made.** These rules also apply when you are making appointments with dentists or tax men or hairdressers. Be sure to set the time under the same phase of Mercury as when it was made.

If you have people in your family who have computer-related jobs, you can hear them doing a lot of swearing with Mercury ℞. Anybody whose job is linked to cars, computers or telephones will be tearing their hair, particularly when the stations hit their natal charts. The plethora of small, irritating difficulties is like being nibbled to death by a man-eating bug. It isn't the quantity that annoys you, it's the persistence.

Mercury also has another function on the higher levels of awareness, according to some older authors. It was the capacity of the human mind for wisdom, as Venus was the capacity for true charity, in the sense of wide love for all mankind, not just one's own family and friends. Since these two planets were inward from the earth toward the Sun, they were considered most important, according to some of those older writers.

Mercury is the planet most apt to alter its expression depending on which planets aspect it in the natal chart. Since it is so neutral of itself this should not come as a surprise.

Aspects to Mars improve mental speed and assertiveness. Throw in the Moon and you have the motor-mouth. This is very good for memory and speeds recall but it increases the tendency to talk endlessly, sometimes unkindly. It ups the irritability factor into the ozone. Aspects to Venus are helpful in artistic concerns but since the sextile and conjunction to Mercury are fairly common, it's considered a mildly nice but not particularly important aspect. Venus does not seem especially likely to affect the memory.

Aspects to Jupiter give a special facility of expression. Good for foreign languages and story-telling. Wonderful for a comedian. The ability to remember a good joke is a genuine talent and the skilled are often known for their huge collection of jokes. Aspects to Saturn mean that what is learned stays there. It's superb for memory and number skills but it can lead to bouts of depression, particularly if the aspect is a square.

Aspects to Uranus make the mind extremely high-powered and inventive. This produces what used to be called a "nervy" type or somebody who is "high strung," fidgety, nervous, quick with details everyone else has forgotten, and often has a high IQ. Aspects to Neptune are creative and imaginative but sometimes not truthful. In combo with Venus, they are excellent for the arts, and with Jupiter, good for fiction. But if memory fails, Neptune is apt to get creative.

An aspect to Pluto can mean lots of material in the mental stash, but periods of forgetfulness, sort of like a computer with random purges of odd material. This "random purge" effect, as I call it, has nothing to do with age. It can happen all through life. Anybody I know with a Mercury-Pluto aspect knows exactly what I mean.

It's almost as if the brain decides which items are not worth storing and simply refuses to bother, while other things one finds mildly interesting, such as why fireflies flash, are remembered forever. Words I have ever seen once I can remember if I see them again. But a credit card number just won't register in my head, even though I shop with it all the time. It's as if the brain is arrogantly saying, "Don't waste my space—look at the card." One man I know has a Mercury/Uranus/Pluto conjunction and can remember any kind of number—such as phone numbers of friends from 20 years ago. But he also has had the "random purge" experience—sometimes with words.

I would give Saturn governance of long-term memory but loss of memory seems to belong to some combination with Pluto. The "purge" is definitely Plutonian. Recall problems I think are sometimes connected to the Moon and Mars. Those who are fans of such mercurial hobbies as daily crossword puzzles may notice that the transiting Moon determines how quickly they can recall the words necessary to work them. So obviously the Moon has recall impact. Any transiting Mars aspect and the puzzle gets done pretty quickly. People who have vague memories may not have a lot of Mercury aspects that help it function. On the other hand, if there is no Pluto aspect, at least there's no purge either.

I once was in the process of knitting some fancy mittens: definitely a Mercury project. I started the first one with Mercury ℞. and then frantically worked on mitten no. 2 to complete it before the direct phase resumed. I knew it would take me twice as long to finish if I didn't. I know how this works. Both mittens needed linings, so I saved those for the direct phase. One learns to cope with Mercury ℞.

Mercury is usually very strong in the chart of any business with a double letter in its name—Yahoo, for instance. This works the same way with people's names. If somebody is known by a name with double letters—Willy, or Debbie, etc., there is usually a strong

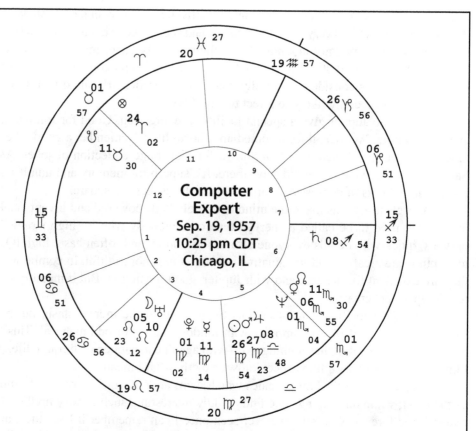

The modern world offers an irresistible lure of computer technology to those powerfully ruled by Mercury. This man's angular Mercury was one day after a station and rules both his Ascendant and his Sun sign. His job title reflects his role as chief architect for the companies he works for. He designs new technology and is often in demand as a trouble-shooter for systems on the cutting edge. He also has a law degree but has never used it.

Mercury component in the chart. The former U.S. President Jimmy Carter refused to give up his name for any other version of James and he was known for being a micromanager and extremely picky with small details, all Mercury qualities. Above all in our modern agenda, is the computer which is a Mercury tool. The chart above is of a man who is an expert in computer technology of all kinds, and it shows a powerful Mercury, indeed.

When it comes to hiring and the jobs world, those without computer skills are seriously handicapped today. We are simply living in the information (Mercury) era and the computer is the god of the information world. A look at career possibilities for anyone with a pronounced Mercury influence has to put computer technology at the top of the list.

How to Use Retrograde Mercury

If you can start and finish a project during a retrograde Mercury period, it works fine. If you don't finish then, you'll likely either wait until the next Mercury ℞ period or not finish it at all. OR, there will be so many changes that you'll end up starting over anyway. We're not talking routine things here, but special projects.

I think the stationary direct time —the 24 hours or so just after it—are excellent for getting all Mercury things off the ground. I have a lot of things I save up to get done at those times to make hay while the Sun shines, so to speak. When transiting Mercury turns retrograde, it's the people who have powerful Mercury influences in their lives who are the most distressed by it. The Gemini and Virgo Suns, those with Gemini or Virgo rising and those with angular Mercurys seem to me to be the most vulnerable.

The people who seem the least annoyed by Mercury ℞ are people born with Mercury ℞. They are not people who talk a lot about what they think or what bothers them, UNTIL Mercury goes ℞. Then it's Katie bar the door—out comes this flood of information. They chatter away for days and don't shut down until Mercury's retrograde period is over. If you didn't get an important question answered by then, you'll have to wait until the next retrograde period.

A bridge near me was undergoing some reconstruction started during Mercury ℞. Right. I knew I could count on that one taking forever while engineers tinkered with the specs. It was not completed until a much later Mercury retrograde period. It took nearly two years, well past the time it was scheduled to be completed. And a new "department of the government" announced during a Mercury ℞ period? It somehow never happened. Too many people changed their minds about it once Mercury went direct. What was finally established bore no resemblance to the original plan.

Mercury ℞ is an excellent time for certain things—re-initiating a project is a classic. Sometimes things you started under previous Mercury ℞ phases can finally come to a conclusion under this one. I had a knitting project for a linen tote bag I unwisely started under Mercury ℞ (even smart astrologers are stupid sometimes, and I just hadn't thought to check before I got into it) and didn't finish. Every time Mercury went retrograde I'd pick it up again, mess with it a while and put it aside again. Finally after three Mercury ℞ periods I gave up. I just unraveled it, wound the yarn into balls and put 'em away. Lord knows if they'll ever get used but that project was never going to get done. Still hasn't been, for that matter.

The rule is that anything you "go back to do" or "re-do" under Mercury ℞ is favored. Of course, there are exceptions, as I just mentioned. Just remember, if you start a project under Mercury ℞—especially one like a knitting one that is string (Mercury) and fingers (Mercury) be sure to finish it before Mercury changes direction.

One learns to cope with Mercury ℞.

Chapter 8

All the things we love
Venus

Some have said wisdom is knowing what is good to choose and Venus is caring enough to choose it. Venus is exalted in Pisces where love means giving of self unselfishly. Taurus and Libra, its two signs, offer a great deal of scope for Venus, ruling as they do the financial and sensual arenas so vital to ordinary happiness. Sometimes we get so involved in the lesser meanings of the signs and planets we lose sight of these basic qualities, I think. Once in a while we need to ask where we're going with all this stuff we know and how much good is it doing us. After all, if we don't "live" what we know, we're no better than jackasses carrying a load of books.

The traditional interpretation of Venus is that when Venus is rising before the Sun as the morning star it acts like a masculine, warrior planet, and when rising after the Sun as an evening star is feminine, soft and peaceful. That seems to be true in a vast number of charts, even though not evident initially.

Thinkers like Immanuel Velikovsky, who wrote some very interesting books, suggested our Venus might have entered the solar system late in a rather violent way, perhaps destroying a planet that once existed between Mars and Jupiter (and which is the source of the asteroid ring there now) and that this long ago event lingered on in the tradition of Venus as a warrior. Certain ancient peoples did not think highly of Venus in her so-called peaceful image. To them she was violent and bloodthirsty.

The late, great American astrologer Evangeline Adams had quite a lot to say about the difference between Venus in Taurus and in Libra, too. She saw Venus as necessary for the continuation of the human race, and in Taurus has all the deep, earthy, fecund imagery where it can produce a rich seeding for the future. It is tactile and sensual and desirous of the sexual pleasure which brings forth the young. In Libra, she said that Venus is also necessary for the continuation of the race, but in a different sense—that of creating partnerships and human relationships and the principles that allow people to live and work together harmoniously, thus fostering a happy home for the young to develop.

Libra does not give Venus the sensuality that Taurus does but it provides a way for the sensuality to enhance human relations. Taurus does not give the aesthetic sense that Libra has but it provides the powerful underpinnings of creativity and the fertility of the soul. In Taurus there is a love of music and quite often a good singing voice. In Libra there is a broad artistic hunger and appreciation for beauty. Venus in either sign understands the other quite well. Venus spends less time retrograde than any other planet, only 40 days every other year, so it functions constantly to provide the pleasures that keep us going.

I have seen a very strong natal Venus in the charts of successful race car drivers. It's obvious that Venus transits reinforced a natal chart promising they would be winners. Venus is also the sheer joy they feel in the driving experience. Venus deals with what we love, and that can be anything we do that gives us pleasure. Jupiter, which is honor, may bring championships and titles, but Venus represents money and satisfaction.

I wonder if the singer Mick Jagger knew someone with an afflicted Venus position or had trouble with a progression. His natal chart does have an afflicted Venus, and his song, "Can't Get No Satisfaction" is definitely a lament over Venus troubles.

The ancient Mayans used Venus movement as a primary predictive cycle and her rotations over a period of years in very large cycles they used concluded in 2012. A new Venus cycle commenced at that time. So what was called the world's "ending" actually marked the position of Venus returning to what the Mayans believed was its starting point. Venus was seen as a threatening planet in Mayan cosmology. The Mayans, among the best astrologers of ancient times, were aware of her different functions when Venus was rising before or after the Sun. But they were among those who didn't particularly trust any "peaceful" manifestation. I always wondered if they weren't confusing her with Mars.

The kidneys come under Libra and Venus. There is some question about the gall bladder. I think it is Venus-ruled, but there is a school of thought that wants to give it to Jupiter or even the Moon, because it is a "bag" and bags come under the Moon's rulership. However, both the liver—the body's largest internal organ—and its companion, the much smaller gall bladder, function to purify the body of toxins. They even use a common bile duct. They illustrate perfectly a greater and lesser benefic pair, in my opinion. The ovaries are also Venus organs. They have the job of allowing eggs to mature in the female which will provide the potential for reproduction.

Venus is the principle of harmony, an obvious tie-in to both the musical talents of Taurus and the people skills of Libra. Progressions which involve Venus urge people to find partners, seek emotional satisfaction and even wed. It is above all the planet which deals in partnership and marriage. When marriage fails, of course, it is divorce.

When harmonious relationships between nations fail, Venus deals with war. The sign Aries is that of the soldier but generals come under Libra, probably because of the tactical and logical skills needed to conduct military campaigns successfully. The air sign Libra is one of logic, rationality and the ability to function well in an emotionally detached manner. Dwight D. Eisenhower, the supreme commander of allied forces in World War II, was a Libra Sun.

Venus also rules law and the lawyers who practice it. It rules negotiations and ambassadors and those who seek peace and agreement between opposing parties. When agreement cannot be reached, Venus falls back on the law. But Venus also rules broader human issues than just formal partnership. It is the glue of society, dealing with soft words and courtesy that smooth out all human interaction, kindness, affection, friendship and the beauties of daily life. It deals with good clothes and the "fine feathers" we all want for special occasions. It is jewelry that adorns us, fancy hats and the comfort of underwear that fits and

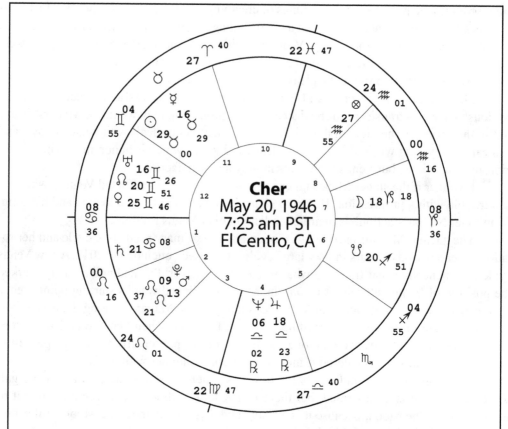

Lovely Cher has had a long and successful career as a singer, with platinum records in each decade for 40 years. Her Venus is trine her Part of Fortune and her cardinal angular T-square has produced the drive to be outstandingly successful in the varied careers she has had. In film, she is an Oscar winner.

nightwear that welcomes us when we crawl into bed. Venus is tasteful homes and pleasant rooms, elegant sculpture and art that adorns our walls. It is our comfortable chairs and the sweet smelling lotions, perfumes and after-shave liquids we use on our bodies. It's records in our collection, music we choose to listen to and the richness of the land that nourishes us.

A land of plenty, with crops in the field and fruit in the orchards, gardens of flowers and vegetables, nuts and berries are all part of the Venus bounty. In early summer it's easy to see the Venus effect by driving through a wide array of neighborhoods. How much, or how little, each home is adorned with flowers is a good tip-off to the owner's Venus. Most of us find some way to brighten things up, even with a pot of purchased petunias. It's the human hunger for beauty and a little of it tends to show up wherever people are.

Think of the lack of Venus in a military barracks (the Mars life) and in prisons where the failure of the inmates to respond to their fellow man with any Venus treatment is "adjusted." Soldiers are trained to kill each other, not make friends and convicts are essentially told that all kinds of Venus satisfaction is denied to them.

In its guise as a financial planet, Venus rules banks and earnings, and the prices we pay for precious things. Of course it is money and those who become intensely interested in

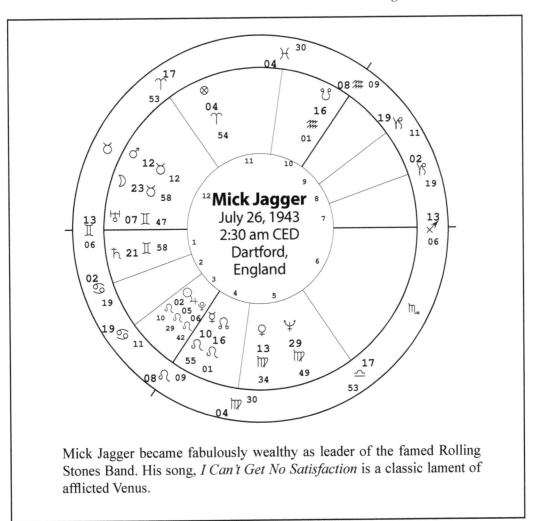

Mick Jagger became fabulously wealthy as leader of the famed Rolling Stones Band. His song, *I Can't Get No Satisfaction* is a classic lament of afflicted Venus.

finance and the markets usually show a sharp streak of Venus activity in their natal patterns.

It is, above all, the planet which describes our values and whatever we count as important to ordinary living. It rules the sense of smell, and the discernment of the connoisseur, whether in food or wine or the arts. But it is also all the goals most of us have for happiness in this world—people we love who love us back, joy in our work and the pleasures of leisure and hobbies.

This world would be a grim place indeed without Venus.

Chapter 9

Dealing with danger
Mars

Mars is always dangerous. It deals with knives, and weapons and the process of cutting things. It is soldiering, which involved swords in the old days, and surgery. Anything that is hit or thrown or torn or blown up is Martian. People who have a strong Mars in their charts are comfortable with weapons and sharp pointy things in general. They are also comfortable with danger.

Butchers are Mars-ruled, as are any other occupations that require "cutting"—lumber jacking come to mind, for instance. Professional football players are among those who hit and run into others as part of their job. Athleticism, the pure joy of movement, speed and power are Mars. High speed driving and boxing are sports that are particularly Martian. Anything that involves hitting, shooting, or throwing covers a lot of sports—baseball, golf, football, archery and tennis. And above all, Mars rules tools, usually made from the Mars metal, iron, which has been forged into steel.

All of the uniformed services come under the zodiac sign Virgo, whether police or fire fighters in a city or the military of a nation. EMTs, paramedics and the like are also in Virgo occupations. However, the tools they use and the courage they display using them when confronting dangerous situations are Mars qualities that have nothing to do with a Sun sign.

Anyone who chooses a Mars occupation is someone who has a potent Mars position in the natal chart. That can be both good and bad, since Mars is not a disciplined planet but rather a hurry-up-and-get-it-done one. The result can be scars on the body from accidents or the simple process of living. When Mars gets one going there is little likelihood of worrying about every little bruise or bump.

It takes very little to push Mars, the planet of energy, past proper behavior. We would all like to think that those who represent us use their Mars energy in the right way. The truth is that all the legendary Mars tales talk about this as a violent, abrupt and uncontrolled force. While the Romans, whose conquering spirit created the greatest empire of the ancient world, loved Mars, the Greeks, who called him Ares, just thought he was mostly trouble.

It takes other planets, particularly the Sun and Saturn, to help with the job of civiliz-ing him. Without a strong Saturn to keep it under control, Mars easily gets out of hand. The

Sun tends to give Mars a channel to constructive use, though in some charts that doesn't work. Conjunctions are good, squares are not so hot. Both Sun and Saturn symbolize authority and in the military or in the police departments, rule those of higher rank who simply MUST stay in control to prevent gratuitous violence from happening.

The truth is that you won't get good fighters or killers without Mars and the danger always exists that it can get loose. Mars is rather like an attack dog—handy in the yard where it can deal with intruders but it needs a lot of training before it's fit to come in the house.

The very fact we got out of bed this morning was Mars at work. We probably heard a loud noise (alarms are Mars) which woke us up and urged us to get up and start the day. Beginnings are particularly Martian. Everyone uses Mars, men and women alike, though it is considered masculine because of its action.

The whole notion of discipline, which is training, is the measured persistence of Saturn which focuses and enhances that power. This is why Mars is said to be exalted in the sign Capricorn, where Saturn's focus and limitation ups the ante on the Mars power. Most outstanding athletes have some link from Mars to Saturn. The very best athletes in the world are always the hardest workers. The ceaseless practice, the hours on the ice or the basketball court, or the putting green reflect a level of personal commitment that is intensely focused and disciplined.

All of the planets do not exhibit their qualities in the same way. If Mars is in an air sign it is mental in expression. It can yell and shout about its anger before it actually does anything. In water it is emotional, and may cry a lot before acting, but it is still Mars—the energy we have to work with. In its worst expression, it can let anger fester and that's not good. Mars in earth is direct and prompt. No sitting around thinking about it. But for sheer quantity of energy, it's fire, hands down. People with Mars in fire don't seem to run out. However, one simply cannot attribute qualities to Mars that belong to other planets whose influences modify the Mars expression.

Mars deals with accidents which can cause cuts, bruises and abrasions. In the body it rules the head, the face and the blood. It's the color red. It is surgery and the scars left by it. It deals with temper, as well as panic and bravery in the face of overwhelming odds. People with scars on their head or face are often apt to have a Mars-ruled Sun sign or have Mars rising in their natal charts. If Mars is square or opposed to the ascendant the same thing can occur. Additionally, red hair shows up, which is why redheads are assumed to have a hot temper. Many do, of course.

Accident proneness is usually a combination of Mars and Saturn, which can come from suppressed anger, resentments, guilt and depression. In the old fight-or-flight decision, Mars is fight, Saturn is flight. Mars is the "aggressive sexual-fight-injure" energy. Frustrated, it brings anger and resentments. Saturn is the "defensive-flight-control-to-avoid-damage" energy. Saturn's problem, fear, can lead to depression and guilt.

Both malefics symbolize part of our human nature and both can also be part of other things, such as the sexual experience, just as much as Venus, which is the "yield-submit-soothe-please-redirect" energy.

When both Saturn and Mars together operate, Saturn prevents Mars from fighting and Mars prevents Saturn from running, but the energy has to go somewhere. Sometimes that is outward toward others and sometimes inward toward ME, where it is driven down into the body where it leads to accidents, or illness. So much for the fun Mars and Saturn together can provide.

Mars is not a good position for celibacy in any of the earth signs. Earth signs find great comfort in sexual activity and usually have a lot of stamina as well. Actually, the whole notion of celibacy is pretty difficult for Mars types to deal with since it is the most active of all the planets except Mercury and sex is one of its two primary drives. The other is also a sensual appetite, but has to do with food. Mars food is strongly flavored, hot and spicy and involves meat. Vegetarianism is not usually a first choice for a Mars type. It may not be a second or third one, either.

For centuries—millennia, really—Mars was said to be the daytime ruler of Aries, the sign of Me and the nighttime ruler of Scorpio, the sign that deals with the "seed" of life, the transformation of it into new life, and the murky areas of "recycling," explained in the sense of leaves becoming soil, bodies returning their elements to the earth etc.

The cult of Mithras in ancient times and the legend of Pluto are both VERY Martian. Mithras was a god specifically for soldiers and his rites were often held underground when facilities either natural or manmade were available. Pluto was the god of Hades, the underworld (the Greeks actually called him Hades. Pluto was his Roman name), where souls went after death.

Pluto is said to deal with the process of restructuring elements. There is a modern tendency to think regeneration, transfiguration and deep transformation is a new thing. Not so. They simply used different analogies and different words in other times, but the principles were the same. And, they belonged to Mars-ruled Scorpio. Even in the New Testament there is a "transfiguration" episode. Just because we fling all these words around today and connect them with Pluto doesn't mean Mars is not still the owner of Scorpio, in my opinion. It just means the planet Pluto seems to have affinity with the sign. But then, it always did.

Years ago I read an astrology book that said bluntly the universe was all about sex—positive and negative energies and how they interact. I was mildly annoyed by that idea at the time. Silly me. The older I get the more I realize the author knew something. In addition to the sexual act itself Mars rules the organs of sexual activity in the body as well as the anus and rectum which are used to eject wastes.

Here are a couple Mars stories from my journalism days. I'll never forget the picture we had on page one after a big area 10K race one year. Here came the winner, legs pumping and the details of his anatomy coming out of the bottom of his shorts. Some women noticed. The men just saw a man running and winning and thought the picture was a "good angle" on his efforts. The horror among the men in the newsroom —after the papers were printed and shipped, of course— when the women in the office started giggling was something to behold. About as funny as the time we ran a big picture on page one of an Amish barn raising with a bonneted woman in the crowd scratching her bottom rather graphically. Luckily her part of the picture was very small and we hoped people wouldn't notice. Mars is not a planet that rules tact or tactful behavior. Oddly enough I never thought at either time to check the Mars aspects but it had to have been pretty strong those days to cause the furor it did.

When it comes to health matters, sometimes people with a weak Mars don't like exercise well enough to do it long enough to benefit from it. Mars is the planet that rules exercise. There was an interesting study reported on TV recently about why some people benefit more from exercise than others. The study concluded that those who benefited the most were those who actually did some of it. I was stunned by that bit of insight. Exercise, they said, was most beneficial when done:

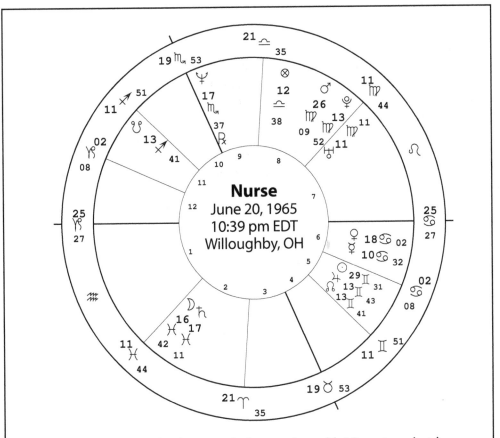

This woman wanted to be a surgical nurse, but with Mars strongly trine her Ascendant, she found her niche in the labor and delivery areas instead. The grand trine which has the 8th house planets forming a kite pattern and Neptune on the MC with trines to 6th house placements tie the medical houses into the pattern.

1) More often and longer
2) Involved things of pleasure, such as games and sports
3) Was continually being varied to include many different things to alter the routine
4) Always included some weight lifting. Apparently weight lifting strengthens the body faster than anything else.

Saturn rules weight lifting, Mercury is variety, Venus is pleasure and Saturn (again) deals with things we do longer and more consistently. So it's easy to see how other planets help Mars function The old rule about the two classical malefics is that Mars is more trouble when retrograde and Saturn is less. Mars is a direct, completely unsubtle planet—"Ugh, me see target, me hit 'em."

When Mars is retrograde, it's "Ugh, me see target, target won't hold still, me gotta hit something, me hit anything that moves. Me get headache from being slapped down after picking on wrong guy." It's a bad time to launch any sexual relationship and should never be retrograde in the wedding chart of two people who have not yet had an intimate relationship.

One year a young couple planning to wed came to me for a chart comparison and help in picking a date for the wedding. They wanted to learn what to watch out for so they could make their marriage happy. And they wanted a good head start with the date. They told me about their date selection and when I looked it up I realized it had a retrograde Mars. With great delicacy I said that it looked like a good day although Mars was retrograde and I explained that it was a not good for those who had not yet begun intimate relations. I was greatly relieved when they said that was not a problem. We were all glad.

Among other things to be cautious of during the retrograde phase is purchasing machinery, especially a car, which can overheat and catch fire. This also includes furnaces and other things that produce heat, such as irons, hair dryers and the like. It applies to cutting tools, hedge clippers, electric shavers and knives as well as weaponry of any sort.

The Mars influence in the medical field is obvious. The surgery involved is directly Martian but the 8th house and 6th house influences contribute strongly to the careers of those who choose any health direction. Aries influences are less often seen than Scorpio and Virgo ones, I think. That is my impression, simply based on the charts I have seen in my life, not any careful research. When it comes to health matters, sometimes people with a weak Mars don't like exercise well enough to do it long enough to benefit from it. Mars is the planet that rules exercise.

Chapter 10

Big and beautiful
Jupiter

Jupiter, the largest body in the solar system, deals with fat—fat of the land, the fatted calf and the principle of expansion. It deals with social benefits and rewards as well as the extra poundage we pile on during the holidays. As the Greater Benefic it is considered a big help when angular, in a good sign and not retrograde. One of the best key words for Jupiter is "big."

Most of us would like a good Jupiter. People with it prominent in their natal pattern travel widely and often internationally. They teach and console others readily and often are attracted to helping professions and the clergy. It leans one toward ethical behavior and charitable giving.

It is usually pronounced in the charts of successful people who depend on personal contacts and the exchange of favors. They are generous friends and merciful to their enemies. They are "lucky" in the classic sense and always seem optimistic about life. Other people never think they have problems. They do, of course, but they're quiet about them. These are the ones who laugh easily and a lot and know great jokes. They are the optimists of the world and can cheer us with their boundless enthusiasm for life. Jupiter is the planet of hope, hope for a better tomorrow, a better outcome than we fear, and kindness from others. It is above all the virtue of forgiveness.

Or, Jupiter can also come with a large streak of hot air, self-importance and pomposity when under stress. A Sun square Jupiter person often has a largely inflated opinion of him or her self. They take over conversations and all the extra space in the house and are always astonished that people get annoyed with them. They can get awfully self-righteous and sometimes act as if single-handedly they can solve all the problems of their friends, neighbors or the government. They know this because things have always worked out so well for themselves. Occasionally they get downright disdainful about people with problems which aren't solved promptly.

Its less pleasant side is know-it-all and condescending. Jupiter knows how to pull itself up by the bootstraps. When poorly aspected it is very judgmental about those who cannot.

Jupiter has an opinion about everything, and many opinion writers and speakers are strongly Jupiterian. They are found in every level of political and religious belief and are capable of talking about their knowledge and opinions at great length. They come with a built-in soapbox from which to pronounce their truth to the world.

Jupiter is the planet called "the Preserver," and in the old days it was said that a good transit of Jupiter saved lives. To this day ships carry life "preservers" for passengers and even row boats come equipped with life jackets.

A Jupiter transit over the Ascendant is traditionally a time when the body absorbs nutrition more readily, responds promptly to medicine and recovers quickly from injury or surgery. Nowadays, in our affluent world, we also say it makes us fat, but if we were struggling for food just to stay alive, we might see it differently.

Isn't it curious that in some fundamentalist religions (Jupiter, of course, also rules religion) that solidly converted people are considered to be "saved" or "preserved" from sin? Regardless of one's belief system it always fascinates me that people unconsciously choose words to express concepts that fit the astrological patterns.

In any chart Jupiter acts to encourage and preserve the benefits we have. Its transits of any house tend to bring favorable events and opportunity unless Jupiter was severely afflicted at birth. It deals with the principle of hope and optimism. It believes that things will get better. Sometimes people with a good Jupiter setup in their natal take their blessings in life for granted and get a mite cavalier about dangerous pursuits. Dare devils tend to forget this.

People with a strong, well-aspected Jupiter, such as the music professor whose chart is seen here, usually get a good education, achieve some sort of professional status and end up with a title in their job, sometimes more than one title. They also attract honors and recognition quite readily. Later in life they usually look around to see what they can do to help others. Sometimes they start their giving at quite a young age.

Jupiter has always been regarded as the "good luck" planet because it bestows so many blessings on those lucky enough to have it. Since it also symbolizes the "givers" of the world, it is no wonder those blessings flow their way in return. But if Jupiter is harsh, they misuse opportunities and sneer at the law. Then, of course, they may end up in Saturn's hands, a much less congenial place.

In the body Jupiter seems to be heavily involved in cancers, which are cell growths that don't know when to quit and expand out of the norm. Cysts, moles and other types of non-malignant growths are part of this syndrome, as well. It also deals with the largest part of the leg, the thigh, and the principle of movement. It rules the hips. The larger vehicles of transportation and those that are operated by leg movement (bicycles) come under Jupiter. This would include trains, large trucks and even large horses, which were transportation necessities in the world before the mechanized era began. Hot air balloons which depend on the principle of expansion in order to rise are clearly Jupiterian. Shipping and ocean-going ships as well as cruise ships, which are quite large, are other examples of Jupiter transportation.

Jupiter rules the body's largest internal organ, the liver. I noticed it was stressed in most of the charts I once collected of AIDS victims and those with HIV virus who had not progressed into full AIDS. Since one of its major functions in the body is producing antibodies for disease, a breakdown can quickly be expected if one has been exposed to the possibility of a serious disease when the natal Jupiter does not offer sufficient protection.

Jupiter's role in celebration is well-known and Jupiter-ruled people love a party, a good drink and a great joke. Many of them have a whole bagful of funny stories and anecdotes they like to share. Diseases of excess, such as cirrhosis, gout and the complications of obesity come under Jupiter.

Jupiter is involved when anything "goes too far." Since those with a strong Jupiter love to go too far, particularly if it has the word "foreign" about it, this can happen readily. They can go too far in generosity as well. I once knew a Pisces woman who ruined herself financially trying to give to every cause that ever sent her an appeal. And of course, you just know that all the good cause people passed her name around.

On the negative side, Jupiter is active in the charts of those who seek to cheat others, through games and gambling or get-rich-quick schemes. The pleasing personality which hides a crook may be due to the misuse of Jupiter. Most Jupiter people smile readily and often but when the smile becomes too artificial it can reflect a less-than-honest intention.

When big business or large banks or those who try to use their friends in high places to get special privileges try to undermine the rules of fair play and concern for others, it is often due to a poorly aspected Jupiter in their natal charts. Jupiter has a powerful influence over personal ethics.

Jupiter has a special function in our solar system. It is a gas bag planet, without sufficient density to be solid and not solid enough to blossom into a star as our Sun has. A very little more mass and we'd have a second star out there beyond Mars. It would be too uncomfortable to live nearby, however. Like the Sun, Jupiter emits its own energy and many think it acts like a fly wheel to keep the other planets moving around the Sun and help the solar system maintain its equilibrium.

When Jupiter is in good aspect to Mercury it brings word skill and even writing ability. When the aspect is not good, it seldom lets the facts get in the way of a good story. When retrograde it promises more than it delivers, which can be very annoying to those who have to deal with people with such an aspect.

Venus-Jupiter combinations provide open doors to opportunity, luck and money. Any harsh aspect with Mars can get one into trouble, though the trine provides energy and enthusiasm to the personality.

Sun-Jupiter rises to the top, professionally, though the squares and retrogrades can provide excessive self-satisfaction. Conjunctions, sextiles and trines are more pleasing.

With Jupiter in aspect to the Moon the childhood was comfortable and the parents –particularly the mother— considered moral values important, along with education and religious training. Any good Jupiter aspect usually shows a privileged upbringing.

If Jupiter is in a good aspects to Saturn it stabilizes the entire chart and makes one a solid, respectable citizen. These are the "salt of the earth" people one relies on to do and be what they say they are. It also gives a strong drive into the occupation in life, and those with Jupiter positive often know at quite a young age what they want to be.

Jupiter's aspects to Uranus give a broad perspective and are one of the best combinations for management ability. It helps one to put the pieces together. This aspect tends to show up in political charts as well. With Jupiter-Neptune the religious drive is emphasized and may be pronounced. Those who have Pluto with Jupiter could end up quite wealthy if other things in the chart agree.

Jupiter often relates well to the animal kingdom. When Sagittarians or Pisces people visit the home, the family animals are quick to notice. Since those people often have animals of their own, it's no surprise. Many choose careers where they can deal with animals, or have hobbies that do, such as horseback riding, or dog breeding and training. Pet shops are classic Jupiter places. Those who are Jupiter-ruled or have any good Jupiter aspect often find ways to help strays and homeless animals as well.

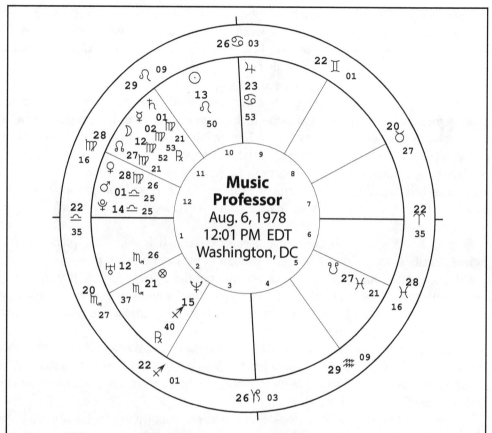

This man is a music professor in a large American university. His power-ful and exalted Jupiter on the Midheaven is a dramatic indicator of the excellent education he received. It also shows his own outstanding talent as a choral in-structor. The chart is AA from his birth certificate.

Jupiter's role in giving by both the wealthy and the average person cannot be over estimated. While Venus deals with gifts we give to each other in person, Jupiter deals with philanthropy, the broader social giving that often needs an organization of some sort to manage. A great many successful people, particularly those who have provided generously for their own families, go on to establish foundations which manage their organized giving.

These foundations provide grants to the arts, public television, schools, churches and universities. They support community projects and many help keep outreach programs going to the poor and troubled. Free clinics and traveling ships that carry doctors to foreign ports to help the under-privileged reflect Jupiter's involvement. Foundations build hospitals and buy equipment, provide money for research, scholarships and endowments of all kinds.

The huge movement in the 19th century in the U.S. to establish free libraries in every community was launched by the giving of a single wealthy man, steel magnate Andrew Carnegie. Parks, land grants, nature preserves and organizations to defend the rights and needs of animals have all been based on charitable giving. Groups that protect the environ-ment and huge public gardens have often been started by the wealthy who continue to sup-port them. Many eventually are turned over to public ownership when their benefactors die.

The same thing often happens to beautiful homes owned by wealthy families, which do not fit modern lifestyles but which may be loaded with art and furnishings of great value. They often end up as tourist attractions with fees to visit, thus helping supplement the grants that keep the doors open. Some become museums and preserve the history of the past.

Many organizations do public health work, attacking problems of specific diseases and the like. These rely on broad support from the public as well as grants from foundations. Bill Gates, the founder of Microsoft, has put much of his vast wealth into his foundation which is currently attacking the problem of malaria around the world.

The international Nobel prizes, which were started by Alfred Nobel, the inventor of dynamite, honor those who have achieved something outstanding in such realms as the sciences, mathematics, literature, and peace efforts. Those who receive such honors also have a Jupiter influence in their chart which brings them awards. Many people work assiduously but never receive the recognition for their efforts which Jupiter provides.

These are all very Jupiterian responses to social needs. In the U.S., Jupiter is prominent in the national horoscope which has a Sun/Jupiter conjunction. It is also conjunct Venus, which explains a great deal about the support given to orchestras, theater renovation and preservation projects, and museums.

But not only the wealthy do charitable giving. There is much silent and unheralded donation of funds by average people who see needs and support organizations such as Salvation Army, Red Cross and disaster aid. Indeed, many such organizations would wither on the vine without the cash that arrives in the mail from ordinary citizens of no great wealth. Without Jupiter stirring the giving impulse, our world would be a much poorer place.

Chapter 11

When times change
The Chronocrators

The Jupiter/Saturn conjunction in Taurus in 2000 was a dramatic finish to a long series of such conjunctions in the earth signs and like all such events, altered the world. When the two great chronocrators ("time" keepers) Jupiter and Saturn conjoin, times change. And there is no sense trying to swim upstream afterwards. Think about what happened in the years after that.

Taurus is about things of value. It rules money, the earning of it, banks and financial institutions which help manage it. Around the world, all those issues fell into a maelstrom of crisis in the years ahead. This was largely because the world's economic house had gotten into disorder and debt and escalated dramatically because the convenience of paper money led government to just print more of it when its excesses got too bad.

The whole world experienced an economic slowdown and many corporations went bankrupt and out of business and the world's money and relative currency values became a major issue in all the markets. The value of the dollar, the coming of the Euro and later its possible fall and the problem of fiat currencies preoccupied nations across the globe. There were cries in the Middle East and even in Russia urging a return to the gold standard.

China and India woke up and joined the developing world with far-reaching consequences. China began a manic effort to stockpile gold –many thought it was an effort to corner the market— and India upped its traditional buying. Times were fearful and there was little confidence that paper money would hold its value. Much of it was due to the combined efforts of those who borrowed too much, speculated too much and who robbed those who relied on their business skills or who trusted them to invest for them. A great deal of it came from the very nature of a fiat— or paper—currency backed by nothing but faith in the issuer. This prompted the huge surge in consumer credit, indeed in the credit generation that easy money created. Unlike a fixed amount of gold, paper wealth could simply be made by the printing press. It enabled huge spending on wars by governments and vast social programs as well as continued budget "deficits."

The Aquarius square from transiting Uranus to the conjunction point at 23 Taurus first launched the "tech wreck." Tech had been the profit mobilizer in the U.S. and consumers spent themselves silly on equipment. By the midpoint of the Jupiter/Saturn cycle, when tech had recovered and far outdid its early days, people forgot that. But it was the first sign of things to come. The near collapse of the world-wide banking system in 2008 shook those in financial positions around the globe.

The collapse of the U.S. airline industry (this was not a new development by the way—it's been a serial story for many years) was almost inevitable, given how close to the edge they had been operating for years. It continued to survive but there were consolidations and merges and new alignments and some well known old-line names vanished from the ticket counters: TWA, Pan American and many more.

The Capricorn angle (provided by Saturn's actions) marked a sharp return to conservativism in governments and fashion. Long skirts, classic styles and black black black in clothing took over for a while. Fashion is a good tip off to the world's mood. And of course, Taurus rules the art of colorful plumage by male or female.

The Sagittarius angle provided by the Jupiter element brought transportation issues to the fore. Roads, bridges, trucks, buses, etc. were replaced and repaired and overhauled. In the US, rail service made a comeback as trucking changed and oil problems multiplied. Religion issues became part of the political mess as foreign affairs tied knots in the Christian, Jewish and Muslim worlds. And it was the conservative point of view that held dominance. Some of it was from the extremists, as they had their day.

I had been warning people on various astrological lists for some time before the 2000 conjunction that the economy (at least in the U.S.) was in trouble and events during the next 20 years were to be a shocking confirmation. The two biggest world economies as the period began were the U.S. and Japan but 10 years later Japan had fallen far behind as China took over. India and Brazil surged forward as their economies grew.

The U.S. financial mess was coming to a boil. It was underplayed or underestimated by the powers that be for a long time. Big banks, big business and big interests are very good at hiding information the public needs but which may prove embarrassing. As soon as the first major events began to happen, students of astrology began running around looking at the Uranus stations and the Aquarius transits for answers, but events were plainly triggered by far larger movements of the planetary cycles..

In 1999 we had an eclipse at 19 degrees of Leo so bad and so powerful that it was in effect for years and was followed by that Jupiter/Saturn conjunction in Taurus at 22 degrees in 2000 within range of a square to that position. In 2001 we got a major eclipse that fell on the summer solstice itself and people were shocked by all the subsequent developments. Those three elements alone were the most destabilizing to life-as-it-has-always-been which had been seen in decades. When times change, we need to look at the Big Stuff. Those were the Big Stuff.

The 2001 destruction of the U.S. Twin Towers, which held much of the U.S. financial community, was an eerie confirmation of more that would lie ahead for the U.S. Its premier position as having the world's reserve currency and the world's most stable money, the dollar, was in serious trouble only 10 years later.

The view of money itself was undergoing a reappraisal. While the U.S. continued furiously printing its newly redesigned fiat money in a vain attempt to stay ahead of the escalating debt crisis, gold and silver exploded onto the world stage as people sought something more stable than paper. Their value soared as metal markets woke up. Fiat money is backed

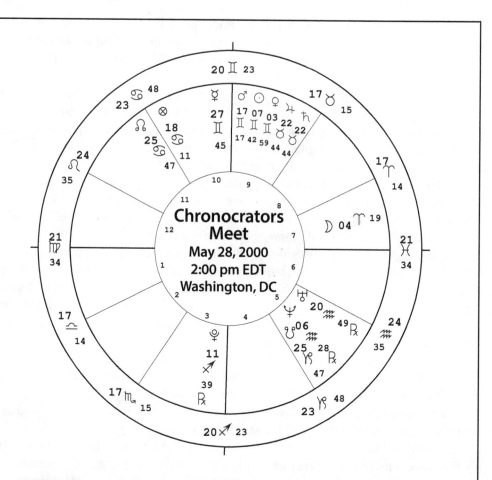

20 ♊ 23

23 ♋ 48

♌ 18 ♋
25 ♋
11 ♋
47

☿ 27 ♊ 45
17 42 59

♂ ☉ ♀ ♃ ♄
17 07 03 22 22
♊ ♊ ♊ ♉ ♉
44 44

17 ♉ 15

⊗ 24 ♌
35

17 ♈ 14

11
12

Chronocrators
Meet
May 28, 2000
2:00 pm EDT
Washington, DC

10   9
8
7

☽ 04 ♈ 19

21 ♍ 34

1   6
2   5

21 ♓ 34

17 ♎ 14

3   4

♇ ♀ 11 ♐ 39 ℞

♅ ♒ 20
♆ ♒ 06
☊ ♒
25 ♑ 28 ♑ ℞
47

49 ♒ ℞
24 ♒ 35

17 ♏ 15

23 ♑ 48

20 ♐ 23

The meeting of Jupiter and Saturn every 20 years marks the beginning of each new generation in human history. This conjunction in Taurus is the last in a series of meetings in earth signs and shows the vast changes that would occur in world finance and money. The planet Uranus throws a strong square to the two, showing many of the changes would be unexpected. The next meeting will be in Aquarius in 2020. There will be eight more in the air signs before the cycle shifts again for another 10 meetings in water signs. The first air sign meeting occurred in 1980.

only by the faith and credit of the issuing nation and the dollar had left the gold standard many years before. World central banks which had once sold their gold as an unnecessarily troublesome responsibility changed their minds and began trying to get it back. Banks collapsed across the globe, but not in places like Switzerland which had always kept huge gold reserves. However, some of them were caught off balance, too.

In China and India, where gold has always had a special position, tons of the metal were bought and stockpiled, by the governments as well as the banks and the ordinary investors. China took a long look decades ahead and started an enormous commitment to gold which would astound the world in later years. It bought mines and bullion everywhere.

This period also marked the rise of silver on the world market. Silver, a Moon-ruled metal, has always taken a back seat to Sun-ruled gold but had not been reevaluated in decades and lagged far behind. Previously, during most stable monetary times, its average price was about 1/16th that of gold, though in some periods that rose to 1/13th.

Midway through the 20 year cycle silver began to climb again, though it has a tendency to go up and down in the marketplace. Unlike gold, it has a great many industrial uses as well as for jewelry and coinage (where gold is clearly supreme). It has always been considered as the "poor man's gold." When the US began to remove silver from its coins in 1965, and even copper from its pennies in 1992 it signaled to the world that metal was no longer to be the measure of value. Henceforth there would be "fiat" money. The word fiat is Latin for faith. There has never been a fiat currency that has survived very long. The U.S. dollar is probably the longest. However, even the US had tried fiat currency before and found the idea wanting. Experience in the 18th century was against it, but a new generation forgot the lesson of its own history. Fiat money was first begun in Rome, with the denarius, and later with France, Germany, China and Japan.

The first paper money in the U.S. was the Colonial note issued in Massachusetts in 1690, supposedly backed by commodities such as grain and cattle. The other colonies quickly jumped on the bandwagon and within a short time too many notes were printed and it became valueless. Next was the Continental instituted at the time of the American Revolution in 1776 to raise money to fight the war. The crash of the continental was spectacular, and the phrase "not worth a continental" was coined. This brought on a distrust for paper currency, and until 1913 none was used in the U.S.

But then came the Federal Reserve in the 20th century with its monopoly on money and interest rates which backed the paper dollar. Paper made a comeback, leading to the new fiat currency, despite all evidence that it did not ultimately work but led instead to inflation and collapse.

Although the money was "officially" backed by a gold standard until 1971, it wasn't a true gold standard. When the government found it inconvenient to have a gold standard, it just made it illegal for U.S. citizens to hold gold or exchange dollars for gold as before. Foreign entities could still show up at any U.S. bank and convert their paper dollars to gold and too much was being sent abroad. Under President Franklin Roosevelt gold was actually confiscated and citizens were ordered to turn in their gold in to the government in 1933. The government promptly reestablished the value of gold. The final link to gold was finally broken under President Richard Nixon in 1971.

The dollar has not fared well since then. It has lost over 92% of its value since its initial issuance in 1913. After the revaluation in 1934 alone, the dollar dropped 41%. As the world's primary reserve currency it has held up surprisingly well for a long time, doubtless because others believed it was backed by U.S. military and commercial might in lieu of gold. But the U.S. engaged in huge and costly military actions over the years and by the end of the 20th century there were underlying stresses that began to show. The wars in the early 21st century set a new standard for lavish spending.

The Jupiter/Saturn conjunction in 2000 reawakened the world to the need for a stable currency and genuine coinage. By 2008 frightened officials in Washington faced a banking crisis that could bring down the government, and nearly did. While that scary scenario does not seem to have penetrated the average person's understanding of the financial ramifica-

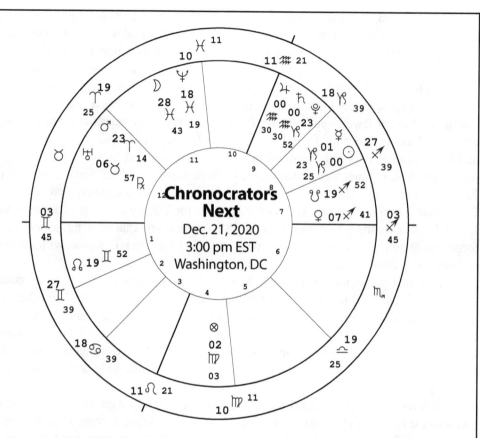

The next meeting of the Chronocrators will continue the theme of a square from Uranus when the cycle fully commences in the air signs. The Mars/Pluto square in cardnal signs which accompanies the conjunction in the 9th house promises violence and struggle over religious issues and the fall of a major religion.

tions, the huge government funding that went to the banks to keep them in business made the point clear.

As this book is being written there are several years to go before the effects of the conjunction are over, and they promise to be very unpleasant before restructuring is finally achieved. Europe is teetering on economic collapse and countries around the world have financial problems. Gold and other precious metals are soaring in value as individuals and nations buy, seeking to protect themselves from financial loss. The prospect of horrendous inflation ahead should the dollar collapse terrifies many financially savvy advisors.

This is a dramatic and easy to see effect of the Jupiter/Saturn conjunction in Taurus. Above all else, Taurus is the sign of material wealth, things that are real and can be touched and held in the hand. Paper money backed by nothing at all except a government's promise is not likely to survive the 20 years until the next conjunction.

The next meeting of the great chronocrators will be held in an air sign, at 0 Aquarius, Dec. 21, 2020, and the world will see changes based on ideas, human relationships and

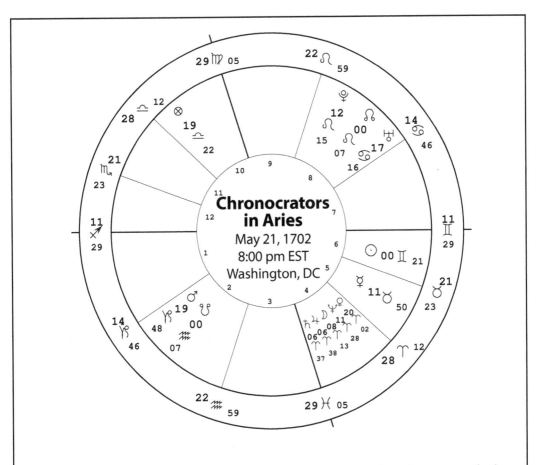

The beginning of the current cycle of Great Conjunctions in Aries was marked by several favorable aspects as well as a powerful T-square in the cardinal signs.

communication. (See chart above.) Each conjunction ahead will be part of the air series that will last for 200 years as the Chronocrators meet and part again every 20 years.

Each great conjunction lays its stamp on the society of its time. Over 800 years conjunctions will occur in all of the earth, air, fire and water signs before returning to earth once again. The most important of them is the one that occurs at the beginning of Aries, which sets the keynote for the coming 800-year period. The last one occurred in May of 1702. (See chart above.) Before each 200-year period begins a conjunction or two happens in the oncoming cycle. The 1980–81 Grand Conjunctions were in Libra, which introduced the air cycle just before the last conjunction in earth of 2000. Historical development clearly corresponds to the cycles. During fire conjunction periods, there is global exploration, conquest and discovery as well as movements seeking independence and personal freedom. The last ones recurred in the fire signs in 1603 and 1623, then from 1663 to 1782, and in 1821.

In the earth period there is wealth creation, land settlement, territorial disputes as well as development in agricultural and biological areas. Better food animals and better crops are grown. And, of course, our current issues, finance and money, step on stage. The conjunctions began in the earth signs in 1802, then went from 1842 to 1961, and in 2000, which concluded the cycle.

The coming air conjunctions will mark rapid social change, intellectual development and new ideas. A more universal sense of personal involvement in the lives of people everywhere happens. The internet development after the 80-81 conjunctions in air was the forerunner of the next stage of growth. The previous conjunctions in the air signs were in 1186, then from 1226 to 1345, and again in 1385 and in 1405

The Jupiter/Saturn conjunctions in water which will follow the 200-year air cycle, will spawn an artistic reawakening as the last ones produced the glories of the Renaissance. Those conjunctions occurred in the water signs in 1365, then from 1425 to 1583, and in 1643. The period also fostered new spiritual movements and social assimilation on a large scale.

The Libra conjunction of 1980 sparked a great deal of emphasis on "fairness" in the legal system and in relationships of all sorts for the next 20 years until the final earth conjunction of 2000. Its 20-year period gives some clues as to the oncoming air series beginning in 2020. Like all struggles between opposing points of view, it was fraught with tension and angst of various sorts. Libra is the sign that deals with contracts and agreements and negotiation and deals between nations and pressure groups. As one of the "people" signs, it gave the edge to "people" interests at the expense of everything else. Sometimes the spirit of the law gets lost as we argue for the ever-tinier minutiae of the letter of the law.

The Taurus conjunction launched a mini-restoration of a bit of "earth sense" and reawakened an interest in the land and growing things. But Taurus rules a lot more than just flowers and veggies and farms (which are so important to our survival, of course). It has fundamental rulership over resources of all kinds and our very value systems.

Whenever there is a Jupiter Saturn conjunction, the first half of the 20 year cycle belongs to Jupiter and the second half to Saturn. Thus, we saw big Jupiterian growth and widespread expansion in the electronic world as the conjunction squared Uranus, with the bill coming due 10 years later when Saturn took over. One of the developments was a planet-wide emphasis on restoring forested areas and halting destruction of jungles. Taurus rules wood and a new movement began to value it more, not only for its utility and beauty, but for its stabilizing qualities in the ecology.

In my library is a book written by George C. Noonan, called *Classical Scientific Astrology,* which he published in 1984 through the American Federation of Astrologers. I bought it when I attended one of his lectures and I still had the notes from the lecture and the handout on fixed star positions he mentioned. Among the topics he discussed was the historical pattern of Jupiter/Saturn conjunctions. He described how astrologers several hundred years beforehand had predicted the rise of Islam and most of the major events or battles to establish its bona fides. He said such predictions were based on the Jupiter/Saturn cycle's reliability.

He also talked about the work of the Arabic astrologer Mash a allah, who pointed out that every 800 years when the cycle occurs in fire there comes the rise of new ideologies. The fire conjunction of 26 BC heralded the era of Jesus and Christianity. The fire series which began in 809 marked the rise of Mohammad and Islam. The one of 1603 launched the democracies.

Noonan expanded on the meanings of the series in water, which he said bring periods of cold climate to the earth. One cycle began in 571 AD (lasting until the 809 shift to fire) and a second occurred in 1425, only decades before Columbus sailed to the New world. He linked earth cycles to improving the lot of workers and practical inventions. The series which began in 1802 marked the rise of technology. Other earth cycles began in 154 and 988 CE.

Air cycles should concern us most, since we shall recommence in 2020. Air cycles also were begun in 332 and 1186 and dealt with monasticism and the shift to religious feelings, Noonan said. He expected to see a return to more "godliness" under the cycle continuing in 2020 and lasting until the next water cycle begins in 2218. I found that reading the notes brought some of his comments back and I am only sorry I didn't tape the lecture.

I don't remember where it was held, unfortunately. I think it was at a conference but I am not sure. Only that the room was so packed many people stood to hear him and he ran out of handouts. It was one time I was greedy and kept mine tightly locked in my fist, ignoring all pleading eyes.

The study of the chronocrators will give us many insights into the future of our world.

Chapter 12

The old dog
Saturn

A wonderfully scary short story I read many, many years ago—and I wish I remembered the name or author of it—was about a woman who hated her bones. They would always ache and stick out and she gradually began to think that if only she could get rid of them she would be a lot happier. Of course she meets a slimy man who offers to help her with her problem in exchange for her soul, I believe, but at any rate, he pulls all her bones out through her mouth and she gets her wish.

The story ends when somebody comes into her room, sees a gross, ugly puddle of gooshy stuff on the floor and throws it out in the garbage can. Of course that gross, ugly thing is all that's left of her once her bones are gone. We always want to get rid of our problems but like the bones, which are ruled by Saturn, they may have an irreplaceable function in our lives. Our job is not to throw them out but to solve our difficulty. And difficulties also come under Saturn. All paranoia and conspiracy terrors come out of fear. And that's Saturn's department, too.

Now obviously when Saturn is part of a stress pattern—particularly to the Moon, which rules emotional reactions and to Mercury, which has to do with how the mind works—the fears can get out of hand. What things are we afraid of? Well, throw in Pluto, Neptune or Uranus and you can get conspiracy, secret organizations and messages received by your bridgework (in about that order). That same stress pattern of Mercury, Moon and Saturn often reflects a pattern of lying.

Why do people lie? Usually because of fear: whether of blame, or punishment, or the simple truth. When fear gets out of hand, the truth is often the first thing to go.

When houses in the natal pattern that rule the mind (3 and 9) are part of a stress pattern, particularly from the 12th house of secrecy, things can get pretty sticky. Neptune can be responsible for the endocrine gland system going haywire, for instance. When the thyroid gets overactive (6th house stress maybe) and affects planets in or ruling the mental area, you can get really weird mental reactions. Throw in Saturn and bingo—conspiracy fanaticism. I've seen some of in a few clients and when the physical was corrected, so was the mental. But they are so closely linked, that it's no wonder the reasons often go undiagnosed. One woman was thought to be suffering from Alzheimer's, until a thyroid problem was diagnosed. And believe me, she had a bunch of conspiracy theories and was an incipient fanatic. No, I take that back: she is a fanatic—about lots of things. Conspiracy fear is just one among many.

The mutable Virgo-Pisces polarity is pretty finely balanced and involves the health/sensitivity sign and the imaginative/endocrine gland system and when you throw that into the package you are downright guaranteed to have paranoia. It seems to be part of a lot of paranoia cases I've seen. Of course the mutable package does not do it all alone, but mutable planets in succedent houses under stress to Saturn have a built-in likelihood of fears.I know a Virgo woman with a Pisces Moon squared by Saturn who suffered from anorexia, which is a condition with a complicated set of factors that cause it, and is characterized by an eating problem. There is often a desire to be "perfect" (the Virgo compulsion) and thinness is equated with being more nearly perfect. The late musical figure Michael Jackson was another with such a signature of Saturn stress (a controlling father problem) and the Virgo-Sun/Pisces-Moon package.

A well-aspected Saturn seems to guarantee mental balance because one stays so closely in touch with hard reality. It also deals with the kind of self-discipline we impose on ourselves to structure our lives when necessary. For some people structure provides freedom. For others, freedom is the structure.

The virtues of patience, endurance, hard work and the shouldering of responsibility come under Saturn. However Saturn may point to the use of its energies in other ways. People who love old things and work with them, such as antique dealers, may have a strong Saturn, particularly when it's rising. Many of those who haunt garage sales and adore the bargain hunting of auctions are Saturn children. They hate to spend money if they can get things cheaper, and they know exactly how much things are truly worth and what a real bargain is.

Saturn often shows up in the charts of those who are accountants, bank examiners or people with a gift for management. It deals with order, method, systems and patience. Saturn rules reliability and guarantees. The expression common in places like India to express a certain approach to life, "It is written," –meaning foreordained—enchants me as a good example of a Saturn principle.

In the body Saturn rules the largest organ of all, the skin— the outer limit of the body, and also the bones, particularly the knees. It is the principle of hardening or crystallization as well as contraction. This is one of the reasons that a difficult Saturn transit forces us to condense our lives and "get tough."

Indeed, Saturn rules all limits and people who are easily imposed on, manipulated or are abused are often said to have no understanding of their own rights and the limits others should respect. This is often because something in their childhood was poorly conveyed to them. The power to say, "No," is the power to establish one's limits. All too often over-controlling parents refuse to allow the child ever to say "No." A big mistake, in my opinion. It's much easier for a parent to let the child save face and still establish rules.

I once had a client who told me her grandchild really minded her father and would never leave a room she was placed in or disobey any order. She casually noted that the father really "put the fear of God" in her. The child was 2, as I recall. I have often wondered what the cost of such obedience was and what kind of life that daughter was going to have one day.

Saturn rules Capricorn, which is preeminently the sign of the father, as Cancer is that of the mother. Psychologists tell us that the way a father treats his daughters has such strong effect on her self-image that it can even affect her sexual relations with her husband when she is an adult. Now that's a pretty far-reaching effect, but it tells us how deeply Dad matters to girls. Girls who have good relationships with their fathers seem to do better in their careers than others, just as boys who are highly successful tend to have had good relationships with their mothers. Capricornian Elvis Presley was a classic example of that. Most of his problems apparently became much more serious after his mother's death.

Hillary Rodham Clinton has insisted all her life on keeping and using her maiden name Rodham because it was her father's, and she said she did so to honor him. Despite her marriage to U.S. president, Bill Clinton, she certainly was successful in her own right, both as an attorney in private life and later as Secretary of State under President Barack Obama.

Boys whose fathers are so Saturnian that they never give them praise or approval are seriously handicapped later in life. They may succeed in careers, and often do, but their success may come from a driving need to find the self-esteem their fathers withheld. In short, fathers matter, and the best gift a man can give a child is good fathering.

Since Saturn is one of the two indicators for any adult males in the chart, it becomes enormously important in how children relate to authority. The Sun, of course, is the other. When adult males mistreat a child of either sex it can lead to severe emotional difficulties. This may happen from words or actions. In the sexual realm it is devastating to the child. An afflicted Saturn can show this. I have seen many, many charts where there has been a negative sexual event when Saturn was in House 12 natally, particularly if it afflicted the ruler of 12 or the Ascendant. Often there was molestation as a child. I have the chart of a woman raped in her teens by an escaped convict who has it there.

But I also did the chart of a woman with that Saturn placement who, as a 12-year-old, chased a would-be molester around the dining room table with a butcher knife in her hand. Needless to say she was not molested. It was her mother's boyfriend (where have we heard that before?) and I understand the relationship between the two adults was a dead issue after that incident.

Above all, Saturn is time. We are told that time heals pains and sad memories. That seems to be true as many memories soften and the memory of trauma fades as we age. Saturn's children are traditionally those who are most happy as senior citizens, their weight of responsibility to their families and work behind them. Capricorn Sun types and those with Saturn rising tend to have most of their hardest problems in youth and find that they become more and more contented as middle age and old age arrive. By that time they've seen it all and have learned how to deal with it.

Weights and measurements of all kinds are Saturn's business. The entire notion of fair play and justice is Saturn's, and a scale weighs everyone the same. They are what they are. Saturn's scales are both the kind that tell us about our food indulgence and the kind that fish have since they are a hardened protection for the fish.

A friend of mine told me that in Japan, it is said: "the stake that sticks up will be pounded down," implying that people would discourage differences and that an independent person who might draw individual attention would be subject to criticism and/or jealousy. This is so Saturnian a viewpoint it's hard to believe. And yet some cultures have embedded these old ways tied to the past for centuries. Another Saturn idea is that "we do things this way because that's the way we've always done it."

Saturn is always the authority in life and the "powers that be" in the community at large. It is the place we occupy as adults and the amount of responsibility we may have. Whenever one takes on a hard job of any sort, whether voluntary or for pay, Saturn has a hand. Saturn is payback as well as what we earn in a broad sense. If work has been done well Saturn provides rewards. If not, of course, the outcome is much less pleasant.

Leo Sun writer Alex Haley spent 10 years tracing his family heritage (something Saturn rules) from the days when his many-times-great grandfather was kidnapped in an African forest and sold into slavery in the American colonies. Despite the number of slaves that once lived in the U.S., such a family heritage had never been traced before. The conditions of slavery made even the names of one's relatives often unknown as members of most black families were sold away and relationships were broken irrevocably. Unfortunately, the success of "Roots" prompted a lawsuit by the author of "The African" and Haley paid $650,000 to settle the law suit in 1977 when Saturn was on his Leo Sun. (See his chart on page 75.)

When "Roots" came out, it was a worldwide best seller and the television series later made from it made history. He, of course, became a huge celebrity though he did not live very many years after his enormous success. Nevertheless, Saturn rewards were showered on him as well as the lawsuit. Saturn rules projects that take a long time, and this one took years to accomplish. It is one of the great achievements in modern literature.

When Saturn goes retrograde, it's like, "Oh, let's see, shall we do some damage or not? Aw shucks, let's wait a while. In fact, let's think about it a looooooong time and then be careful we get what we're after. Maybe tomorrow. Or the next day. Or what's wrong with next month?" It's no coincidence that the old ruler of the "mañana" sign Aquarius (That's Spanish for "tomorrow") is Saturn. Maybe procrastination should be ruled by retrograde Saturn. It's true that Aquarius deals with tomorrow as Capricorn deals with yesterday. It is the Aquarius vision which brings the best of Saturn's attributes to the fore as knowledge from yesterday is used and becomes the invention of labor-saving devices of the future.

Saturn's odd, double-dealing with time was symbolized as far back as Roman times—and perhaps earlier—with the idea of Janus, the two-faced god who looked both ways at the end of the year. The festival of Saturnalia held at the time of the winter solstice allowed servants and slaves to put down their burdens and join in revelry. It was much like the more modern Mardi Gras celebrations. Saturn's lessons are of immense value in our lives and it provides us both the carrot and the stick that lead us to accomplishment and the wisdom of maturity.

I found it quite interesting that women with Saturn ℞ are often heavily involved in "support roles" in business. While this information did not come out of an organized poll, a number of my friends told me of their experiences with this. I would be quite interested to know if a) they are paid commensurately with their responsibilities and/or b) they are given recognition for it.

Here's why I say this. Bear with me a minute. Saturn deals with boundary issues. When a child is two years old, it first discovers the word "no," which is an attempt to establish its boundaries—its identity as a sovereign individual. Children who are prevented from saying no or are punished for it, develop a lot of confusion about boundaries and have to learn about them in other ways, as I mentioned earlier. Boundary issues establish our right to be ourselves and our right to ask—no, demand—fair treatment later on in life. We don't stay two forever, but that's the age at which we should be learning that particular lesson. Obviously, it's a key one for us all.

The father is a very important figure in child-rearing, and fathers who are absent or unloving affect their child in important ways. The Saturn ℞ often shows this. But it also shows that the absence of the father can be hard for the child to deal with. I, too, had Saturn ℞ at birth and adored my father, who was a loving man all his life. But, he worked very long hours when I was quite young and I still remember the rare occasions when he took me to work with him for part of a day in those years. His absence later when he traveled on one particular job was very upsetting to me.

Fathers teach their children about responsibility, but they also teach about structure, duty and security. Children with Saturn ℞ can take those lessons too much to heart. Some become insecure and do more than is expected of them to get "rewards" from their dads. The reward they want is approval, of course. They apply a lot of good behavior. Perhaps this sets up girls for those support jobs I mentioned.

One thing the child often doesn't do is "stick up for itself" as a way of getting approval. It's "see what a good girl/boy I am" by behaving in "nice" ways. I see this a lot in the behavior patterns of those with Saturn ℞—they are unsure about themselves, unsure about the whole boundary issue thing, unsure about how much they should do for others and when to say "no." They can get imposed on.

A woman with Saturn rising—direct—had a clear sense of boundaries when she was a first grader. She was a quiet child and never picked any fights, but the class bully got in back of her in line one day on the way to the cafeteria and made a big mistake. He grabbed her braids and started yanking her head. She spun around and without a word swung on him, bloodied his nose, and then turned back and resumed walking. He, on the other hand, squawked loudly, crying like he'd been mortally wounded. The teacher smirked later when she spoke about it. This is not the behavior of a retrograde Saturn child.

Retrograde Saturns are sometimes picked on because they aren't sure if they should defend themselves and if so, how far they can go. They don't know where "the limit" is. Sometimes they will befriend a bigger child who will stick up for them or help them avoid bullies. Sometimes their way to deal is to be so "useful" they are left alone. That may or may not change later in life, particularly if Saturn changes direction.

We are all in the middle of several interwoven cycles at any given time in life. There's the lunar node cycle, the Saturn cycle, the progressed Moon cycle, the effect-of-the-last- eclipse cycle, the retrograde whatchamacallit over the dingus, etc. You name it, something is always going on.

So where do we go in Saturn's cycles? We judge as we always have: try to do the best we can at the tasks in front of us, take advantage of the good things in life as much as possible without hurting anybody else, try not to get too excited when the Jupiter high time doesn't last, and remember that no Saturn cycle lasts either. If we make mistakes the only solution is to get back up and get back in the game—which brings us back to my all-time favorite Saturn saying: Good judgment is the result of experience. Experience is the result of bad judgment.

This goes with a principle that the late American astrologer Grant Lewi postulated: that Saturn's cycle of worldly success and experience begins with its transit of the IC when the individual launches a new start in life. It develops as Saturn moves through house 4, 5 and 6, and comes "into the light" when Saturn moves up over the Descendant.

As Saturn moves through house 7, 8 and 9, we are perfecting our efforts and growing

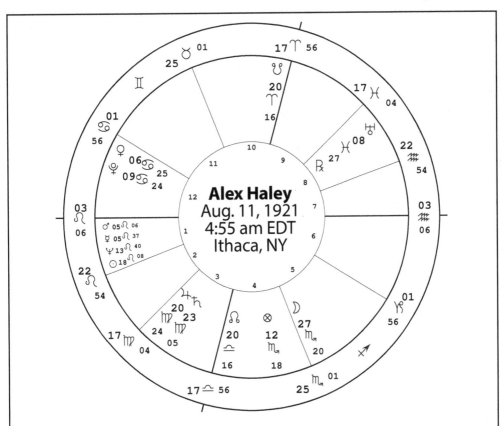

Author Alex Haley spent 10 years researching the history of his family during the slavery era in the U.S. His book, *Roots* became a worldwide best seller when Saturn came to his Leo Sun. Unfortunately, he was also sued for plagiarism that year by the author of *The African* who charged he had copied parts of it for *Roots*. Haley paid $650,000 to settle the suit. He became world famous and the miniseries on the story set records unmatched in U.S. television history. He also wrote *The Autobiography of Malcolm X*. His chart is AA from AstroDataBank.

in importance. When Saturn hits 10 we are at a peak period of authority, responsibility, success, etc. As Saturn moves down through Houses 11 and 12 we continue to reap rewards for efforts we have sown in the past. Then, when Saturn hits the Ascendant, things end or stop dead in their tracks and we reassess. As it moves through house 1, we begin throwing things out of our lives that we no longer need or can't keep up with anymore. The cycle from house 1, 2 and 3 is a retreat into self, a reflective period and a change-over time until Saturn hits house 4 and we start over again.

That's a very brief summary of Lewi's idea, which has been used very widely since he came up with it 40 or 50 years ago, because it works and explains a lot in life. It seems to be particularly significant in the charts of politicians who must run for office or people in the public eye who need public approval. Those with a "rising" transit of Saturn—between 7 and 10—have an edge over those with a "descending" one—between 10 and 1. Those with Saturn between 1 and 4 are behind the curve, seen as dated, etc.

One thing Saturn's children need to be careful of is trying too hard to control others. When any one has planets square the Ascendant /Descendant angle, they may attempt to impose their will on others. Mars square, for instance, can be extremely bossy, demanding and aggressive in getting its way. Saturn uses coldness and every controlling weapon at its disposal when it is square the line. Since the Asc/Dsc line is about our relationships with others, you can easily see that what the individual reaps from that behavior is loneliness and isolation. Everybody just wants out of any relationship with a person so desperately intent on making everyone obey his or her wishes. When Pluto and Uranus are square they can demand compliance to some really unusual "needs." Pluto is compulsion and Uranus is kind of off-the-wall stuff: not a happy outlook.

Luckily Saturn ties us to reality. For all the flaws we see in the way it works, it can be our best friend. It is a lifelong teacher and the testing process that tells us what we have learned. Think of it as the clothespins that tie us to the clothes line before we float off and end up in trouble.

If we step too far away from its rules and regulations and try to become the one who makes our own rules, the karma is never very pleasant. When we live the ethical life, the rules are no barrier to happiness and the rewards are as sure as Sunlight.

After the 2nd Saturn return

The 2nd Saturn return at about 58½ introduces us to the creative, liberating years of old age. I am convinced that the more one lives a steady, duty-oriented life, the greater is the freedom in old age: hence, the reason so many Sun-sign Capricorns or those with strong Saturn placements or aspects in their birth patterns truly have "golden" years. Many people first discover their personal freedom and creativity in the leisure years of retirement and thrive on it.

We live in a time when there is an eruption of healthy, long lived senior citizens having fun, developing new interests, taking courses at area colleges, traveling and exploring volunteerism, hobbies and social life. In any tourism area you will see busload after busload of seniors at restaurants, shopping meccas and the like. Go to the opera, or the ballet in the afternoon. Try the matinee performance of your favorite orchestra. They'll be crammed with seniors. Some of them are likely to be ushering as a way to enjoy all the cultural offerings cheaply. A lot of seniors develop new mental interests when they aren't burdened by the "musts" of life.

The seniors today are all part of the WWII or post-WWII-Korean War generation, of course. Many worked hard for at most one or two employers and many were limited in their opportunities by the world they lived in at the time A lot of the women had few educational and recreational chances because they were married in the pre-pill era and had babies to raise. Later in life many even went back to work at jobs they really hadn't prepared for or hadn't done for decades. Now that they are retired, if they have any financial security (and sometimes even if they don't), they are going at the goodies with a vengeance and loving every bit of it. Many of them are so energetic they leave the rest of us in the dust.

I think we should look to Venus and Neptune to see that burst of creativity as it makes aspects. A lot of seniors learn to play music or study music or the arts. I have a friend who paints and who is always taking some art course or other. Maybe they're just doing some pre-planning for the next lifetime, for all I know. The great psychic Edgar Cayce, who brought reincarnation into public awareness, said this was often the case when some new interest developed late in life.

It seems to me there is also the spiritual aspect of life to consider. We are creatures of more than flesh and bone. After the working years when we operated on high-powered Mars and dutiful Saturn, we move to retirement with Venus, the gist of our loving nature still strong. Neptune, the soul, and Uranus, the spark of the divine within, speak to us all. Some of us are lucky enough to hear those voices while we are younger, but I suspect we all hear them somehow, even if it takes the senior years to improve our inner hearing, just as some of the outer hearing goes.

Obviously for some of us, Neptune brings ill health and Uranus brings disruption to our comfortable years in old age. Venus problems can show up as tight incomes. But maybe these are the ways the Universe helps us to break our psychological ties to the body and our habits of behavior so we are free to move on at a later point.

Whatever, I think the senior years have some very interesting developments and I think those 65 and older can say plenty about the new country they explore. Ask one about it, some time.

Retirement

Retirement marks the ending of one's life work, not a beginning, so look to Saturn and the natal 10th house rulership and what is happening to see if it will occur early, late or at the usual time around 65. Nowadays people work longer, and may also pursue a second smaller money-making career after the formal retirement so it can be confusing.

If the 10th is ruled by either benefic it indicates one might not completely retire but would pick up another job in the future, even if only a part-time one. Venus likes the sociability of work and Jupiter enjoys the opportunity for learning and sharing. Mercury in or ruling 10 is often the mark of someone who has always had two areas of work and retirement for either may occur at a different time than it does for the other.

A retrograde planet in the 10th could indicate unhappiness with the inactivity of retirement once the planet goes direct.

It's always good to keep an eye on the 2nd and 8th to see if a return to work is likely after retirement Some people with stresses there may often extend their work years because they either have not prepared very well for retirement financially or there are other problems, such as the debt load, which can frustrate their plans.

Should the natal 2nd and 8th be too difficult, or if Saturn is in 6 natally and stressed they may never retire. A lot of 6th house problems keep people on the job in order to get better medical benefits when they aren't really financially stable enough to retire.

Chapter 13

Surprises are good for us
Uranus

Uranian people are great at poking pins in balloons and pointing out the feet of clay on idols. But spending their time doing that is really a waste of Uranian energy and purpose. The strength of Uranus is the future and its ability to break down the boundaries of the past in order that progress can occur. It is, above all else, the planet of surprises.

There are three planets that involve change, the Moon, Mercury and Uranus, but the ones Uranus brings are the most dramatic and far reaching. They take us out of the ordinary paths of life and put us in scary new situations that prove how well we can cope. There's a saying I like, that "life is what happens when you had other plans." Uranus is the new plans.

Most people go along in their ruts in life and do things the way they've always done them. Unless somebody challenges the way things are, nothing changes. And many things in life may have slipped into unprofitable and negative patterns from simple inertia. But then a new path opens up and we strike out into the unknown, sometimes to our own great surprise. It's usually good for us, though sometimes we don't see that for years.

Uranus is said to rule astrology and a great many astrologers can verify the fact that a major Uranian transit first prompted them to investigate astrology. Those of us with strong ties to Uranus in our natal patterns may end up in the field professionally, and those with weaker ones may be the people who study it and seek its wisdom.

But it also deals with something as different as politics, and at least in the U.S., most successful politicians have it strong natally, sometimes in the 11th house of the legislatures where political careers are shaped. On the local level, many people take public office when spurred by a Uranus transit but may lose interest when it is past unless their natal pattern favors such public service. It can be tricky to forecast elections strictly on its activity since it can just as often mean a loss..

Inventions of all kinds come under Uranus since it is a mental planet which seems to build on the past in order to construct new tools for the future. It rules airplanes and outer space and technology of all sorts. Back in the 1960s when Uranus and Pluto formed a conjunction in Virgo, it marked a new era of miniaturization and the start of the technological revolution. It was launched by a need to develop tinier and more efficient tools for the space programs. But the conjunction also brought astrology out of the closet, so to speak, and made it part of the new era. While many people were born with this conjunction in their natal patterns, it affected the entire generation of those who would grow up to lead the way into the high-tech era that is still growing today.

Today's society is permeated by young people who are comfortable with the high tech equipment everywhere. The computer spawned the internet and the dramatic linkages we all have now with people around the world. It also began to undercut the print media, as news became more available than ever online and the entire world of communication shifted away from paper to the electron. Now it is the tiny telephone combined with the all-purpose gizmos that play music, games and quotes on the stock market.

Depending on how the Uranus-Pluto conjunction was aspected in the natal chart, it had major or merely strong effect on the life. Whether the aspects were good or bad also counts a lot. We are all products of the time and place in which we are born, and these big conjunctions color that with a unique shade.

Uranus-Pluto in Virgo had an enormous and sweeping effect on several areas of society symbolized by Pluto's discovery in Cancer in the 1930s. Pluto had a great deal of influence in family and women's matters and this is the era which produced "the pill." Young people today have no real awareness of the huge changes this made in the lives of women. Before that there was very little a woman who was sexually active could do except have a baby when she got pregnant or conversely, find an illegal abortionist. And there was real fear involved when a period was late. If it was worrisome for a married female it was far more so for a single woman since a child out of wedlock was considered a horrifying family disgrace. Those were not tolerant decades. Unwanted pregnancy made the world of jobs very insecure, and is the real reason women were so slow to become self-sufficient and independent for so many years. No employer could count on keeping a young married woman and older ones usually were too busy taking care of a brood which could grow every year to have time to start a job. Once the babies started coming, hang it up as far as a job went.

This Uranus-Pluto conjunction, however, launched the sexual revolution, in which women could be free to play without paying the high price of the past. Of course, many other problems followed in its wake, but those were different than they had been before. Uranus changed the way women could live, and that was an enormous step forward. It was a time when many medical issues soared into focus, and the very beginnings of what we see today in terms of things like cloning and genetic manipulation (tiny changes as the microscopic level, etc...: how Virgoan!). When the sexual revolution led to a soaring problem of sexually transmitted diseases, new treatment methods were begun. In fact, a great many changes occurred in hospitals and care-giving institutions.

One thing you may all have seen in your communities—how the homes for the orphaned and abused children were closed in favor of "foster homes," and many state-run long-term care facilities for the retarded and mentally ill were closed in favor of "community care." Of course the foster homes and the community care mostly failed to materialize to the degree needed and yielded their own share of disastrous effects, but the changes did happen anyway. It was partly a case of the Uranian tendency to think that society can be changed for its own good by fiat. That rarely works.

The hospice movement to provide better care for those at the end of their lives came

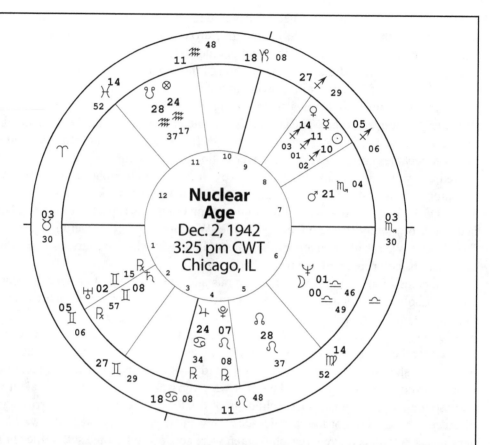

Uranus is rising in this chart of the first splitting of the atom during the Manhattan Project of World War II which produced the atomic bomb. Four planets are retrograde, showing how much public opinion will influence development. Mars direct in the 7th house of war shows the military application, while Saturn's occupation of the 2nd house of the immediate future shows there will be trouble ahead, though that is not apparent at first.

out of this time period, though. Virgo deals with nursing care in general and there were many changes in the work of nurses. The hospice movement has grown every year since, and helps many to live their final days in comfort in their own homes or in a caring situation.

I remember talking with my husband at the time when the conjunction was happening. We were sitting on the screened-in porch on a Sunday morning drinking coffee and watching boat races on Lake Erie. I told him the world of labor and employment would never be the same. And, not long after the arrival of the pill, women swept in to the offices and stores, changing the face of the working world.

The other momentous thing that occurred concerns all of us, because it broke open the world to astrology. It led to astrology being seen as a useful practical tool to help with life. In the years that followed, astrology became very "hip" and those of us who were trained rode a wave of increasing business and social acceptance in its practice.

How did Uranus-Pluto work in terms of the individual chart? Much like any major conjunction does. It blended the planetary influences with the sign where it occurred. In

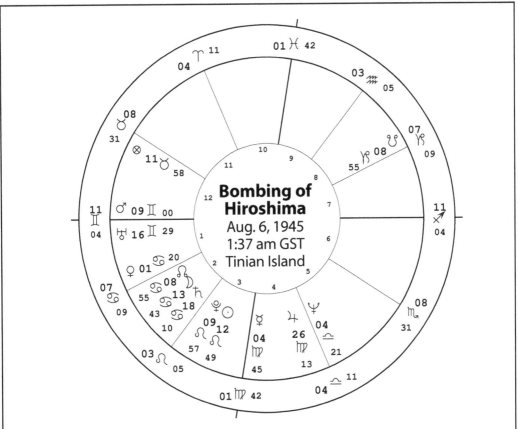

This chart is the time of the bombing run that left Tinian Island for Japan where the first atomic bomb was dropped on the city of Hiroshima. It contains a rising Uranus conjunct Mars and shows a tight correlation to the chart of the first splitting of the atom. A second bomb was dropped on Nagasaki, forcing Japan to surrender and ending WWII. The anguish and suffering caused by the bomb horrified the world later, as it came to light, and despite great disputes in the world, has never been used again.

Virgo it showed an intense mental focus and work issues that needed to be solved in the life. It was the beginning of trouble for the union movement which had altered the conditions of labor decades before but it also made "temporary" jobs a reality.

Uranus in conjunction to Pluto would eventually launch changes in the way death was regarded and burial issues were managed. Cremation was never very popular before this time and the new cause of organ donation began. The right to be in charge of one's own medical care and the right to die at one's own time would become powerful issues in the future. So would abortion and birth control.

As Uranus passed on into the other signs, laws changed to bring more equality and launched the Civil Rights era in Libra. Laws governing marriage and divorce were changed. Above all else, Uranus rules protest and the way protest can succeed in forcing change. It is the ultimate rebel against how things are.

Sexual crimes came out of the dark ages when Uranus went through Scorpio, and the religious landscape was altered as it transited Sagittarius. When Uranus hit Capricorn the

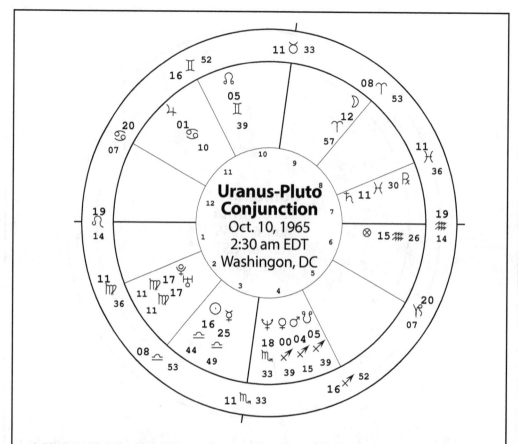

A Uranus-Pluto conjunction occurs very rarely. The conjunction in Virgo of 1965 showed many changes ahead. It launched the era of technological miniaturization which would fuel the space race and ultimately put the computer in homes across the nation and cell phones in pocket and purse.

corporate world got its turn for an overhaul, and then when Uranus moved into Aquarius, the high tech era arrived full-blown.

With Uranus in Pisces, profit in the music world was dramatically lowered as music became more widely available and changed how we viewed movies. No longer were they simply a matter of going to a theater. Now they are seen in the home and even on personal communication devices. Changes in modern drugs and hospital care followed fast and furiously. And the tiny devices of communication that linked us all together proliferated. The cell phone became as common as a safety pin.

When Uranus moved into Aries the social groups on the internet expanded and Facebook exploded. I am sure I don't need to mention that Aries rules the head and face, but of course it was a development defiining the launch of the Aries transit.

Depending on how Uranus is aspected in a natal chart, change is easy or more difficult to deal with. Those with the easy aspects—sextiles and trines—deal best with it. Squares and oppositions may bring harsher changes, largely because people tend to resist change. When change feels forced, as can be the case with hard aspects, they feel a greater sense of trauma.

When a Uranus transit sends a good aspect to a planet such as the Sun, some of the most interesting men may come into the life. Squares and oppositions will bring them in, too, but are apt to reflect problems later on, unless one has a favorable Sun/Uranus aspect in the natal pattern. Such outer planet transits intensify greatly the effect of the natal pattern. A favorable natal pattern benefits from any transit but a difficult natal aspect faces much more trouble. This is the simple rule that allows us to forecast more accurately. It can be called an echo effect—the natal is always set off by the transits and Uranus does this in superb fashion.

People often change jobs when Uranus goes across the MC, or they divorce (if they are going to) when it hits the natal 7th cusp. They move (if they are going to) when it transits the first or 4th Houses. The transit of House 1 is a little less reliable since it may be revoked later on. Generally speaking, when Uranus goes retrograde we may have second thoughts about the changes, but once it resumes its forward motion, we often go ahead or make a second, modifying change.

Uranus rising or angular in a chart can mean a great deal of power, and when it is a natal chart, the individual can be highly contentious and unreliable, unless favorable aspects are involved. In a national chart, Uranus can reflect continual fighting and rebellion.

In the charts of Ireland (Eire) Uranus is strong. In the 1916 chart when Irish nationalists first declared independence from Great Britain, it opposed the ascendant by one degree from the 6th House side. That action launched the Easter Rising. In the 1922 chart it is in the 10th House when the British surrendered Dublin Castle to end the Civil War and de facto independence began. But in the 1949 chart, which marked the complete separation from the British, it is in the 7th House, showing the end of the "partnership."

Such national charts showing an utter refusal to accept anything less than autonomy were a dramatic illustration of a rebellion that would never end without victory. The battling continued the struggle for decades even after that to force Northern Ireland and Great Britain apart. The Irish simply would not quit. Uranus can be a rigid planet when harshly aspected but its real mission in our lives is to open the way to a better era. When anything in our lives is not working a Uranus transit will end it, one way or another.

One of the things I notice in old people is the Uranus return at 84. If Uranus has any tough aspects natally, people don't seem to survive it. My father had the conjunction to the Sun and died a few days after his 84th birthday. I expected it.

Many of the older texts say that natal trines of Uranus and/or Saturn to the Sun give long life. Saturn in my experience seems to improve the pleasure of old age, but I don't know how many years it adds. Uranus I will agree with.

Uranus just plain loves to break any rules if it can.

Chapter 14

Mysterious and spooky; altogether kooky
Neptune

When John F. Kennedy died in 1968, his brother Bobby gave his eulogy. He quoted Jack as saying, "Some men see things as they are and say why? I dream things that never were and say why not?"

Neptune is the planet of the dream of a better life, of the divine within and the creative powers all men have to make their dreams come true. It is the realm of the highest good man can imagine, the ultimate ideal. But it is far more than that. It is all of the unseen influences in life, the pervasiveness of gases and liquid. It rules the air we breathe and the primordial ooze out of which we came. It rules the power of prayer.

Neptune was Poseidon to the Greeks who were considered the intellectual "elite" of the ancient world. For many years after the Romans conquered them, hiring a Greek tutor to teach one's children was the "in" thing to do. Later the Romans decided their own culture needed more respect and they changed the names of the gods. Poseidon became Neptune. But Greeks had their revenge, the tutors lasted quite a long while and their influence and ideas still pervade Western culture.

Modern evidence of earthquake-destroyed cities in the Mediterranean supports the ancient respect and fear of Neptune's anger and ability to produce quakes and volcanos. Even the "liquid" lava that came out of the ground from a volcano was considered Neptune's business. He was called the earth shaker and trident wielder. The trident, a three-pronged spear, was used in fishing and became his symbol as well as the astrological one we use for Neptune.

In the natal chart Neptune can point to an element of confusion and escapism as well as secrets, delusion and less than honorable behavior. At its best, it is also prominent in the charts of saints and psychics and rules the whole world of make-believe. It can be a clear indicator of a con or a con artist as well as as a more ordinary cartoonist or a sublime Michaelangelo. It is a stairway to heaven, but the lower manifestations are not pretty. They can involve chicanery and drug abuse of all sorts, including alcoholism. But the pull to put one's feet on a higher step is insistent. It was quite visible in the late 1960s and '70s when young people by the thousands who had gotten mesmerized by the drug world turned to religion. Many became the "Jesus freaks" of that era. It also marked a pinnacle of popular music which launched Woodstock and huge rock festivals.

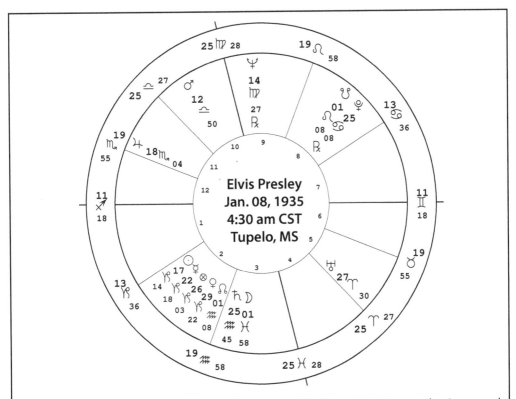

Neptune is often the mark of those who succeed in the entertainment business and Elvis Presley had a string of successful movies and an unmatched record in the music industry. Neptune also shows up in obsessive behavior, particularly in drinking and drug abuse. The music of this "king" of rock 'n roll continues to make money long years after his death of a massive drug overdose. His chart is AA from AstroDataBank.

In today's world the violent drug cartels of Mexico are signs of Neptune decay in that once highly religious nation. The brutality there is the outcome of a desire to corner the market on the profitable drugs that allow addicts to escape the ugliness of this world for the supposedly better but artificial one beyond the senses.

Neptune is glamour, both in the sense of glitz and glitter as well as any form of escapism, from a good book to a trip around the world. It is the shadows of light and dark which became photography, film and movies as well as television. It is the make believe world in all its manifestations.

Neptune in the natal 7th can indicate the individual is naïve about the world, and there can be a lot of idealism in this position. You might see a martyr/messiah complex operating. They are attracted to people who "need" them or who represent some ideal. This could mean marrying someone in prison or someone who then steals them blind, or it could show divorce or separation, sometimes with a weird angle. It may also be the mark of one who seeks to help others, and who may choose a spouse in the healing business—a doctor or member of the clergy. Choice depends a lot on the maturity of the individual.

I have the chart of a physician with a Mars/Neptune conjunction on the MC, and I have charts of musicians and artists and criminals with Neptune in House 7. Often there is a desire to have a "pen name." Many writers and creative people who work under other names than their own have Neptune there.

A well-aspected Neptune and a poorly aspected one do quite different things. Pluto and Neptune sometimes work hand in hand with both good and bad effects, but I would give Neptune to gas seepage, chemical devastation and pollution that builds up. The old tales indicate that Pluto—while powerful— had very constrained limits for manifestation. While Pluto can work quietly a long time before showing effects, I sometimes think we often credit Pluto erroneously with action that is actually Neptunian. Pluto may do deliberate damage, but Neptune's is more by neglect, forgetfulness and wishful thinking not based on reality.

During the years when Pluto actually swung inside the orbit of Neptune there was a great deal of confusion about which planet did what. Only since Pluto moved back outside it into its own orbit have the differences become clarified. If you think about places such as the once infamous town of Love Canal, NY where toxins long forgotten in the ground began to seep into the groundwater, causing terrible birth defects and cancers, it is the Neptune realm. The town's name itself became a bitterly ironic commentary on the situation.

The God Neptune was said to have gifted man with the horse. Sagittarius is the half-horse sign but it is the 12th house of the chart that rules large animals such as horses. And that resonates more specifically to Pisces. One of the worst racing bettors I ever knew was a Pisces. She made lots of money in her life but she lost it almost as fast and would have died broke except for the pension she had from a government job. It's impossible to miss the connection Neptune has to Pisces. Many Pisceans find gambling irresistible and every person I have ever known who got involved in a questionable get-rich scheme was either a Pisces Sun or had the sign prominent, such as angular or with several planets in it. That's not to say others may not be vulnerable, but Pisceans seem to zero in on a lot of this.

Most of the people beloved by the camera seem to have good Neptune aspects, especially to their Ascendant. If you look at a lot of the charts of film and TV people you'll see strong Neptune in their camera appeal. It's also the Neptune link that shows all the boozing and drugs among the creative types but hey, you can't have everything.

When Neptune occupies the first house at birth the individual is a walking mystery show. People with this placement usually don't know who they are, so they adopt whatever image they learn, unless the parents are very careful. They usually get the Neptune "look"—those big, melting eyes you sometimes see. Winona Ryder comes to mind—she always has the haunting gaze. And who can forget Omar Sharif in Dr. Zhivago?

I once had a friend with Neptune rising who had the most gorgeous blue eyes big enough to hold Olympic swim trials in. She was very psychic as well, another Neptunian characteristic. Neptune can make us seem better or worse than we really are. Sometimes it just makes us think we look better or worse. How else can you explain why some women think they are "fat" when they can barely squeeze into a size 6? Or the man who thinks he's a stud with a 4-day beard and a potbelly the size of New York?

Watching Neptune transits go by is illuminating. When Neptune passes through a sign, you can identify it easily by the fashion industry, or the entertainment industry. When transiting Neptune went into Aquarius a few years ago the fashion magazines were suddenly showing absolutely wild colors and peculiar designs in sharp contrast to the Capricorn flavor of the previous few years. Under Capricorn, black was so pervasive even children's wear was black.

The first year after Neptune left Capricorn we had dark greys and browns wake up. The next year they started showing light grey as a "basic" in clothing and paint for interior use. The following year, with Neptune well into Aquarius, fashion went berserk. Color was back.

The same happened in the movies. With Neptune in Capricorn we had a lot of "imitation" stuff—classic oldies being redone in new formats, for instance. Ted Turner launched his Turner Classic Movies on cable and the old wonderful films were being shown again. A lot of it in (what else?) black and white. We also had business stories, (remember that one with Harrison Ford and Melanie Griffith playing a secretary who moves into her boss's role while boss is away skiing?) and people on the job, or making job decisions (Doc Hollywood was the one on medicine) and career excitement (Wall Street stories and powerbroker stuff and big business manipulating things for —gasp—profit). We pretty well wore that topic out by the time Neptune was done with Capricorn.

Then times changed. Once well into Aquarius, Neptune's influence became cyber-stuff in the cultural milieu. Aquarian themes were everywhere, from the blast of new businesses dealing with the high tech world to the cultural images on the internet. Over the length of the transit the music business was devastated by the high tech world which allowed copying without pay to the artists and the rise of the home movie became ubiquitous. Hollywood, considerably smarter than popular musicians, eventually capitalized on it and released movies into the home viewing market. The music industry has still not recovered.

Along with the oddballs represented by Neptune in Aquarius, space became big news again. Our Mars shots were going weird on us. Some of the images in *Vogue* magazine (*Vogue* is always on the leading edge in some way) were of women in shiny cloth, metallics and the like, almost as if they were aliens to earth or wrapped in space suits.

Before the Capricorn transit, big fantasy had an upsurge in popularity and the first outpouring of mythological themes in literature happened during the Neptune in Sagittarius transit. During the Neptune in Capricorn period we had stories with trolls and gnomes and dwarves who live "underground" and the explosion of interest in stones and crystals, and magic linked to the earth itself.

When Neptune was in Aquarius, there was a shift in some of the literature—away from the ideas of the past into the futuristic magics and stories written in the present day somehow making magic through modern technology. It introduced what was called "urban fantasy." Interesting to me to watch.

During Neptune's Pisces transit as I write this there are vampires and ghost stories galore, with the psychic front and center on television and in the movies. Neptune is especially visible because its influence all shows·up in the imaginary realm. Since it spends 14 years in each sign that it transits, there is plenty of time to develop a clear influence.

People who have strong Neptune positions, particularly the angular ones in the natal package, may come out of a family with secrets or creative talents when it is in House 4. In House 10 the influence moves into the career areas of medicine, the arts and music.

Neptune is involved in the medical field with its strong link to the 12th house of "rest and repair" which rules hospitals, nursing homes and rehabilitation facilities. But it can also be the researcher who works alone, the historian of the past or the undercover agent who takes on many personas in the process of acquiring information.

Well aspected, Neptune in a chart gives a spiritual hunger. Favorable ties to Jupiter or Sun produce a lifelong commitment to the spiritual, sometimes religious, life. 12th house benefics show a person who does lots of kindness behind the scenes that comes back to them when they need it. If Neptune is also there, a desire for life away from the spotlight is clear. Sometimes these people end up in cloistered situations, working in forgotten realms or with the needy.

The story of Father Damien, a Catholic missionary priest born Joseph DeVeuster in 1840 who ministered to 600 lepers on the island of Molokai, once a quarantined home for those afflicted with the disease, became famous. It is a classic example of Neptune at work. He was assigned to Hawaii and went to Molakai in 1873. He remained there 15 years caring for the ill until he died from leprosy himself after finally being infected by the disease. The story prompted many later researchers to find a cure for leprosy which is no longer the sentence of death and mutilation that it was in those years. Prisons, quarantines and ghettos are Neptune's realm. The idea of putting any group of "undesirables" in a special place which they cannot leave is Neptune's work.

House 12 malefics are often signs of powerful enemies that you can't really confront and if those planets aspect Neptune it is even more difficult to find out who is the problem. The entire 12th house is an area of private matters and the past and malefics there are usually people you've dealt with before or had a problem with that was not resolved. A progressed Neptune turning retrograde in the 12th may show a change in your 12 house affairs. If these have been unimportant in the past, they now become important. Or, if you have been up to your neck in sick/needy people in the past, they will vanish in the future.

Anytime Neptune—or any other planet, for that matter—changes direction by progression, there is a notable effect on the house it is transiting at that time. The station of Neptune will last several years and intensify all Neptunian events and people who come into one's life.

With Neptune in the 5th your children may need your help because of health, or job problems, perhaps. In the 6th you may have health problems that are difficult to diagnose and treat. In the money houses 2 and 8, Neptune may mean a lot of trouble. In House 2, it may be serious loss or thoughtless spending that ruins your budget. In House 8 it can mean lapsed insurance policies, or unwise investments or dealings with people who are not ethical. In Houses 3 and 9 Neptune may mean trouble with relatives or vehicles. It could mean that things you've written come back to haunt you. It could be called a "change in the wind" of your life.

This current generation is the first generation in many years to grow up with smoking as a diminishing interest. Unfortunately, hard liquor sales, which dropped sharply for a number of years while interest in wine grew, are climbing again. All drugs, including alcohol, are Neptunian, though smoking is also strongly Martian.

There is only one kind of alcoholic—one who drinks compulsively. All the rest are simply rationalizations—as many rationalizations as there are people. The way each person rationalizes his or her drinking may reflect a pattern in the birth chart, but that's because the way we do anything reflects our birth charts. The patterns of alcoholism reflect a desire to use chemical means to escape consequences of reality, along with the frustrations of life— there is always a Neptune problem. I have the charts of many alcoholics I have known and the patterns repeat endlessly. Men often have a Neptune aspect to both Mars and the Moon. Women may get it to Venus and the Moon instead of Mars, but Neptune is always—repeat, always—involved in a stress pattern. Alcoholism is a self-inflicted disease. Any alcoholic can begin to recover by not drinking for one day. Easier said than done, of course, but that is the basis of the work of Alcoholics Anonymous—choosing not to drink for one day. The modern obsession of drug abuse is similar. Only the means are different than booze.

There are lots of reality avoidance methods other than booze or drugs, of course, and some are much more positive. But all escapes are Neptunian, in a sense. And we all use one or another. For example, I adore fantasy and sci-fi literature. I am a retired newspaperwoman and after some 30 years in the business I have read all the stories I ever want to read about crooked politicians, venal clergymen, child abusers, murderers, sex criminals, mega-thieves and the like. Stories about witches and elves and space travel are just dandy for me. For escape, I want a world that I know is fantasy and where the bad stuff isn't true and everybody gets a happy ending. Does that make me nuts? No, it's just one way I find some relief from life's daily routines. There are many other escapes people use, of course. We all have ways we deal with stress. It can be a card game, a night at the movies, a good nap or a whodunnit. Some choose an active sport to work off a day's tensions. Some people all but dive into the television set and stay there until they feel better. As long as our choice takes us away from today's stresses and gives us a time-out it is a good thing.

We all have Neptune somewhere in our charts. Whether we choose to use it to become wise and loving and giving or we settle for booze and partying every night of the week is up to each of us. No excuses. We are what we choose to be. People with Neptune in hard aspect to Ascendant often have a very slim tolerance for alcohol—either they can't drink at all (or very little) or they don't because they don't like the effect. They may like the taste, however. Alcoholics often dislike the taste but like the effect. And I know that's true—I've known a zillion alcoholics in my life and they've told me so.

A man I know whose wine cellar is his pride and joy and who has a huge capacity and tolerance for wine has Neptune in tight conjunction to the Ascendant. Neptune to Ascendant shows his love for his wine, I believe. A conjunction is not always considered a hard aspect, but a square definitely is. However, there are many people who have a "high tolerance." Some of them eventually cross the line to compulsive drinking after 20 or 40 years or more. Why? I don't know, but there is some thought in scientific circles that the mechanism that keeps us free of compulsion can break down from too many "assaults" of high levels of alcohol. Also, I should point out, that many people who have drinking problems start off with that high tolerance, which deserts them later in their drinking careers.

I am not saying any particular person is an alcoholic. That's way out of my realm of competence to judge and certainly not just because someone collects wine. The world is full of wine collectors who aren't alcoholics. I think it would benefit anyone with questions to read some Alcoholics Anonymous literature or books (available in any library) or any of the studies on alcoholism. It might offer illumination. The astrological aspects are usually seen in Neptune stress aspects to Sun, Moon, Mars and/or Venus. It won't be a single aspect, but a combination that sends one off on that road. Oh, and people with the hard aspects to Ascendant from Neptune also have difficulty with other chemicals in the body—weird reactions to novacaine, or difficulty with anesthesia, many allergies to antibiotics, etc.

And as to the higher manifestations of Neptune, psychics, mystics and deeply religious people also have strong Neptune positions. Prayer is Neptunian and the belief that there is a better if unseen world is Neptunian. The idea that there is a reason we were born and a "mission" we have on earth is a Neptune concept. And lest we think that Neptune itself thus invalidates those things, we should mention the beliefs that goodness, human decency and ethical behavior are not false concepts. They merely belong to the unseen realm of ideals. And prayer is a reality of that higher world. After all, as the old saying goes, "More things are wrought by prayer than this world dreams of."

Chapter 15

Use it up, wear it out—
Pluto

Pluto is the planet that forces us to eliminate things in whatever area of life it is transiting. It also helps us restructure our lives to make them better. The title to this chapter comes from a saying I learned from my mother, which is undoubtedly one from her old depression days. It was, "Use it up, wear it out. Make it do, or do without."

Sometimes it indicates people who are leaving one's life, and sometimes it ends the time of childhood as babies arrive in our own lives. Pluto seems involved in both birth and death. But of course, there are many other things it deals with.

Pluto, like all the major planets and most of the minor Moons and large asteroids, is named after a mythical figure of Greek or Roman origin. In this case, it's been dubbed with the name of the god supposedly in charge of the afterlife. Since its discovery in the 1930s it has altered our society in many ways, forcing us to change.

Modern scientists in 2006 tried to eliminate Pluto from the pantheon of planets because of its size after the discovery of Eris out beyond Pluto. They said it was a 'planetoid' which was even larger. Ceres, the largest of the asteroids, and nearly Pluto's size, is now also considered as a planetoid. Regardless of what anyone else says, however, astrologers think Pluto is more important and consider it a 'planet.' There are a great many scientists around the world who were annoyed by its demotion at the time, and disagree with the "official" label. I don't have any material in this book on Eris because I haven't yet worked with it, but I have considered Ceres extremely important ever since its discovery.

A lot of us build up wasteful spending practices over the years. Sometimes we buy far more shoes than we need, or excess clothes, or trade cars too often, etc. We don't bother with budgets. We live from payday to payday. When transitting Pluto moves through a house it pushes us to get rid of the outmoded in our life and rejuvenate what we keep. I see Pluto prominent in the natal charts of people who like to refurbish old furniture, resellers of auto hub caps, antique store owners, used car lots and second hand clothing stores. It is also strong in those who manage money and who manipulate money well to their own benefit.

Any time transiting Pluto makes an aspect to your Moon you may get the urge to clean the closets, or the basement, or the attic. Sometimes it cleans out your pocketbook. One woman I know with a Moon/Pluto conjunction buys and sells "vintage" clothing on eBay. She helps other people clean out their closets. Sometimes it helps you discover buried "treasure" in that housecleaning.

But when transiting in a financial area, Pluto will force you on a sound financial footing one way or another. It will help you restructure your attitudes toward money and spending and giving and keeping. If you have a beneficial aspect from Pluto natally to the ruler of your 2nd (or a planet in it) in your birth chart, it can be a big boost, possibly even a big jump in income. The old word for a very rich person is Plutocrat. It's not used much these days, but it's still descriptive of those whose wealth can hardly be calculated. Rupert Murdoch's net worth has been estimated in the billions. Another vastly rich man is Bill Gates, who founded Microsoft.

Go on a budget system as soon as possible when transiting Pluto heads for your own House 2. Start paying yourself first by putting cash off the top of your income into a savings account. Cut your spending and overhaul your finances. You'll still have to clean up your debts, but it will leave you better off. If Pluto heads for House 8 before you have that done, the clean up can be serious, even leading to bankruptcy, if that natal House 8 is in bad shape and you have neglected to make it work better. For several years there was a tendency for some careless spenders in the U.S. to see bankruptcy as an easy way to get out of debt and still afford the high life. I had a client who was on her 3rd bankruptcy when I met her. Congress finally overhauled the bankruptcy laws after the big credit card companies beseeched it for aid.

There is always an element of overhauling with Pluto. Sometimes it is a major trauma in life if the transit is angular or hitting a key natal planet. A 10th or 4th House transit can show the death of a parent. Or it may be the loss of something we counted on or the birth or death of someone else important to us. Pluto has the quality of being irrevocable once it gets in gear. It forces action that has been underway for some time and finally comes to fruition.

What ordinarily happens at death, aside from the dying itself, of course, is very Plutonian. All of one's possessions are cleared out and redistributed. Perhaps that's why people who sense that death is nearing worry about who will get grandma's cut glass and start passing around family heirlooms, and updating the scrapbooks. Some people also try to load the family history onto the next generation. I know some who have. Occasionally when the transiting Sun or Moon goes over natal Pluto we do some of the same thing, or life does it for us. It may be some aging person or troublesome element in business, on the job or in our romantic life. It's not a good time to buy something because the purchase will mean you will have to get rid of something else, even before you need to.

Example—you buy what you think will be a piece of "back up" equipment for your business on sale. And before you know it the new takes over because it is so efficient everyone wants to use it instead of the much bulkier older equipment you thought had another year of life in it. Instead, it gets pushed out the door. Or you keep the old equipment as the back up and by the time you ever need it, it has become obsolete.

Sometimes that monthly transit of the Moon over natal Pluto results in a day when we clean out the knife drawer, or rearrange the linen closet. Not all transits are momentous. Occasionally they just help us to get a job done.

Does Pluto have a Scorpionic flavor? Yes. Am I happy to see it assigned to that sign? Indeed. But co-rulership? Perhaps. Anyway, lest anyone think I don't use Pluto with Scorpio, I do. I think of Pluto as more the renter in the house than the owner, though. I feel the same way about Neptune with Pisces and Uranus with Aquarius. I object to folks trying to oust Mars, Jupiter and Saturn from places they've had since antiquity.

I see Pluto having a function in the birth/death process quite different from that of Mars and yet the sign Scorpio definitely seems involved. Pregnancy usually has some strong Pluto aspects indicating it, from the women's charts I have done. It helps to spot pregnancy possibilities as well. Pluto-Moon aspects in a woman's chart natally can often trigger a full family.

Perhaps in 100 years we will realize more about Pluto's actions. Pluto's discovery was only some 70 to 80 years ago, so we are hardly in a position to judge completely. We haven't even seen a full cycle of its action. Pluto has an eccentric orbit, not on the ecliptic as the other planets but at angle to it. It also swings inside the orbit of Neptune (closer to the Sun) and outside it at other times. A move by astronomers to demote Pluto from planethood to the status of planetoid, or "dwarf planet" junior member of the solar system has largely been ignored by astrologers who know it works just like a full planet anyway. Which brings up another interesting fact I notice with Pluto, and that is the tie to the Moon and Saturn cycles.

The Moon takes 28-29 days to circle the chart. Saturn takes 28 -29 years to do the same thing. Pluto takes nearly 10 times that to circle the Zodiac. It's not an exact match, of course, but it is closer to those two cycles than any others. If there is any correspondence there, it has to be this: the Moon is in charge of giving form. Saturn crystallizes or hardens form. Pluto breaks down and re-forms. Mars just likes the breaking part. I think Pluto is much deeper and subtler than that. But do I want to give Pluto full title to the sign yet? No, not yet.

Tenants often act as if they own a property and it is in fact their "home" and most law treats it as such, but that could be subject to change if they move out. Meanwhile they use the address as "theirs." I have no problem using Pluto themes for House 2, for example, if Scorpio is on that cusp. Pluto is deep pockets and Mars just likes to spend the shiny stuff. Having Mars there is nearly a guarantee of careless financial attitudes. It is the classic "hole in the pocket" characteristic. To understand how it works for a specific person, you have to look at both Mars and Pluto. But Mars first. Pluto second. And when in doubt, use Mars.

I use Mars for the Scorpio ruler in horary unless the question applies to something we generally attribute to Pluto in particular—such as a nuclear power plant, or a sewage treatment facility or a recycling program or something of the like. A compost pile in your garden, an old septic system in the back yard and anything that converts matter to a new form comes under Pluto. That probably sounds like I'm trying to have it both ways and I have to admit that I am. But I think we all use Pluto as a Scorpio modern ruler, and this has been intensifying in the last 30 years. But there is too much emphasis on Pluto and too little on Mars, in my humble opinion, and all I want to do is remind us that Mars did not abdicate, to my knowledge, and still has the primary clout in Scorpio.

The main story from antiquity about Pluto (his Roman name) is from Greece, where he is called Hades. On a trip to the surface, Dark Lord Pluto saw a lovely girl named Proserpina (in the earlier Greek myth, Persephone) and wanted her in the worst way. So he drove his magic cart up through the lawn, grabbed her and took her home with him, so the stories said.

Ceres (Demeter in the Greek myth), goddess of the grain crops and the weather, was so upset at the loss of her daughter that she caused drought to nearly wreck everything on earth while she mourned her loss. Finally the other gods protested that she was ruining things by killing off their worshippers. So her brother Jupiter (Zeus in the Greek myth), ruler of the gods, made a deal with her that she could bring Prosperpina home if she hadn't eaten anything at all while she was in the underworld with Pluto (Hades). Pluto, after all, was Jupiter's brother, so it was a rather awkward family situation all around.

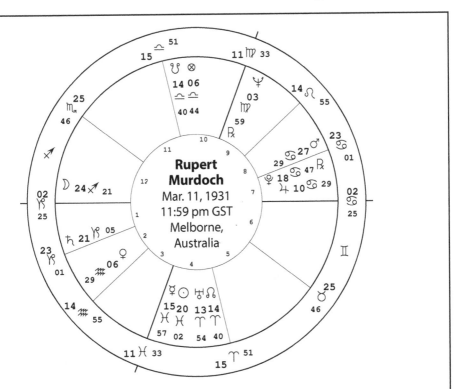

Australia media mogul Rupert Murdoch is hugely rich and owns major news and entertainment properties all around the globe. His chart ruler Saturn is involved with a Mars-Pluto combination in the 7th and 8th houses, which also trines his Pisces Sun and Part of Fortune. Jupiter fall close on Pluto's other side. Pluto has a way of intensifying the effects of other planets that it contacts, particularly when it is angular.

When Ceres arrived in the underworld, she discovered that Proserpina had eaten one tiny pomegranate seed, but when she threatened to reinitiate the drought, Jupiter and Pluto made another deal with her. Proserpina would spend part of every year with Pluto, but could come home to mother for another part. So every year there is winter and Ceres is unhappy. But, part of every year Proserpina comes home, and Ceres lets the world bloom.

By the way, the story does not say what Proserpina thought about all this. But she didn't have her mother's heavenly clout and apparently Pluto and Jupiter didn't feel she needed any opinion of her own.

Pluto seems to have an extra strength in all birth charts I've worked with that appears to give added impetus to whatever planet it contacts. Pluto is particularly strong when direct, but shows strength even when retrograde. Since Pluto has an erratic orbit and swings inside Neptune periodically, it's not too surprising that it should have other unusual properties.

Not all Plutonian events activate natal Pluto. Sometimes transiting Pluto, which is so strong because it is slow, brings major events when it passes through the angles, or across the Midheaven.

Chapter 16

Coming up roses
The Ascendant

The Ascendant is the single most "personal" point in your chart. Think about this for a minute—everyone in the world born on your date has the same general set-up of planets—everyone born close to you in time probably has the same Moon but only someone born exactly when and where you are has the same ascendant degree AND the same planet package. Others around the world can have the same rising degree but not the same planet package with it because that changes with time to suit their locale.

The Ascendant is like the door you use to come on stage for this lifetime. It sets your "costume"—the physical equipment you are born with—and points to which part of the "show" you will be in. If it is Cancer rising, you will have a different "role" than if Aquarius is rising.

The Sun sign describes the "you" that you become more fully with every passing year and the Moon as the way you start out in life: your childhood, your sense impressions, your emotional package and your family relationships. Many children start out as timid, fearful people (Capricorn Moon, for instance) who become strong, self-assertive adults (such as a Leo Sun). However, the Leo Sun person has developed a different "overlay" with a sensible, practical, conservative Capricorn flair than if there were a breezy, optimistic, easy-come-easy-go Sagittarian Moon.

But the ones who come through the Gemini rising stage door will have different roles to play in life than the ones who come through the Taurus ascendant door. The ascendant shows, I think, what area in life will be an important function for you to develop and how you will do that. Virgo rising will have a health/efficiency/work/6th house focus that will be there regardless of the Sun or Moon. Something about all that will be crucial. Also, the body will have a "Virgo" look and the "costume" for the show will be practical and quiet, rather than loud and impulsive as if Aries were rising.

Taurus rising will be born with charm. Money—the lack or the abundance of it—will be important. Look at Michael Jordan, the great basketball star. The Aquarian Sun man was called "his Airness" and he left a fabulous record in his sport. But it was his huge money-making ability that set a new standard for athletes and endorsement earnings. He was single-handedly credited with causing the stocks of companies that endorsed him to rise and fall depending on what he did. This was something new at the time.

If the Ascendant is your "role" then the ruler is the "script," perhaps, to carry this analogy further, the words and the action. I had a Cancer rising client who was a classic appearing Cancer with thin legs, heavy upper body, round face. Her Moon was afflicted in a T-square by both Pluto and Uranus and she never knew how she felt about anything — the up and down mood swings of Cancer are ferocious and she had a twittery, fluttery personality that reminded me of a moth bashing against life. Her stomach was always upset by something or other and digestion was very delicate. Motherhood of her large family was obviously the most determining factor in her life path. Cancer was neither her Sun nor Moon sign, but it certainly told about her life.

The sign rising will show its problems. Headaches are common to Aries. The last degree of Aries rising often has a lot of migraines but without the physical resilience of the sign and may suffer more effect from them. The individual 29-degree Aries will look more Taurean, perhaps, or seem more Taurean, than Aries. Heavier, for instance. It's the oncoming "new sign" effect, when you realize the entire first house is occupied by it.

The 29th degree Scorpio may run into problems in the Scorpio career choice and not settle down until it switches to a Sagittarian type career. One nurse I know (Scorpio is one of the medical signs) was never happy in a hospital—constantly at odds with the rules and management. She ended up doing one of those medical ship trips to Africa, worked her tail off and found what she really like doing. Now she's a medical missionary for her church and goes all over the world. Both signs, Scorpio and Sagittarius, showed the arena of her life's work.

The Ascendant determines your physical body but how do planets there strongly modify the basic costume? It's like having a blue dress. The world is full of blue dresses. We need to know: casual, dressy, two piece, long sleeve or short, a-line, empire, etc., etc. All the modifiers are the planets and the rest of the chart. But it is still a "blue dress."

Pisces rising will often face the problem of ill health and the need to follow a loose medical regimen for instance, something this rather forgetful sign may have trouble with. The life path may involve helping to deal with the needs of those who are themselves ill or handicapped or poor, perhaps.

Libra rising—in common with Taurus—has a sweet look and a bow-shaped mouth. The body is almost always pleasing and appears to be in proportion whether it actually is or not. If Libra Ascendant is accompanied by a strong Venus placement the individual can be considered truly beautiful, whether male or female. A good aspect from Venus to Ascendant preserves the looks into old age. A good aspect from Mars can mean endless amounts of energy. Of course, the harsher aspects are apt to destroy or minimize those blessings.

Aquarius rising always seems to be surrounded by people whether there is a desire for solitude or not. They often tend to be leaned on in life, though sometimes they are the leaners. Both Libra and Aquarius rising give good legs, often with long, elegant ankles. All the air signs have a need to discuss things endlessly. They enjoy the play of ideas, news and information of all sorts.

Red hair and scars on the face are quite common when Mars is strong or aspecting Ascendant. I have both—and Mars is in opposition to Ascendant natally. Although, I can think of an Aries rising type whom I know who has no scars, but she does have a very reddish cast to her hair and a very weak aspect of Mars to her Ascendant. It can be tricky to spot sometimes. That's true of any Ascendant. Another Aries rising type I know with a strong Mars aspect to Ascendant has the typical flaming carrot hair and boundless energy.

Thinking of the husky, whispery voice of Virgo rising. I thought of Jackie Kennedy, but she actually had Scorpio rising and all the magnetism of the sign. I still remember the late President Richard Nixon going all husky and whispery under stress and then recovering and going into the strong, clear "politician voice." He had Virgo rising. I always notice the fastidiousness of Virgo rising. Things are always neat and where they're supposed to be. Men's ties are precisely centered, the collars are straight, etc. When I was very young, women still commonly wore hosiery with seams up the back. Mine were a constant struggle but I knew girls whose seams were always dead straight and dead center. They were the ones with naturally curly hair, too. This has to have been Virgo. No wonder I hated them.

There are all different kinds of looks we can attibute to Ascendants. The rising sign has a ruler and if that ruler is afflicted or in a sign that is not compatible, the rising sign will not manifest well, meaning in an attractive way. If the ruler is well-aspected it will present the better side.

Libra rising can sometimes seen in people who part their hair in the exact center so both sides are even. This is more common among women than men. Simply fashion, of course.

Scorpio rising tends to have very straight or very curly hair, sometimes very fair or very dark, deep set eyes, pronounced brow, thin lips and prominent chin. Billy Graham, the famed minister who has a Scorpio Sun, has the sharp nose-sharp chin look of the sign.

Sagittarius rising usually has a clear, open face and strong, well proportioned body. But, for example, what if Jupiter is debilitated by sign, or square Ascendant? That could be a doubly unfortunate package. You may get a gangly, awkward body and a horse face with long teeth that is not particularly attractive. It can run to hump backs and stoop shoulders. But that package might also be that of a well meaning, rather clumsy person devoted to helping others who sort of lights up from the inside and presto, the longer you know them, the "prettier" they get.

Now that I've picked on Sag Rising, let's have some fun for a minute and think about the worst possible rising sign look for the other eleven signs.

Pisces rising can give you the person who lacks a chin, or has the wide, almost blubbery fish-mouth look, with bug eyes as well as pasty skin and a soft body.

Aries rising gone sour? Eyes too close together, skimpy, scraggly hair and/or beard and a nose only a mother could love. Cavernous cheeks, missing teeth, and slope shouldered.

Taurus rising—excessive hair, double chins, no-neck, googly eyes or a piggy-looking face with beady eyes—sausage tied in the middle.

Gemini rising—case of the squints, a nose that wanders, peculiar ears that stick out, bad teeth and a sly, crooked expression. Knock-kneed.

Cancer rising—Fat face, big boobs down to the knees in the women and downright noticeable in the men, bellies out to wherever and thin, disapproving lips. Big Adam's apples and vacant, staring eyes.

Leo rising—harsh appearance, like a scarecrow with bulimia, rat face with sharp teeth, or teeth all rotten and bad skin. Limps and wears padding everywhere to look normal. Or goes the other direction and weighs 400 pounds in grade school and has terminal acne.

Virgo rising—Ski nose, bean pole body, huge ears, unmanageable hair, skinny body or one with no waist, flat busted in women and no shoulders in the men. Small pot bellies.

Libra rising—Good ankles and that's it. Everything else is misshapen and out of proportion. Head on you can see the eyes don't match, one side of the face goes up, and one down, the too-small mouth is hidden by pouting cheeks, the skin is pitted and baldness follows puberty by about 6 months. The nose is too large.

Scorpio rising —looks suspicious just standing there—sullen, with low hairline, primitive, apelike appearance and protruding bone over the eyebrow line. Hands like claws, arms too long, big hips or flat butt, lips look too wet, eyes peer out from under heavy eyebrows that grow together and the jaw is wide. Teeth don't come together right.

Capricorn rising—scrawny and ill-shaped, little hair and that unmanageable or too oily, crooked face and limbs, sway backed and bad complexion. Bunions and flat feet. Buck teeth.

Aquarius rising—funny colored skin, hands too big, feet too small, gaunt cheeks, owl eyes, perpetual sweats, freckles and pimples.

Is this awful enough? I had some fun here thinking about how bad it could be. Luckily, most of us don't get the worst. On the other hand, people who find us delightful company ignore even the worst appearance. We are all beautiful on the inside, if we choose to be. And sooner or later the inside shows on the outside. Somebody once said that at 20 we have the face God gave us, at 30, the one we are making for ourselves and at 40, the one we deserve.

A tip off can be the profile. Aquarians usually have pretty classic looking profiles and Pisces will have a lack of chin, or sometimes a double chin. Remember Don Knotts who played the man who became a fish in the Disney movie *Mr. Limpet*? If ever I saw the look of a Pisces Ascendant walking it was Don Knotts. He also played the deputy in Mayberry. When he'd get excited his head would pop forward and his eyes would bug out and *sohelp-meGawd* he looked like things I have taken off hooks with worms in their mouths! He did not have a Pisces Sun or Moon and I was not able to find a birth time on him to verify my description of Pisces rising. If he was born with another sign rising, of course, he might have had a strong Neptune influence. It would only prove my first principle of astrology: **Everything modifies everything else.** A water ascendant is *de facto* sensitive and leery of the rough and tumble of large crowds.

One of the things that may help pinpoint an Ascendant is noting physical characteristics. Dental problems or back trouble are common with Leo rising, but allergies (Hay fever or hives from some food) often show up with Virgo rising. Capricorn rising usually has good teeth and bad knees. Gemini rising people tend to look younger than they are and, as a rule, the men keep their hair as they age. Leo rising women may comb hair straight back without a part and wear it in a large "mane," where Virgo rising likes it parted, under control and neat. Small hips show with Leo rising, and high arched, pretty feet also show with Virgo rising. The body is average to slightly under average in height and looks youthful and compact. Leo rising is taller and has strong, straight shoulders and good posture.

Men with Cancer rising can be quite tall as well as very short and tend to accumulate weight in the abdominal area in middle age. Women may have either the round, cheeky full-moon look or sharp, hatchet-faced thin-Moon features. The health may be weak in childhood but very strong in old age.

Leo rising women use lots of cosmetics, particularly as they grow older. Libra rising wants the latest thing, but tends to simplify with age. Sagittarius rising hates to bother with cosmetics at all, though will if pushed. The best characteristic Sagittarius rising gets is a tendency to smile readily and see silver linings in every problem. It's a tall sign and sometimes develops a stoop in old age. It can also get much heavier in middle age, though will stay slim if they develop the habit of exercise early.

Jewelry is sometimes a giveaway if all else fails. Leo rising is the gold lover and the women adore adornment, often big, or dramatic in style. Virgo rising likes tiny, neat earrings and "unobtrusive" jewelry, preferring a simple look. Cancer rising wears family pieces and things that are "meaningful" and probably have been in the jewelry box for years.

Scorpio likes one potent piece of jewelry at a time. Gemini will have the latest thing, even if it's a plastic or a "mood" ring, which was a fad in the 1960s because it changed its appearance with body temperature shifts. Capricorn rising wants the real thing, never paste or glass or imitation gold or silver. It prefers family pearls or inherited gems. Taurus rising will often do without anything if it isn't real gold or silver. Aries will sometimes wear iron or wood. They hate to follow trends anyway. You can often spot them moving in a hurry as they tend to lean forward "into the wind" almost as if they can win a race by the nose, as horses are said to do. This sign also get scars on the face or head.

You never hear about all the dental problems and broken bones Leo gets. It never fails to amaze me. I do not know a Leo Sun or Ascendant without some of these. After I realized how many Leos had major teeth problems or broken arms or bone damage of one sort or another I began to ask why. The clue is the solar set-up for Leo which puts Capricorn on the 6th. Saturn deals with bones and teeth.

On the other hand, Sagittarius rising gets stubborn,—persistent Taurus on the 6th—and can be quite healthy. If it does get ill it can reflect a Venus problem, such as strep throat or kidney infections. Libra has Pisces on 6th and can develop real and continuing health problems.

One of the things we have to watch is the similarity between the solar or natural houses for a Sun sign, and the natal pattern which puts a different sign on Ascendant. Usually Leo rising will have Capricorn on House 6. Even if the Ascendant is Aquarius, which also has a powerful Saturn input, you may find it. However, the Aquarius/Leo polarity will tend more to the circulatory problems—artery hardening, varicose veins, etc.

With the Sun sign there is always a polarity operating, which is why Aquarians sometimes pick up on Leo problems and vice versa, but you don't get that with the sign on the Ascendant. The polarity, of course, comes from the fact that the earth actually occupies the sign opposite the Sun at birth. It's why Capricorn Suns work so hard at a nice home and Cancer Suns chase around doing community service, for instance.

Whenever you think about what affects a Sun sign or a rising sign, keep that 6th house in mind. It is a big help to analysis. Also, watch what aspects the Ascendant. That's another thing people tend to overlook and I have found it a big flashing light, particularly on the physical level.

Chapter 17

A tale of the dragon
The Moon's Nodes

The Moon's north node has been called the dragon's head for centuries. It is the place where the Moon crosses the equator going north on its slightly winding path around the earth. Its south node is always exactly opposite, marking the place where the Moon crosses back to the south. These points change.

The Latin terms are Caput, or Caput Dragonis, for the head of the dragon, and Cauda, or Cauda Dragonis, meaning tail. For those who have never seen the dragon, a Mercator map of the earth with the Moon's path drawn will illustrate it vividly. A Mercator map looks like the skin of an orange peeled off and flattened, with none of the tidiness of a square or rectangle. The path of the Moon across it is a serpentine, S-shaped trail. No wonder the ancients considered the Moon mysterious and called its nodes "The Dragon." The Arabic astrologers of old also called it the dragon and their terms for the head and tail were Catahibizon and Katababazon. I mention them only because the names have a kind of bounce on the tongue and if you're going to study something you might as well enjoy it wherever possible.

The nodes move backward, both retrograde and direct and even stationary at times, at a mean, or average, motion of about 3 minutes per day. The north node was traditionally believed to be benefic, with the quality of Venus and Jupiter. The south node was of the nature of Mars and Saturn. Another way to consider them is that the north represents growth and the new development of the future while the south represents the way out, the past, or things we already know how to do. The north node is intake of new material and the south node is release of the used waste.

The value of the node to astrology is immense. First of all, it allows astrologers (and astronomers, for that matter) to forecast eclipses. A new Moon or a full Moon that occurs close to the longitude of either the north or south nodal point is an eclipse. If it is very close, it may be a total eclipse. This is because the Moon can block the Sun's rays from the earth (at the new Moon, creating a solar eclipse) or the earth can block the Sun's rays from the Moon (at full Moon, producing a lunar eclipse).

A solar eclipse, when the Sun and Moon are conjunct, can only occur when the Sun is less than 18 degrees, 31 minutes from either node. It is total if closer than 9 degrees, 55 minutes. An annular eclipse is from 9 degrees 55 to 11 degrees 15 minutes and partial runs from 11 degrees 15 minutes to the limit of 18 degrees 31 minutes. The lunar eclipses, at full Moon, have a narrower margin. A partial lunar eclipse must be 12 degrees 15 minutes or less from one of the nodes and a total eclipse must be closer than 9 degrees 30 minutes.

In the birth chart of a person or an entity such as an organization or a nation, the dragon has some very specific uses that no planet provides. It can indicate fame, recognition, success and opportunity, as well as disgrace and public humiliation.

Keywords are helpful here. The nodes are particularly responsible for the "knots and ties" of relationships. When two people are looking to the astrologer to see if their romance is going anywhere, the nodes will tell the story. All enduring relationships of any type that I have ever seen have some kind of strong nodal ties from one chart to the other. Any relationship without them simply does not last. I have seen this repeatedly in decades of doing charts.

When the nodes of one person lay across the Acendant/Descendant line of the other, the node person will stick like glue to the other. Such contacts are lifelong ties and no matter how much time has passed since people have seen each other, the power of the node will reawaken the relationship very readily. In the charts of family members, the closeness is intense. When the nodes contact planets, the relationship takes on the quality of the planet. For instance, a nodal tie to Mercury often initiates a conversational tie or a classroom introduction. Today's internet is definitely a Mercury contact and when an acquaintance is begun there, expect to see some Mercury activation. If the relationship develops and deepens and endures, look for the nodes to be at work.

Marriages that endure always have strong nodal ties between the two people. Sometimes they are node to node, or one person's node to the other's MC/IC axis, showing they share the same goals in life.

Nodes to Saturn have special meaning. Anyone whose Saturn falls on your North Node gives you good advice and will be a help to you at some important time in your life. These are excellent contacts between you and someone who serves your needs—a nurse, a financial advisor, a lawyer, or the like. Saturn to the South Node is a practically unbreakable tie in this life. It shows some important lessons will be learned through the relationship and it will bring heavy obligation at some point.

I recall seeing such ties between a man and his wife who had what could only be called an "open" marriage for several years before it eventually settled down with the birth of a child. I would feel sorry for any woman who expected a fling between her and the husband to lead to his divorce. It never would. His South Node fell on his wife's Saturn. Her South Node fell on his Saturn. I believe they are nearing at least 40 years of marriage.

When the North Node falls on the Venus of one person, it shows benefit to both. When the South Node falls on Venus, it shows the Venus person does a lot of giving. The node person has to work hard to match it, or the relationship gets lopsided quickly.

One person's malefics to the other's South Node can be a warning to the South Node person—Neptune can lie, Mars can injure, Pluto can blab confidential information, Uranus can vanish forever at the blink of an eye.

Sun and Moon contacts to the nodes provide instant sympathy/friendship and usually benefit. They insure strong relationship possibilities. The North Node is best. If the contact of the planets is to the South Node, the planet person does more of the work in the relationship. Any meeting where the nodes occupy angular houses or contact Sun or Moon in the event chart can be important in the life.

When there are no nodal ties between two people, they may have a pleasant relationship but it will be "out of sight, out of mind" when they aren't there. People with planet/node ties etch their names on your soul in some way.

I'm not sure the nodes are involved with money as such. What they do seem to mark, I think, are events that the birth chart promises. Timers, if you like. If there is a financial windfall indicated in the birth chart, or at least not a denial of that possibility, then the nodal transits can point to the time it will occur, whether from gambling or contest winnings. Jupiter doesn't really rule money, but is usually involved in "big" wins (Jupiter deals with big opportunities) so the nodes are also involved in big wins.

In practice, the nodes can lead to new relationships, and people who steer us to certain things that turn out to be blessings, even in "bad" times. One might be a physician who finds a cancer before it metastasizes, (maybe the natal nodes were in 6 and 12) or the advisor who finally helps us manage our finances (nodes through 2 and 8), etc.

There are many other things to say about the nodes. One should always pay attention to the house, sign and aspects of the nodes as much as one pays to those of a planet. They tell the experienced astrologer volumes. But it is in the birth chart of a single individual that the nodes become invaluable. Where the nodes are in relation to the angles can smooth the path of life or make it more difficult. Contacts to planets by the nodes or in the same degree in any other sign, show that affairs ruled by the planet will get special attention in life. An example might be a node/Jupiter contact in the chart of one who travels a great deal, or whose work involves teaching or import/export of foreign goods, or philanthropy (working for a charitable institution, perhaps).

The North Node/planet contact shows the area for possible growth and beneficial future development. A planet conjunct the South Node shows the individual pulled by the hopes and experiences of the past who will reap less benefit from the activity it indicates than would otherwise be the case. Often, events ruled by the south node contact bring failure or one's efforts fail to prosper.

Planets in the same degree anywhere in the chart are a warning that affairs ruled by the planet will be a lifelong headache. For instance, Mars in 12 Taurus and the nodes at 12 degrees of any sign point to trouble with the things Mars rules in the birth pattern as well as things Mars rules in general, such as a hot temper, surgery, injuries, falls, and so on. In a particular chart it might also rule the tenth house, for instance, in which case temper or an accident could harm the career. In a woman's chart, such a Mars would be one of the indicators of trouble with men. It will also indicate the part of the body that may suffer through injury. In Taurus, it would be the neck, in Gemini the hands, or the arms or even the finger nails perhaps, and so on.

The North or South Node conjunct the Moon itself rates several stars in terms of importance. It always—without exception—brings public recognition, notoriety or even outright fame at some point in life. Sometimes it is a continual process. I recall the chart of a young woman who had never completed high school, came of a poor family, married a man with little education, had a couple kids and lived in rural semi-poverty. She nevertheless became a household name in her part of the state as a murder victim. She had the Moon conjunct her South Node. Not all Moon/South Node people are murder victims, of course, but she did fulfill the pattern for receiving public notice.

Another man I knew had North Node conjunct Moon in his 12th house. He was a simple blue collar worker who was always in the news. Every time his Moon/North Node was hit by major transit or progression, up he popped. He might be stopped as the 1 millionth person to cross a bridge, or the winner of the first new sandwich made at a fast food restaurant, or be the only witness to a plane disaster. But it was regular as clockwork. There he would be—half the time in his old truck in work clothes—and news photographers would take his picture and he'd get another 15 minutes of fame. He had a huge scrapbook.

A third man I knew was a priest whose work was always in the news. He had a poor parish in a poor neighborhood and was assigned by his bishop as an advisor to students on the side (probably to beef up his salary) and was always getting publicity. He never understood it. Neither did his colleagues who struggled in vain to get attention for much larger, more important projects that failed to capture public interest. Unfortunately, they didn't come into this world with Moon/ Node contacts in their charts. One aside here: his lunar contact was to the South Node, and jealousy or criticism from others sometimes followed his recognition.

The next thing the nodes do that is unique is provide one with the habit of getting "credit" for one's accomplishments. There is a "line of advantage" that runs through the chart and the credit predominates on one side of that line. The north node at birth must fall on the favorable side. The line of advantage runs from about 9 degrees west of the MC (in the ninth house) to 9 degrees east of the IC (in the third house). The north node must therefore be in the east, and rising, if the individual is to get the most benefit. Those born on the favorable side win awards easily, get good grades in school, stars for good behavior, and applause when they do something well. They learn about the spotlight of approval very early in life.Those born with the north node on the other side seem to labor in vain when it comes to applause. What they get is often attention for their failures instead. They may even be geniuses who leave the world incomparable music or art, but they seldom get the recognition during their lifetime.

This does not always work, of course, and there are always people who find exceptions to any rule. In astrology, any iron clad rule is the first one to go. However, it is one of the rules from ancient times and works quite often. A classic case of someone who got no credit during his lifetime would be that of the artist Vincent VanGogh, whose own brother considered him a failure. Contrast him with Pablo Picasso, whose every little pencil doodling was pounced on and pronounced the work of genius. But VanGogh is nevertheless, a painter whose work is immortal.

Not everyone with a node on the wrong side of the line of advantage is going to reap posthumous fame, but it does explain why "credit" eludes some of us, no matter how well we do. People who have the nodes working for them may be keenly aware that some of those who operate on the other side do better work than they but are less appreciated. They may even try in vain to share the spotlight with them. It doesn't matter a whit. The nodes dole out the goodies as they will.

A word about transiting aspects to the angles: These are crucial in that they show when and how well efforts are rewarded. The nodes have a 19-year cycle and can also show recurring events that nothing else explains. I once had a student who asked me to show her in her chart why lightning had twice struck small outbuildings on her property in her lifetime. The events happened several years apart and she could not find similar aspects to explain it. When she told me they occurred 19 years apart, I knew where to look. The South Node transited a 4th house planet in both cases. I told her to make sure she kept a small, unimportant shed there until the next time the south node passed through or the next time the lightning might hit something important like the house.

In the charts of politicians running for office, a rising North Node is a blessing. If it hits the MC or travels through the tenth, it marks a high-water point in life. This is when one experiences the proverbial "tide in the affairs of men" that leads on to victory. The South Node uppermost at such a time brings failure or loss, or election to an office in which efforts will fail or be unsuccessful, at the very least.

It goes without saying that being born with the North Node uppermost is an advantage. When the transiting nodes cross the Ascendant/Descendant line it marks a key period in partnership matters. If the North Node is in House 7, the individual is eager to make a partnership work. If it is in the first, house partnership matters are going through hard times, and perhaps changing or ending, but the individual is experiencing a renewed sense of personal potential. Times of marriage tend to occur when the transiting North Node is in the 7th.

The next thing the nodes do in one's birth pattern is show whether or not the individual will experience progressed eclipses. This can only happen when the nodes come after the Sun in the order of the signs because as the Sun moves forward by secondary progression (a year for each day after birth), it can come near one of the nodes. Then, as the progressed Moon opposes or conjuncts it, a progressed eclipse (partial or total) can occur. A good way to see this is in the ephemeris of the birth year. If an eclipse occurs within three months or so after birth, it will show in the chart if the individual lives that long. Obviously, four months (roughly 120 days) means a person would have to live 120 years or so for the aspect to form. Few of us will do that. These are landmark years when eclipses occur by progression. Watch carefully for them. If such eclipses land on planets, it can mark the major events of a lifetime. Aspects such as squares or trines are far less important than a conjunction, of course.

Many cases of progressive blindness in life seem to be indicated by progressed eclipses in the chart. It is always wise to keep a careful eye on contacts to Sun or Moon (which rule the eyes) by the nodes in any case. The South Node can definitely indicate weakness.

One author who wrote on the nodes in 1927, George White, said that certain nodal patterns affected height. I have not found that so, but perhaps he was working from a larger sample. It would be worth studying and perhaps prove to be fertile ground for contributing to astrological knowledge. This brings me to the subject of fate, or destiny. Moon's nodes operate in such specific ways that they often point to far- reaching consequences when they show up in the charts of events. Malefics on the South Node in the chart of the onset of war, for instance, is a dire warning. The aggressor is making a big mistake.

Consider the chart of the first nuclear test in Albuquerque, NM on July 16, 1945 (5:30 am MWT). Fifteen degrees of Cancer rises with Saturn at 15 Cancer and the North Node at 9 Cancer in the 12th house. It is in the same degree as Pluto at 9 of Leo in the second house of the future. A profoundly disturbing pattern. Worse yet, Neptune is in the end-of-the-matter fourth house and the Moon is there, squaring Saturn exactly. Without examining a single other thing in the chart, the bomb's power to do great harm is obvious, despite the fact that initially (north node in the area of advantage) it would be greeted with great cheers by the U.S. This event has a "destiny" signature, if you will, pointing to some hard lessons down the road. However, that north node rising also indicates to me the potential power of nuclear energy for good. Nevertheless, the lessons of Chernobyl are implied.

Another important nodal example closer to our own time is the NATO attack on Pristina in Yugoslavia in response to the ethnic "cleansing" of Albanians by the Serbs which occurred during the time when Bill Clinton was the American President. The north node falls in 10 and the south node conjunct Uranus—showing important change would be part of the outcome. The south node says the "change" of residence experienced by the fleeing Albanians would attract great attention, but would not be seen as a good thing.

But it also foreshadows the time when the Serbs would lose all patience with the Yugoslav president Milosevic and his posturing and would, as they say, "throw the bum out". An uprising of people angry at his attempt to steal another election turned the country upside down and forced him out of office.

Another indication of nodal influence I learned when a Hispanic astrologer told me they also had an effect on the digestive system, particularly the bowels, and that stresses at either north or south could show trouble developing. He said its usage was common knowledge among Spanish-speaking astrologers. I had not seen this myself so can only verify it by watching it in the future and recommending that others do so also. He said that it can point to diverticulitis, hemorrhoids or ulcers, so it is definitely worth the time to investigate.

An individual's fate or destiny is most profoundly affected by how he deals with the events of his own life, rather than what those events may be in themselves. Fate may deal us the card, but the game is won by those who play it most skillfully.

Van Gogh could have quit his painting, taken the opinions of his colleagues and critics to heart, and never left us his brilliant skies and Sunflowers. Picasso could have doodled his life away getting praise for amateur cartoons and never become the dominant force in modern art. Instead, both men devoted all their lives to the beauty they saw in their mind's eye and worked unceasingly to create it. True, one got more applause during his lifetime. But was he the greater? I leave it to the viewer to decide.

I can only urge readers that the Moon's nodes get at least equal billing with the planets. We simply must pay attention to them or lose invaluable information. The quality of "attention" or "coming into the light," is ruled by the Moon, and the nodes are the key we need to shed light on our efforts.

Chapter 18

Symbols of the Planets

Symbols of the planets are intended to convey information in a clever shorthand, just as the zodiac conveys information in a longer and more comprehensive way.

☉ The dot in the center of empty space symbolizes the individual entity. When circled by the Sun of creation it is given form. It is the symbol of spirit and the unchanging reality of existence.

☽ The Moon is half the circle, thus a reflection of only half the light, which comes to the embodied soul. The half circle is the soul, which receives inspiration.

✝ The cross is that of matter—the horizontal line is the horizon, and the vertical line symbolizes the soul's descent to the earth, thus the cross is matter.

☿ Mercury is the cup of intelligence descending to the spirit which rests on a foundation of matter.

♀ Venus is spirit above matter, the circle above the cross, demonstrating love.

♂ Mars is spirit with the cross of matter at an angle, indicating aspiration, or the desire to achieve.

⊕ The Part of Fortune, a circle containing a square, is the spirit containing matter, or embracing it.

♄ Saturn is the cross of matter over the spirit, showing the difficulty of the individual incarnation.

♃ Jupiter is the Moon over the cross, the soul surmounting the difficulties of life.

The outers are a combination of these things. Since they came along much later than the earlier symbolism they are somewhat less clear cut.

Pluto is the symbol of Mercury with the circle of spirit centered in the cup of the soul, which supports and fosters its appearance. ♀

 Neptune is the cup of the soul penetrated by the cross of matter which expresses itself in a new way. Ψ

 Uranus is the circle of the spirit under the cross of matter, much as Saturn is, but with two cups flanking it: one is that of the soul and the other is that of the intelligence. ♅

There may be many other ways of looking at these things of course. Among the more interesting symbolism is that of the Tarot, which also refers to the various planet and lights.

Chapter 19

The Part of Fortune

Everybody learns how to cast the Part of Fortune, the most widely used of the ancient Arabic parts, in beginning astrology. But instructions on how to use it differ widely. I think of it as indicating the "life support system." It is whatever it takes to keep one going. In a material sense, that means money, of course, but also it means other kinds of support—emotional and spiritual—we need to survive as viable human beings.

Many of the Arabic parts are based on the notion of a solar chart—with the Sun's degree rising—and the parts represent the positions where the planets would be in such a solar chart. The Part of Fortune shows where the Moon would be, for instance. Some parts are based on a lunar chart, with the Moon rising. Thus, Fortuna is an indicator of the relationship between the two lights, the most important factors in the chart. In antiquity they cast it a bit differently for births by day or night, putting the Moon on the Ascendant at night and calculating the Sun's difference from there.

There is a modern discussion going on as to which we should use and there are smart people on both sides of the argument. Since I am hardly dogmatic about astrology I suggest you try them both and see what you think.

My rule under any and all circumstances is this: Try what seems good. If it doesn't seem to work, throw it out or find out why and fix it. Maybe you have misunderstood how it is supposed to work. Study harder. Or try somebody else's method. There are no absolutes in astrology or in life and we learn as we go along. Good aspects to Fortuna enhance its ability to give us help in life. Harsh aspects limit it, of course. This is a simple rule that will stand you in good stead in many astrological techniques.

Some people have **Fortuna in the first house**. They are their own best advocates and their own best advisors. They should not take anyone's word for anything about their behavior or choices. They need to judge for themselves. When it comes to taking care of themselves, these people are the best at it. They always seem to have an instinct on how to accomplish their goals, whether that is simply keeping the wolf from the door or achieving outright financial success. They are self-reliant in the extreme.

They were obviously born shortly after a new Moon. That means Sun, the ego, is potent and strong. Moon, the personality and emotions, is vulnerable and weak. So the person often starts out life as a timid child but evolves into a potent, self-confident adult. Moon is always more significant in childhood than Sun.

Those who have **Part of Fortune in the 7th house** are Full Moon types. Their reason for being and their success often come in partnerships or marriage. They need to relate to others in a very specific way. Here the personality and emotions are powerful and out-front and the need for self-dramatization to attract attention is often quite strong. Sometimes that need for attention can be tiresome to those around them.

Often they deal with the public (the 7th is the house of the public at large) and may find that jobs which deal with the public in a way that brings recognition are their best way to make a living. Advertising, the entertainment business and marketing come to mind. Strangers often help them at critical times in their lives. These are people who need others in all ventures. They also benefit from marriage in ways other than merely financial, and may be wed to someone who is their "best friend," or "biggest fan." Cooperation and conciliation lead to success. They probably shouldn't marry other full Moon types. It would be a constant battle of whose emotions get top billing.

If you were born when the Moon was at the first quarter or not too far beyond it, your **Part of Fortune** may be in **House 4**, and the family is what keeps you going. Early in life it is the parents and siblings, but later on it becomes your children and the entire extended family. This gives a talent for making money in real estate, by the way, but also in working out of the home or in taking up a "family" trade. One of your parents (probably the father) is always your ace in the hole and manages to help you whenever you are in dire straits, whether from a flood in the basement or a catastrophe that strips your bank account.

When you need it, resources may be found through members of your family even if they don't help you directly. A family reunion is an excellent place to network. Somebody always knows somebody with the answer you have to have, or the job that will suit you or details on the small carpentry job you started. It is one of the marks of inheritance, of course.

There are many forms of inheritance, by the way. I have the handmade bedspread my mother loved, and a chair she knew I always wanted. My dad sent them to me after her death. To me those things are more valuable than money and if I gave them away, it would only be to a sister, or maybe—maybe—to one of my children.

If you were born when the Moon had reached its last quarter, you may have **Part of Fortune in House 10,** a strong indicator of career success. You will do best preparing for your career early in life and setting your sights high. You will attract a mentor quickly and people in powerful positions are often drawn to help you. Your key to financial stability is through your career. This is a position that also may indicate strong help from a parent, most likely the mother. Sometimes the mother is the best career mentor or motivator and will steer you to people who can help you succeed in life.

The tenth is the house of public office as well, and if you have a chart with other favorable indications, **Fortuna in House 10** is a help in getting elected. It is excellent for management positions. The 10th also rules our reputation and Fortuna there is a big boost to keeping your good name. If you don't have a career or a public life, perhaps you take a strong role in community affairs as a volunteer. Many volunteer types swing clout far beyond expectations. They run the city's arts board, or the orchestra, or serve as fundraisers for urban renewal projects and the like. True, those may not appear to be lucrative. But powerful people may share information or tips on investing or the like which pay off in the long run.

Sometimes the powerful person is Dad. The two parental houses, 4 and 10, often switch genders, depending on the individual chart. After marriage occurs, they will indicate

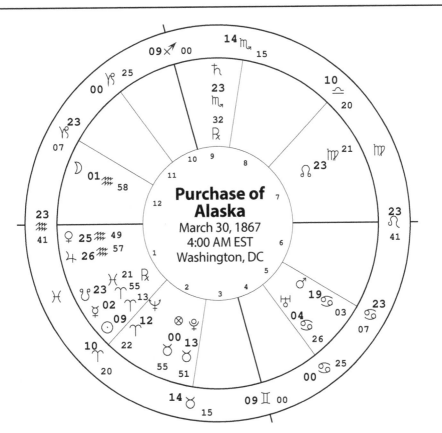

This was called Seward's Folly when the U.S. Secretary of State William H. Seward first proposed buying the "useless" land in the far north from Russia. But it doesn't take a genius astrologer to make a favorable forecast with both benefics on the Ascendant and the Part of Fortune in the 2nd house. The Moon rules the 5th house, which is the price of the 4th house-ruled land and it contains Uranus, a surprise in the future. It would prove to be the incredible resources, including gold, which the U.S. bought so cheaply. Congress argued over it and recessed before deciding, but President Johnson called it back into special session to vote again, and when he signed the bill (this chart) the U.S. got 586,412 square miles for $7.2 million. It was a bargain for $12.27 per square mile. AA from Congressional Records.

a mother-in-law or a father-in-law, as well. It's a good thing to remember. If you have a problem with assigning the 10th house to the mother, it's no problem. A lot of people think she belongs to the 4th house with its Cancerian influence. I have always used the 10th for the mother as the earliest and most lasting authority in life and the 4th for the father who provides security and our "roots." This has some traditional usage, by the way. However, I will be quick to tell you that I have charts where the 10th is clearly the father and the 4th is the mother. I'm inclined to think it is an individual response to parenting rather than something ordained on high.

Fortuna in the 2nd house gives skill with money, the handling of it and acquiring of it. It is a good position for the self-employed and for establishing one's own business. I once had a co-worker whose favorite saying when he got a pat on the back from the boss or an added job benefit was, "Put it in the paycheck." It always amused me. Of course he never said that directly to the boss, but money was definitely his prime (if not only) motivator.

Second house people who can help you? Bankers, for one. Take their advice, if you trust them, but never let anyone else actually manage your money. You know best for you. Keep it in mind.

If you have **Fortuna in House 3**, siblings back you all your life. You fight the neighborhood wars as kids side by side and grow up looking out for each other. A brother or sister may be a pipeline to a job when you need one, or just happen to know someone who can help you when the chips are down. Your close relationship with at least one sibling will be lifelong. They are your best counselors and your best friends. The neighborhood itself is your friend, too. Neighbors are full of gossip and conversation that is of benefit to you. This is also a good indicator for success with autos, or in any career that features travel, transportation or communication skills. It blesses you with sales ability.

And writing. Ah, writing is often a source of income. Or it will shift into one of the other communication skills, such as advertising or the media. If not the skill, then perhaps the industry. Printers can benefit, and even paper delivery pays.

Fortuna in House 5 is a good position for those who are athletes and can bring medals and awards in competition. It is good for gambling or speculation and careers in recreation, sports, the arts or entertainment industries. This is excellent for somebody who runs a fishing boat service, or manages parks, or who is a high school coach.

One's own children will be of great comfort in later life as they grow to provide companionship. This is particularly helpful for those with many children, because they like and enjoy their families and are enriched by those relationships in turn as they age. In large families there is often an aging parent who may need to live with someone at some point and if you are that elderly person and have POF in 5, you'll enjoy life readily with one or more of your children.

The 5th is the house of the creative idea and the hobby as well as projects we may undertake in life from time to time. They, too, pay us dividends in one way or another. Sometimes a special project one has undertaken at work leads to honor or recognition or even better jobs that pay more. Sometimes a hobby leads one to begin doing it for pay and perhaps eventually it can become a second source of income or even the primary source. This is particularly true for crafts which can evolve in quite lucrative directions. Remember Grandma Moses, the famous artist, who painted all her life but never sold a thing until she was in her 80s? Her art was her "hobby."

Fortuna in House 6 gives success in the military or in public service jobs such as police, fire, health care and the like. It is the house which draws one to jobs where there are helpful co-workers who turn out to be important in one's life. Nursing, medical technologies of all sorts and even library science are good possibilities.

It also gives one a knack for finding the right plumber or the best mechanic to fix your brakes. Sometimes this position indicates that you are the person who does those kinds of things. It is excellent for veterinarians and dog trainers. These people need a pet and find some of their greatest comfort in life from one. Agents or representatives or envoys of any sort come under this classification.

This is the best position for always being able to find work that pays. Usually people

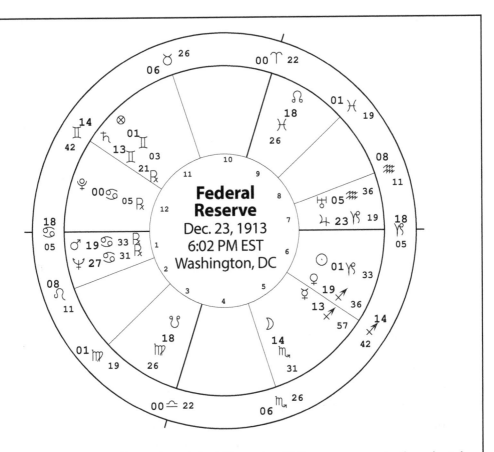

President Woodrow Wilson signed the bill turning U.S. money over to the privately owned Federal Reserve for its services every year. However, the stability never occurred and instead, the dollar's value has been decimated in the years that followed. The Part of Fortune with its aspects to the Sun-Pluto opposition shows how profitable the arrangement would be to the powerful banking forces in control behind the scenes.

with Fortuna in 6 have a lot of resources to draw on and in times of financial need when jobs have vanished like fog in the Sunshine, those pay off. House 6 Fortuna is also a good indicator for management since it tends to give one good judgment about employees and who can do which task best. It is also one of the best indicators that you will get good medical care and if you must be hospitalized, you'll get assigned the best nurses. Fortuna in 6 brings you all kinds of good care givers when you need them. Co-workers benefit you if you need it, too. When you're too broke to afford a new roof, one who Moonlights as a roofer might offer to do it cheap "after hours." Or maybe you want to find a new job. Ask around at the water cooler. That's mighty fruitful territory for a 6th house Fortuna.

House 8 Part of Fortune shows a likelihood of inheritance. It is the most superior position of all for those who manage other people's money or finances. It will sometimes indicate a wealthy spouse or one with a very good earning capacity. Perhaps the inheritance comes through the spouse, but there will be family money if either Sun or Moon is there or ruling the house. People who deal with the affairs of the dead—such as morticians and insurance salesmen—also benefit. It is the house of taxes and settlements from law suits as well as the profits one makes from invested money. Fortuna here gives one a definite edge. If you must sue someone for damages, you are likely to get them.

This is also a good position for accountants, bankers, and brokers who advise others. If you don't work yourself, these are people who can help you find your way through the morass of red tape in life. Often a person met through such an initial contact will be important in some way. Besides, it's an excellent indication that you'll benefit from saving money or any long-term investment you make. You may get a long term CD with a good rate just before the rates fall, or you learn you got the last great mortgage rate before the rates went up. Tax breaks provide you with extra cash and when the flood wipes out your neighbors you find your homeowner policy had a flood coverage option you signed up for without remembering it and you're covered.

Fortuna in House 9 gives preference to the benefits of education. You may choose to stay in academia in some way, either as teacher or janitor, but some element of the education world is likely to provide you with a living or help in achieving job training. Or, you may benefit through the travel industry or the export/import business. Fortuna in House 9 is good for writers, translators and publishers—the book business is good for you.

This is also the house of in-laws, and your brothers- or sisters-in-law will back you in ventures or provide a sounding board when you need one. If they borrow from you, they'll probably pay it back. They are friends more than merely relatives. It is also one of the cadent houses which refer to aunts, uncles and cousins and they can be helpful to you. Sometimes those collateral relatives belong to your spouse. Don't underestimate Fortuna's power because they will benefit you when you need it. Sometimes in life a friend who will make you a cup of tea and sit and talk when you need to talk is priceless. Occasionally one of those relationships is a lifelong treasure.

The **11th house Part of Fortune** is a good one for those employed by the government. If you have Fortuna there, check out Civil Service, if you are in need of a job. It gives an "in" at any level—community, state or federal. It could be as a building inspector or a mail carrier, but the door is open for you. But friends are without doubt your greatest asset in life. They may not be many in number but the ones you have are solid gold. You participate in networking like some people breathe and may find you have skills in dealing with groups. Whether you run sales parties or manage conferences, you can succeed. This is the politician's mark. You understand them and may even be one of them. You certainly know how to use them. People with Fortuna in a social house are always the recipients of help from others when they need it.

The **12th House Part of Fortune** is the house of last-minute help and confidential maneuvering. It shows you have a knack for dealing with those behind the scenes of any situation and they will help you in turn, as long as you don't blab about it. It also can mean success through various institutions, whether those are medical, philanthropic, or even penal. Perhaps just the town library. People who work in them are your friends. Any bread you cast upon the waters of life will come back with butter and jam on it. You yourself may prefer to work behind the scenes of larger ventures and you do it well.

The 12th is also the house of things we are owed and where untapped resources abide and we can quickly take advantage of them. People with Fortuna here often are surprised by times in life when they are saved from catastrophe by last-minute aid. A sky-diver whose parachute didn't open found his spare worked beautifully. That's a good illustration of Fortuna in 12, when disaster is averted. When transits and progressions contact Fortuna by conjunction or parallel, benefits will come your way. You can even plan for them, and this is one of the more helpful elements to include in electional work.

Whenever Fortuna is linked with a planet, it adds additional information about the "who" and "what" that can be of help. The Sun is men of importance, particularly those in authority and those who have social prominence or wealth. The Moon is women. and any man whose Fortuna is conjunct the Moon or in good aspect to it probably already knows that women at any level will help him. This is doubly true if the planet conjunct Fortuna is Venus, which additionally adds money to the mix. Venus will often benefit one in both ways—women and cash. Can't beat that.

Jupiter brings additional opportunity, often through church membership or religious figures as well as those whose lifestyles are different from our own, or those who may actually be foreign or have interests abroad. Jupiter always opens doors to opportunity, and sometimes that is exactly what one needs. It gives you an edge in dealing with important people. Those who climb from obscurity to great success in life often have prominent Jupiter positions and if it aspects Fortuna, it is a powerful help.

Saturn, of course, can link us to old friends, and older people. Always be nice to senior citizens—you never know. It reminds me of the story in the news a few years ago about a lonely and wealthy older man who left his entire fortune to the kind young waitress who always took time to chat with him when he came to the small diner where he ate breakfast every day. I've often wondered if she had Fortuna with Saturn. She didn't know he was anybody special, but she did know he was lonely and appreciated her kindness. She became a sort of surrogate family member to him and he rewarded her.

Mercury is young people. It never pays to dismiss them from consideration, either. Teens grow up and they remember kindnesses and unkindness, too. They see more than many people realize, so those with a Mercury contact to Fortuna should take special pains to listen to what they have to say. Perhaps that older man had his Fortuna conjunct Mercury. The young waitress certainly provided him with some emotional support and good morale for his last days.

Fortuna is the treasure chest we all have in our charts. It well repays us for giving it a few minutes of attention and can often direct us to the things we most need. It truly can be the map to our life support systems.

Chapter 20

Forecasting
Progressions and Solar Returns

The response to the forecast often depends not on the astrologer but on the person hearing it. I am sure that there is always going to be some effect caused by the way the astrologer phrases a comment to a client. For many years I have been keenly aware of the fact that if I snap off a quick remark about a chart to someone they may remember it forever. That's a heavy responsibility. You learn not to do those quick remarks.

Many predictions go in unexpected directions and a lot of people forget that every specific forecast simply does not have the same effect on every person. This has to do with the internal dynamics of their specific charts. In a very real way we are always dealing with a chart we have never seen before and forecasting about aspects or their combinations which are new to us and which we have no precedent by which to judge. In other words, we operate blind, to some extent. That shouldn't come as a surprise to any of us. We are always dealing with some unknown or other. The best we can do is keep our basics in mind and tread softly.

People born under Cancer know when the Moon is nearing full—not from an ephemeris, but from simply being too restless to sleep well or having very vivid dreams for a couple of nights every month. This can happen every month for a lot of Cancerians.

Venus returns may do zilch for you. But for some people, they work great. The people who get the most reaction out of Venus are strongly Venus types (Suns in Taurus or Libra, or with Taurus or Libra rising, or with an angular Venus, particularly in the first house).

The people who get the most out of Mars returns are those Mars types—Sun in Aries or Scorpio, or those with Aries or Scorpio rising or Mars angular and powerful in the natal pattern. You would think such obvious effects would be common knowledge but it is amazing how often such logical pieces of information pass some of us right by.

Jupiter does its best work for those with a strong natal tie to it, Sagittarian or Pisces Sun or ascendant and/or an angular Jupiter. Mercury favors the Gemini/Virgo package, Sun or ascendant and those with a powerful Mercury. (Angularity and/or a stationary condition confer power. So do a high number of aspects from other planets.)

Saturn is a surprising benefic for the Saturn-ruled among us. Their Saturn problems come along in time to be solved before they get out of hand. They are seldom caught by complete surprise by the planet. Usually difficult situations develop well before the aspect is exact and sometimes that exactitude ends the problem. It all has to do with the amount of "echo" a transit or progression has to the natal pattern.

And we can't overlook the aspect intensity. Planets that give or receive aspects from many things in the chart become more powerful and can manifest sharply and surprise us if we don't pay attention to them. It isn't necessary to use fancy mathematical calculations to see this, though some astrologers do. All you have to do is count up the number of natal aspects and when you are on both hands or starting over you have a powerhouse position and a major event when a transit sets it off, no matter what else it's doing or where it is in the chart.

Sometimes a single planet swings the entire action of a chart. It may fall into the traditional "basket" configuration, but it doesn't have to. Watch for these. Such planets are an education.

Our Bad Days

Are there times we as astrologers are less effective than others? Should we do readings then? That's not a dumb question, you know. Somebody once asked that in a group discussion and it prompted me to do some thinking.

There are days the plumber doesn't do as good a job as other days, or the electrician, or the businessman. What, should they all stay home if they have bad aspects? Don't think so. As a working astrologer I can tell you that you don't quit working because it's a bad hair day, you're catching a cold or your dog just died. You dig down and do the best you can. That's the difference between the pros and the amateurs. The pros can still do a good job when they aren't in the mood, the weather's all wrong, and it's Monday morning.

Reading the Chart

Aspects and transits are read in terms of what the planet means all by itself and then also what the planet may mean in this chart. For instance, Jupiter transiting the MC is often a promotion or an honor. Saturn in good aspect to the MC could mean additional responsibility. But you also need to ask what Jupiter and Saturn are doing natally to the natal MC. If Jupiter rules the 7th, it can mean good things for the spouse. If Saturn rules the 11th, there may be a heavy load in an organization one belongs to, or loss of a good friend because of a job change.

All natal charts are the root out of which the tree grows. If there is a badly stressed Jupiter or MC natally, even though Jupiter usually gives opportunity, then this aspect could bring something less desirable. Astrology is very logical.

Secondary Progressions

The Major Aspects for the Year

It will pay to list these. All that are applying and which reach perfection within the 24 hour period which symbolizes the year should be noted. Those that are separating but still within 30 minutes of arc should also be noted. They can still be set off by a lunar progression.

Calculate when during the year the aspect they are forming will become exact. That is the month to watch for an event. If the Moon triggers them a month or two before or after that you will get a secondary event. Sometimes those events are part of a larger development and can mark a stage in its effect.

Any year in which a planet reaches a progressed station is important. All by itself it may color the year, since stations are times of intense emphasis on the planet's action in the chart. If the planet rules the 7th, something about the marriage or partnership will happen. In the 6th it can be a work situation or a health one. Anything to the angles, natal or progressed, is significant as well.

Always draw the progressed angles on the outside of the natal chart for a progressed year. Signs of short ascension will pass over the ascendant quickly so you will probably need to calculate exactitude for the month things become exact. Signs of longer ascension will be slower to arrive and depart and one doesn't have to be quite as quick to make sure the month is known. Events may stretch out, oddly enough.

Be sure to note the declinations of the progressed planets and angles as well as the natal ones. Any progressed angle coming to a planet in the natal chart is important, whether by longitude or declination.

The Progressed Moon

The secondary system is based on the year-for-a-day concept. Each year after birth measures to one day in the ephemeris. It makes it easy to count ahead to the current year and see what's going on. The Moon during each day moves rapidly, of course, and can vary from less than 12 degrees per day to more than 15. Each degree of the Moon is roughly one month in that year. But, if the Moon is moving faster than 12 degrees, it may travel 1 degree 4 minutes per month. You won't know that until it's calculated.

The progressed Moon is one of the more reliable indicators in prediction. One absolutely must calculate the current year and the next year to see exactly how fast it is traveling and where it will be during any given time period. Just guessing "a month or so" per degree is not good enough in my book. I want to know exactly.

In addition to the longitudinal aspects it makes, one must be aware of its travel by declination. The difference between next year's position and this year can be divided by 12 to see where the Moon makes an aspect to a planet if you are hand-calculating. You can do it on your computer if you wish. Most programs are highly precise. These can be quite specific, I find. A hospital trip can be indicated by a simple progressed Moon forming a parallel (the name of the declination aspect) to Neptune. An argument can show up with a parallel to a Mercury/Mars combination.

One simply can't ignore declination. It was far more commonly used in earlier times, usually in combination with aspects in right ascension, though moderns tend to give longitude priority. Once it becomes a normal part of your forecast routine you'll find it valuable, too.

Saturn Hunting the Moon

Transiting Saturn is said to be "hunting the Moon" when it is conjunct the progressed Moon. It is a combination that has a terrible (and quite justified) reputation. Luckily, it can't last decades, as some people fear. The progressed Moon keeps on going. The transiting Saturn will station and go retrograde after a few months, giving the Moon a chance to pull ahead and get away. I have had some cases among my clients when this happens and while it's in effect, it's brutal. Luckily, as I said, it doesn't last long.

My first experience with Saturn hunting the Moon came with the chart of one of my students who had a litany of woes happening to her. Her alcoholic husband ran out on her, left her with a house, the mortgage and young kids and just disappeared. He never did come back. The kids were sick, her job didn't pay much, money matters were a disaster, etc. etc. I saw her progressed Moon conjunct transiting Saturn, where it had been for several months.

I do not use orbs on progressions. In my book, a progression is exact or it isn't in effect at all. Saturn hunting the Moon has to be on the position by less than 30 minutes of arc. Preferably less than 15 minutes. Anyway, I was pretty sure that when Saturn stationed shortly she would start to pull out of the problems, and at the very least, no new ones would fall in her lap once the progressed Moon had moved one degree away from Saturn. That's what happened. New bad things stopped occurring. Yes, she still had to deal with the old ones, and some of them took years to sort out, in true Saturnian fashion. She eventually had to go to court to have the hubby declared legally dead in order to sell the house she had paid for and cared for nearly 20 years.

I think when we use orb on lunar progressions we are setting ourselves up for error. I allow a Venus/Mars aspect, for instance, to be primed for action when it is within 30 minutes but not a degree and a half. Even then, the aspect only manifests when it is exact unless a lunar progression ticks it off again a month or two early or late.

Sometimes it is a parallel that ticks it off. Again, I do not use any orbs. All the problems that woman had eventually worked out in her favor, but she was a tough, determined Scorpio who refused to give up and that helped.

The job she had led to a felicitous meeting and a happy marriage to a wealthy man years later. The children she raised alone adored her and made her later years rewarding. The house had a mortgage payment that turned out to be teeny after the whopping inflation of the 70s, allowing her to raise her family, pay it off and live surprisingly well on that not-too-sensational pay check and so on. Saturn gave her what she earned in all those years of unremitting toil. But during the "Saturn hunting the Moon" months, life was a mess.

Residential change

I think it's important to keep the word "change" in mind whenever the progressed Moon makes a major aspect. Consider a case where an older man was thinking about a residential move. His progressed Moon conjoined his natal Sun/Saturn conjunction in the 4th, suggesting a possible change of location. The natal eighth house was ruled by the Moon, and his natal Moon in 2 made it appear that it would be a financial decision aimed at solving a problem. As a confirmation, his progressed Ascendant was conjunct the natal Moon. Again, an aspect of change. Another confirmation of residential change was his progressed 4th cusp conjunct natal 7th. The 7th is the house of "moving" or relocating, because it is 4th from 4th. The 4th is where we live now and the 7th is where we move to. There you have it—three clear confirmations of residential change.

However, as is the case with all men, the Sun also ruled his fundamental health and he had natal Sun/Saturn square the natal Moon. This progression, which echoed the natal set-up, therefore also signaled a change in the health pattern. He was over 60 and at his age, this is common. We all start looking like used cars around 60 and our time to get better acquainted with the medical community kicks in. He had Uranus in 6, so such health changes always caught him and everybody else by surprise. Additionally, he had Saturn transiting his natal 6th accounting for the medical problems that had been showing up for the past two years. Venus ruled his 6th, however, and in Pisces was uncomfortably close to a (transiting) Saturn/Pluto opposition which set up later in the year. He could expect some lung problem (bronchitis perhaps) and some difficulty walking because of a problem with the foot or leg.

The chart stresses on the Moon also pointed to his wife—or rather included her—but since his natal Moon position and his seventh house ruler were not under attack at the time she would likely sidestep the problems. Nevertheless, the pattern showed he'd probably be grouchy anyway over the coming changes in his life, and that's no fun to live with. On the other hand, a man with a Sun/Saturn square the Moon is no picnic to start with.

The change occurred in the family and the residential move was postponed until his health improved. That took quite a bit longer than he expected but it eventually materialized.

Other Aspects

Sometimes the progressed Moon making a conjunction to the natal south node can bring an "attack" of some sort. While usually verbal, it can also show up as losing a game to a more aggressive player, or the like. Not good for athletes or politicians.

In natal charts progressions of Venus to the natal angles often mean legal steps of some sort. If divorce is being contemplated it is the time when the papers are filed. It also shows when unions and business partnerships are formed and marriages are held. In a business it can mean a lawsuit over products or safety. Any planet forming an aspect to an angle is significant. The Sun brings recognition and a step one may take to achieve prominence or position. Mercury involves some intense communication or personnel changes.

Uranus throws a curve into whatever is planned but Pluto launches profound change in the way things work over a long period of time. Deaths in the family and pregnancy can occur then. Jupiter is a warning against excess or taking things for granted but may open up an opportunity one should never ignore. Mars is likely to be trouble, arguments and dissension but also sexual attraction when aspecting the ascendant/descendant line. Saturn ends problems or imposes penalties when problems have been revealed. Not good for the outcome of a dispute unless one's chart shows a likelihood of winning. In any case, justice is served. Never trust a Neptune aspect unless one has a well-aspected natal Neptune. Otherwise it can bring in disreputable people, confusion and too much drinking in social events. Its main influence can be in the medical areas indicating hospital care as well.

Oh, how can you tell if your chart shows a likelihood of winning in a dispute? Old rule says if the ruler of House 1 is stronger than the ruler of the 7th house, and more elevated in the chart, the 1st house always has the edge. This is a plus for those who fall into legal disputes. You can enhance this with a good electional chart, of course, but some of us who are lucky just get the pattern at birth.

Progressed Stations

One of the problems with doing charts on computers instead of out of a huge old ephemeris is that you don't always know what year a planet turns retrograde or direct in your chart unless you specifically ask for it.

It's easy to see that when you have a month's movement in front of you on one page. That month reflects about 30 years in the life of the individual. That's why you should periodically survey an ephemeris of your birth year for a bird's eye view on what will change and when. It's quicker and very reliable.

The year any personal planet—Mars, Venus or Mercury—changes direction marks a change in the affairs of whatever house is ruled by that planet, as well as the house where it falls in the natal chart. If you have a 7th house ruled by Mercury and your planet goes retrograde, you will probably marry in that year or divorce, if the chart shows that as a possibility. Occasionally it may mean some change to the spouse, such as a major health problem or something, but it always, always, always means a change from what you have now to what you will have in the future in your relationship matters. This can imply a business partnership as well.

If Mars changes sign and it rules your 4th, it will be family changes, changes in the way you relate to your father or your mother, or changes in the place you live, or a change OF the place where you live. It can be trouble with a landlord or a fire as well. The same is true of Venus. If your fifth house ruler is Venus, it means a change in your children's lives. If you don't have any, guess what—you'll probably get some. If you do, there will be changes relative to their affairs, or to a romantic affair if you are single. Some change always happens with things that the planet naturally rules. Venus deals with money and expressions of love and emotion.

Those with Venus retrograde at birth have experiences during the year in which they learn that love is more important than money, and they learn to express love more openly. If Venus goes retrograde, it marks a year of major disappointment in the love life and usually some financial stress as well. Sometimes the loss is "the love of a lifetime" and the individual never really gets over it. Or, the relationships that do come their way seem more emotionally detached, less passionate, etc. Generally, people born with Venus Retrograde have a hard time understanding other people's emotions and feelings. It's almost as if they are divorced from their own, or get skewed ideas. Emotional appeals of any sort are lost on them, though they may go through the motions. They have to be carefully trained as children or they don't even bother with ordinary courtesy.

However, most people will eventually have Venus go direct in their life and the year it happens is a year when they first really get hit with feelings. They fall in love and suddenly all that "stuff" becomes comprehensible in a way it never did before. One man I knew was married to a woman in his profession and he called her his "best friend," but ran around on her ferociously. The year Venus went direct he ended a relationship with another woman, his wife got pregnant and he renewed his relationship with her. He completely lost his heart when the baby was born. It turned his entire life around.

Many people have Venus go retrograde by progression, and this can mark a time when financial issues loom large. It's obviously not a great time for designers or creative people whose output may fail to attract the public as it did before. They get "off track," and it may be years before their new style is vindicated. If they are at all ruled by Venus natally (Sun, ascendant, angularity, etc.) it can be much worse.

Mars changes how you work, from mental to physical and vice versa. In sexual matters many women born with Mars ℞ suddenly discover that sex is not threatening as they thought, but downright enjoyable when it goes direct. If Mars turns retrograde some years after birth, it can mean loss of a sexual partner or a problem in the sexual area that restricts or limits sexuality in the life. For men with Mars ℞ at birth, the direct shift may be a welcome relief, freeing them from several hangups, or limitations they have experienced.

Mercury is verbal expression. Some writers start writing when Mercury changes direction—or go back to it. It also deals with how we communicate with others, particularly the people in the houses Mercury rules. Obviously the other planets also create some effects when they change direction by progression, but the three personal planets are the most noticeable as a rule. As an example: a client has natal Venus ℞ in the 10th. She counts forward in the ephemeris 34 days from her birthday to when Venus turns direct. So at 34 she will probably have a year in which an event triggers a more open emotional nature. In the 10th it could have something to do with a parent or marriage or even a job change which unlocks a softer side. Or, someone has natal Mars direct in House 7. It turns retrograde 65 days after the birthday. The client asks "I do not have a spouse. So does this mean that at 65 I may get one?" The answer is no. With Mars going retrograde, it may change your desire for one or you may go back to a past relationship. Marriage is always accompanied by a Venus aspect, so look to see if you get a Venus aspect that year. Then, indeed, it could be marriage.

Solar Returns

If you obtain Alexander Volguine's book on solar returns you may find it gives you a lot of clues that are helpful with this technique. I strongly recommend it. I think it's better than any other book I have read on the subject. The entire Solar Return is a transit and all the planets in it are transits. They are transits for the birthday, which is why they have special impact.

First of all, you can cast it for where you are. If you are living very far away from your birth location, use the location where you live now. If it isn't too far from where you were born, then just use your natal locale. Remember, your birth locale is always the "default" position anyway.

Secondly, see where the degree and sign of the Ascendant of the solar return falls in your natal chart. It gives you the focus for the year. Suppose you have a natal Aquarius Ascendant. This year, the solar return has Capricorn rising. It will fall in your natal 11th or 12th. Then do the same for each house. The blend is how you interpret the chart. Solar return 2nd falls in natal 7th means partners may be influential in the way you make or spend money this year, or you may begin doing consulting to make money, etc.

Next, look for conjunctions of solar return planets to natal placements and see if any angle of the chart hits a natal placement exactly. This is a biggie. One year's solar return put my natal 9th house Neptune on the MC—guess where I spent a chunk of the year: in a hospital recovering from hip surgery. But I also went to Europe and Canada lecturing. Check to see if any aspect that is forming in the solar return becomes exact within 24 hours. That aspect is important for the year ahead. Most of the other aspects will not close during the 24-hour period the solar return covers and become just so much background noise.

Try using these rules a bit and see if your solar returns make more sense:

1. Planets that are angular in the solar return chart are more important.

2. Any major planet which is forming a conjunction, square or opposition

to the Sun is obviously a key planetary influence for the year.

3. The signs of the solar return Ascendant and MC are significant, because they show where and how the year's action will develop.

4. When you have any repeat of a natal pattern, it is an important year for whatever that pattern rules in the natal chart. It means one has more freedom of action than usual and it is the time when what the natal indication "promises" occurs.

I don't think it always pays to try to avoid the indications of the SR. There are astrologers who disagree with this point of view, I know, but I don't think leaving the area for a day or two at the time of the SR to get another Ascendant is always the answer. You still go back to the place where you live and I think the SR for that location kicks in anyway. At best, the relocation for the solar return can "soften" the indications.

The 8th house can mean surgery when the Sun is there in the solar return—or it may indicate a legacy from a death, or that one takes on a load of debt or tries to unload it, perhaps through bankruptcy. If the Sun was in House 8 and well aspected natally, all will turn out well anyway. If not, the person was bound to face such a problem sometime in life, and apparently now is the time.

The solar return Sun in aspect with Saturn says one will deal with a burden brought about by affairs of the house that Saturn rules natally. We can't alter the patterns that we're born with. Sometimes astrology just helps us recognize when they become active. We will all have a "natal return" pattern more than once during our life times. The solar return angles are near to the spot they occupied at birth and some of the planets are in the natal position as well. These can be quite significant years when the life steps off in a new direction and one has more "say" in how to shape it.

There are many astrologers who use precessed solar returns or feel that any solar return (SR for short) is strictly a siderealist's technique. I used to agree with that before I learned how to really read them. Now I find that a simple un-precessed tropical solar return is just dandy and yields a lot of information. We live and learn.

I don't claim to be an authority on the solar return but I can offer a few tips that may help you:

- If the SR Moon is void of course in the SR chart it merely means that the affairs of the house ruled by the SR Moon won't be prominent in big events or key events of the year.

- SR Moon, Mercury and Uranus positions reflect the areas of change. In 3 the Moon can mean a new car, events in brothers' or sisters' lives becoming important in your life or their lives changing sharply or that you will do some mental re-arranging of your own thinking. It is always a mark of a lot of running around or short trips. In aspect to Neptune, for instance, it can involve you in the health affairs of yourself or others etc.

- If the Moon is void-of-course (VOC,) this will probably be secondary to other things going on in the chart this year. Separating aspects to the VOC Moon signify events that are concluded.

- The SR Sun, Jupiter & Saturn falling in natal house 6 would indicate an emphasis on health and/or volunteering or part time work; or matters having to do with pets or the like. The 6th house involves us in lots more than just health. Any service we provide or that others provide for us or any item that serves our needs (clothing, for instance) comes under 6. A seamstress might be interested in donating help making kids' Halloween costumes, or doing a lot of sewing or mending for a sick relative.

● A health regimen of exercise and diet, could begin. Maybe joining a health club or taking up bee-keeping (all small useful husbandry skills come under 6), or selling garden produce could be the result.

● Keep your mind open to lots of possibilities. If the SR 6th falls in the natal 5th it will be different than in natal 10th.

● SR interpretation is a blending of current influences with the natal and a drawing out of the natal potentials.

● When a new pattern meshes with the natal, it has greater effect.

● When a house rises that is an angular one in the natal, or when a planet is angular in the solar return that is angular in the natal, it has a stronger effect. Also, some of this has to do with transits of the outer planets going on at the same time to key natal positions. For instance, a solar return which features transiting Uranus conjunct the natal Sun is going to be a dynamite solar return. Ditto if it is conjunct the Moon, or a natal angle.

● If you have a seventh house planet natally that sits on the MC in the solar return, it probably indicates formation of a partnership, which can mean that this is a "key" solar return.

● If your natal nodes are 16 degrees of a sign and you have a natal planet at 16 degrees in any sign, it shows you will have some difficulty and stress in life with whatever that planet rules in your chart. Sometimes a great deal. A solar return emphasizing that degree means "pay attention." It's remarkably consistent and reliable as an indicator. But only to the exact degree.

While the precessed solar return was commonly used when I began to use the technique, I did not find it a great deal more help than the ones without it. Indeed, sometimes I found the angles not nearly as sensitive to transits as the simple solar return without precession. I would encourage anyone who wants to use this technique to try both techniques and draw their own conclusions. Until I began to give Volguine's techniques serious consideration I didn't find either system very useful. Volguine gave me the key to better forecasting techniques and I stopped using precession.

Since the solar return is a solar technique, it is only common sense I think to watch the transits of the Sun to the chart. In addition to using the ascendant as "the birthday" and the first house as the whole first month after the birthday you can also just follow the Sun as it goes around the chart in reality. Both systems will give you some insight.

Another good way (probably the best of all) is to calculate the following year's SR, and measure the distance this year's MC must travel to reach the next year's MC. (It's not the same each year.) Then by dividing the distance, you can move the MC at a daily rate of speed and watch as it and the ascendant conjunct and oppose various planets in the SR. Some will tick off immediately, others will wait and some will not be touched at all. Planets in angles get the fastest action because they are the first to be contacted.

The Ascendant, of course, moves at a different rate of speed. You can easily see this as you look at a table of houses and watch the shifting angles. This is due to the obliquity of the Ascendant, but makes a fun thing to watch happen anyway. Some computer programs that feature actual visual movement of the angles in the progressed chart are equally fascinating.

Suppose Mars is nearing a square to Mercury within a few minutes and it becomes exact within 24 hours. In secondary progression, that 24 hours represents the whole year, so the exact aspect is significant for the year and will occur sometime during it.

But Saturn is separating from a trine to Venus. That's not as important. Or Venus is applying to a conjunction to Jupiter by 3 degrees. Venus doesn't move fast enough to conjoin Jupiter during the 24 hours which symbolizes the solar return year. It, too, is nice but is a less important aspect. However, if either planet was significant in the natal pattern, then this year could mark a favorable development in the financial affairs or the career.

It's interesting, now that we have so much computer technology, to spend half a day running your entire life's solar returns, and then match the years to important events. I did that as soon as computer development allowed me to do it, and it taught me tons about how they worked! It also helps to have a good diary of your life—or at least a list of the highlights. I made one to show the years of moves (houses 4-7), marriage (house 7), surgeries and illnesses (house 1), job changes (house 10), etc. Things that would reflect events ruled by the angles are always easier to spot. Try it and see. It's worth the time!

You can't cast an accurate solar return without accurate birth time, and the divergence becomes worse every year, so this forecasting technique is a a dead loss for those who have an unknown time. (See Chapter 41 on rectification.)

I can't resist a comment here on a Sun and Moon conjunction, or close to it, within a solar return chart. It is more significant if applying, of course. I find that it always indicates a major life shift in activity into the area of life (house) where it occurs. It will be of fairly long duration—several years—until another "New Moon" aspect forms. For instance, a New Moon in the 6th of your solar return chart points to an obvious focus on the 6th house of health, co-workers and work, volunteer or paid, as well as all the other peripheral things the 6th house deals with, such as pets, tenants (if you are a landlord), employees, contract labor, etc. This focus will shift the emphasis of your whole life for its duration, and explains why some people have nothing but 7th house events happening for years, for instance, or nothing but 10th house, or 4th house activities.

This New Moon is the single most important aspect in a solar return, I think. Once it occurs, expect it again in 29 years as the Moon repeats its cycle, returning close to the same position on the same day. The conjunctions don't have to be tight—8 or 9 degree orbs seem to work just fine. It's like anything else in astrology, though—**closer is better and stronger.**

Progressing the Solar Return

There are two good ways to progress the SR.
1. You start out the year with Sun in its birth sign and degree but probably in a different house than in your natal chart. That house is going to get the major activity after your birthday as the transiting Sun passes through it. You can use Placidus or equal house to see when it "leaves" the house of the SR. Then the activity shifts into the new house.

The solar return is a **Sun** vehicle so of course the transiting Sun sets it off. It is the very best way to use it for timing, I think. It also confirms natal timing. If it were off consistently, the chart would need rectification. I use an orb of no more than 3 or 4 degrees. 10 plus is way too far. Some charts are highly sensitive to the solar transits over SR planets. Others don't seem to notice. I have seen this vary from year to year, too (although that sounds like heresy). When transiting Sun passes over a natal planet, it usually combines with the meaning of the planet in the natal AND in the SR. Those with strong natal influences in Leo are always more affected by the Sun's action.

Example: Mercury in the natal rules the 7th. In the SR it rules the 4th. When transiting Sun crosses the SR Mercury, the spouse does some work on the house. If SR Mercury is afflicted, maybe the spouse has to do it to fix something broken, or perhaps there is a problem with a parent and the spouse gets involved in it. Keep a small diary of your own for a couple years and watch how this works. It is very illuminating. If Mercury in the natal is **before** the SR Mercury, maybe that's when the problem showed up. If Mercury in the natal is **after** the SR Mercury, maybe there was a secondary problem that had to be taken care of.

Example: Suppose the MC moves to contact a 10th house planet and that brings the Ascendant to a 2nd house planet at the same time. It doesn't take a genius to figure out it's probably going to mean money from your employment. If one or both are benefics, you get a fat raise, or make a bit extra from something like an extra project, or lecture on the side, etc. If the area shows likely problems in the SR you will end up losing money or spending it on bills. Or, Maybe it contacts a planet in the 7th—a competitor or partner has some effect on your work.

Now, if you are doing a bunch of these SR charts, you will notice that there are many years when the angles will not contact all the planets in the SR. In some years there are lots of hits—some years are more active than others.

These are both useful techniques and quite different from the ones used in natal progressions. This may sound more complicated than it is. Do a few different years' charts and look at the angles from one to the next. Just look at the shifting and you'll immediately see what I am talking about. The year ends before all the chicks get counted. It's almost as if the SR promises action in some areas but doesn't quite deliver it. (That shouldn't surprise anyone who pays attention to politicians.) Lack of action in some areas of life can be a blessing if the area that isn't hit had stresses in it. It doesn't mean the year won't have stress, just that there may not be major events linked to it.

Now, as to why people say they only have 5% accuracy. That's like complaining that a screwdriver only hits the nail five times out of a hundred. Maybe a screwdriver is not the right tool. Try a hammer. Most people have never heard of this perfectly sensible way to progress a solar return, or if they have, they try to use the wrong kind of progression on it. Of course it doesn't work as well. One of the comments you hear a lot of in astrology is that astrologers should use "whatever works for you." This implies that the tools are nebulous things that only a special brand of ESP can handle. Instead, I think it's a simple matter of not using the right tool. Not every technique is suitable in every situation.

Does the progressed SR work in my life? It used to, when I paid attention to it. I don't pay that much attention to my chart anymore. I do it at the beginning of the year and if it doesn't threaten outright chaos, I ignore it the rest of the time. I really don't bother unless I need to know something. Then I haul out the tool box and see what's happening. I try to use screwdrivers on screws and hammers on nails. Makes for much more effective forecasting.

I think I did about 50 years' worth of SRs once to learn how this stuff worked when I was first studying it. I learned which angles meant trouble for me and which let me sail through. I think every natal chart, has its own rhythm but when you get a feel for how they change and shift, it really helps you analyze them all better. And of course, like everyone else, I used my own chart to see how it worked.

This brings up another topic. I used to think "how egocentric" when I stopped to realize I only used my own chart to test out all the new things I learned.Then I realized that this was really the best way to do it. First because it's your own chart, you pay more attention to how things work, and secondly because it's about you, you remember the lesson better. So now I think "how intelligent we all are" when I hear other astrologers say they did and do the same thing. Our instincts take us to the right place.

Returning to my comments on solar return interpretation:

The natal 12th to the SR Ascendant almost always brings hospital contacts and/or things out of the past to you. Depending on the rulership and the comparison to the natal, it could be a member of your family, or even a co-worker.

One year when I was metro editor I had this in my SR, and two or three of my reporters were hospitalized or ill for some time and it meant additional pressure for me to staff their beats, visit them, spread their work around, etc. I also visited a couple of friends who had surgeries or babies that year. There were also some health problems in my family but I stayed perfectly healthy. However, an old problem that had been put on hold for a long time resurfaced and had to be dealt with. All of these are typical 12th house effects.

This is some of what you can expect. There is a special meaning, however, if one of the SR angles is conjunct a natal planet. That entire year will be colored by the meaning of the natal planet in itself, and what it naturally rules as well as its house position in your natal and the natal house it rules, as well as the SR house it rules. That sounds like a lot of trouble, but it is probably the dominant theme to the year when it happens, so worth taking time to understand.

A station in a Solar Return can be the dominant influence of the year. If it actually aspects or conjuncts a point in your chart, it will indicate one of the key events of the year.

A Solar Eclipse conjunct the Sun on your birthday is the single most important aspect one can have in the solar return, I believe. It always shifts the main focus of your life in the direction of the house where it falls in the SR. A 12th house solar eclipse can involve you with sick or needy people, things out of the past, a time of private work, or isolation. A 2nd house solar eclipse is a financial indicator, showing your efforts will be intensely focused on money—getting it, keeping it, figuring what you need to do with it—and so on. These eclipses do not occur very often. However, they always refocus your life and change your interests and your labors.

Also, with such a Solar Eclipse, remember to protect the eyesight (get an eye exam promptly) and check with the doctor any symptoms which can be related to the back or the heart (solar organs), especially if there are other indicators of health effects. For instance, it may be time for blood pressure medication, or cataract surgery. Both Sun and Moon rule the eyes, so pay attention. One of my clients had a torn retina after such an aspect. Others just need stronger glasses.

Relocating the Solar Return

I read Noel Tyl's chapter in one of his books on how he tried to relocate his solar return to avoid a back problem, I believe, unsuccessfully. It merely seemed to have changed the timing. That figures, frankly. I thought about this and I have a few things to share. I've also used them and they work. One is that events shown by the internal arrangement of the planets cannot be avoided entirely. However, timing shown by the angles CAN be softened. Location east or west shifts the emphasis of trouble or protection.

A man I know had a solar return showing major difficulty with his immediate boss, a somewhat ineffective person who had just been brought in over him as part of a political play elsewhere in the company. The boss's boss, however, favored the client. He was dismayed when I told him about his solar return and asked if there was anything he could do. I said we could try something if he was willing. He was. By spending a few days on the East Coast at the time of his birthday, he came up with a solar return putting the significator of the immediate boss in a weak, cadent house and putting the significator of the boss's boss in an angular one, with more power in the situation. So he took his family east for vacation then.

In his birth location, his solar return 10th showed harm to his reputation from the dealings with his boss. That is not what happened. Yes, he had problems with the boss. But the boss's boss was happy with him and his year ended with some awards from the company for outstanding performance.

With a temporary relocation on his birthday, he had successfully shifted the 10th house stress out of House 10 and into House 9, where any threat of harm to him at work would not be indicated. Does this change of location always work? To be honest, I don't know. I haven't done a thousand of these, only a few in cases where any softening of an angular problem was helpful.

These relocated solar returns are like any relocation charts. You don't change who you are, just what you meet in this new place. I have used the technique a few other times and have run up against difficulty analyzing solar returns, if I did not know that the individual had spent the time surrounding the birthday in some other area. That alone proved to me that there was something at work here.

Lunar Returns

Just a few words on lunar returns. While I don't use them much, I do know that they have a "foreground" and a "background" theme. The foreground is the angles. Planets in the angles are the main theme for the month. Planets in the background are relevant only insofar as they relate to planets in the angles. These charts put a great deal of emphasis on each person's natal Moon position, obviously, so in a way, you can get a good look at how your Moon functions by doing an equal house natal chart with the Moon on Ascendant. Then each lunar return may give you more clues on how it works. The comparison makes an interesting study.

If you are a strongly lunar person (angular natal Moon or a Cancer Sun sign or rising sign) you may respond to these lunar returns more than other people do. But all of us have lunar concerns—family, home, moods, emotions, public contact, etc. etc., and the Moon is the most personal of all the planets in some ways.

There are many, many useful techniques in astrology. Nobody has enough time to use them all or to become really good at them all if they plan to eat and sleep and have a normal life. This is one of the useful ones and often allows people to forecast events to the day, using the quarter Moon weekly cycles, as well.Some astrologers—like me—are too lazy to work that hard, but those who use them can be ungodly accurate.

Nodal Returns

I had an interesting case a few years ago of a student who had lightning strike her home twice several years apart. In each case the lightning actually hit an outbuilding rather than the main house—one was a storage shed for the lawnmower and another was an old detached garage. Both were destroyed, of course. She asked me where it showed up in her chart because she couldn't see it. I asked her when the first one hit and she told me. Then I asked how many years later the second strike occurred. The answer was 19 years. Aha—the exact time of a nodal return. In both cases she experienced a nodal return to its natal position with the South Node in House 4. I don't remember if there was an aspect to Uranus or not but it sounds like there should have been.

My advice to her was to make sure she always had an outbuilding on the property especially 19 years after the second strike (which would have been some years in the future at that point). Better the outbuilding than the main house.

Planetary Returns

These planetary returns I find amusing because everyone who does one does not necessarily find it helpful. Unless you are strongly Venus-ruled (Ascendant, Sun sign or Venus rising) you may not get a lot out of a Venus return. Maybe you are an Aries Sun with Scorpio rising—in which case, a Mars return is going to do you a lot more good as far as being a useful predictive tool. I know a man who has Venus rising in one of its own signs and his Venus returns are very evocative in terms of forecasting. Most of the big events of his year tend to cluster around the date of the return, even if not exactly on it.

I ran Venus returns for myself for a few years and discovered zilch. I simply don't respond to Venus that much. I discovered this is true for a lot of people. We respond to the most powerful influences in our natal patterns and some of us are Mercury ruled, or strongly Jupiterian, or have powerful Saturn influences in the birth chart.

It's the same principle at work with transits. Mars transits are terrific timers for some people. They are simply ignored by others, whose charts respond very quickly to the Moon, for instance. When the nodes of the Moon are in the same degree as a planet anywhere in one's natal chart, it points to a major area of stress in the life. That one seems to work for all of us.

Declinations

One of the things I always (well, I think always—some may have waited for intermediate groups) taught my beginning classes was declinations. I have used them for years, long before I had the pleasure of knowing famed declination queen, the late Kt Boehrer and read her book.

Declinations used to be one of the great neglected areas in astrology and I was often surprised by the ignorance on them that I found when I did lectures. It was like "where did that thing come from?" to my audiences every time I mentioned the word.

Now I will confess that I don't use all the nodes of the planets, but I always use the

Moon's nodes. Nodal ties are another thing that often get overlooked.

I was teaching classes and using declination in the '70s also, although I never did any work on the out of bounds (OOB) planets that Kt Boehrer made famous. A planet is out of bounds when it exceeds the Sun's maximum declination at 23 degree 25 minutes. Kt's work on the OOBs added a great deal to my own work with declination.

Truly there is nothing new under the Sun except humans. We each have to relearn it all, or at least all we know. There oughta be a better way. On the other hand, if we passed along knowledge like we give our descendants blue eyes I might have a brain cluttered with things like how to trim a mustache and how much salt to use for the pickle barrel. Better I learn these things only if I need them. Meanwhile, hurray for declinations! And to learn about them, read Kt's book!

Orbs

All symbolic movements should be used without orb. I don't use any orb at all on progressions. They are exact or they are nowhere.

When Saturn transits through your Sun sign or your rising sign you'll probably feel it all the way through as a general "downdraft" in the atmosphere. When Jupiter transits it will be a general "updraft" and I notice that Uranus seems to affect an entire decanate at a time when it transits. However, specific events during those "general atmosphere" times require tight orbs. To give an example: say Mercury is moving 1 degree 45 minutes for the year. The progressed Moon will make an exact trine to it sometime during the year. When? Depends on when Mercury gets to the exact point where the Moon can hit it, and you need a bit of math to figure that out. Don't fuss, just do it. You need to know.

Say the progressed Moon at 21 will not form an aspect to the 28 degree Pluto until it's traveled 7 more degrees. That's 7 months, if the Moon is moving exactly (or close) to 12 degrees for the year. But suppose the Moon is fast for the year—moving at 14 degrees 12 minutes? It will get to 28 faster than 7 months. That's when the action occurs. Pluto moves about 3 minutes per day (or progressed year). For all intents and purposes you don't need to worry about progressed Pluto moving much. But some years the Ascendant moves faster or slower, so you need to know how fast it's going and you need to know exactly how fast the Moon is going.

When Ascendant exactly contacts Pluto, expect action. When Moon exactly aspects Pluto, expect action. When Moon contacts any planet you will get action. ANY progressed aspect that is exact will provide an event.

I get very annoyed by people who say an aspect is approaching for a degree and separating for a degree on a progressed chart. That's two years, folks. Well, duh——you're bound to have something happen in two years that you can say you predicted, but it sure won't make your client happy when you are doing a one-year forecast. Oh—and yes, I use progressed to progressed and progressed to natal. But I use them **exactly.**

Progressions in Summary
When forecasting, look for:

1—**The current Saturn transit.** As it moves through the houses of the chart, forming aspects with natal planets, it creates clearly visible stresses and events.

2—Stations of the planets. Create a handy check sheet so you can see when planets go retrograde or direct and when each year. They help time events.

3—Eclipses for the year. They are ranked in order of power, from a total solar eclipse visible overhead to a partial lunar eclipse. Their aspects indicate how malefic or benefic they will be.

4—The current lunar node transit. This will indicate in which grouping (cardinal, fixed or mutable) the eclipses will fall and has special implication in the natal chart.

5—The year's most outstanding planetary aspects. Some years this is a series of conjunctions formed as planets retrograde and return to direct motion. Other years it has to do with planets entering new signs. In 2001 it was the Saturn/Pluto opposition series which concluded in 2002. Sometimes it is a change when the planets move into new signs such as Jupiter's entry into Cancer or Saturn's entry into Gemini.

6—Solar arcs. I use the mean solar arc, which is one degree per year of life applied to any planet or angle to see what new aspect forms. It is a symbolic direction, sometimes called the "age arc." Others use the exact solar arc. Equally valid.

7—Mars transits. They set off specific patterns. A massive earthquake in India in January was one such event forecast a year and a half previously by the "Millenium Eclipse" at 18 of Leo in August of 1999. Mars was exactly square the eclipse point when the quake occured. The path of totality of that eclipse passed over the quake site.

8—Past eclipses which may have left sensitive points in the chart. (Such as the Milennium Eclipse). Make a note of any total solar eclipse point in the last two years which is close to exactitude on the chart in question. It may act again.

9—Transits of the planet which rules the particular chart in question. Always watch Venus in a Libra rising chart, or Jupiter if it has a Sagittarian Sun.

10—The solar chart. If you can't do it in your head, draw it. Planets act in solar houses as well as natal houses.

11—The secondary progressions—Notes: Keep in mind some keywords. It helps to memorize words that trigger associations. For instance, think of Uranus as "change" and "sudden" since its transits or progressions often force change or facilitate it abruptly or in an unexpected way. Think of Jupiter as opportunity and important people. Think of Saturn as responsibility and delay and so on through the planets. Get in the habit of using partile or exact aspects. You'll be happier if you do.

Chapter 21

Missing elements

When one sits down to count up the number of earth, air, fire and waters in a particular map, it can be quite a jolt to see that one entire element might be missing—no water placements or no air, for instance. This is not a catastrophe but it points us in the direction of things to consider before interpreting a chart.

One of the pluses of having no earth in a chart is that it gives an individual the power to step outside the box of tradition and what is expected of them in life and do what will succeed in a novel, or non-traditional way. These people often acquire money by making career choices that will lead to money and authority.

The birth pattern is like a bowl of water—nudge it anywhere with a transit and the whole thing vibrates or makes waves. But like a bowl of water, the energy flows into any empty areas to fill them up. The lack doesn't mean the individual is weaker, merely that he or she will try to fill the void.

The missing air person can be constantly on the phone to someone talking or asking questions and pestering everyone he knows for answers. It can be tiresome since these types seldom bother to do their own research, which would have the advantage of giving peace to their friends and neighbors. If there is little fixity in the pattern they can be asking the same things over and over through life. It's almost as if nothing "sticks" in their heads.

Missing water is emotional at the drop of a hat, wants everybody to be sympathetic to its needs and weeps buckets over you. But of course they probably won't visit you in the hospital when you get your leg cut off in an accident, or something equally awful. "I can't STAND hospitals," they will tell you. This is the person who over-dramatizes their lot in life and demands as much as possible of your attention. One should never mistake their crocodile tears for real sympathy. Some feel it, of course, but there is an element of this in the makeup of all those who lack water in the chart.

People missing fire often take on jobs they can't manage to handle and try to do more than they should. They are constantly running from one thing to the next in order to cope with all of life's demands. They try to do one thing at a time but there is always something else waiting for them when they finish a job. And it's usually critical in time or energy. It is a lifelong struggle for them not to get on the horse and ride off in all directions. A major modifying factor can alter any of these well known generalizations, of course.

Sometimes Void of Course Moon can squelch the emotional expression of a missing-water person. But, sometimes it's a lot of other things, as well. Missing-earth people don't always go after the money, for instance—sometimes they have a lifelong love affair with ceramic figurines, or want the best book collection in town. But there will be some drive in the Venus direction. Missing water can use the emotional drive in another way, such as acting or psychology.

But true genius always seems to reflect extremism in some direction and usually in the direction of finding what is missing in the chart. For most of us, a missing element is more an itch we have to scratch somehow than a huge deal, but it does give us food for thought..

Chapter 22

How Aspects Work

The single most helpful skill in astrology is understanding of aspects and how they work. Planets seldom act alone and their signs and houses are part of the story in every chart. Aspects are the rest of it and probably represent the biggest part of it.

The Parallel

I list it first because from antiquity it has been considering powerful, despite its lack of attention in recent times. It has been returning to prominence in the last 20 years and is worth paying attention to. I have always used and taught the use of declinations but I disagree with the common contention that they always act like conjunctions when two planets share the same declination. I don't think so.

I find that declinations "echo" whatever aspect is already present between them in longitude and make it more powerful. An example is a semi-square reinforced by a parallel, which sits up and talks in the birth pattern. Or a wide trine where the parallel exists that makes the trine seem a lot tighter and more potent. Conversely, conjunctions that don't have a parallel operating don't have the traditional conjunction punch, I think.

This is my rule: When two planets are in parallel of declination, it reinforces whatever longitudinal aspect they have and makes it more powerful. If square by longitude, they do not act like they are conjunct, but like they are a more powerful square. When two planets are parallel but in NO longitudinal aspect, the parallel brings them together like a weak conjunction.

I find parallels important in progressed aspects. A progressed Moon parallel natal or progressed Neptune, for instance, will mark a hospitalization when there is no other aspect to explain it. The contraparallel business comes because oppositions in longitude are usually accompanied by parallels with one planet north and the other south. And so they act like more powerful oppositions. However, I don't think of them ever as "contraparallels."

A parallel is a parallel is a parallel.

The maps of the progressed Moon's declination that astrologer Carolyn Egan has so brilliantly brought to the public awareness are a wonderful, simple way to see the parallel operating in a visual manner. I can't praise her enough for this work. It echoes that of the late astrologer Kt Boehrer, who tracked the progressed Moon's travel north and south and who first started to convert the declination to longitude for another look at its effectiveness. Her book "Declination" is hard to acquire but worth having for study.

When the parallels of the Moon in a given year in the progressed chart are heading to the north, it usually casts a social, outward tone over the year. When the Moon is heading south, it focuses action more inwardly and one has issues to deal with. As it crosses the 0 degree point, this becomes pronounced. Often the month when this occurs is significant.

Using a computer program's visual chart of the progressed Moon to see this is a handy way to understand it. When the declination is heading north from zero, the individual's perception is that life is "improving." When declination begins heading south, things begin cooling off in life and sometimes those periods are welcome. Other times they show a shift away from further expansion of a given life style. **Changes are always significant.**

Sextiles and trines

Sextiles have the quality of air and of fire—all the sextiles starting from the ascendant would fall in house 3, 5, 7, 9, and 11 in a simple Aries-rising chart. Thus they have the need of air for mental stimulus—read "interest" —and fire's energy—read "pursuit." People with many sextiles simply can't hold themselves to any one path. They have too many interests they want to chase down. Even a single sextile will lead one to pursue the interest, if only as a hobby or an avocation. They are also in a sense unfinished trines, being half the sum of a trine. They resonate to the lesser benefic, Venus, the 6.

Trines, on the other hand, would fall in Houses 5 and 9 from that Aries Ascendant and tend to be in the same element, such as earth or fire. The exception comes when a trine occurs late in one element, say water, and a planet occupies a very early degree of the next element, which would be fire in that case.

A trine anywhere in any chart reflects a full-blown talent. It is something an individual has to such a pronounced degree that it is all but ignored unless in use. One simply feels that one "is" a Sun trine Mars, or a Venus trine Neptune. In times of stress or need, the talent is there, like money in the bank, to be used or spent.

People with too many trines are like people with old money. They don't need to shout about what they have but can't imagine not having a way to accomplish what they want. So they take a lot of things for granted and can sometimes be downright lazy with their assets. What activates use, of course, is a dandy little square or two somewhere to one corner of the trine or another. An opposition will do just as well.

The sextile has its own rationale and doesn't need to be activated. It is already in action because it represents the development phase of talent. It's the farm team, in a way.

As an example, consider piano playing. A trine is like someone born with a perfect ear who can play by ear—whatever they hear they can play. Will they explore its full potential and become a virtuoso? Maybe, depending on whether or not the trine is pushed sufficiently by those other aspects I mentioned. A sextile is the soul who yearns to play, finds music fascinating, goes to endless concerts to hear how it's done, just loves having a chance to play scales or learn how to read a score, etc.

The so-called Solomon's seal which King Solomon is said to have worn on his shield in ancient days to intimidate his enemies was a double grand trine reflecting the fire/air power. It is the interlocking six-pointed star of Judaism. But it is also the full series of sextiles, and represents to those who understand its significance, a daunting array of ideas and energy to solve any problem as well as the completed trines of power and talent.

Sextiles are very nice to have. They keep you from being bored in life. They also keep you from being boring. I have very few charts of people with only trines and no squares— one belonged to a butcher, the other to a factory worker. Neither man seemed to have any other interest in life besides job and family. Exceptionally "boring" people. Both are dead now, unfortunately, or I could ask them if they found life boring. The great psychic Edgar Cayce, who discussed the idea of past lives, said that some people apparently get "resting" lives after stressful ones. I've always thought that was an interesting remark. Maybe that was the case for those two men.

I have another chart with almost all trines that belongs to a young man who sold drugs and went to prison for several years. He finally got his act together and made a successful life for himself but it took some pretty strong pressure (the prison term) to make it happen. As I said, too many trines are lazy. Talented, but lazy.

Trines are not only complacent, at times, but those who have them can get self-righteous about their own lack of difficulty, a rather unpleasant habit. Trine people can slip through life tweaking things just enough to avoid many of the problems other people develop. It's almost like the difference between an adult who can speed read and a child still learning to read. Trines are a very good thing to have, but one needs a dose of humility and appreciation to use them wisely.

Squares

Squares are the single most dominant aspect in the charts of those who succeed. Learning to solve problems develops grit and determination to accomplish something in life. People who have squares often become truly outstanding in whatever field they choose.

Basketball star Dennis Rodman's chart is one of the most stressful I have ever seen, with many heavy squares angular in fixed signs. They form a fixed grand cross. But his athletic record is astounding. He is truly one of the all-time greats in basketball.

A chart with too many squares and oppositions and no trines or sextiles is like someone besieged on all sides in life with almost no way out except to fight one's way through whatever is going on. Usually a chart contains both good and bad aspects. The harsh aspects force us to struggle in order to overcome problems and grow thereby. The good aspects provide opportunities and talents to do it with.

Rodman's career resulted in a handful of championship rings as well as wild violence, womanizing and misbehavior. His athletic career is over now, but most people remember his bad boy behavior and his habit of dyeing his hair wild colors, rather than his superb athletic talent. He helped win those championship titles on three different teams, including the Chicago Bulls during the Michael Jordan era. He later tried to jump-start a movie career, as so many athletes do to capitalize on their sports fame after retirement, but it wasn't very successful. He even became a pro wrestler for a while. Reading about his life is an excellent way to see the squares at work.

Many people with too many squares have difficulty "getting it together." While some stress in life seems to be good for us, too much seems to be defeating unless the individual works very hard. Dennis Rodman's insecurities and inner angers certainly were the fuel to spark his talent. He is still in the spotlight these days in Las Vegas as I write this and I hope he finds a greater peace with himself as the years go by. He may finally do so in old age.

This is a curious fact about squares. If we survive their pummeling in youth they power a better lifestyle as the years go by. We take the challenges of life and win, and the universe sits up and takes notice. Our "reward" is that the squares seem to act more like trines after 60 and we confidently move through the stresses that would have buried us at 20.

Oppositions

The opposition is a problem in human relationships or the clash of desires and requirements. It takes consultation, communication and cooperation or conciliation to solve and almost always means confronting oneself in the process.

The see-saw pattern which Marc Edmund Jones wrote about is based on a series of oppositions in a chart. A see-saw is a very good analogy. When one is faced with a dilemma of choice between goods, and is forced to choose, one often finds there is no simple choice allowed.

Here's a good example. An opposition through 4 and 10 almost always involves a problem between one's job and the needs of one's family. It has become almost fashionable in these days for politicians and those who lose their jobs or walk away from them to say they wish to spend more time with their family. Cynics may so, "Oh, yeah?" while the rest of us nod because we know how it goes. Many hard-working people truly long for just a little more time to loaf with their spouse on a beach or go to the kids' ball games and music recitals.

Over a lifetime of working I marveled at how many young women juggled the needs of the job and their families, often with very small children, in order to keep their world balanced. It isn't always easy.

Other oppositions through Houses 1 and 7 involve people in dealing with the needs of their marital partner while also taking care of their own and that is usually a lifetime balancing act. It's no wonder some of them end up divorced only to walk into an identical situation in the next marriage. The only way to deal with the opposition is to find a way to cooperate and work together and that effort to solve problems may take years to accomplish. Running away doesn't work. Maybe an opposition runs between Houses 5 and 11. Here we find the desires we have for our own pleasure (5) and the needs of others, such as one's friends or the larger group (11). It's very like the sports challenge of either playing for oneself to attract the spotlight or playing to help the team win even if you don't get credit.

I know of many friends who have traveled together and often think of one elderly man who told me he went on a tour of the American southwest with a lifelong buddy after both men lost their wives. Unfortunately the buddy wanted to spend a great deal more time in the bar or around a pool than touring the Grand Canyon and visiting the spectacular desert scenery of the Southwest which the first man wanted to see. Neither was very satisfied with the trip and it put the friendship into a permanent limbo. The case was a classic study in the opposition between Houses 5 and 11. House 5 rules vacations.

Oppositions between Houses 2 and 8 can involve the conundrum of spending or saving. Worse yet is the one between credit and cash—and people with these oppositions sometimes end up in terrible trouble with borrowing unwisely and bankruptcy when the debts they incurred to fuel their spending urges become too much. Credit cards simply are not the all-purpose blessing they are purported to be. These people need to solve the puzzle of their value system. One doesn't become more lovable by spending too much on others. One only becomes broke.

Oppositions between Houses 3 and 9 can be stress between what we say and what we really think. This can easily get out of hand. It's the mark of those who can be all sweetness and light about politics or religion but turn nasty when it gets serious.

Problems between Houses 6 and 12 can be stress over the need to take care of others and the need to take care of oneself—not easy to solve until one confronts the issue of guilt and learns to say no sometimes. Or, they can be stresses involving health and medical personnel. This is also sometimes called the "serve or suffer" package, which prompts so many to take up volunteer work as a means to help others. Sometimes they choose helping careers. Those who don't, become the ones who need the help.

People with oppositions have to be careful about judging others too quickly. They may end up in their shoes one day and have to revise their thinking.

Conjunctions

I don't consider a simple conjunction "hard" as much as a "blend." Let me give you an example. I made some lemon bars for dessert for my son and his wife when they came for dinner one day. It was the first thing my son learned to make in the kitchen when he was a little boy and I stumbled across the recipe when I was looking for something else and decided to make them for him. I know it had been at least 20 years since he had the things.

Anyway, the recipe for lemon bars calls for the juice of real lemons to be mixed with Eagle brand evaporated milk and then spread across layers of graham crackers in a shallow pan. The milk is a rather sickeningly sweet concoction that nevertheless makes wonderful baked goods. Lemon juice and that evaporated milk are sharply different but are needed to play off each other. The layers are repeated until you run out of crackers or the lemon/milk combination. The top layer is always crackers.

Once the bars are made they have to be frosted with a butter cream frosting. I use real butter and real vanilla with the powdered sugar. Now butter and vanilla are also quite different, but they blend in the taste buds and most of us find anything with real butter and vanilla very tasty indeed. I consider they make a great conjunction. And, when you put the lemon juice and that gooey evaporated milk together in a recipe, THEY make a great conjunction. You can also put lemon with butter—a great combination. Ditto the vanilla and evaporated milk. And, the graham crackers are an inspired conjunction.

Conjunctions teach us how we take diverse qualities and merge them to create something new. Cooking is often about the ways we put dissimilar elements together to create something wonderful. And all that from a batch of lemon bars simple enough that a child could make them. They have to be covered and put in the refrigerator for a few hours but then they are ready to cut and eat. Oh, and my son loved the rerun of his childhood cooking lesson.

Another aspect, a Mars/Jupiter conjunction , which comes along fairly often, every 2 to 5 years, was feared by the ancients, who greatly distrusted Mars when it got a boost from its buddy Jupiter. Two fire planets were considered like two teen age males—better off apart than together plotting mischief.

Think about all the things Mars rules—warfare, arguments, hitting, shooting, cutting, biting, hurting, pain, anger, resentment, retaliation, hot weather, fires and more. Jupiter's influence adds the element of "more." No wonder this transit can be annoying!

Transits of the outer planets are much more significant since their conjunctions come more rarely. Their effects can change lives and mark big developments in society at large. If you are watching them, you will also notice that their parallels may form both before and after the longitudinal ones, thus extending their influence and giving additional timing tips.

Any chart with multiple conjunctions is about power and the individual comes equipped with a great deal of it.

Combust and Cazimi

The words Via Combust are Latin for "road of fire," or Fiery Pathway and refer to the fact that a number of important fixed star positions fall between 15 degrees of Libra and 15 degrees of Scorpio. That area of the zodiac is called the Via Combust and is particularly significant in horary work. The term "cazimi" refers to a planet within 17 minutes of arc from exact conjunction to the Sun. Mercury, for instance, at 10 Taurus 15 minutes is cazimi when the Sun is 10 Taurus 12 minutes. The term "cazimi" means being "in the heart of the Sun." This gives Mercury far more power than it otherwise would in conjunction with the Sun. Usually a conjunction to the Sun overwhelms the planet, but when it is cazimi it becomes dominant. This is an aspect that also has special relevance to horary work.

In my experience, planets that are combust (conjunct the Sun by 3 degrees or less but not cazimi) in a natal pattern take on a solar character and tend to sharply color the career and health (for a man) and affect a woman's relationships with men and her career (if she has a career as opposed to a job). In other words, they link with the Sun's characteristics. The Sun's qualities (by sign and aspect to other planets) color how the planets express themselves. People with such aspects tend to be easily influenced or persuaded by more powerful personalities and may not initiate very many actions on their own.

When combust, Saturn isn't as selfish, Mars is not as violent (but may be more physically active), Venus is kinder, etc. Jupiter can have a strong social conscience and Mercury isn't as chatter-y, but is more thoughtful. However, combust planets are read somewhat differently in a horary chart and follow those rules in that type of work.

In cazimi, however, the planet's natural characteristics tend to become stronger. The individual seems more Saturn-like, or more Jupiterian than Sun-like. When the Sun is strong in a chart, the person often seems like a Leo, extroverted, straightforward and generous. A Sun-Jupiter person doesn't seem like a Sagittarian or a Pisces, however, unless Jupiter is cazimi.

In the case of the Moon, a conjunction to the Sun weakens the Moon in some way. It is simply overpowered by the stronger Sun. In a woman's chart, it usually means health problems. Particularly with the female system or the nervous system, the problems may be lifelong. In a man's chart, he either has difficulty really understanding women and/or has women with difficulties in his life—again, often with health problems.

Conjunctions to the planets on the other hand, usually intensify the manifestation of the planet's energy as a blend with the Sun. The Sun is colored with the shade of Venus, or Mars or whatever. I know women with Venus Sun conjunctions who are tasteful and artistic in everything they do—up to and including the wastebasket— and Sun/Mars types who put tremendous energy into the career, and who collect antique weaponry.

A planet can be combust or conjunct the Sun within an orb of 12 degrees. "Under the Sunbeams" is another horary term meaning within about 17 degrees of the Sun but not combust or cazimi.

Cazimi is a different case. It shows the meaning of the individual planet dominating the life. Mercury for instance could be a writer who is intensely focused and driven to write to the exclusion of everything else. Beyond that I think the combustion, cazimi, or Sunbeam business is really a horary thing.

Unaspected planets and minor aspects

The traditional meaning of "affliction" in a chart is harsh aspects from the malefics, Mars and Saturn. In modern times the squares and oppositions from the outer planets are also often considered malefic.

A completely unaspected planet is a rarity. When it occurs, it has a pure energy, unmixed or diluted, unlike the energy most of us receive from a planet which is modified by aspects from other planets. Such an unaspected planet dominates the life and may actually provide a type of genius in its expression. Traditionally it must have no major aspects and I would include the parallel as a major aspect.

However, when it comes to inconjuncts and semi- and sesqui-squares I think anything beyond a 3 degree orb either side is out of touch. There are a lot of astrologers who get into semi-sextile and quintiles and bi-quintiles and stuff and frankly, I'm not one of them. If I can't figure it in my head and there is no aspect in one of the major ways, I think it is too picky for me and I don't use it.

The problem in astrology is the multiplicity of tools one can use. At some point you have to choose what to work with and if you keep piling tools into the bag, eventually it gets so heavy you can't lift it and the result is you do less and less useful work. You may spend hours calculating minutiae, but you don't get more out of it. Stick to the classic aspects, keep your orbs fairly snug and you won't go wrong.

I see planetary interconnections in a chart like a row of dominoes. This is especially true of a stellium. Tap one end of it and all the planets are set off sequentially. This is also the principle behind "whole" charts and people who "never seem to get it together."

In what I call "whole" charts all the planets are linked in a series of interlocking aspects, good and bad, which allow their energy to become focused and operate smoothly. These are people who are what I call "whole" or mature types whose lives enrich others.

Those who don't seem to have a cohesive personality often have one or more isolated complexes that never interact with other complexes and it's like a split personality. They spend their whole life preoccupied with themselves and their needs and have difficulty making the machinery all work as a unity. When you've done a zillion, charts you begin to see how some of this works.

An isolated, unaspected planet stands outside all the unity or disunity, however, and has another mission in the life altogether. That mission is to blaze a trail for the individual to follow in the search for personal meaning and accomplishment. It is a huge beacon to lead the astrologer toward seeing how it manifests. It is rare, but well worth watching for.

Out of Sign and Orbs

I don't necessarily find that out-of-sign aspects are weak when they are close in orb. Some astrologers don't like to use them, but after doing a lot of charts over a period of nearly 50 years, I think they work just fine.

Orb is not a fixed thing, however. It varies with the planets involved as well as with their power in the chart. Angular relationships have wider orbs, and when we are considering Sun, Moon or Jupiter, orb grows. It can be 12 or 14 degrees with Jupiter and the lights. As a general rule of thumb, 8 degrees is good for the major aspects and 2 or 3 for the minor ones. The smaller the aspect, the tighter it needs to be. Semi-squares and inconjuncts need 1 or 2 degrees at most.

However, I use exact aspects only in all progressions (none of this "approaching" and "separating" stuff), and I prefer a natal parallel of 30 minutes, except to Sun or Moon. However, I know that others may use larger orbs. The best rule to use is like romance— "closer is better."

Like a lot of rules there are modifications. Interlocking aspects can be like a block of gelatin. No matter where you stick the spoon in, the stuff wiggles because it's all hooked together.

The T Square

This is the most dynamic of all the complexes that can be formed. It is an opposition combined with a third planet that is square to either end and links three parts of the modes of action, such as cardinal, fixed or mutable, while leaving the fourth one "open."

The open spot is the key. The planets in the tension of the opposition and square fuel the drive. The focus is the open side, where the energy is put to work and things happen. Wherever in the chart a T-square falls is important and provides the main clue to the astrologer about the individual's drive and accomplishments. Should the T-square fall in cardinal signs or angular houses the ambition, drive and determination come very young and have specific goals in mind. People with T-squares simply will not be denied. If there are any good aspects elsewhere in the chart to any of the T-square planets, the person will readily grasp and adopt whatever tools they provide.

This is, above all else, the aspect of action. People with these patterns in their charts don't sit and contemplate the world before deciding what to do. They tend to just make it up as they go along and are quite apt to take everyone they know along with them.

The downside of the T-square is that it can be hard to live with and if gets too compelling, those who have such aspects can end up smothering others. People with these aspects need to back off a bit sometimes in their human relations so as not to spoil what they most treasure.

The Grand Cross

People with the Grand Cross mostly go along just fine but when anything—progression or transit—sets off any part of the natal pattern, all hell breaks loose in their lives and the roof seems to cave in on them. Everything feels affected, major change happens and major trauma is involved.

This is because the Grand Cross involves the rulers of so many houses, in addition to its own dynamics as a straightforward pattern. The oppositions of both arms of the cross form squares as well, involving not only the houses each planet is in, but also the houses they rule. People with this configuration often see no way out except to fight. Somebody. Anybody. Everybody. Hence, my choice to show you the Rodman chart. (See next page.)

The Millennium eclipse of 1999 (see chart on page 27) was powerful for precisely the same reason. First, it involved both lights and both malefics, as well as Uranus. Secondly it was in fixed signs (which are capable of very long-lasting effects), and thirdly, the aspects between the planets included almost all the houses no matter what location anywhere on earth for which it was calculated. It doesn't get any tougher than that. Additionally, the middle areas of the fixed signs are THE most powerful in the zodiac. This is because their reflex points, or solstice points, also occur in fixed signs, doubling up the power in regard to events occuring then.

All the malefic indications in that 1999 eclipse chart were close in orb. The benefics were around but Venus was afflicted by Pluto and debilitated by sign, and Jupiter was not happy either. I consider this chart to be the worst single eclipse chart I have ever seen. I'd looked it years before, and was afraid of it then. The earthquake in the Pacific which launched the huge tsunami that killed a quarter of million people followed. Aspects between the two charts, Millennium and tsunami were close. The Millennium eclipse chart was still quite active for the World Trade Center catastrophe two years later. It warned of earthquakes, war, devastation, disease, oil problems, nuclear posturing, religious fighting and political change. All of those followed in the wake of that eclipse, within in the zone of maximum effect.

But a grand cross in cardinal or mutable signs can be nasty, too, whether in the natal chart or as part of an eclipse. It just functions a little differently. Personal effects are easier to see in the natal pattern.

When it occurs in cardinal, the person leaps into action to fix things. Any kind of action will do. Sometimes it's exactly the wrong kind of action, which puts the individual back in the soup instead of out of trouble. However, it never passes quietly. Cardinal stresses are "noisy" because they quickly expand into dramatic effect.

By contrast, the fixed cross has an inevitability about it. It's the difference between a hot car with a loud exhaust, like the cardinal cross, and a huge bulldozer, like the fixed cross. The mutable grand cross is equally annoying but has a slower effect than the cardinal and less power than the fixed cross. It's the quiet truck that goes where the driver points it.

The cardinal cross acts immediately and its effects can be healed or reversed with the right action. The mutable has a more leisurely time of manifestation but a lingering effect on ideas and behavior. It can leave behind chronic problems.

Damage done by the fixed cross is permanent. It can be soothed or eased but it remains in effect. The work of the fixed cross lasts and lasts. And lasts.

The reason that people born with grand crosses hate to see trouble come is that once

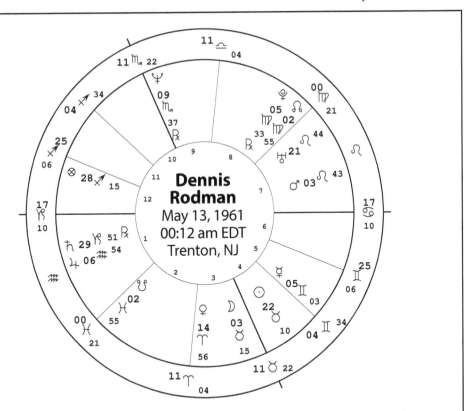

Dennis Rodman's chart contains a powerful grand cross in fixed signs and angles, from Jupiter to Mars to Neptune to the Moon. It includes the rising Saturn out of sign. His Sun is square Uranus, also angular. Such powerful aspects create an enormous drive for survival in a tough world, and the talent to succeed. He has a superb athletic record and a handful of championship rings, despite his antics, but is often best remembered for his habit of dyeing his hair bright colors for basketball games. Chart is AA from Astrodatabank.

the squares are triggered, the action continues until the final aspect is concluded and that can take many months or years.

Two things are typical of Grand Cross types:

1. Life goes along just fine until one thing goes sour and then EVERYTHING goes.

2. The Grand cross implodes in the personality. Unlike the t-square which sends its energy into the "empty" area and is a dynamic, action–oriented aspect, the grand cross is a stubborn aspect that may cause the individual who has it to just hunker down and hold on when things get tough. They like to outwait trouble if they can. They usually can't.

Also, a lot of the problems in most of our lives involve other people. Sometimes we're really just spectators. For the Grand Cross person, it's ALL personal since the cross focuses all the action inward onto the person lucky enough to have it.

Here's an example of Grand Cross with an ordinary chart:

Your uncle gets arrested for DUI and the whole family knows about it and tut-tuts over it. He pays his fine or serves his time or whatever penalty is involved and that's the end of that. You're a member of the family but you aren't involved.

If you're a grand cross person, the uncle is stopped by a cop that's related to you. Your uncle hits you up for a loan to pay off the fine, ignoring the fact that you told him a long time ago you wouldn't loan him money if he got into trouble again. But he tells the judge you're financially responsible for his debts and the judge believes him, orders you to pay the fine and your uncle never pays back a dime. In fact, he screws up your credit rating. Then your mother wants to know what kind of a person you are to get involved with the ne'er-do-well of the family and gets into an argument with your dad over it. They both quit speaking to you and your kid brother doesn't invite you to graduation over the uproar, etc., etc., etc. Grand cross people get very uptight about problems. Still, dealing with the problems always end up in their laps, no matter whether they should or not.

The Grand Trine

This is considered as a favorable aspect by many people and it is, in many ways. However, it is an easy aspect—even a lazy aspect. Those born with grand trines have tons of talent and potential but may never live up to it all unless there are severe pressures in life to force action. And,when the pressures ease off, the grand trine person can happily return to a life of slug-dom. It is, above all, an aspect of self-sufficiency. The result is that other people see that as strength they want to share and may zero in with an attempt to feed off it. They often rely on the grand trine person to come up with solutions to whatever problem arises, and then to implement those solutions, as well.

Self-sufficiency comes in many ways, but one common one is the comfort with one's own company. Grand trine people are often content when they have gobs of non-social time, since they can usually find things that they like to do or that interest them. If there are a number of sextiles that also relate to the grand trine, the interests can be very wide ranging.

The simple trine in any chart shows a talent. The grand trine shows lots of talents. Sextiles to any of the planets show more interests. But it is a closed loop—the energy of any planet aspecting the grand trine is funneled around the trine and may not be objectively used without another planet drawing it out.

An opposition to one planet in the grand trine creates what a lot of people call the "kite" formation, which gives the grand trine a great deal of dynamic energy and sets up lifelong ambitions and goals.

Squares to any of the planets in the grand trine bring problems that need to be solved, thus stirring the grand trine out of its lethargy and manifesting those lovely talents. It's like a big lion sleeping in the Sun when along comes a rat that wants to eat leftover food between the cat's paws. If the cat wakes and sees the rat but isn't interested in the leftovers, it may do absolutely nothing. But if the rat accidentally stirs the cat, it has sealed its doom. The big cat simply demolishes the rat with one swat.

Sometimes it takes a lot of rats to get the big cat energized sufficiently to stand up and wipe out the entire crowd. And there may be a whole community waiting for just that to happen. The community cheers its hero for the day and may try to get more out of the cat while they can, but usually the cat just nods at them all or takes a bow and goes back to sleep.

Some Grand Trine people with plenty of squares or oppositions are so used to the dependency of others and their inability to solve problems which Trine people see as easy that they can't say no to anybody. And the "anybodies" always show up. Grand Trine people are then quite likely to work unceasingly and may desperately need down time. They love down time when they can get it.

People with the Grand Trine which gets no squares or opposition expect life to be easy. They are always surprised when a difficulty shows up and may be given to extensive whining about it before doing anything. Some will take the easiest way out of their problems rather than use any of their talents and may end up in trouble if the easiest way out is not precisely legal. I have seen this happen.

However, when his consequences proved to be uncomfortable, one grand trine person buckled down, turned his life around and went on to become a success. But it was his own idea and was prompted by his own discomfort. That's always the key to grand trine people.

One good spur is a lack of money. Grand trine people will often adapt to increasingly smaller amounts of resources until they "hit bottom" and start to look around to see what they can do about things. Again, once engaged, their talents emerge and they can become successful as well as more financially secure.

But unless the spurs continue they will stop short of outstanding because it takes too much effort. Wealth could be within their reach, but like that big cat, they will yawn and settle down for a good nap instead and a more modest amount of resources. It's just a lot easier.

Chapter 23

The Houses
Doorways to Experience and Their Tensions

There is a natural tension that exists between houses that oppose each other. They concern, superficially at least, the same things but from different viewpoints and needs in the personality. All the houses on the bottom of the chart, from 1 to 6, relate to the individual whose chart it is. All the houses on the top of the chart, from 7 to 12, relate to other people. This is why so many individuals with charts heavily focused on houses 1-6 only want to do what they want to do in life. The needs of others don't concern them, or if they do, they certainly are not the primary motivators of their actions.

The reverse is true for those whose planets focus above the line in houses 7 through 12. They are motivated by the needs of others and respond best to those concerns.

The eastern side of the chart, houses 1, 2, 3, 10, 11 and 12 are primarily self-directed. A heavy preponderance of planets in those houses gives a tendency to initiate the action to be taken and to be successful at it. Those whose planets fall on the western side of the chart, houses 4, 5, 6, 7, 8 and 9, tend to wait for the proper time to react to events and effect changes. They are much less self-determined in that way, where those on the eastern side of the chart seem to be able to produce change any time they choose.

The first house is the house of "me." The seventh is the house of "you." Both deal with how the individual will fit into the world, firstly as him or herself and secondly as that person will deal with all others, and particularly those in the closest of all relationships, a partnership. The second is the house of what I have and the eighth is the house of what others have. Both first and second houses are about money, the earning and the spending, but in different ways. The second is also about values one has and the eighth about the values others may have or that one assigns to their possessions. Tensions between these two houses in a chart can develop into the classic struggle of love vs. money.

Houses three and nine are about what we know and can find out. The third is about information and the tools we use to acquire it. The ninth is about what others know and how we put our information together with theirs thus forming our opinions and philosophies about the world. Four and ten describe our place in society. Four is our roots, our home, our inherited family and what kind of status that family has. Ten is the place we seek to make for ourselves, with all its struggles for recognition, reputation and responsibility as a member of the society in which we live. It may be different from the one in which we were born. These houses particularly talk about the influence parents have on us.

Five and eleven are about finding and expressing our identities as individuals. The fifth is what we love and like to do. It is play and creativity. The eleventh is who we choose to join us and whose society we seek. It is our peers and their approval of us. It is the playground and self-expression which others choose.

Six and 12 are the "serve or suffer" package. Six is where we find out how to care for ourselves and others. Twelve is where we go for repairs, restructuring and rehabilitation. Six deals with all the services we perform for others or others perform for us, but twelve deals with failures and successes no one else may see but our selves. Tensions between houses are somewhat different when they are in square to each other.

Houses 1, 4, 7 and 10 form a natural framework for structuring our lives. These are similar to cardinal signs. It is not easy to fit into the houses which describe parental expectations and to find a partner who will eventually replace them as our primary relationship. Many difficulties can occur when people representing the 4/10 polarity dispute with the 1/7. On the other hand, the square shows the need the individual has to break free from 4 and reach for 10 while accommodating the needs of 7. It's no wonder teens struggle against parental control as they assume responsibilities they must carry as adults and that marital stress is one of the big problems of adult life when parents get their fingers in the pie. It also explains why tensions on the job can affect marriages and why stresses at home can undercut careers.

Houses 2, 5, 8 and 11 are about possessions and the value system. There are choices we all make about what we earn, what we save, the pleasures we seek and the people we choose as peers to share these things with. The wastrel, the miser and the troublemaker are those who have made bad choices. Finding constructive ways to balance these forces is part of learning to be human, too. These are fixed houses and attitudes formed in early life become exceedingly hard to change. Only the individual's own discomfort will lead to reform and then the reform is only as viable as the individual's own efforts to change.

Houses 3, 6, 9 and 12 tell about our ethics, our values and what we do about them. This is the true "wisdom" focus in life as we form the abstract concepts which will rule so much of our behavior later on. These are the "mutable" houses and we tinker and modify them constantly through life. We continually take in new information, which can alter our philosophies and lead to new ways of service to others or new decisions to amend our direction.

Houses that form the natural trines in the chart can be the links to show where we can smooth the path of our progress. These are the earth, air, fire and water complexes. One, 5 and 9 are about our persona and what it finds most congenial in terms of self-expression and self-definition. Houses 2, 6 and 10 are about the work we choose in life and where that takes us. It helps us understand the elements of satisfaction and our place in the work world. Houses 3, 7 and 11 tell about the ways we deal with people, what we say, who we choose to say it to and the relationships that are pure choices, not inborn. 4, 8 and 12 are the emotional side of the self as well as the things that lie closest to the heart and those that are the most private.

Examining the houses from such perspectives as these will lead to new insights for the astrologer. They can be very fruitful material to share with clients and those learning about their own charts and their own psyches.

It is often more helpful to lay the chart on the table and talk about what "it says" than to speak to someone directly about their problems. The chart can provide a marvelous element of detachment which helps in the process of insight.

handwritten notes: 1st house – weak/strength in body parts.
handwritten notes: – Virgo – health/work – cancer – family – Libra – proportioned risn

Doorway to Life
House One

Life officially starts with the first breath, which provides enough oxygen for our opening salutation to the world. It's usually an angry cry, typical of Aries, which has a kind of correspondence with the first "house" in the traditional natural zodiac because both deal with the start of things. We even come out head first (as a rule) and Aries rules the head. Some babies do not and that seems to mark them as cantankerous from the start.

It isn't easy to be born. The mother's work is called "labor" for a reason. It is accompanied by blood, sweat and pain, sometimes for the child, always for the mother. But life demands the expenditure of effort. The determination to survive and thrive is a first-house concept. Life is indomitable simply because it knows no other way to be.

The first house deals with whatever it takes to get things underway. In a way, it is the Big Bang of each life and each action in life. It symbolizes the cracking open of a seed, the first letter on the page.

This is the doorway each of us has into the life we will lead and it is shaped to fit us specifically. An individual's birth pattern vibrates to the tune of all the energies at play in the world at that particular moment but especially to those on the eastern horizon which form the ascendant and first house. We are like records being grooved with the imprint of the hour.

The first house is a description of the body, its type, general appearance, health, assets and liabilities. It is also personal interests in life and actions we take to suit ourselves. It is the start of that road map for the life ahead, describing the way in which the individual is apt to initiate activity and what type of activity that will be. It even points to the arena in which we will act. Those who were born with Virgo there will focus on health and/or work issues. Those with Cancer have an assignment in the family circle and so on.

The house talks about the parts of the body that will be strong or weak and the ruler's condition tells us precisely what those are and how strong or how weak and in what way. Libra rising usually gives a pleasing, well-proportioned body. Never mind that it won't fit the standard clothing sizes off the rack, or that the legs are too short or the arms too long. The beholder sees the body as "just right." Perhaps Venus gives the illusion but everyone else agrees to it.

The first sign of the Zodiac, Aries, particularly has dominion over the head, the face, the eyes, the brain, the mouth, tongue and jaw. It deals with the senses of vision and taste. However, the "taste" that is meant is not that which is affected by smell (which comes under the second sign, Taurus) but the simpler recognition of whether things are hot or cold, salt or sweet, bitter or sour, wet or dry.

While the house deals with the entire body as a package, when analyzing health matters one often finds that paying particular attention to the head or face is quite helpful. Almost any planet in the first will show a scar or injury of some sort at a particular age, but Mars rising is sure to mark the face. It's one of the dead giveaways to the rising degree. An opposition or square will likely do just as well, of course.

Everything that threatens or benefits the body or affects it in any way will show here. All illnesses, surgery, accidents or physical modifications by diet or exercise have a relationship to the house, and the degree of the ascendant itself. The Ascendant is the single most "personal" point in the chart. It is the "me" point.

Natal afflictions or good aspects to the ruler or planets in the first house affect our ability to act in our world. They tell how much strength we have to be useful. They show whether we like to move fast or slow, quietly or loudly, clumsily or skillfully.

The first house is our outer persona, as people see it and as we see ourselves. When we look in a mirror, it is what we expect to view. That persona is built of mannerisms, choice of clothing, the way we comb our hair and its length or color. It is the jewelry we wear, our most habitual facial expression and the sheer physical presence we project. It is our coloration or even—sometimes—our camouflage. It can attract or repel. It can be designed to intimidate or be easily forgotten. People with Pisces here can often be like chameleons, changing their image and attire to suit the situation.

The Ascendant is like the first impression made by the guest who walks in the door for a cocktail party. When he or she appears, others react to what they see and the individual's assimilation into the group begins. After a drink or two, the individual relaxes and deeper qualities—those of the natal moon sign—usually begin to show. If drinking progresses to the "drunken" stage, the most profound characteristics (the sun sign qualities) emerge as all but the core falls away.

You may notice that fire signs rising walk right in, shake hands, introduce themselves and circulate while water sign rising types approach much more quietly, often preferring to look around at who's there before committing themselves to action. Air signs just launch right into whatever conversations are happening but earth takes its time, looks for friends and inspects the refreshments first.

If you ever attend a boring cocktail party where there's no one interesting to talk to, watch this happen a few times and you'll learn a great deal. There is an onion-like quality to all human beings, layers upon layers, which reveal themselves only in stages.

The first house is the simplest, most superficial layer. In all other arenas of life we are part of the universe of others and must bend or modify our behavior to accommodate them. Only in the first house are we free of such necessity. No one else can make us other than we are. When we choose to act on our own behalf in any way, whether it is getting out of bed in the morning or going for a walk in the evening, the unique quality of self determination is at work and that comes from the first house. Whatever hurts or helps the body comes here, too. Injuries, surgeries and illnesses always involve it. The stronger and better fortified the ruler is, the healthier and tougher the individual proves to be.

Some signs are better here than others. Cancer is weak in childhood but strong in old age. Pisces tends to attract health problems from the start. Count on it. Scorpio can be remarkably tough but die young because it overdoes everything and refuses to accept limitations. A little common sense does wonders for longevity. All three can fight weight battles.

The fire signs (Aries, Leo and Sagittarius) give more physical vitality and an impetuous nature. They will attract injury readily because they are so active. They do best when young unless they continue regular physical activity and then can remain vital for long years. Inactivity is deadly for them.

The air signs (Gemini, Libra and Aquarius) tend to seek out other people and adopt physical activity only as a means to that end. They like exercise as a group activity for the social value and aren't particularly keen on sweat for its own sake. Gemini can run on its nerves and Libra needs heavy doses of rest to balance outgo. Aquarius often just moves slowly and assumes it will get wherever it needs to eventually.

Earth signs rising are stable and tough and quietly go about their own agendas regardless of what others do. They are physically strong and usually sturdier than they appear to be. This is especially true of Taurus. Capricorn has a wiry resilience into the 90s and Virgo tinkers endlessly to keep itself healthy, usually outliving everyone else anyway.

The sign on the Ascendant shows where the weak areas of the body are. In Capricorn the knees, the bones and skin suffer. Sometimes the teeth, too. Aquarius has weak ankles and a tricky nervous or circulatory system. Aries gets sinus trouble, eye problems and migraines. Taurus must watch the neck, and throat. In the old days before iodized salt they warned of goiter, but the thyroid is still vulnerable today. It's just less likely to produce a goiter.

Leo can develop heart or back ailments. Cancer has trouble in the stomach or breast and Sagittarius will have a hip ailment or liver problems. Gemini should never smoke—the lungs will suffer, but difficulties with the fingers and arms or even collarbones can also show up. Look to Pisces for foot malformations, hormonal difficulties and vulnerability to a wide range of chronic complaints. Since it's on the polarity with Virgo you will also find allergies to everything from strawberries to cats and lung complaints.

Libra can exhaust itself readily and the kidneys are vulnerable. Scorpio can develop bowel or bladder problems, hemorrhoids and problems with the sexual organs, the prostate and ovaries. Virgo deals with allergies and sensitivities of all kinds. Cancer seems weak as a child and tough in old age.

Anything that modifies the appearance of the body has reference to the first house and the Ascendant degree. A face lift, liposuction or a tattoo are all first house changes, and most often involve Mars tools (surgery, knives and needles) to accomplish. Other changes might be hair transplants, toupees or dyeing, contact lenses or eye surgeries, breast reduction or augmentation and much more. It takes good aspects by progression or transit at the time to the first house ruler, planet or ascendant for these things to be satisfactory.

Major planets that transit the first house often prompt people to plan such changes in their bodies or their lives. Pluto, for instance, can spark major weight loss through diet or stomach stapling as well as some other type of complete makeover. It rarely passes without some important change in the appearance. Sometimes that's merely in the wardrobe, but something will surely alter.

Uranus crossing the Ascendant is apt to produce a restlessness that can lead one to pull up stakes and move a few thousand miles away. Because the first house is on the axis with the seventh house which deals with moving, this happens more often than one would think. Sometimes other types of impulsiveness arise and one should be careful of urges that can leave one high and dry, poorer and without the object or situation one desired.

Neptune can be a dangerous transit of the Ascendant since it leads into La-la land where decision making is less than reliable and illusion abounds. It sometimes marks a period of heavy drinking or drug experimentation. It's not a good time to run off with one's lover because when it's over, life returns with a thud, leaving gray hair and fresh worry lines behind. On the plus side, it's a wonderful time to take up a musical instrument, write romantic poetry and go on a cruise. Sometimes all three at the same time.

Saturn is not a happy transit of the first house. About all it's good for is weight loss and then one needs to be careful or the weight loss comes from ill health. Take vitamins and nap more often. Avoid overdoing or the ramifications can be severe. Heavy tasks are often assumed during the transit and may not end until the transit is over.

Jupiter is a happier influence when it crosses the ascendant into the first house. One hunts up parties and more recreation—often sports as well—and one can gain weight or add muscle from the physical improvement. It's a real blessing if it happens at a time when there has been ill health or accident and leads to good recovery and a return to health.

In any case, the Ascendant and the first house lead to all the adventures of life. Life does not promise us an endless number of options from which to select, of course. But within those limitations we can say yes or no. The "I" that begins is the one we keep for a lifetime

Doorway to Values
House Two

[handwritten margin notes: value system about external world. ranking system. desires → possession. "money" — self respect. self & Identity. "mine". earning]

As soon as we are born we seek what belongs to us, what resonates to our sense of self and our individual identity. The belonging and the seeking after those "things" are the job of the second house. Almost the first external things that a baby begins to recognize as belonging to itself are its own hands and feet. The child notices them waving in the air. It begins to play with them. It soon discovers these things are "mine." If you have never watched a baby bite down on its own fist or foot for the first time, you have missed one of life's great experiences. Good thing they don't have teeth yet.

One of the most critically important words we all need in our vocabulary is "mine." It illuminates the second house quite well. This notion of possession is born at such an early age that it makes one wonder about social concepts which attempt to deprive the individual of material goods of one's own in favor of a share of collective property. It is like telling people not to eat their own food but only "collective" food. It seems to violate common sense and all human experience.

The second house is where we develop a value system about the external world. We learn to rank things by their importance to us. We learn about the function of desire. Acquisition in life comes when we reach out for something. Anything. First we must want that something. We must see it as a good thing for us to have. Only then do we reach for it.

So first comes desire and then the effort of attainment and finally, possession. All these elements belong to the second house. Venus is the planet that rules Taurus, the second sign of the zodiac which in a way resonates to the second house in the chart, though they are not the same. Venus is the planet of things that are desired because they are considered either beautiful, comfortable or harmonious or have some intrinsic worth for us. Once we get them, we experience satisfaction. A Venus word. Thus, every single thing we have in life that isn't nailed down or too heavy to carry (real estate and cars cover that category pretty well) comes generally under the second house of possessions. This is an important concept in natal or horary work.

This house deals with the amount of money you make and all the things you have as the result of your own labor: money, prizes, awards, bonuses, all of it. It is the cash in your pocket, the savings in the cookie jar, your checkbook, your net worth and your jewelry. It's your wardrobe, your furniture, your spoons and forks and the food in the refrigerator. It's your high school yearbook, the photos of grandma and the old letters in the back of your drawer. In short, it is anything you have bought or keep or value.

The second house is the premier zone of money, of course, or the things used for

Bad - Desires in Life
Confuse love's money

currency or as a medium of exchange. In addition to all the material things of life, the second house tells us about whatever intangibles that we value. Some astrologers use this house to understand how the individual values himself or herself because it is also the house of abstract worth. It's not the house that rules the development or acquiring of such ideas, but rather whether or not they are to be considered important enough to seek.

It is what we can earn that gives many of us that intangible thing, a sense of self respect and which proves to us that we are important. We may express that by purchasing things of beauty and comfort that make us happy about our success. Money, which is both that measure and our medium of exchange, is thus how much we get or have, how we spend it and what we spend it on and why.

Many people get muddled up about the key desires of life—love and money—and confuse them. When people confuse immaterial love with material things, they can develop a frantic need to acquire possessions as a substitute for love. They think people "love" them more if people give them increasingly expensive "things." This may occur when there is too much stress in other areas of the chart, but particularly from the other succeedent houses.

A healthy person knows that love is not the getting of things but rather the giving of self. Children who are well loved grow up understanding that love has no material measurement

This is not so for those who come from cold or unloving homes. Their hungers for love have become perverted, measured by the yardstick of material goods. They develop a greed for things that may consume them. This is one of the lessons that some people take a lifetime to learn, but others know from the cradle. — Dad !

There are two money houses in the natal chart, the 2nd and the 8th. Anyone who has stress in their 2nd or 8th houses should be very careful about credit use. If progressions set that off you can be in a pickle faster than you expect. The 2nd house is money you earn or have and the 8th is money you borrow. It's important to understand the difference in the two houses.

The sign on the cusp of the second house in your personal chart gives a clue to how you see value in life and the aspects to the ruler of that house give added information. A person with Capricorn there is going to value security, for instance, and some of Capricorn's cautious, thrifty nature will be evident in the choices of how to earn it or what to spend one's resources on to get it. There will be a regard for old things with family tradition, or antiques, perhaps. The person will want to get full value if they trade cash for any purpose. They will spend readily for high quality but not a cent more than necessary to get it. They like bargains. They also like to invest for the future, buying quality that will last beyond the expected duration.

If Capricorn's ruler Saturn is well aspected in the chart, money can be seen as a trust to be spent wisely for the good of all: family or the community. Old age often finds such people secure and comfortable and they will probably leave a goodly amount behind when they go. If Saturn is poorly aspected, the individual may have to learn to overcome selfishness and a tendency to hoard possessions out of fear that there won't be enough to provide for their own needs, let alone those of others. They will be highly reluctant to give anything to anyone.

Where Saturn is you will find the vocations and the work chosen in order to earn resources, if Capricorn rules this house. It will also tell you what is the top spending priority. Saturn in House 5? The children, obviously. Or vacations and pleasures if there are no children. Saturn in 8? Investment, savings and insurance will get the first dollars of every paycheck. Saturn in House 4? Fixing the house or buying property. And so on.

Now if it were Cancer on the cusp of the 2nd house, Moon would become the significator of this house of desire and possession, telling you about the earning power and something about the career choices. Moon is a more restless ruler than Saturn, showing many ups and downs in life. It is cyclic in nature. Money comes and goes and if the moon is poorly aspected, it can truly be a feast-or-famine life style. It points to a need for domestic comfort, and spending on items for the home and family—or even food— as a top priority. Perhaps a career choice that provides the income would involve real estate sales, cooking, or hotel management. But often they are just as apt to be self-employed, whether as professionals or as salesman whose earnings depend on how much they sell each week.

Whenever someone has asked me about selling real estate as a choice of occupation I look carefully to see if they like or can tolerate the "feast or famine" approach to income. Most of us like our income to arrive on schedule in an amount we can plan for. But real estate sales is one of the jobs that does not provide that. Money arrives at very irregular intervals and the size of the checks can vary dramatically. Not all of us can live on the edge that way. For many people, a job with regular paydays is preferable to one with fewer paydays but bigger checks.

Perhaps the person chooses to work for a firm that sells furniture for the home or one that builds ships or cans fish. Or perhaps it has to do with the affairs of women, such as child bearing or care of the young. All such work comes under the moon. To find out, look at the natal moon, its sign, house and aspects.

That individual may even copy dear old mom and her ways with money. If the native's moon is well aspected, he or she saves for the rainy day and will always have a dollar stored in some cookie jar or other. Poorly aspected? Money slips through the fingers like water and a lot can be spent on "liquid refreshment" if there is any Neptunian problem.

Each sign has its own unique coloration to apply to the business of values and possessions when it occupies the second house. The second house shows priorities in life. If you aren't sure what yours are, take a good look at that second house and you'll see. Each sign of the zodiac has its own portfolio of interests and importance and when it occupies the second house, colors the entire matter of finances and asset values. There is a vast difference between careful Virgo or enthusiastic Aries there.

Never underestimate the power of Mars to "burn a hole" in one's pocket. A Mars ruled sign on House 2 is a very good warning to watch the spending and the impulsiveness on gifts. A little planning is a big help. Mars actually in the house is a dire warning to learn the lessons of budgeting. In a very broad, general sense, fire signs on the second are usually freer, more "easy come, easy go" in their attitudes toward possessions than are the earth signs, which have an acquisitive, practical streak. The water signs are more emotional about all such matters and their actions can be easily swayed by the mood of the moment. They will often give a lot of money or possessions to others when their emotions are touched. After all, the house that rules "getting" also rules "giving." Air signs approach this house of possessions with detached, logical decisions, making budgets and plans before money is spent. (They may not follow the plan, but they have one.) They decide in advance how much their gifting should cost, for instance. Then they stick to it.

Now obviously all this can be modified by the individual pattern. Always remember my first law of astrology: Everything modifies everything else.

The sense of satisfaction and pleasure in life is the dominion of the planet Venus, a study of Venus in any chart will help you grasp whether the individual requires a great deal in order to find satisfaction in life, or whether small things will provide contentment. Many people with Venus in Taurus find a beautiful landscape they can see every day of far greater satisfaction than an expensive picture of one, for instance.

People with Venus in Leo may value their own identity and physical appearance or the welfare of their children above mere mundane possessions unless those are things which enhance their status or attractiveness. They could sink a lot of dollars into the kids' orthodontia and never notice the house needs painting, for instance.

As it is the house of getting, the second is also the house of giving, and the nature and quality of the gifts we choose are ruled by this house. The world is full of selfish people who never give anything away. They are the first to tell you how nobody gives them—or ever gave them—anything. Such people will have charts showing cramped and grasping second houses, with perhaps a severely afflicted parental axis. These things always come out of the childhood and show how selfishness is a behavior linked to stunted emotional development, mostly defensive as part of an attempt to shore up a fearful lack of self approval or insecurity.

But the world is also blessed with those who share their resources readily with others and who never seem to lack what they need. Such people have a more idealistic second house and many find true pleasure in giving. And of course, the universe seems to send more resources through their hands for wider distribution.

It also shows what you like to donate and to whom, what you like to give and how you want to share what you have. The ruler of money in the third house? Maybe you support ecological and environmental groups. You love to swap a good book or you like finding someone who wants to read the same magazine you just finished so it isn't "wasted."

In the ninth house, you would want to donate money to your college or your church. If Scorpio rules 2, maybe you prefer to save the giving until you're gone and don't need the money anymore. Some insecure people think that's a way to compensate for a lifetime of stinginess. ("I put it in my will, didn't I?")Those are the same people who put strings on their giving so as to still keep a hand on their former possessions, whether it's a family portrait or an antique bowl.

Nothing in any birth chart stands alone and each house must be examined in its turn in order to see the picture of how the individual is put together. The needs of the second house are the things in life which are of greatest value to the individual. It's interesting to see an air sign on this house. These are indications that human relationships are more important than money and nothing pleases more than a gift that brings a hug or a smile of pleasure. Income can be through sales or communication or anything that is a direct cause of interaction between people.

There is a further consideration for this house, however, that has nothing to do with things, but everything to do with events. This is the first house after the rising sign and represents the immediate future in all mundane and horary charts. Individuals born with malefics in the 2nd house have problems from day one. All charts with malefics in 2 show trouble "coming up" in life and events that must be dealt with before progress can continue. This can also extend into House 3. The reverse of course, is also true. Those with benefics in the third house see the immediate future as beneficial one where opportunities abound. These people are quick to believe that the world is their oyster. Their childhood showed them a happy face.

Because resources of all kinds are always brought to the fore to deal with problems or opportunities, it is more than appropriate that the second house should tell us how we handle these things. Often we must spend in order to get. Or we must have before we can invest, or take a chance on the future. Sometimes the resource in demand is our time or energy. These things are also our "possessions" in a way. Thus, a careful astrologer can ascertain why an individual fails or succeeds when challenges come. It is always an education to deal with the second house.

Doorway to the Neighborhood
House Three

It's always a good idea to know where you are, what's around you, who's on either side of you and who watches your back. That's the third house. It is the house of siblings, brothers and sisters, and those who occupy the neighborhood in which you find yourself, whether that be rural or urban, psychological or actual, campus or playground. In short, it is your environment. In order to deal with your surroundings, you need to communicate and this is the house of communication. Here is where you find the elements of speech, gossip, plain talk, letters, notes, signs, phone calls, radio broadcasts, want ads and the amassing of information of all kinds. It is not the house that sorts it all out—merely the house where it is gathered.

The gathering process is part of education. We must see, hear, feel and observe. The basic tools of reading, writing, and arithmetic that enable us to acquire knowledge also come under its auspices. The third house deals with all the tools of communication and learning, the pencils, paper, road maps, magazines, newspapers, and cell phones. It deals with the stop sign at the end of the street and the crossing guard who sees that children get across the street to school. In fact, House 3 deals with the street itself and the sidewalks, as well as all pathways that lead us from one place to the other, whether a hike through the woods or an alley to the parking garage. Its purview includes hallways, corridors, tunnels and aisles. This is how we "communicate" in the spatial sense.

The people of our immediate surroundings begin in the family circle with our siblings. This is where we learn the arts of communication. These are the people from whom we learn. Brothers and sisters are, in some ways, the most important people in our lives. Sibling relationships are lifelong. Parents often die before the end of our middle age, our spouses and children do not arrive until we are well into adulthood and friends come and go during a lifetime. But a brother or sister is practically forever. When we reach old age, often the only people who have known us through all the stages of our lives, the ones who remember us as kids, laughed with us as teens and have watched us become adults, are our brothers and sisters. Good relationships with siblings are among the most comforting and enduring achievements of life.

We do not stop communicating just because we grow up. House 3 is the house of knowledge and the enduring action by which we acquire it all our lives. It is the door to that part of our experience where we learn and share what we know. In some charts, the third house is simply gossip—in others, it communicates information of value—but in all cases, the third relates to that sharing. Some people are reluctant to share what they know. They may see knowledge as somehow proprietary and finite in quantity, fearing that if they give it away, they will have nothing left. Or they see it as a prop to their ego and somehow "theirs."

These are people hesitant to share a pickle recipe or tell you how they put such a nice finish on the chest they painted for the kids' bedroom. They don't want to lose the information race. The rest of us, of course, didn't know there was one. There is a great deal of difference between keeping a business secret quiet and not being able to talk to people about your life or your opinions because you want to keep it all "secret." Some people are so fearful of knowledge, seeing it as a threat to their world view, that they refuse to listen to ideas that do not conform to their own. Somewhere along the line their third house got badly mishandled.

The third house relates to Gemini, an air sign. Air that is kept locked up soon becomes stuffy, bad smelling and unpleasant. Only when the house gets fresh air at regular intervals is it a comfortable environment. The same is true of ideas. They must come into our lives freely and abundantly for us to choose from. Only truth can survive the buffeting of every random breeze and prove that an idea is of value, because it has proven its worth. We talk about what we think, we challenge what others think, we gather, we listen and sometimes we share. It is only in this way that we begin to form a relationship with the world around us.

The rulers of this house and any planets in it and their condition tell us about the quality of mind and how it works. Nothing in the chart will tell us WHAT we think about, but it will tell us HOW we think. Are we logical or intuitive? Do we get information from people or books most easily? And how do we learn?

Because the third house is one of the cadent houses, it relates to the entire mutable cross of signs, those the astrologers of old called the road to wisdom. Before we can become wise, we must first become knowledgeable. This is the task of the third house of the chart. And in order to become knowledgeable, there must be education. Basic education is here—whether it is the traditional reading, writing and arithmetic or how to thread a worm on a fishhook and clean the catch. There is all sorts of "basic" information for lots of things in life. Watch a toddler learn to tie a shoe. That's basic information for life unless you plan to wear slippers the rest of your days.

The third house also tells us what types of environment we will seek out to broaden that knowledge. Where do we best function? Some of us are urban animals and cannot imagine life without a sidewalk where the kids can play. Still others want a world with few neighbors, the potential for wildlife about and plenty of trees and farm land. Some people give the natural environment a higher priority than others. They may join groups or organizations which try to protect the very planet itself and its health. Still others look about them and see trees and wonder if there's any money in that old hickory in the corner. A third group would just as soon cut them down and build a really good shopping mall.

Whenever life runs into problems with neighbors or siblings or those with whom we have contact in our day-to-day lives, House 3 is the house to examine. It is also the house that determines how well our vehicles and tools of communication function. Vehicles, after all, are how we communicate with places—we get there from somewhere and the car, the bus, the train or the airplane is the medium of transport. It tells us what we like in the way of transportation. Even the color of your car is there. Aries on 3? Bet you've bought a red car sometime in life. Or wanted to.

This house also tells how well—or how poorly—we may function linked to iPods or cell phones and other forms of instant contact with others. Some like it. Some find it burdensome. In modern times the internet has become a kind of instant communication system and personal computers hook us up. All of these are part of the 3rd house of communication. But in all cases, the type of response we make to the needs of communicating with others is determined by the third house. The very means of speech come under the third house, as the lungs which give breath. It is our first and most enduring pathway out of self-preoccupation and into the world of other people and information.

Doorway to Home
House Four

The place of safety and security, love and approval, is always a place called home. If we are lucky, it is where we were born and raised. The childhood we get is described by that fourth house. If we came from people who were secure and who had a sense of family and of identity we grow up with those blessings. And if so, we are truly blessed, because not everyone gets them.

House 4 is the entire past of our family identity, in a way. It is the kind of family we are born into, its ability to support us and provide for our needs and the lineage we inherited. It is all the traditions left to us by those who lived before and the accumulated status of our ancestry. It also describes the father, who is the source of early stability and financial security, or the mother who provides the first and most important nurturing. Many say this is the house of the mother, but older traditions give it to the father.

There is some disagreement on this point and frankly, some charts obviously put the father in the 10th house, as the dominant authority figure. Other charts plainly say this is the house of the mother. But I have found that many reflect the father's fundamental contribution as the source of the home, the person who provides the family "name" and whose strength keeps the wolf from the door. In such cases, activity in the fourth house shows the father.

Since the fourth also refers to real estate—the ground on which we stand and on which our homes are built, which usually comes under the fathering agenda—the whole thing can be a bit confusing. My advice is to use it for the father. If that doesn't work, shift to the mother. How's that for waffling?

A well-known astrologer, the late Annie Hershey of Akron and I used to debate this issue regularly. She maintained the 4th should be used for the mother. I had my doubts then and now. I suspect any professional astrologer with extensive experience may admit that many charts simply refer to the father in House 4. Several ancient writers gave the 10th to the mother. I think the majority of people have 10 as mother and 4 as father. Maybe it's like being right handed—most of us are. But there are still lefties in the world. They're just in the minority.

But then, perhaps the key to this issue lies elsewhere in life. In happy families, the parents operate like a tennis match, first one carries the ball and then the other. Sometimes the mother has to lay down the ultimate law and sometimes the father does the cooking. In today's world the roles can get even less sharply defined. Both parents may act together—or, alternately to provide the child's sense of security. For some people, it is the maternal heritage that is the richer and stronger. In other families, it is the father's. And, sometimes it's hard to tell which is which. In any case, this is a house that deals with parenting and how well it is done. In unhappy families, the most stable and loving parent, the "anchor" of the life, is always the fourth.

This business of parenting is so crucial to our lives that it is hard to overestimate its importance. Relationships with each of the parents determines how we "see" those of the same sex in life. While this is sharply affected by the rulers of the house as well as the Sun and Moon, the fact remains that this house is the learning arena for all of us.

If someone asked me before I was born which I would prefer, a happy secure childhood and a troubled adulthood or an insecure, difficult childhood combined with a happy adulthood I would unhesitatingly take the first. Build a solid base in your early days and you can withstand a great many of the blows of life. You can prosper despite it all and contribute greatly to the world. Inner peace comes readily. But to grow up doubting your security, never being sure who you are or where you came from, or even worse yet, to have a violent or seriously malfunctioning home in childhood can spoil all of life thereafter. The struggle then becomes simply for wholeness, some sense of peace and place. A deeply troubled fourth house is always part of the picture where you are examining the charts of people who trouble society at large.

In every chart I have ever done over a long lifetime I would say that the one thing that causes more problems than anything else is the simple lack of love in early life. Children can endure many things surprisingly well. They can have parents who never hug them or tell them they are special. They can live in squalor and under harsh discipline. They can do without many of life's necessities. But they must—absolutely must—have one single thing, and that one thing is love. The knowledge that one is unique and deeply loved as an individual and moreover, that one can trust the parents to do their best for one is simply irreplaceable. Love is the ultimate security which the parents provide and that is the core of the contributions of the fourth house.

If the 10th house is where we are going in life, the 4th is the rock on which we stand to reach for it. The kind of homes we make for ourselves as adults, the places we choose and how we furnish them are all part of House 4. Cardinal sign people like to buy homes that stand out in some way, where mutable signs may prefer condos or apartments. Fixed signs like property they own which has clear boundaries, and many are suckers for fences. Air people want close associations with others, but earth people want to make sure it keeps its financial value.

There is more to the 4th house which one can use in practical matters, of course. Mars there can point to fire in the home at some point, for instance. It's always good to pay attention to a malefic there. Taking steps to make sure fire alarms are always working is one action one can take to mitigate the trouble. But Mars in House 4 can also show that there was a lot of arguing and fighting in one's childhood and can help one understand why peace in the home was difficult to accomplish. Moreover, this house explains the broader pattern of family relationships as a whole, aunts, uncles and grandparents included. It is our beginnings and our endings, so can deal with family trees and the love of genealogy or the type of grave we end up in.

People who invest in real estate often have a very active fourth house—sometimes with Fortuna there—and any improvements to the residence one has show instantly in aspects to the 4th. Like any of the angular houses, it has a powerfully determining effect on our lives and well repays careful study.

If the ruler of either house 10 or 4 is in the 4th, at some point that parent becomes the dominant or sole parent, in charge of the rearing of the child. Not every child raised by a single parent has the aspect, but those that do seem to be more "marked" by it in some way.

The 4th is both the beginning and end of life and while it is where we are buried, it's not necessarily how we die. The manner of death is the 8th house. The fourth house is also our "roots" and where we come from. Neptune there is often the mark of the adopted child, or the child with an alcoholic parent or a seriously disabled one. In old age, Neptune in 4 can indicate a nursing home or nursing in the home or extended disability. It can also show a flood in the home at some point during the life. Some of this can also come from Pisces on that house. Family upheavals always seem to involve both the 4th and 10th houses. For one thing, the two houses are each the 7th house partner for the other person, showing both parents' involvement.

There is a saying in the U.S. that "if Mama ain't happy ain't nobody happy," which reflects 4th house distress when the 10th is "unhappy." And vice versa. It is also noteworthy that when the 10th is disturbed in the individual's life, say for a layoff or a new job—the 4th is usually affected. Either a move comes, or family life suffers from the new responsibility or the lack of a job. These two houses are so naturally interconnected it is sometimes difficult to separate them.

The old rules on drowning involve a water sign on the 8th (which, by the way, may also put a water sign on 4—but not necessarily) and perhaps a water ruler—such as Jupiter in Cancer with Pisces on the cusp, or Moon in Pisces with a Scorpio 8th. Pluto in 8 is said to sometimes indicate death as the result of a major disaster, so I should love to see charts of all the people who went down with the Titanic, for instance. Obviously they were "buried" in water as well as dying from drowning. Maybe a lot of them had Neptune in 4 or 8.

Odd to think of, but John Kennedy Jr.'s body was found after an intense rescue search in a downed plane in the water and then later reburied at sea. I know this is a crass thought, but at the time I wondered what the point was of all that. They spent all that money to take his body OUT of the water and then spent more money to put it BACK in the water. Anyway, Neptune in House 4 has a lot of meanings, but I don't think drowning is one of them.

In examining the 4th cusp and contents it might be worth noting that in addition to the standard end of life ideas, sex is another topic worth a little study. There is a French term, *le petite mort*, known as the little death, which refers to the sexual act.

It isn't much of a mental stretch to see how that introduction to adulthood has an effect on the foundation of identity. Sometimes there is even a change of demeanor in youth after the first sexual experience.

Reading the 4th as the 12th or the 5th one can dissect the sexual impulse. Every house in a sense has a 12th house relationship to the next one. The 5th is the open expression and result of the hidden 4th desire. And if one doesn't take the interpretations too far, it can be a useful thing to keep in mind.

Doorway to Pleasure
House Five

There is a simple rule to the fifth house. It goes something like this, "Be what you are and be that perfectly." That's all there is to it. You have to be who you are. This is the house of love and laughter. It's all the things we do with our hearts and our joy in the art of living.

It's amazing how many different ways people express their individuality and their sense of identity. The fifth house is a very inclusive business, though. It covers everything from sports to spas, children to sculpture, vacations and romance, to all sorts of private interests, hobbies and leisure activity. It is the house of what we "want" to do as opposed to what we "must" do. True, some loves assume the size of "musts" in our lives, and often they are among the creative arts or our children.

Somebody has said that we always find room in our lives for something we really want to do. No matter what that something is. Maybe it's reading a new book, trying on clothes, or listening to music. For those with youth and physical ability it's often sports and competitions of all kinds.

Personal adornment is one way of expressing individuality. Clothing fashions, jewelry and color choices change rapidly in the teen years until by the time one has passed through the adult years one has finally settled on a personal style. Not the creation of clothing, but the wearing of it and the choosing of it as a way of expressing our individuality belong to this house.

A hobby is a particular private interest. Some may pursue the esoteric and become experts in a Babylonian dialect, or a Hindu meditation technique. Other people buy a Harley and the requisite accessories and become biker types on the weekends. Some make jewelry, or play bridge or design quilts. There are those who spend every spare hour at garage sales and junk shops collecting antiques. Some learn to play the piano, or sing ballads. Anything we choose to do or pursue purely out of personal preference belongs to this house.

It is also (obviously) the house of romance. This is where we have fun. We court, we woo, we go dancing and walking in the moonlight. We give flowers and send cards and write notes. We hop into bed together for sexual activity. All 5th house activities. Some people marry late because there is a blockage in this area of their lives. They have to find success in other areas before they feel free enough to learn to play again and find a lover.

Some charts show the individual will spend a lot of time and money on leisure. Others will not. It's almost as if they know who they are and they have no need to put it on display, thank you very much.

And House 5 is preeminently the house of children. Children are the ultimate self-expression. Who has not heard the old comment that a son is a "chip off the old block." This is particularly true for men, who are often harder on their children than women, because they more clearly identify their children as expressions of their own ego. Women, in contrast, see their children as hard work. And, probably because so much of their energy and time is spent on them, they may be quicker to see them as individuals in their own right. But for women, too, a child's success or failure, particularly in the social areas, is a reflection of mom and how well she parented.

A focus in this house can often show a career choice. Coaching sports comes to mind. Horse or auto racing management. Artistic design or music. Teaching children, of course. Anything that helps others find joy and pleasure belongs to this house. Difficult planets in this area can cripple the time or the inclination for fun, or it can hamper the person who is seeking to grow and develop as a human being. No personality grows untended. All require nourishment. In addition to training, there must be pleasure or the training loses its effectiveness. There must be desire. There must be a personal stake in the activity at hand. Without the 5th house of pleasure and its ability to teach us how to play and develop our personal creativity, we do not flourish.

House 5 is where we learn to value the quality of humor. A joke or a quip can ease the tension in the most dire situations and the ability to laugh at oneself is like the pressure valve on ego, keeping it from growing out of control. Clowns belong here, just as the circus does. The stage, the theater, puppet shows and television programs are part of it. But it can also be parades and cheerleaders, drum majors and the tuba player in the band. Pinochle and poker are here, too, along with the checkerboard and balloons.

Anyone can bake a cake nowadays. There are mixes so easy that if you can read, you can cook. It wasn't always so. But the art of decorating the cake is very 5th house. A chef who loves to create ice sculptures or butter doves for the bread board may have explored the craft just for fun in high school. The career may have emerged later, sparked from an afternoon of pleasure and silliness with a friend. Sometimes older adults lose sight of the value of play and the wisdom of having fun. But this is when we explore our potential and try on the various hats of the world's careers. Something we might never have tried if it weren't part of a game in the beginning can turn out to be our life's work and our deepest pleasure.

Among the people who may belong in the 5th house is the first child of a man. In the derived house system this is his "chip off the old block" child. The second child belongs to house 7 and so on around the wheel as subsequent children arrive. While the 5th house in our charts rules all our children as a group, each specific child can be seen using the derived house system and for a woman, the 4th is her first. Her 2nd comes under the 6th house and so on around the wheel.

The 5th house will also show if there were abortions (intentional or otherwise) in the process of child bearing in a woman's chart. One of the malefics in that house can show an intentional abortion. An affliction to a 5th house planet by Mars can mean a Caesarean section.

Of course, some astrologers prefer what I call the "male model" using the 5th house in both parents to refer to the first child. However, the 4th house rulership for women is of considerable tradition. Obviously the work of many ancient astrologers was done for kings to ascertain heirs and women weren't kings and didn't rule. The older the texts that one reads the more one realizes how much astrology was aimed at the male chart.

The first house for all of us can signify, in addition to self, two grandparents in the derived house system. We don't call the first house a grandparent house, but it can be. So the 7th house can be a man's second child, his wife or the other two of his grandparents. Our charts contain tons of information we can get if we use this system. I've used it extensively for many, many years and I think most professional astrologers do. If you prefer to use what I think of as the male model using House 5 as the first child for both sexes, I won't argue with you. You have company. But like all information in astrology everyone should test it over and over again to see if it works. Most of us are pretty pragmatic about these things and we dump what doesn't fit.

When one is looking to see if a marriage will occur in the family, it is helpful to check the 11th house, which is the house of partnerships for our children. A malefic in the 5th house does not necessarily spoil romance, but it can delay finding an enduring love. If the 7th house is happy and the chart shows marriage likely, the 5th house malefic becomes less significant. It simply means a later marriage. It can, however, show the individual takes parenting extremely seriously. Sometimes it can produce a child with a special problem. There are many things that can be indicated.

Saturn in 5 can bring a great pleasure in hobbies in old age and Mars can as well, so the mere presence of a malefic is not going to ruin one's life.

No matter how life batters us the 5th house always shows us the way to find laughter and pleasure to keep us balanced. There's an old saying that the way to shrink trouble is to laugh at it and laughing at one's self is a good antidote to becoming a sour puss. The 5th house is a blessing.

Doorway to Comfort
House Six

The 6th is the house of "function." In order for our bodies to function, the equipment must be maintained at peak efficiency. It is the same rule that works for cars or washing machines. All the parts have to be oiled and moving properly. Health of the body is proper functioning. Efficient work is proper functioning on the job. Maintaining the equipment is a job (nursing, cleaning, dietary needs, repairs of all kinds, upkeep etc. etc.) or a cause or a commitment. Look at a good hardware store some time and you will see a 6th house heaven. All the smallest bits of equipment—nails and screws, for instance—are in their own little compartments where they can be found easily (increasing the efficiency of the buying and selling). In fact, a hardware store contains bits of pieces of a vast assortment of things that are needed by other things to be maintained or restored to proper function.

The human body also has bits and pieces and some have to be added and subtracted for efficiency. How about replacement joints? Removing unneeded appendixes or tonsils? Nurses and massage therapists and those who provide any service one needs, whether physical, mental, business or even social (dance instructors?) all come under House 6.

In the old days people saw small animals as also providing for one's needs. There were the chickens (eggs), the sheep (wool for clothing and carpets and blankets) dogs (herding the sheep), cats (keeping down the vermin) and other pets (emotional well-being, etc.). And information? Think phone books and catalogs and libraries where all the data is kept organized and accessible for use. When you think of House 6 as function, its ramifications fall neatly into place. Properly Virgoan, of course. The sixth sign Virgo is the sign which resonates to the 6th house.

Since the 6th house can be both co-workers or employees it can refer to them. It can also be pets, and often people with aging pets lose them under difficult 6th house aspects. Spiders and helpful insects in general come under the 6th house. Sometimes the symbol of honeybees is seen with Virgo in older texts.

At any rate, the ancient Greek legend of Arachne, who competed with Athena the goddess over weaving, was an important tale. The hard work of creating cloth was of serious importance in antiquity and the notion of a human competing with a goddess over the skill needed captured the imagination of that time. Athena, the warrior goddess, was believed to be the one who taught humans all the fiber arts of weaving, spinning, knitting, crocheting, tatting, lace making and sewing in the Greek tradition. She was in charge of all domestic skills. While machinery today has taken over the task of creating cloth and clothing, the 6th house still rules these things. This house is all the people and the services which maintain our life and our life style.

The spider (as proud Arachne became in the old tale) helps keep the house "clean" by catching and disposing of less pleasant insects. Any small creature with useful traits belongs here. The spider also spins a beautiful web. As a general rule for the creatures on earth, the big ones belong to House 12 and the small ones to House 6. The bites or stings of insects are a Mars/Mercury phenomenon, so the helpful insects like spiders belong to the 6th, while the poisonous creatures belong to the 12th.

House 6 is the long-accepted house of tenants, servants and those who provide for one's comfort. They can be temporary help, such as a yard boy who mows the lawn, or more permanent help, such as a housekeeper, or all those who nurse you when you're sick, repair the plumbing, clean the eaves and fix the furnace. In a broader arena such as the community, it is those who catch the evildoers, defend the community, put out fires and the keep the sewers functioning.

On a national level House 6 is the armed forces, navy, coast guard, army, air force and marines. All "service" people of any kind belong here. One good way to identify them is the uniform. Many 6th house type people wear one, or adopt one.

House 6 is also all the things that make one physically comfortable—like decent underwear, warm clothes in winter, shoes, boots, mittens, and bathing suits or shorts for summer—and people who make those things, like seamstresses, bootmakers and shoemakers. People who repair such things are also sixth house. Above all, House 6 is the house of health. Two medical houses in the chart, 6 and 8, work comfortably together. Eight is the house of surgery and the type of trauma the body must endure sometimes to continue to function. Six is particularly the house of preventive medicine, health spas and vitamins, medicines and the kind of care one person gives another in time of need. Many of those who have planets here are intensely interested in alternative healing methods.

The 6th house also has a strong relationship with the 12th, which is the house of correction. When health breaks down, one must go off to a place like a hospital or a nursing home until the problem is corrected. Or, if the home becomes the place of recovery, it is often a sort of temporary 12th house where we rest and recuperate after leaving the actual hospital. In the old days, it was customary to isolate people sick with communicable diseases and the home could be considered "off limits" and the person in "quarantine." We seldom do this anymore with rapid recovery effected by antibiotics.

People with more than one 6th house planet in their chart almost always have some major or persistent health problem to battle in life. Or it may involve a work issue or a job problem, sometimes directly affected by the health problem. Saturn in House 6 also can indicate remaining in a particular job position for life. Sometimes House 6 indicates the individual will be a landlord, since the 6th can refer to one's tenants. I have had clients with problems managing rental property who have malefics in 6 and I always counsel them to find better ways to invest for their retirement years. Rental property is not their friend.

Those with benefics in House 6 are apt to profit from rentals, of course. They tend to attract good tenants and if a planet in 6 is in a fixed sign, the tenants are apt to stay a long time. This is worth keeping in mind if a client wants to buy a vacation home which will be rented out part of the year. If the 6th house has too much stress on it, it shows that tenants can damage the property or prove to be less than profitable for an assortment of reasons.

Even temporary problems with tenants or the property can show here when progressions or transits stress the 6th. Sometimes it is repairs needed—such as a new refrigerator, or carpeting. This is also the time troubles show up on the job, particularly with a distressing co-worker. And, since it is the house of pets, people may have to bury their goldfish or their favorite cat. I have often had questions from people who have more than one pet regarding the longevity of an aging animal. Stress aspects usually indicate the loss of such a pet.

A word here about the pet issue. Some people in modern society carry the notion of pets to extremes and begin to talk about their dog as their "child." They may even begin to use the animal or animals as a substitute for children, referring to themselves as the animal's "mommy" or "daddy." This often happens to those with no children, and there are astrologers who think it means that therefore the 5th house should be used for pets. I disagree vehemently on that issue. No matter how an owner dotes on an animal, it is never a "child." It is a beloved animal. It requires care from the owner and provides companionship in return. Those are 6th house issues, not 5th house. It's important to keep one's head when dealing with the things a house rules and not to confuse them.

I once had a question about a "co-worker" from an astrology student who had a romantic relationship with the man in question. She said she was not getting information about the relationship from her 6th house. After I questioned her, I discovered that in her company all the workers were called "co-workers" together, but the truth of the matter was that the man was not her co-worker. He was actually her boss. When we clarified the fact that he had the power to hire and fire her, she realized she had to use the 10th house to get information on the relationship. If I stand in the garage and call myself a car, it does not mean I am a car. It simply means I am mistaken in the term I am using. This was her problem. It's the identical difficulty in calling one's pet "my baby." You can call your dog your baby all day long, but that doesn't make it human.

Doorway to the World
House Seven

Teeter-totters and Tootsie Rolls teach us quickly that the world is not a fair place unless we make it so. If you are the fat kid or the runt of the litter, the piece of playground equipment that allows two youngsters to take turns going up and down is off limits. Unless the two of you are of equal weight, you will never ride together. The fat kid is always at the bottom, the runt at the top. It takes ingenuity to figure out a way to "equalize" the weight on either side. The answer is easy, once you know how it works. The lightweight needs to be at the farthest point of one side. The heavier child has to move gradually toward the center on the other side until there is equilibrium and both children can have a turn going up or down. Balance has occurred.

The Tootsie Roll is another childhood lesson. One child has the candy, the other wants some. The child with the candy is not feeling generous. How, then, can the other get any? Again, ingenuity is required. The have-not can trade something the candy owner wants. Perhaps a purchase offer can work. With skill and persistence, the have-not obtains some Tootsie Roll. Or perhaps the child who wants some candy just cries, persuading the one who has it to feel sufficiently guilty or sympathetic enough to share. The art of negotiation has been born.

Both lessons involve other lessons. The teeter-totter is not just about equilibrium, but also about co-operation. One child will never be able to go up as far as the other so it will never be completely fair, but it will allow some degree of satisfaction. Compromise is inevitable. Learning to accept it is another important lesson. The Tootsie Roll teaches conciliation, the art of persuasion and trade. Both lessons involve convincing someone else to see things "your way." These lessons require use of the mind, an air function, and are the province of the seventh house, which has correspondence to Libra, the sign of the scales. To be successful, the individual must put aside emotion for the moment and concentrate on problem-solving.

But the seventh house is far more than just deal-making, although that is one of its primary functions. This house is the doorway to the rest of the world—those we haven't met and who are strange to us—and how we relate to them. It is the house of human relations in its broadest, most fundamental sense.

Take a piece of paper and a pencil. Draw a line horizontally across the page. Doesn't matter how long. Label the beginning "Me." Label the other end "You." This is what Carl Jung, the famous psychological thinker, called the fundamental "I-Thou" of all human relationships. We all occupy a unique "me" position in our worlds. There is only one "me" in it. Everyone else is a "you." Use that simple line as the Ascendant/Descendant line of the horoscope and it clearly defines the challenges and opportunities of the seventh house, where a single individual relates in the most direct way to every other single individual. Because House 7 stands in opposition to the house of Me, the seventh represents both a challenge and a desire. It is a doorway we must pass through to reach the world of people. It is both partnership and enmity at the same time, love and hate, peace and war.

In one sense, we are all competing with each other for what we want in life. Inherent in all relationships is an implicit antagonism, because both ends of the line exist at the same time and have different needs. On one end is the desire to satisfy self. On the other end is "the other person," who has different needs than we do and who is also seeking satisfaction.

The seventh house solution is through conciliation, cooperation and finally love, where one is capable of truly identifying with and being concerned about the welfare of the "you." The way in which we do that colors all of our relationships in life. And relationships can make us happy or unhappy.

People go through life with one of two attitudes: Push or Pull. Push is the Me approach of force, and willpower. Pull is the gentler approach of attraction and social approval. The seventh house tells which way each of us chooses and is a textbook on human relationships.

One of the first lessons infants learn (after learning to cry, of course) is a Venus technique, a smile, to please the person who feeds them. Another early lesson is the Venus one of courtesy. "Please" and "thank you" acknowledge our need of others and our awareness of their cooperation with us. It's a stage on the way to the development of relationship." And courtesy oils the way in dealings between people. From the lessons of the teeter totter and the candy bar we progress to all the other levels in which we function as we enter the world and find it filled with "others." We can't fight them all to gain everything for ourselves, no matter how much we want to.

One lesson children learn is "taking turns" in an attempt to defuse the competitive "push" instinct of "me" and learn to "make a deal" with the "you." If that doesn't work, another, less helpful idea, that of "getting even," may surface. It is the teeter-totter solution gone awry. The seventh house deals with that, too.

Because the seventh house deals with the whole world of "others" it is the house of public relations and image. If we are to be most successful in dealing with others we must make them want to help us/like us/love us/work with us. Others are most willing to do that when they feel some tie to us, or have some stake in our lives.

Public relations teaches us to put the best, most attractive "face" on self. It is the why behind the smile and the handshake as strangers who start out as "me" seek to reassure the "you" that they come in peace. The 7th is the house of image-makers, spin doctors and make up. It deals with dressing for success and dressing to attract as the Venus-ruled tools of attire and personal appeal come into play.

The closer the "you" gets to "me" the more apt we are to seek equilibrium or balance.

The more like "me" I think "you" are, the more likely I am to see your point of view and to feel I share it. Thus, public relations tries to point up similarities and/or positive feelings between people or people and abstract entities such as business companies and to create relationships that did not exist before. Whether we like the idea or not, we are all doing our own public relations every day. We learned the principles on the playground.

The seventh house is, in a way, the fat kid being moved closer to the center of the teeter totter to be more like "me." Don't forget the teeter totter. In life the weak must find a tool to deal with the strong. The fat must find a tool to balance the runt. The male must find a way to connect with the female. The haves and the have-nots must make a deal.

The more we see others as desirable, likable or having something we need/want/admire/love, the more willing we are to accommodate them. The more we reach out to them, the more they see desirable characteristics in us, the more they reach back in our direction. Prejudices of all kinds are failures of this vision that we are "like" others. When fears of various kinds occur it is often all to easy to see people as enemies. Certain classes of them become "those people" with whom we do not associate. It is one of the negative 7th house responses.

This is the house of love but also of simple courtesy. There will be many people in our lives we will not choose to love or even to become closer to. One of the ways we can deal with them is through courtesy and civility, which gives us time to decide if we want to intensify this relationship to friendship or pass on to other, deeper ones where we can find greater meaning. Lack of simple courtesy—the snub—has always been one of the ways we declare certain "you"s are not like us and we don't intend to be like them. Civility we can extend to all, love we tend to reserve for special people.

Love is an element everywhere in the chart, of course, and the seventh should not be confused with houses which deal with particular people in our lives, such as parents or brothers and sisters. The seventh is the house of ALL relationships generally. It is the house of partnership specifically.

The entire art of growing as a person involves the journey from "me" to "you" until it becomes an "us." And the seventh house deals with US. A most effective way to learn this is through partnership and this house governs every imaginable level of partnering, from sharing a sand box game in childhood to marriage. There can be informal partnerships to play a game of cards or highly structured ones, such as businesses form to create conglomerates. There can be permanent partners, as in marriage, or temporary ones, as in tennis. All call for some degree of acceptable behavior (Venus) and cooperation (Venus).

Achieving balance is not easy. When any relationship goes too far in one direction a reaction occurs: there is a swing back to the other. Nature itself seeks equilibrium. What goes up, must come down. The teeter totter again. But the seventh is a house of continual change and turmoil because nothing ever reaches perfect equilibrium. There are merely times when the imbalance is less, so there is some degree of satisfaction. No human relationship ever satisfies any of us completely. Like the famous song, we all feel we "can't get no satisfaction" with certain people. We must all settle for less than perfect, even with our most dearly loved. With effort, we get closer and closer to the ideal. With practice, we ignore the imperfections in those we love, or convince ourselves such imperfections serve to make them more lovable.

The seventh is the house of war and the house of peace. When two entities are in harmony, a seventh-house concept in which relative balance is on-going, there is peace. When the harmony has become too disturbed there can be an argument, a fight, a divorce between marriage partners, or war between nations. War and divorce are the failures of the seventh house and their penalties are found in the eighth house. So, too, are the rewards of seventh house success.

Human relationships are not easy for any of us to learn. It takes a lifetime of effort for most. The planet of time, responsibility and effort, Saturn, is exalted in Libra, the natural seventh sign of the Zodiac, which resonates here. Saturn says to all of us that we get what we give, we reap what we sow, we are responsible for how we treat others and they are responsible for how they treat us. We are all in thrall to each other.

In another sense, the seventh is the house of the stranger. Anyone who is not "me" is a stranger until he or she becomes known. Strangers who never relate to "me" may pass on, forever remaining strangers. One who will not make use of any Venus methods to contact others often remains alone in life, until the unhappiness of such a condition prompts them to try the Venus tools to build some relationship with others.

Those who refuse to use Venus methods may try the Mars tools of "me"—the "push" relationship—but merely create antagonism and make enemies. The seventh is the house of open enemies, those with whom our relationship attempts have failed. But even if all we wish to do is buy a piece of clothing or food, we must somehow form a relationship with someone who has what we want.

Buyers and sellers come under the seventh house. Which is which in a particular situation depends on who initiates the action. The initiator of the action is always represented by the first house, leaving the seventh for the one who makes the response. This is important to keep in mind when you are making a major purchase, such as a car or house. If a seller reaches out to you and makes the first contact, the seller is the first house person in the chart. If you have reached out to the seller, than you are the first house person.

All trade and negotiations—whether diplomatic, business or personal—and the rules governing them are seventh house matters. Even the rules of war and peace to which the partners or opponents agree, are seventh house matters. Thus, the legal system, which is the outgrowth of rules governing relationships, is a seventh house profession and its symbol is that of Libra, the scales of justice. The seventh house deals with many abstract ideas, the very principles of what is fair, what is equal, what is just between two entities. Without these concepts there can be no true love or respect in partnership, which must come between equals. Otherwise, the relationship is of some other kind, but it is not a partnership.

This is also true of our relationship with the broader community in which we live. There are rules we must obey to have peace and tranquility. This is true on the job as well as in the home and neighborhood. Wherever there are others to be considered, there are principles of relationship.

The rules are needed when less desirable characteristics, such as coercion, confrontation, and manipulation in ugly, unpleasant ways occurs. Outright abuse and mistreatment we call crimes. But in all cases where a relationship has gone awry and become a dispute, the courts become an option for restoring "balance." All law suits which seek some sort of redress come under the seventh house. The concept of seeking justice is a seventh house idea.

In all disputes there is an element of something "not right" or out of balance. The notions of balance and equality imply conditions which are not balanced and not equitable. We can't get away from the challenge of the teeter totter. So the seventh house also deals with contradiction and the principles of contrast: pleasant/painful, love/hate, thoughtful/ thoughtless, kind/cruel, giving/taking, buying/selling, black/white, Yin/Yang. The Yin/ Yang symbol is a particularly apt one for the seventh house. Each of the two sides of the circle contains a dot. Each "you" is also a "me."

Given its quality as a mental air house, the seventh does not operate blindly. It considers the needs of both sides and how best to accomplish goals. It is one of the cardinal houses of action and leadership but it is also a house of thought and discrimination. House 7, like its natural correlate, Libra, is about clear judgment based on careful consideration. Its great virtue is the same as its great liability, the desire to do the right thing, using the correct principle or rule, making the correct decision. It can often seem indecisive, vacillating and confused, as those born with a strong emphasis in this area seem to take forever to ponder their options. It's been said that the best way to drive a Libra Sun type crazy is to give him or her a really big menu.

Once a decision is made, however, action is swift. Getting to the sticking point, as Lady Macbeth said, is the problem. Getting there means pondering the ramifications of any scenario and making a decision. That implies constructing a plan of action, a stratagem. Strategy is a seventh house skill.

It may seem curious that military leaders come strongly under Libra, but in a way, it's inevitable. Plotting the best way to achieve peace, using the least amount of force for greatest effect with the smallest loss is the best way to end a war. Those who fight may be Mars-ruled, but those who plan the battles and direct the course of events are the Venus-ruled strategists. This is also the house of mediation and mediators between two "me's" who cannot connect and rules all forms of counseling and the consultants who offer their opinions on what to do.

Opinions belong to this house and are considered a legally protected form of expression in the U.S., though not in all nations. Many statements (an air function ruled by the third house) are called libel and may prompt law suits, but the idea of opinion as a statement of position is uniquely seventh house.

The seventh also encompasses the notion of cease-fires and truces for peace-making in times of war . During peaceful eras, it has to do with the ambassadors who seek to keep relations between nations harmonious. It deals with peace treaties and trade agreements, amnesties and pardons. Above all else, it is the house where the issues of love and war are sorted out. During the 1960s and early 70s, when the outer planets transited Libra, the expression "make love, not war," and other Libra sentiments were popular. The Smiley face was on buttons and posters and "Flower Children" offered strangers blossoms as war raged in the southeast corners of Asia. An entire generation grew up imbued powerfully with Libra sentiments. "Not to decide is to decide," was one such statement in wide use. Young people wore friendship beads and sent each other sentimental cards with statements about their relationships. Marriage, however, was another matter. In typical seventh house fashion, divorces soared as the rules of partnerships changed. Women went to work by the millions, earning their own money and altering the balance of power in the domestic scene. Civil rights cases clogged the courts as issues of equity long neglected were redressed. House 6 makes use of all tools intended to improve or correct relationships, whether it is a sentimental card saying "I miss you" or a legal decision.

Planets in the seventh house tell us much about how successful each individual is in his or her human relations, how the world sees them. This is, after all, the house of justice and what goes around comes around (another Libra sentiment). As we do unto others is what is eventually done unto us. The scales must balance. All human beings instinctively understand the ideas of justice and fairness. A desire for equal treatment seem to be basic human equipment, seen in the smallest of children. The principle of stern justice—the eye for an eye of the old Testament—as well as the gentler notion that one gets rid of an enemy by making him a friend, belong to the seventh house. Both retribution and reconciliation are in the seventh house.

In a way, we are always looking for 7th house people as we go through life. The 7th house is all the "others" in our lives, not just the spouse, although that is the closest "other." The sign on the 7th tells the most about what you need in a partner. If it is a Mercury ruled sign, for instance, you need somebody bright, intelligent and talkative, interested in lots of things, or ideas. A Venus ruled sign says you need somebody to calm you down, show you the gentler side of life, give you emotional security and often financial common sense, introduce you to the arts, the social life around you, etc. A Mars ruled sign there says you want somebody stimulating, intense, who stirs you physically and sexually and who "kicks you into gear" when you need it.

The condition of the ruler, house, sign and aspect, will tell you what specifically you want from partners. A Venus-ruled sign with natal Venus in 11 says you want friends, a social life, etc. A Mars-ruled sign with Mars in 3 says you want somebody not afraid to argue about an idea, who likes fast cars or lots of running around and who can keep up with you mentally.

And so on with all the houses. The aspects add additional information. A trine to Saturn from the 7th house ruler? You want stability and reliability and security, and probably will find that in an older person or somebody with a really serious outlook on life. A square to Neptune? Watch out, you are attracted to unreliable dreamers or people who drink too much or who have serious physical or mental problems and you will end up providing the help.

The signs can provide further information. One good way to find out what you are looking for in life is also to think of the "natural" ruler of the 7th sign from your sun. All Cancers are looking for a Saturnian Capricorn type in some way, all Libras need a Mars partner, all cold-headed Aquarians want the Leo warmth and so forth. Now that's a pretty broad category, of course, but you will find, if you examine it more closely, that the partners we choose fit into a very specific spectrum and include some of the qualities associated with the "natural" seventh sign.

We are often attracted to partners who are all of a "type" in a general way. One morning I was having coffee and flipping around after the news, stumbled on an old movie, "Heart Like a Wheel," about Shirley Muldowney, the first woman top-fuel drag racer in the 60s and 70s. Now she's obviously a Mars-Mercury type and both the "important" men in her life had some Venus qualities. She herself was born with a retrograde Venus, an obvious sign that she did not value that side of life nearly as much as the Mars side. Her husband ran a gas station and the racing star Connie Kalitta was her long-time rival. Both men helped her racing, although her husband apparently wanted her to be a housewife with a little hobby, which ended that marriage fairly soon. He wanted a comfortable lifestyle without any big stress in it. Definitely a Venus type. Nevertheless, they remained friends until he died. Her second husband managed her team, though the marriage ended in 1996. Shirley pushed and worked until she got three world titles, but got fed up with Kalitta after one party girl too many, kicked him off her team and three years later ran him into the ground in a match race for the NHRA title. If that isn't a Mars-ruled woman, I never heard of one.

Curiously enough, in a racing accident, she was burned (Mars) on the face (Mars) and arm (Mercury). Both planets deal with fast cars. Mercury itself rules driving and the hands need to be very sensitive for a top racer. She was born with a Gemini Sun.

We hunt for what we need—the other half of ourselves, in a way—and the 7th house shows us that. The 7th is partnership, but also the house of open enemies—people who hate you, fight with you, sue you or try to kill you in public. The 12th is the house of secret enemies—those who hate you, smile at you, pretending to be your friend, or who ambush you from in hiding. House 7 is the random killer who is a stranger, or the soldier in the army fighting against you who will shoot you. The 12th is a sneaky criminal who tries to do you harm but works in hiding. This criminal can break into your house or your bank account and seek to rob you.

There is often confusion today about 7th house live-in partnerships that are not legally sanctioned. Many astrologers make mistakes reading for clients who have had such relationships in the past. The 7th rules the first partner but that may not be a marriage as such. This is where you need the "3Bs rule." If the relationship includes sharing the 3 Bs,—bed, board and the bills— it qualifies as a marriage astrologically. Some people who do not want the restriction of marriage may have had several of these, and the astrologer needs to be clear on how this works. If one is merely a guest in another's home (with or without bed privileges) but no responsibilities for food or providing cash for the establishment (gas and heat, etc.), it is not a marriage. Marriage is a partnership.

Plenty of long-time marriages didn't get legal sanction. In many primitive societies there was no religious or civil ceremony. People simply moved in together and that was that. But if there is any agreement on who manages what share of the common needs for electricity, telephone, grocery bills or meals, it's a marriage. The three Bs are the decider. An overnight visit, or weekends together are not the criterion. Moving in together, closing out all other living arrangements, keeping your groceries and toothpaste there and arguing over who has to do the dishes is quite different.

A long-term romance is not the same thing. In those one may spend hours and hours together but in the end you go to your home to do the laundry and get your mail. It's intense, but not a full partnership. A clincher might be a joint checking account. Or sharing hospitalization coverage. etc. Anyone you "lived with for a while" and shared the 3 Bs with should be counted as a spouse. All interpretation is a blend of things. The sign on the 7th is the generic description. The planets in the house get specific about the details. Subsequent relationships still go back to the 7th—they merely are the new people one selects to fit the profile of the house.

One Libra-rising woman I know described her first husband as an overly aggressive Mars type male, reflecting the Aries house rulership on her 7th. He didn't have to be a Sun-sign Aries or Scorpio, just reflect the qualities she was looking for. Her second husband is also a Mars type (actually a Sun-sign Aries) but a writer and thinker. The first spouse reflected her Mercury in 7 position in a more negative way—that of immaturity. The second was a more mature Mercury influence. Her 9th (which is the 2nd marriage) has Gemini on the cusp and she said her 11th (any 3rd marriage) has Virgo.

She likes men with active Mercury positions but wants a strong male type (Aries on the cusp). If she were to marry a third time she would again go for Mercury influence, I suspect. Perhaps a younger man or one with two careers, or a physically active type to reflect the Mars.

If you are an Aquarius rising person you have Leo on the 7th. Leo has a lot of traits you are seeking.—a strong ego, a romantic personality, a need for attention and a generosity of spirit. You will seldom be attracted to people who are stingy or excessively picky. Leo can be possessive but on the 7th cusp is almost always a sign that you want someone whose demonstrations of love and affection are clear and unmistakable. This house also gives us information about changing residence. The fourth is the current home. It is always where the person actually lives. But the 7th is the house of moving—the next home, if you like. Aspects in transit charts or progressed charts to the 7th often show the timing on a change of location.

The 7th is one of the angular houses of great power in the chart. It is truly the doorway to human relationships. It is the challenge and the opportunity that beckons to us all. It is the doorway to love.

Doorway to the New Country
House Eight

This is the house of trauma in the zodiac and its primary characteristic is to force us into situations that we can deal with only by calling on our deepest reserves to produce growth. It rules some of our most fundamental physical functions and our most sublime spiritual ones and can truly be called the "house of necessity." It is best symbolized by a doorway which takes us out of the familiar world and into a new landscape.

House 8 deals with things we cannot escape: birth, death, debt, taxes, surgery, sex and a lot more. Trouble in this area can cause violence and perversion, while beneficial aspects can produce a healing or an inheritance. In all cases, such events have ramifications which change the individual, altering the progress through life. They become turning points on the road.

In a purely physical sense the eighth house deals with the organs of sexual reproduction and elimination. For this alone it justifies its crown as the source of most humor. Humor helps us deal with uneasiness in the face of what scares us. Both sexual and scatological jokes deal with these bodily functions that can give us so much concern and are the most personal and private.

This house governs all things that have become useless and unnecessary— and the process of dealing with such wastes. Every male can probably recall his first "wet dream" and every young girl remembers the onset of menarche. Both were events which rid the body of unneeded material but yet were events that had emotional impact. They could not be escaped. The body does what it does and does not ask permission. Even the traveler's experience of diarrhea or constipation can be a painful memory. But the "trash" had to be removed, even if the body's way of doing so was unpleasant.

In a social sense, the eighth house deals with trash and garbage of all kinds and those who collect it and process it. We must somehow deal with wastes. There is no option. In an earlier time it may have seemed easier, but in today's more crowded world it has greater urgency. All city water purification plants and waste treatment plants and dumps where trash is placed come under the eighth house. Many city landfills have become "new land" which is turned into parks or golf courses. Break-walls along shores that protect beaches and docks are often constructed of debris and become new reefs in their turn.

The house deals with garage sales and the recycling process, because all that is waste is eventually broken down into its component parts which are then rearranged for another use. Manure becomes compost which becomes organic material for vegetables and flowers in gardens. Waste must decompose if there is to be a world that is reusable. In all of this there is the element of "necessity." These things simply must be done somehow. They are not options.

Any device which breaks down waste and turns it into something else comes under the eighth house. A septic system qualifies. So does the disposal in the kitchen sink which chops up the food scrap. So does a wetlands which cleans nature's liquid runoff and turns it into clear water and habitat for living creatures. Companies that sell jackets made of the fiber that once housed liters of soft drinks are doing eighth house work. These tasks have become necessities as our world fills up with leftovers.

House 8 is in charge of the sex act which leads to new life and it rules death, the recognition that the body itself has become a waste product. It deals with the "expelling" of semen, which is needed to produce a fetus when joined with an egg to create new life. It rules the process of birth which rids the body of the infant now ready for independent existence.

In its supreme role as arbiter of life and death, House 8 determines manner of death and the ways in which we deal with and benefit from the deaths of others, whether financially or simply as the end of a difficult period. Planets in 8 speak clearly, not about the final period of life, but the manner of its ending. The sign on the cusp, its ruler and planets in the house can be quite specific in detail. Death comes to all of us in its time. We cannot choose a life that does not include it. The kind of death is often shown by the 8th but it is not nearly as simple to decipher as some of the text books would have you believe. As examples: One man died in a hospital while he was getting some care by a nurse. His 8th house ruler was in the 6th of nursing. It was in Libra, but had nothing to do with the kidneys, merely the location. However, it was quick and gentle, and Libra is cardinal sign. That's a stretch, of course. Another died at home. His 4th house ruler received a trine from his 8th house ruler but was not otherwise very explanatory. These were certainly not helpful in forecasting. The dying itself is often connected to aspects of the 9th house of journeys as well as the 4th of endings. There are interesting correspondences for those who look at a lot of charts.

I have charts of two murder victims. There did not seem to be much connection to the 8th, but a lot to the 12th house of hidden enemies. One was definitely believed to have been a professional killing by underworld types who were never caught to this day. Much of his involvement in a variety of illegal activities was revealed as a result, however. The second was a drug dealer who was apparently killed in a botched deal of some sort and also remains unsolved. The first was the husband of a client. The second had been a client many years before. Their deaths were not easy to see from looking at their 8th houses. But of course, both deaths were involved with the issue of money and profits.

Pluto in House 8 is said to sometimes indicate death as the result of a major disaster, so I should love to see charts of all the people who went down with the Titanic, for instance. Obviously they were "buried" in water as well as dying from drowning. Maybe a lot of them had Neptune in 8. There is a difference between the 4th and 8th houses in deaths. The 8th is the cause of death or the dying process itself. The 4th deals with the entire last period of the life as well as the place the body "ends up." This can mean burial in the earth or in the sea. It can also refer to cremation.

As one of the water houses, the eighth is bound to be a house of emotion and in its polarity with the second house, which resonates to Taurus, it deals with shared resources of all kinds and our feelings about them. Taurus is the simple house of "mine" but Scorpio is the complex house of "ours." When "I" marry "you," I give "mine" to you and you give "yours" to me. We reveal our resources to each other. In a simple way, children express this by the perennial "I'll show you mine if you show me yours." They can be talking about what's in a pocket or their homework pages or their bodies.

Thus, as the house of joint resources, House 8 deals with all complicated finance beyond simple possession and earnings (which come under the second house). When we invest, we allow someone to use our money and they pay us for the privilege with "interest." When we want to use theirs, we borrow it and pay them the interest. Therefore, the house deals with loans, mortgages, mutual funds, money markets, annuities, insurance, credit cards, stocks, bonds and all inherited money. But loan repayment is not an option, and investing or saving is a necessity if we want to have a secure old age. Inheritance is outside our control.

In a social sense, House 8 deals with taxes—one of the "inescapable" things in life—in which we contribute a share of our resources for the common good. It deals with pensions, in which an employer shares resources with us. It deals with the spouse's finances, of course, and tells a great deal about how our spouse handles money and how much he/she earns in the first place. In a business partnership it has the same function.

Since this house is so closely tied to sex and money, it is no wonder there are serious ramifications in marriage and in society when problems develop here. Marriages may not be made in the bedroom and the checkbook but they can be broken there. Confusion about "sharing" or "buying" or "borrowing" can make a hash of psychological attitudes. This is why some people equate love with "things." They learned as children when their parents didn't share time or love with them but substituted material possessions. They grow up judging value by price. They argue over family inheritances because that is how they judge how much they were "loved." They examine gifts for the dollar amount and rank all relationships that way. Confusion between love and sex can arise. The eighth house doesn't deal with love, but rather the sharing that love requires. The sharing is needful. There is no other choice if partnership is to be viable.

The eighth house, like the eighth sign Scorpio, has a Mars overlay and deals with cuts and wounds and forceful openings, such as childbirth. Thus, all trauma medicine comes under this house as well as anything that spills blood. All surgeries qualify as trauma. An emergency appendectomy is easy to classify this way, but so is the removal of a cancerous kidney or the sewing up of a stump where an arm was cut off in an industrial accident. In all cases the body must heal after a difficult experience.

In another sense, surgery reconstructs life by preventing the waste of the human being. Some surgery simply removes waste, such as the diseased appendix, but other surgeries actually deal with repair and reconstruction of damaged organs. But they are all trauma, and in all trauma there is the question of "necessity." Or perhaps this word: inevitability. If you have a cancerous kidney it has to come out. There is no other treatment option, at least at present. You do it or else.

The eighth house rules instruments of surgery as well as those of death and a mortician's tools. Because it is the house of death, it deals with instruments of mass destruction such as bombs, as well as things which can improve the production of life, such as fertilizer, a reconstitution of a formerly waste product. These reflect the Pluto influence in the eighth. This is the house that remakes things into other things.

Seeds, the ultimate end product of the life of a plant, which contain the future of life after the plant itself has become waste, are eighth house matters, as is the kind of genetic manipulation that alters the next generation. Hybrid plants and breeding programs of all sorts, whether to produce a faster horse or a prettier rose or to avoid inherited disease, come under the eighth house. DNA, the genetic code, is a matter of the eighth house.

Unless change occurs, what has happened before will happen again. The genes will replicate and the next generation will be like the first. It is the business of the eighth house to interrupt this otherwise static state of affairs. It does this through events that are traumatic but needful. Mutation is one way nature creates change. Something has been changed into something else. In a way, it reflects the principle of Chaos (action) as the second, symbolized by Taurus, reflects Entropy (stasis). Again, it is the irresistible force on our immovable object. When there is a collision, things take a new direction. And so we come to the eight house's chief claim as the house of necessity, the trauma which remakes our lives. Trauma is inescapable. We have to deal with it. We can face it bravely or try to run away but the fact is there is no way out. We must pay the piper. We recognize this with the old expression "You can get out of everything except death and taxes." The eighth house will have its due.

A woman in childbirth is a woman in trauma. It is necessity which holds her in its grip and she cannot escape. The child must be born or she will die. There is no other option. This is trauma with a capital T. Trauma is any event of such physical or emotional or spiritual power that it breaks down our old parameters and forces us into new ones. Whatever happens to the woman in childbirth, she will never be the same again. Neither will her husband, for that matter. Whether they lose the baby or take it home to be raised, the result is the same: Their lives are changed forever.

In every life trauma comes. It cannot be avoided or denied. Thus, the eighth is the house of turning points, beyond which lies new country, unexplored and unknown but which we must enter whether we will or no. Trauma is the doorway. Many eighth house events contain inherently the kind of power that becomes traumatic, sending us into that new country. Any psychologist knows that even toilet training the very young child can be a pressure-filled event that alters mother/child relationships and can leave a deep mark on the psyche.

Sex—the good kind or the bad kind—forces us out of childhood and into a new kind of dealings with the adult world. The first sexual experience has great power to determine the quality of all subsequent relationships. Rape or sexual abuse can so damage the spirit that the victim requires years of therapy and even so may never completely recover. Sexual abstinence until marriage can give sexual experience transcendent meaning and intense power. Pregnancy can provide a traumatic event to both parents. But the experience of sexuality comes to all, whether through activity or inactivity, choices are made, experiences are met. All humans have gender and must deal with what that means. The gender issue is inescapable. There is a clear difference between the sex implied in the 5th and 8th houses. The 5th is the house of romance, of lovers and play. Sex there is part of the relationship. The 8th house, in a sense, is sex divorced from all other considerations. It is simply "the act" of reproduction, not a relationship.

Peril, threats and danger are all eighth house matters. They are a form of trauma. If we do not have sufficient peril, threat or danger in our lives, we are apt to introduce it with roller coaster rides, scary movies, and mountain climbing. Some individuals require more of this than others, but who has not read a ghost story or watched a murder mystery on TV? All the instruments of peril or threat or danger to the life also belong to the eighth house—such as knives, guns, and the like.

Surgery or wounding (in war or anywhere else) with its concomitant pain and rehabilitation and recovery can force us to take another look at ourselves and our lives and build coping mechanisms. We must find our courage, learn endurance and deal with fears and impatience. We must enter new territory as human beings in order to deal with the experience and the experience, in its turn, alters the territory of our future because it has happened to us. Many great and powerful people have written books or developed new desires or philosophies of life during such times of recovery from some trauma that led them to shattering conclusions and new, far-reaching personal decisions. They moved into "new country."

Even the financial matters of the eighth house can be seriously traumatic. A spouse whose spending sends one into bankruptcy, a parent whose legacy is a shock (for good or bad) to the child, the education in financial matters required by one who comes into a money windfall or a terrible loss are all traumatic events. Then, some people actually have problems if they have too much money. It's a question of fear, and that is always a Saturn problem. Those with strong Saturn positions in their charts are already cautious by nature and if Saturn is in one of the money houses, it can set set up a fear of abundance as well as fear of poverty.

One woman told me that as long as she is behind on what needs doing and she is a little bit anxious over having enough to pay her bills, she's fine. But if she has extra cash at the end of the month or there is some possibility of making a lot more money than she is used to, she goes into a panic. The fear of abundance can also be Saturn in the 8th, since that house rules other people's money.

Most of us never think that interest on a bank account or the growth of an investment is "other people's money," but it is. The idea of having "extra" money that you didn't earn is akin to the "other people's money" idea and it triggers the old Saturn alarm.

Saturn in 2 is fear of famine. Saturn in 8 is fear of feast. That's because we have to "do" something with the excess—save it, or invest it or something, if we don't actually spend it instantly on the leaky roof or the broken-down car. And of course, that puts it in the other people's money department. When you've never had any spare cash, excess can come as a threatening shock to the system and means learning a whole new language that includes "savings accounts," and CDs and even more. It's why a lot of people who win the lottery develop big problems. They go all to pieces with all that cash. Either they think it is an endless stream that won't run out (and they get quite a shock when it does) or they are so terrified of losing it that they put it all in a bank earning teensy-tiny interest and sit on it like a hen on an oversized egg.

The key thing to manage feast vs. famine is to just calmly put one chunk at a time in a savings account or a bank CD and then buy a good book on how to manage the rest. And follow the rules. The journey of a thousand miles starts with one step, in the old adage, and that goes for managing extra money, too. Start with a piggy bank and go from there. As one woman I know put it, take "baby steps."

One of the unspoken problems of having Saturn in the 8th is that sometimes financial counselors can steer you wrong. A good rule is never to let anyone have control of your money but you and have more than one person giving you advice. That way you can compare ideas. If you have come into sudden money, whether through inheritance or a lottery win or an insurance settlement, you especially need to keep calm. Follow some simple steps. First, take 5 or 10 percent and indulge yourself. Buy a car, take a vacation, whatever. Then quit spending for a while and do some long-range planning. At least 40 percent should go to safe places—real estate, bonds or CDs (which count as cash). That leaves about 40-45% for stock investments. You should never have more than 10% of your total portfolio in risky investments. After your heart has quit its daily palpitations, you may want to make other decisions. Don't rush. Go slowly and do it a bit at a time.

That's a simple rule of thumb and there are others that various experts will suggest. Just don't make quick decisions. If you have trouble halting your spending, put most of the money into investments where you can't get at it easily.

A lot of people get in trouble when they turn their cash over to a money manager and say, "Manage it for me." That's an invitation to disaster—especially if you have Saturn in 8.

Lawsuits are ruled by the 7th, but their financial outcome is the 8th. That can include child support—the result of a 7th house divorce matter. The eighth is the house where we pay for the justice of the 7th. In that sense it is also atonement or "repayment," and has a karmic element. In any case, we cannot escape the penalty we have incurred. Even bankruptcy, so often chosen as an attempt to escape repayment of debts, has its own set of inescapable penalties and ramifications. In trying to avoid one necessity, we find another.

Trauma doesn't have to be bad. Good trauma is still trauma and forces change. Many tales are common knowledge of those who inherit wealth and are crushed by it, frightened by the responsibility or intimidated by advisors and fearful that all those who express any simple kindness or friendship are "after my money." But there are many who are invigorated and renewed by windfalls, who lose weight, get a hair transplant or a facelift, buy new clothes, take up new interests and rejoin the human race after years of drudgery and discouragement. They have welcomed trauma. In both cases, necessity, the unavoidable event, the death of another person and their gift of a share in their resources, has brought the individual to the door into the new country and change follows.

But all transformation has a metaphysical side and can become spiritual in its dimension. The butterfly and the principle of metamorphosis has become symbolic of such work and is one of the best known symbols of the eighth house. Even the New Testament contains a vivid description of what the apostles believed was a spiritual transformation they said they witnessed as Jesus was filled with light and appeared superhuman in an episode upon a mountain. There are records of such transformations all through the spiritual literature of many religious traditions in which these things are said to occur to advanced yogis, saints or teachers. Perhaps they are meant to entice us to travel the road to the new country of the spirit. Some take such a road by walking away from everyday life into a religious world. They do not escape trauma, however. Spiritual writers speak vividly of the rocks and stones along such a way, the struggles they will face which will be too much for many. These are the tasks of years, or a lifetime. Even such a man as Mahatma Gandhi wrote searingly of his struggles against the lure of the flesh, his own eighth house challenge.

Some spiritual crises—of faith or belief—can also produce turning points. They have a ninth house connotation. In such times one often turns inward to find answers, and that can be a matter of the 12th from the 9th — or the 8th. Thus the eighth house has power to force us into agonizing reappraisals of our destiny, in a kind of spiritual or emotional trauma. One great mystic of the Catholic tradition, St. John of the Cross, referred to such times as "the dark night of the soul." An apt expression for the eighth house.

In all astrological work we deal with the total human being. The eighth is only one house of the chart, but can be a pivotal point when aspects and transits or progressions bring it to the fore. Some birth patterns say specifically that traumatic events will force major change in the destiny. But all lives contain some necessity and all lives will have some trauma.

Any planet in House 8 will produce trauma during the life. The kind of trauma will depend on what the planet is and what it rules and what it aspects. Its depth of transformation and its quality are also shown. Pluto, dark lord of the unknown, sends its natives deep into the new territory when it occupies the eighth. How well the individual copes with that trauma, and what kind of journey he or she will take into the "new country," can be seen by examining the rest of the chart.

Necessity and trauma are destiny's handmaidens which lead us where we otherwise would not go. They bring us to places where we can grow and thrive and become better human beings. When we realize we have passed into some kind of new country many times on our life's journey there will be less to fear when we reach the last doorway of all. We will walk confidently into a final "new country." The kind of death is often shown by the 8th but a lot of us are rather limited in our thinking about that. It is not nearly as simple to decipher as some of the text books would have you believe. To give you an example: One man died in a hospital while he was getting some care by a nurse. His 8th house ruler was in 6th of nursing. It was in Libra, but had nothing to do with the kidneys. However, it was quick and gentle, and Libra is cardinal.

Another man I know died at home. His 4th house ruler was getting a trine by his 8th house ruler, etc., etc. These are not always fail-proof for forecasting, believe me but offer food for thought and might lead one to accumulate enough data to provide a new viewpoint. There are a great many areas in astrology crying out for such study.

The dying itself may be connected to the 9th house of journeys as well as the 4th of endings, in my experience. You will find interesting correspondences when you look at a lot of charts. I have charts of a couple of murder victims. Neither has much connection to House 8 but a lot to the 12th house of hidden enemies. One man I am thinking of was pretty definitely a "hit" by unknown underworld types. The crime is still unsolved but there were many hints his life was not on the strait and narrow to begin with. The other was a drug dealer who was believed killed in a botched deal of some sort. His case also remains unsolved. The first was the husband of a client. The second had been a client years before. It isn't always easy to see.

Doorway to Understanding
House Nine

All of the experiences we have in life, all of the information we acquire, all of the data we analyze, is meant to help us form a spiritual and mental focus, giving our life direction and meaning. The ninth house opens the door to understanding. It tells us about our spiritual hungers. It deals with our desire to comprehend why we are here, what we are supposed to be doing here, and where we are going, both now and later. It is the house of hope and hopefulness.

On the simplest level, House 9 deals with just "going" and is the house that rules travel and the things we find when we travel. The people and places that are strange to us are symbolized by this house. It has to do with foreign languages and foreign ideas. It rules all places with a culture different from our own. In earlier times, anything more than a day's journey away was "foreign" but in an era of high-speed jets, it is less the length of the trip than the kind of place we find at the other end. In a large city one can go across town and find a more alien life style than one can have after a 1,000 mile jaunt within the borders of one's own country.

But the ninth house has much deeper meanings than merely those related to hitting the road, no matter how exciting and extensive that might be. It rules all of our horizons and the things beyond them, the unseen and unknown that are "over the next hill" in a way. It is the house of discovery and the house of the seeker. It rules all our journeys, whether of body, mind or spirit. It is the realm of the explorer.

Thus it is the house of higher education, which introduces us to the unknown idea, the foreign concept, the new vista we have not yet seen. It is termed the house of "higher" education, because it is more than merely acquiring the tools of learning, which we do at a much younger stage. That earlier stage of reading, writing and arithmetic, the tools of learning, is the territory of the third house. In the ninth house, education is the process of synthesizing what we know and what others think and know. We arrive at meaning.

Thus, the ninth is the house of religion, in which our spiritual growth takes place, and where we seek to know the meaning of life and how to live it. It rules churches and religious training and the moral values they inculcate. It is the house of philosophy, where we expand and broaden our ethical system and moral principles. Also it is the house of political opinion, and social ideas, which are based on those very concepts we have formed.

In the zodiac, the 9th sign is Sagittarius, the archer, who is symbolized by a centaur, half man, half horse. The horse was the earliest form of transportation allowing humans to travel farther and faster than their own legs could take them. Both education and religion take us beyond where we already are. The mythological teachers of the Greeks of old were said to be centaurs, who took humanity, symbolically, to the next level of understanding. The centaurs studied the heavens, another potent symbol, urging humankind to look beyond the here and now to a distant goal, a wider vision. The centaurs, in short, urged man to stretch, to become more, to become greater than he thought he could be. Moreover, they urged man to believe in a power greater than himself. This is the house of the Divine and the seeker of the Divine.

Both the 3rd and 9th houses deal with seeking and finding and traveling, but in quite different ways. The third is the means—the car, for instance—the roads and sidewalks and paper maps and signs and gas stations and all the minutiae of travel. The ninth is the long distance road itself, that mysterious one that starts at our front door and that leads us where we never thought to go. Many of the most successful books are written about journeys. Two wonderful modern classics are *The Hobbit,* by J.R.R. Tolkien, and its sequel trilogy, the *Lord of the Rings.* Both tell tales of personal change, how the individual steps out onto that mysterious road and in the process of going somewhere to accomplish something, discovers himself. And it is the discovery of the inner territory that is the true tale. The process of travel forces first Bilbo (*The Hobbit*) and then his nephew Frodo (in *Lord of the Rings*) to grow, to change, to find and use inner resources, to confront moral decisions and develop spiritual courage. The body is toughened, the mind is deepened, experience is broadened and the spirit grows wiser and stronger. At the end of the journey, neither is the same person who began it.

Every generation has its "journey" story. The biblical *Old Testament* has Moses, and Jesus roams Galilee in the *New Testament.* Even the Puritans of the early days in the U.S. had their *Pilgrim's Progress.* Dante's famous travelogue was *The Divine Comedy*, the exploration of heaven, purgatory and hell. All such stories belong to House 9. In fact, books themselves are devices of the 9th house. Stories and tales are a form of oral teaching and can have many layers of meaning. Even our childhood fairy stories were intended as travel guides to life. True, the big bad wolf is not always apt to go on four legs, for the world is full of tricksters who do not have our best interests at heart, as *Little Red Riding Hood* learned.

The study of any topic at a deep level belongs to the 9th house. Study is a mental journey. Learning the language of another people in order to find out where to get a meal is a third house "tool." But learning about why some people use chopsticks for eating and why they cook rice belongs to the ninth house. Paper may be a 3rd house matter, but the book which examines an idea belongs to the 9th house. Publishing thus comes under the 9th house, and so does a college degree, or any degree, which we achieve as the result of exploring knowledge. The perennial student, the spiritual seeker, the footloose traveler, the hobo, are all 9th house types. All are trying to "get it together," to find a cohesive whole that will give meaning to their life, to decide which philosophy they can believe in. Even our slang phrase, "get it together," is a ninth house cue.

The principle of Jupiter, ruler of the natural 9th sign of the zodiac, is expansion. The ninth house of the chart correlates quite plainly with that expansion of our self, our mind, our spirit, and sometimes our body. A powerful Jupiter influence in a birth pattern often enlarges the body and makes it stouter in middle life even as it coaxes us to stretch and expand our minds.

Jupiter is said to rule "hot air," and many of those who are seeking answers to why things are the way they are can be accused of too much of that as they talk out their philosophical notions to others. Many expound at length. It is almost as if the more they hear themselves talk, the sooner they will understand what they think and mean.

Conversely, those who have found their answers and think that, like a suit of clothes in "one size fits all" their answers should be just right for everyone, so are often accused of endlessly proselytizing. In a way, House 9 is those who "sell" a point of view—whether it is a politician with a stand on gun control, or a clergyman who wants to save souls. All are 9th house approaches. They participate in the concept that because "I" have found my meaning, it should be "yours" too.

And so we get the missionary syndrome—let's go to foreign parts and convert the natives. It's sometimes a way of convincing ourselves that we have found "the" answer instead of the process which will lead us to answers. It merely substitutes a physical journey for the spiritual one, leaving the spiritual hunger on hold, perhaps for the next lifetime. Sometimes, of course, it is the genuine expression of one's whole approach to life. I think of Father Damien, the Catholic priest who created the first humane colony for lepers on the Hawaiian island of Molokai in the 19th century, or the 20th century Virgo "saint," the late Mother Teresa. She went to India as an educator but soon began helping the most desperately poor to have a clean and comfortable place to die. Her mission became much greater than that, of course, but that simple concept was the start of it all. Nevertheless, part of both their missions was the journey to a far place to accomplish a goal based on living out their philosophy and religious belief. They are not unique, of course. Countless religious groups and missionaries go abroad. All ninth house notions.

Of course, there are journeys with other kinds of moral purpose. There was Mahatma Gandhi's famed march to the sea for salt, which aroused millions in India and was a milestone in the campaign to force the British to leave. There are groups like Doctors Without Borders, who circle the globe to provide medical care and healing to the most destitute of peoples. In the U.S. there was the Civil Rights march on Washington, and there were parades of Orangemen in Ireland. All were political, but all also reflected the ethos of their time and place.

The centaur of Sagittarius, symbol of the 9th sign of the Zodiac, shoots an arrow into the heavens. The poet who wrote, "I shot an arrow to the air, It fell to earth, I know not where," obviously implied that he intended to go look for it. But the Sagittarian is the hunter of more important game than merely a dead animal or a lost arrow.

To seek, to find, to understand, is part of the human mission. The other part is to teach, to share what we know with other seekers. Some of us must stand at the byways and the crossroads and at the doorway like circus barkers, saying, "Here's what you're looking for. Step right this way." It has been said that teaching is the highest expression of human wisdom, which is of no value if kept to oneself. Thus, all the houses of higher learning are staffed with those who teach, who have come the journey and returned to bring us messages and encourage us to travel along with them.

Also, people of the 9th house are among our collateral relationships. This is the house of in-laws and speaks of how well we deal with them. It is also the house of grandchildren and our relationships with them as well. Many people have better relationships with their grandchildren than they had with their own children when they were raising them. Perhaps this reflects the "wisdom" they learned through their own lives. House 9 is also about all the teachers in our lives, all our politicians, all our clergy and how well we get along. It tells us what we learned and what we shared.

And lastly, the ninth house is the house of prayer. Prayer is the desire of the human soul or spirit to journey on an unknown road to be in touch with the ineffable, the divine, the Supreme Other. It is, in short, a communication reaching a vast distance, to the heart of creation. But like any long distance call, it travels on a party line, connecting all of us with each other. The loving, prayerful concern of each of us for the other is expressed not just through sharing and teaching, but also in prayer. Even those of us with no belief in an ultimate authority in the universe often have a desire to "think good thoughts" for others. Prayer is as much the cry of the spirit as the hunger for knowledge is the cry of the mind and adventure is the cry of the soul. Each ultimate destiny is unique. Each of us must travel a road of our own. The journey of discovery, its pain and its joy, belongs to the ninth house.

Doorway to Honor
House Ten

This is the house of praise and dignity, of status and position and responsibility. It deals with reputation and achievement, the career and the amount of regard one has in the community. It is the pinnacle we have reached in life and the judgment of others on our deeds. Whatever the outcome of the effort of one's life is in this area of the chart, it is both a glad and fearful place. It is where we fit into society.

Some people find the tenth house one of comfort where the rules are clear, the responsibilities are plain and the rewards are sure and specific. "Work hard, keep your nose to the grindstone, and you, too, shall one day rule." That is one of the commonest mantras of the climb to the top. Another is: "As you sow, so shall you reap." Sound a bit Capricornian, doesn't it? Certainly Saturnian, and there seems to be a strong corollary between the signs and houses. This is the house of who we become and how we achieve it.

Because it is so important in life, House 10 is also one of the parental houses. It symbolizes the first and most enduring authority figure in life, and is therefore most often the mother. However, it can be the father and some charts clearly prefer it. It seems to be more fluid than other houses and may reflect the child's response to parenting more than anything else.

This is the house of our life's career and is intended to reflect the work that gives us the most profound sense of the rightness of things. If we have chosen wisely we should be able to lose ourselves in that work and find deep and satisfying pleasure when it is well done. House 10 reflects career, in the sense that it is work that requires training, as opposed to a mere job that does not. Whether we choose to become a professional in any field is reflected there. Oddly enough, House 10 is also our name—that name by which the world knows us.

The tenth also has relevance to our family and its position. Some of us are born into families that have good reputations or standing in the community. Some of us aren't. Those things can affect not only our beginnings but also our later lives once we become independent and make new choices for ourselves.

Family upheavals always seem to involve both the 4th and the 10th houses. For one thing, the two houses are each the 7th house partner for the other person, showing both parents' involvement. There is a saying in the U.S. that "if Mama ain't happy ain't nobody happy," which really reflects the 4th house distress when the 10th is "unhappy." And vice versa.

It is also noteworthy that when the 10th is disturbed in the individual's life, say for a layoff or a new job—the 4th is often affected. Either a move comes, or family life suffers from the new responsibility or the lack of a job. If the 4th house is too stressed, some individuals seek to escape the family influence and may even adopt a new name to change the 10th house perception of themselves. This is where aliases and alter egos and names adopted by writers come from. Sometimes it's simply a good way to protect one's own family from too much notoriety. Sometimes it's the career one seeks, such as the movies, where new names used to be common to get away from what might be seen as too ethnic or unusual or wimpy.

In all ways, each house of the chart reflects to some extent the affairs of the one opposite on the wheel. They are the yin and yang of events and people. So it shouldn't be surprising that when we are born the 10th reflects our family standing, just as the 4th reflects our family heritage. Later on, the 10th shows the company we work for (or own, if we have our own business) and the kind of role we play there.

Many years ago I did the chart of a teen who was a drug user and, like many in the '70s, also sold drugs to his friends. When I looked at it I saw business written all over it, with a Taurus MC and both Venus and Jupiter there, among other things. At the time I was involved with a drug drop-in center and many of the young people would talk to me if I did their charts because being an astrologer was so "cool." I told him I thought he had the likelihood of a higher calling, so to speak. He was a charming kid who always looked well turned out and the last I heard he had dismissed the entire drug world from his life and was running a shop to sell women's clothing. Successfully, I might add. I have often wondered whatever happened in his life after that. I was certainly happy he put all that talent to work in a more legally lucrative field. It was often the case in those years that young people "sampled" drugs and the fast life but moved on when it proved unsatisfying to them. With both benefics in one of the parental houses it was a clear indication he came from a good home and probably a financially stable one with a high income. He was not the kind of person who would long be happy in a dingy, low class environment with very few comforts. It wasn't his "scene."

The drug era was, like many such time periods, heavily affected by the movement of the outer planets which gave definition to it and those who got caught up in it too much had charts closely tied to those outers. This young man did not, but he took advantage of circumstances, briefly, as so many did then.

Planets such as Venus and Jupiter, which are benefic to start with, give the urge to have a place of some respect in adult life when they fall in 10. Venus can bring one into the art world, or the music world, or—in Taurus, which likes the good life—the business world or the financial world. Jupiter is often involved in publishing or education and I have seen it show up over and over the in the charts of those with such roles in different businesses. Of course it can also show up in religious vocations and philanthropy but whatever role one seeks, a Jupiter or Venus in 10 is a big boost.

Both Jupiter and Saturn are social planets and their presence (singly or together) in 10 say this person wants to be, or will end up being, a pillar of society. Jupiter has a certain luck there but Saturn reflects the likelihood of hard work to get there and sharp punishment if one strays from the straight and narrow.

I once knew a married woman with Jupiter in 10 who was having an affair with a much younger man. She told her friend over coffee that she had met him at the airport quite openly when he came to visit and her friend remarked in horror, "But what if somebody saw you?" "They'd never believe it was me anyway," she said. The affair never did come out, but that remark struck me as coming from someone who was taking a rather risky advantage of Jupiter's beneficence.

Many cardinal planets in the angles of the chart, and the 10th is certainly a powerful angle, can show a great deal of what we might call adventure in the life, but in any case they may also show the child becomes independent and leaves home at a very early age. If there is any talent, the child can go on to become renowned. The singer Cher has such a chart, and she left home and went off to marry Sonny Bono in her teens. It was the kind of connection one would term hasty in those years but her angles were heavily tenanted.

The fixed planets often point to business, as the young man's benefics in Taurus showed. Planets in mutable signs there choose careers focused on people and their needs, or education. This is often true also if mutable signs occupy the angles. Cardinal planets just want to run the show.

Mercury in House 10 is apt to choose some type of communication field. Mercury has rather expanded its portfolio in recent years with the rise of computer technology and the internet and the like. It is sales and talking and driving. Mercury loves to travel. If it rules the 10th you will see that, whether it's driving a truck or being a traveling manufacturer's representative. There are many vehicles we can "drive," and I have the chart of a train engineer with Mercury ruling 10. Mercury is also a double occupation and I have many charts of those who made such career choices. The two occupations may be quite different. Mercury often needs more stimulus than most and such doubling up may bring them more true satisfaction than it would for those who don't have such a need.

Earlier I mentioned that the 10th was the doorway to honor. All those who receive honors of various sorts do so when their 10th house planets or rulers are triggered. Honors—such as the Nobel Prize, for instance—are a recognition by someone else that you have done outstanding work in your life. There are also medals for bravery, which come under the 10th house since they show how well men behaved in their jobs as soldiers. The military comes under Mars, but so does medicine and I have the charts of a couple doctors with Mars there. But honors can also be the little gold star a small child receives for good behavior, or a tidy coloring book or learning one's letters. Those with benefics in or ruling 10 have an edge in receiving such favors.

Any planet in the tenth will tell a great deal about the career and whether or not there is one. In the case of those who never have a career, the planet often reflects the community interests the person has, or the status of the spouse, if the spouse is the family breadwinner. If there is no planet there, of course, one uses the ruler of the house to get this information. This is true of every area in the chart. However, a tenth house planet is like a lighthouse. You can see the effect from a long way off. This is the light that one doesn't "hide under a bushel basket."

I should also mention the notion that House 10 is the house of karma. Karma is the idea that we get what we have deserved in life. Some people, who believe in reincarnation, think it also reflects a carryover of talent and obligation from previous lives. Whether that is true is immaterial since it certainly reflects getting what we have earned in this life.

The woman I mentioned who leaned too heavily on her Jupiter for the "luck" in her life may find herself a bit short of it in some other way later on, perhaps. I don't think it's wise to try to fool the Universe. I love the expression that "what goes around comes around." It's probably truer than we know.

Doorway to Reward
House Eleven

Nobody quite knows what to do with this house. And yet, it holds the key to some of our most normal satisfactions in life. It is sometimes called the house of hopes and wishes. It is the place where we seek the rewards of our actions as well as the rationale for some of them. It isn't the house of accomplishment (that belongs to 10), but it is the house of approval. And because such rewards must come from others, it is the house of our peers, those who are most like us. These are the people who approve of us and who like us. It is also the house of those who don't, but we won't talk about them for a moment.

It is clear that we choose very little in our lives. Our parents, our appearance, our talents and abilities are a sort of package we receive at birth. The universe hands us our walking papers and our little tool box and sends us off on the journey of life. But there's one thing we do choose for ourselves: our friends. This house deals with all the myriad groups we select in life—the world of friends—from the Brownie troop or Scout pack in childhood, to the ball club or glee club in high school, the sorority or honor society of college, and the professional organizations of our mature years. It deals with church circles and Kiwanis. It is the charitable civic organization and the AMA. It can be as purely social as a 40-year-old bridge club and as exclusive as that of some people who entertain only a few friends for lunch once a month in a sort of rigid rotation.

But the House 11 can also prompt as casual an event as a pickup game of poker on Tuesdays, with Joe sitting in when Jack has to work. It is a regular luncheon with friends and the evenings out. It's the ladies bridge game and the alumnae teas. It is the golf game and the bowling league. It's the breakfast meeting before work with buddies we only see there.

Now obviously every friendship in life does not belong to a group as such. Many friendships are single ones. But every friend is a freely chosen association and thus comes under 11th house auspices, whether it is the janitor with whom you have coffee every Wednesday, the neighbor who borrows the lawn mower when hers breaks down, or someone who works for a competitor. The 11th house represents a person who cares about you for some reason and whom you care about, regardless of all else.

The house is not that of intimacy, particularly, although many friends share profound moments in each other's lives. People with whom we live are intimate in a deeper way and those relationships are more than friendship and come under other houses. Friends are not relatives although some relatives may be friendly. The same rule applies to lovers, who come under the opposite 5th house. Some people try to use this as the house of those we like and also sleep with, but it's a mistake. A friend is not a lover and a lover is not a friend. One may "graduate" from friendship into intimacy, but the reverse seldom occurs. An ex-lover becomes part of our past and that's the 12th house.

The 11th house is thus geared to the peer group and lends itself to the art of social engineering. Who among us has not modified his or her behavior or attire to "conform" to the expectations of the group to which we belong or wish to belong? It started in our teenage years. Choosing clothing to "fit in" to the peer group is an obsessive adolescent preoccupation we were all guilty of at one time. This is the house of team work, and represents the team itself in sports. The sport is 5th house but the team is 11. Adults all value those who work well with others and the training for this is often developed in the sports arena or the social scene. Human relationships, after all, help us in every avenue of life.

It is a common adage that it is not WHAT you know but WHO you know that counts when it comes to getting ahead in life. It is an obvious reference to the tenants of the 11th house. Because this house is opposite to the fifth house, it shares certain polar relations. As the fifth is where we express individuality and in a sense "stick out,", so the 11th is where we "fit in." Different societies at various times in history have put more or less emphasis on group behavior and group contributions. It is obviously a powerful influence on behavior. It would overwhelm most of us without the dynamic tension of its opposite, the individualistic 5th.

As the 5th rules our children, so the 11th rules the children of others and this house reflects how well or how poorly we deal with them. It is the house of step-children, or those that we inherit with a second or third spouse. We are not related to them but they become part of our life anyway by virtue of the marriage. In a way, we have "chosen" them.
In truth, we have chosen their parent, but in the end it boils down to the same thing. We have agreed to have them as part of our life. They may or may not ever become part of our true family. We may not even live with them. But nevertheless, as part of our extended family they must "fit in" some way. Friendly relationships are sometimes the best that can be had. That relationship quality is part of the dynamics of the 11th house.

Such "children of others" accounts for relationships many of us have with nieces and nephews or the friends of our children. Many adults end up in a sort of informal foster parent relationship to the poorly parented child who comes home from school with their own child and who stays for dinner and life lessons. This is the house where adults get involved in the activities of children generally, from the Scout troop leadership to the coaching of neighborhood games. Sometimes it is as simple as helping children in the neighborhood learn to ride a bicycle or do a tough homework math assignment.

Many manifestations of our work in the social circle are informal but they belong to this house. Others, of course, are far more structured. As this house follows the 10th house of career, it also reflects the business and professional organizations to which we belong. It is the house of alumni groups and political involvement, as well as neighborhood block watches. An excellent example of a professional peer group is the Hollywood organization which produces the Oscar awards for outstanding accomplishment in the film industry. This is an 11th house group—both in a social and in a professional sense—which provides the recognition that fulfills the "hopes and wishes" of those who labor to entertain us.

Truly, the recognition by our peers for the excellence of our work is the pinnacle of achievement for most of us. Career promotions are one thing, but praise is another and this is the house of praise. Only our true peers know all we did to achieve our goals because they seek the same ones, in a sense.

Other kinds of 11th house relationships enter the political arena. Some work can be for city council, a church council, or activity in a political party. Many figures in government have a focus in the 11th house which pulls them into legislative bodies. If you examine the charts of many politicians you will see emphasis in the 11th. Often it is the planet Uranus, which deals with governmental issues.

All organizations that have a board of trustees or a board of any kind operate under the 11th house. So do many quasi-governmental agencies that have a community service or social element, such as a historical society or friends of the parks and the like.

This house is not a career house, but it does deal with groups of people who work together, particularly those in semi-social settings to provide for the needs of the community, either on a paid or non-paid basis. True volunteer work comes under the 6th house, but the 11th house provides both the incentive and the reward for it. It is the framework which allows the 6th house service to be provided. Philanthropic groups belong here and people with active 11th houses are often involved as volunteers in some type of "organization" work that helps others. They may support the arts or battle to restore a city landmark. The appreciation they receive and the social contacts they make are sometimes what they consider fair value in exchange for their work for the common good.

Sometimes membership in something like the Red Cross evolves into participation in an even more special and exclusive task, such as an elite disaster team. Both activities come under the 11th house insofar as they are chosen for their social values, even though they appear to shift into the sixth house of volunteer service. As I say, the work one does may be 6th house, but the social element is definitely 11th.

But many hobbies (5th house matters) can also shift into 6th house endeavors. Consider the desperate need for ham radio operators or snowmobilers in times of catastrophe. The hobbyist provides a (sixth house) lifeline for those in need. The later honors banquet and the plaque from a grateful community, however, is 11th house praise and approval.

The 11th is a house of complex, interconnecting human relationships. Some people have only a few friends in life and are not what we call "joiners." For others, the social air is the only kind they breathe and they are involved in a multitude of activities with others. But whether the peer group is structured or casual is immaterial. The rewards we seek in life—the intangibles, not the money we hope to earn from our work—come from our peer group.

The satisfaction of a job well done is a personal thing. The gold watch or trophy and the banquet to honor one's efforts come as recognition from our peers, a treasured reward indeed. By the same token, the 11th house rules those who judge their peers. The notion of juries to decide criminal matters is an 11th house concept. This is house of social condemnation as well as a legal one of the individual who has refused to "fit in" to the rules of society.

We should not forget the devastation of social disapproval, though. The "shunning" practiced by some religious groups of those who have beliefs or actions that violate group standards has been known to split families and force people away from loved ones.

Prejudice against those who are not part of "our" group is here. Racial and class bias of all kinds are misuses of 11th house principles. This can start young, when groups of boys decide against girls, or groups of girls decide to dismiss boys. Most of us evolve beyond this and part of the reason occurs as puberty and the inevitable glandular changes refocus our views of the opposite sex. But racial and class bias, which are often taught in the home, may linger. It's one thing to disapprove of a single person; it's another to cut an entire body of people out of our lives because they aren't quite "like us."

The power of the 11th house tends to be underestimated or ignored by a great many people in astrology. But it is here that we seek power by joining with others to effect change or strengthen our own social position. This house deals specifically with the power to manipulate behavior and 20th Century tyrants have given us good examples of how to use political organizations and youth organizations to mold community values and allegiances.

In such extreme situations, the group mentality overrode individual common sense and ethical values. A good example of 11th house power gone awry is seen in the classic film "Citizen Kane," or in the George Orwell books. Part of their fearfulness was the loss of individual worth and potential. These are classics that clearly expose the dynamic tension between houses 5 and 11. In real life, the Nazi preoccupation with Aryan "purity" was a deliberate attempt to foster the "us vs. them" mentality. Because this house opposes 5, where individuality is paramount, the fear of losing identity has a particular horror. Many born under the 11th sign, Aquarius, have a veritable compulsion to continually do things to assert their own individuality, as if they found the peer group both irresistible and threatening.

The 11th house is where we are least like ourselves and most like others. It is the house where we become our brother's keeper, or our brother becomes our keeper. This is the also house that tests the value of our ethics by holding up to us the mirror of our friends. We can see how far we have come by studying whom we choose to befriend. The 12 apostles were a peer group, after all. Birds of a feather do flock together.

Doorway to Judgment
House Twelve

This has an ominous sound, and we haven't even started yet. But there are all kinds of judgment and this house deals with judgment in a particular way. It's where we get our truest grades in life. Most of us get C's and some of us get F's. But there are also a lot of A's to be handed out. And for a very few among us, the A plus, which implies outstanding achievement. This is not a public thing but a very private one.

The 12th is where events and people of the past are always hanging over one's head waiting to be dealt with. They keep coming back until you do. And they bring problems with them if they haven't been solved yet. The 12th house is like a closet where you store things you don't want to deal with just now. Like Scarlett O'Hara in "Gone With The Wind," we tell ourselves, "I'll think about that tomorrow." Psychological hang-ups and fears, old debts and unresolved issues, are all stored in the 12th house, keeping you from accomplishing more until they are resolved. You have to drag them out into the light of day and examine them. You have to fix what is bothering you or you can't go forward in life. They hold you back.

If you think reincarnation is a valid explanation for how the universe works—the 12th house may also deal with past lives. I don't think you have to believe in reincarnation to understand it, however. The 12th is your "hidden weakness" and your "unused potential." It has also been called the house of "self-undoing," where we ourselves create the conditions that hurt us. Sometimes the process of opening the closet is brought about by trauma and many people experience it as deeply unpleasant. It needn't be. When done voluntarily, a piece at a time, it is much more manageable. It is doubly important for people who have the same sign on the first and the 12th houses to deal with their problems. Ignoring them is like issuing an invitation to a trauma party.

The 12th is also a house where our desires for solitude come from. Many people who do work behind the scenes in life, or research or anything that isolates them from others will have strong 12th house indications in their natal patterns. It is the house of the hermit and those who step aside from the world to learn more about themselves in solitude. Many great religious and social figures have had periods in life where their progress came through solitary reflection. These were 12th house activities even if their natal patterns did not mean a lifelong commitment to the process.

This is also the house of prison, of course, or hospitalization or quarantine. Quarantine is something that has gone out of fashion in these days of antibiotics, but isolation was once considered the only safe treatment for highly contagious conditions. The 12th is the house of repairs. In any case, for all of us, where the ruler of the 12th is, you will find one of your major life challenges: In the 7th, it might be your marriage; in the 4th, a family member, or a parent, or your property; in the 5th, a child, and so on. The 12th is the house of the past generally. Anything we are done with belongs in this area of our lives. Ex-husbands, former lovers, old friends and people we once worked with qualify. Anything that we are owed is here, and if we are people who scatter largesse with a generous hand, it comes back to us in times of need.

A benefic in the 12th is a sure sign that you will reap old benefits. I have always thought of Jupiter in the 12th as the "ram in the bushes" aspect. You may recall the biblical tale of Abraham taking his son Isaac to be sacrificed after God's instructions. The bible says that when God saw he was so obedient he would actually go through with it, He stopped Abraham and told him instead to use the "ram in the bushes" for the offering.

There is an old principle that what you send out into the world—good or bad—comes back in triplicate. The chickens always come home to roost. Best they come back as fried chicken or chicken soup, right? Of course a ram in the bushes is nothing to sneeze at either. The 12th almost has to be understood in terms of all the other houses and our actions in them, but particularly the other cadent houses, 3, 6 and 9. The polarity of 6/12, especially when there are planets in both houses, is sometimes (and not so humorously) called the "serve or suffer" package. It implies that we must take care of the needs of others or we end up needing others to care for us. It also means we have to take care of our own bodies or they break down and need to go in for repairs. The 12th is the house of repairs—the ultimate makeover shop.

But the 3/9 polarity is of equal importance, defining as it does our attitudes and thinking processes, our opinions and ideas in life. The 9th is the house of our spiritual aspirations and comprehension, and the process of reaching those new comprehensions can push us into a needful 12th house experience. The third house reflects our need to learn something new in order for more progress to be made.

Traditionally the 12th is the house of the institution, the house of confinement, the house of isolation and secrecy. It is the house of limitation. It is all those things, of course. Most institutions that come under the 12th house are intended to "fix" us in some way—either to conform to proper behavior in society or to return us to useful function, or to provide refuge when we have no other. Prisons are where we put those who have not passed the classes of life experience and have instead harmed others. Hospitals are where we go when our bodies have ceased working properly. Old age and nursing homes are the final refuge of those who can no longer care for themselves and who have no family to fall back on.

Quarantine, largely an outmoded response to contagion nowadays when vaccines and antibiotics work so rapidly, is also a way to isolate a problem until it can be repaired. The "time out" of modern days to solve problem behavior comes from this idea. But prisons and hospitals still use isolation or solitude to "fix" problems that prove intractable. It's even used in sports and schools.

Other types of institutions, such as orphanages, mental hospitals and those for people with special needs, such as the retarded, or the elderly, are all places to amend a situation of some sort, whether one of need, or breakdown, or simply the deficiency of age. Thus, all the people of such institutions come under the 12th house. It is a medical house as well as a house for the social misfits among us. It is the house of last resort for the feeble and the needy.

But lest misconceptions occur, the 12th is also the house for those who outdo the rest of us in some way. This is the house where genius resides. It is where people try to reach beyond the norm. Truly brilliant people are seldom social butterflies. Many times they have agendas that require a great deal of private work. The entire principle of privacy comes under the 12th house. Whether privacy refers to our bank account or our inventions or our original ideas or creations, it is a necessary component of those things.

In modern society we are losing the sense of privacy as an inviolable right. Despite the struggle in society to retain that right to personal privacy, the tools of the information age have stripped us of anonymity. Anonymity and privacy are enormously valuable commodities we appreciate only when we lose them. Ask any famous person if anonymity would be nice for a while. The 12th is where we seek to disappear. Many people do, both as a kind of refuge from stress but also as a way of shutting out the world and its demands. It can happen before or after other more public events in our lives. Sometimes it is as simple a thing as going into a quiet room and shutting the door. Other times it may involve a true retreat from society as a whole.

It often seems that those destined for greatness go through a kind of 12th house preparation. Perhaps to "fix" deficiencies before success can occur. Think of the great artists of history who labored long in anonymity and often poverty and isolation. Michelangelo was not on display when he painted the Sistine Chapel. He worked alone, on his back, high above the floor.

Many great political leaders who have changed history have done some of their most seminal work in prison and even used the time to write books—Gandhi, Nelson Mandela and even Adolph Hitler. In addition to continuing his extensive political and spiritual correspondence, during his imprisonment, Gandhi of India also developed his ideas about non-violent confrontation that eventually drove the British from his conquered nation.

Adolph Hitler of Germany planned to take over the world. He wrote his book *Mein Kampf* in prison. He obviously didn't use his "time out" in a positive fashion. Nelson Mandela of South Africa tried to heal his nation and provide a new government to represent the black majority as well as that of whites. In his case, too, his non-violent approach gave his opinions a spiritual power and moral efficacy they may have otherwise lacked. Hitler developed a type of power and moral persuasion. One thing he wanted to do was rebuild his nation. He took that rather literally (he was a Taurus, after all) and erected a great many important buildings in Germany. But some of them were concentration camps in which he kept all the "undesirable" human beings he planned to exterminate. He had a very narrow definition of desirability, unfortunately. He built furnaces to burn the rest, alive or dead.

It is no coincidence that some of history's most influential books have been written from sick beds or prison cells. The famed *Count of Monte Cristo* was one such volume. Its author Alexander Dumas knew what he was writing about. Robert Louis Stevenson was a semi-invalid most of his life, and almost all his writing was "12th house" stuff. *Alice in Wonderland* was written by a man who had a drug problem and was in rehab at the time. Lewis Carroll was trying to shake a cocaine habit.

The very notion of "time out" is a common one for those in the sports world or in education. It's interesting that in many progressive schools or educational settings such as games, the idea of a period of inactivity when one is not allowed to participate in the action is seen as a "corrective measure." That correction can provide a rest for the body or a time for the individual's emotions to return to normal. Occasionally, of course, the time out has its own priorities.

And so we come to the spiritual adventurers and all-around weirdos. We have the hermits and the yogis and the saints. There were eremites who spent their lives on the top of stone columns or in caves in the desert in ancient times and those who entered cloistered monasteries and abbeys, both then and now, to spend their lives in prayer. There have been the wandering Sufis and fakirs of the East and the Tibetan lamas of former eras who passed their lives on mountain tops in meditation. There are still orders of monks and nuns who live such intensely private lives. It is the isolation and privacy implied in the 12th house which allows such aspiration to come to fruition.

But then too, in a reverse application, some of the most famous people in history have left their pinnacles of accomplishment and retreated to this kind of intense solitude and have left the world to seek an inner destiny, perhaps to "fix" the loss of time for contemplation. Or perhaps, to take the next step forward in spiritual growth, one which cannot be shared with others, although the fruits of its experience may be. In the spiritual sense, it is the house of faith. The seeking of one's belief system belongs to the 9th, but this is the 12th house where one accepts the reality of things unseen.

The very principle of contemplation is 12th house. And so is that of spiritual growth. Unlike the 9th house which explores the direction and path to understanding, the 12th insists one do more than merely grasp the notion, or "talk the talk," as sometimes occurs in the 9th house. The 12th insists that one live out one's understanding.

The 12th is a house of more mundane secrecy, too, of course. It deals with spies and organizations which use spies and profit from their work. But for all of us it is a house where we hide, or attempt to hide, our deficiencies or whatever parts of our opinions, thoughts and actions that we do not want others to see. It is "behind" the first house, which shows us openly to the world. It can be as simple a desire for privacy in the matter of our financial affairs, or the keeping of a tale of family misdeeds for generations.

Because it is also the house of last resort, it deals with places of refuge. In ancient times there was a notion of "sanctuary" which was very real for those in trouble. One who reached a church was safe from legal authority or punishment as long as he was on the church grounds. This was, I hasten to add, first a pagan and then a Christian notion which does not seem to have been adopted elsewhere by other religions. All Christian churches before the Protestant Reformation (and all the Catholic ones still do) made use of another 12th house function. They had small dark closets parishioners could enter to confess their sins anonymously to a priest sitting behind a concealing grill. This confession concept targets the guilt which is so often found in the 12th house and provides a way for spiritual healing and forgiveness to occur when the priest gives absolution in the name of the Divine.

The 12th house conceals, but not always. Many times correction of a problem can only occur after the secrecy of the 12th house is broached. Crimes are usually secret misdeeds and the criminal is only brought to justice when he or she is brought out of the dark corner into the light where another judgment can occur. This is also the territory where psychiatry and psychology function. Fear and guilt and secrets are the enemies of the whole and healthy spirit and helping the individual learn to deal with these things is as valuable (perhaps more so) as helping the individual agree to lifesaving surgery.

The 12th house is one we all visit one way or another. And the experience is usually good for us. The 12th is a house of the past, one's private life-long struggles, handicaps and difficulties (as well as other things, of course.) and the Sun there can show a struggle with health issues over many years.

Sun represents the father, and when it falls in the 12th he will be one who is a big help or no help at all in childhood. People who are either secret helpers or hinderers or just outright failures in their relationship to us show up in this house. It is a karmic house and is said to be the house of past lives (if you believe in them) and to indicate what we bring to this life with us. The Sun there says our view of ourselves was set pretty firmly in past lives.

The 12th house position for a planet is one of hampering and limitation. It shows hangups and problems we don't reveal and where the individual most needs to learn lessons that will help growth. The ruler of the 12th and its natal position is the key. Where it falls shows the arena in which we will deal with our difficulties in life. If the ruler of 12 is in the 7th it can be marriage. In the 5th it is a child or children. In the 10th the career or the needs of a parent. If the sign on the 12th has the double influence of both a classical ruler and one of the newer outer planets, such as Scorpio, both will be involved but I find the old ruler a better clue.

It's amazing how many of us find our greatest challenge in marriage. But there are those for whom the career seems to have a karmic element. And there are parents of handicapped children who learn through helping their child. How about Helen Keller—or her famous teacher?

The same sign on both 12 and 1 shows that the hidden side of life has great power in how the individual deals with personal growth. This seems to refer to unfinished business from the past, with special skills brought to this lifetime to complete a task or accomplish a goal the individual has. Now obviously a life mission is a complicated thing, and we use a lot of other areas in the chart to analyze this. The Ascendant sign is one focus. The Moon's Nodes show another. Saturn is a third. But don't forget to check out the ruler of 12. It shows what we most need to learn. You'll find some answers in its location.

For some people the talents shown in the 12th are never even used in the current lifetime. But like money in a forgotten bank account, they can appear in times of emergency need. The 12th is also the house of earned benefits. Jupiter there has been called the guardian angel aspect. Venus in 12 often brings money and other aid when things look bleakest. If the ruler of the 12th is in 12th, it's time to solve old puzzles, learn to deal with your hangups and discover the virtues of solitude occasionally.

Mercury in 12 says you need to talk about your issues. Venus says you need to explore your emotional nature and commit to loving someone even when it's hard. Both planets say you will find you are your own best friend and can best recover from stress when you have time for solitude and contemplation.

Saturn is not a happy influence in 12 and can sometimes indicate a childhood in which sexual abuse played a role. An afflicted Saturn can show it precisely. But a well-aspected one can be the reverse. One client with such an aspect fended off a lustful boyfriend of her mother's. The man attempted to molest her, but she picked up a butcher knife and chased the man around the dining room table until he left the house. She was 12 or 13 at the time.

But, lest we think the 12th has only a psychological portfolio, let's consider a more practical one. Horses and the larger animals belong to the 12th house. The 6-12 polarity in the houses was intended to give us clues as to the creatures in our world. The small ones provide many necessary services for us—think of bees, and rabbits (often kept for their fur or eating), dogs, which guard the home, or cats, which keep rodents under control and the like. They all belong to the 6th house. The larger ones, such as horse, cows, buffalo and camels, yaks and llamas were also part of the labor package. They were said to fit into the house opposite. Back when the traditions were being formulated, there were few pure "pets." Even today, many farm people tend to have animals with dual purposes—cats may be nice to cuddle but they also keep the barn clean of mice, dogs do herding, etc. 4-H youngsters may make temporary pets out of their lambs and calves, but they sell them for meat just the same. Seeing eye dogs and sheep herding dogs and police dogs are classical 6th house types—they provide a distinct service for us and are not big enough to fit into the 12th house category. (I can't imagine a seeing-eye camel, for instance.)

House 12 also has a special relationship to things of the past. It is the house where we keep track of our history, in a way, by "saving" it. All the relationships in our lives that are over and no longer viable come under this house. Old lovers, friends, one-time teachers or colleagues and ex-spouses are all found here.

But yoga, meditation and prayer periods are fostered here, too. So is ruminating over one's past, which old people start to do and often discuss with others. This is a natural state of unfoldment, in which we begin to analyze the actions we took, the reasons for them, and find some clarity about a lifetime of choices.

The old seem to be trying to boil down life's experiences, see them from new perspectives and choose what is worth saving out of their years and what heritage they wish to pass on to others. This is the house of memory and souvenirs and old lore. Things that are hidden or stored—for whatever reason—are part of the 12th house. It is the closet, the attic and the storage areas around the house. It is all your scrapbooks.

It's been my impression that people with 12th house planets have 12th house issues to work off and like all such indicators, show that we will attract people who will help us do that. Sometimes they are people who have solved the problem we are working on and it's almost as if the universe has provided us with a "tutor." Sometimes they have a problem we deal with quite well and bingo, guess who's the tutor. Not all of this is positive, but not all of it is negative, either. Wherever a planet falls in our chart is where we need to learn the wise use of energy. For instance, all of us have the ruler of our 12th in some house. That is where we should be working on our growth patterns because this is the area which provides us with problems to solve and limitations to deal with which help us clear out the 12th house debris.

But when planets are IN the 12th there are other issues as well. People with benefics in 12 often notice the needs of others and quietly, without any fanfare, they move to help. Sometimes they help anonymously. When one thus becomes a "secret friend," one is expressing the highest qualities of the 12th house, in my opinion. What is a secret friend? Well, maybe you hear that a co-worker is in desperate need of a loan for heavy catastrophe expenses (not covered by insurance) and is nervous about approaching the bank's loan officer. The officer happens to be a friend of yours and you casually mention the case to him at the weekly card game, and recommend your co-worker as a solid citizen. The co-worker gets the loan and you smile and say, "That's nice." Or you see a woman on the bus with terrible varicose veins and swollen legs who is obviously unwell, so you spend the day saying prayers for her whenever you have a few minutes. Maybe you never see her again.

The 12th is the house of the cloistered individual who prays for the healing of the world as well as the house of those who suffer health problems that limit their ability to function. It rules the miser who hides his money in the walls and the hermit as well as the person who secretly drops a gold coin in a Salvation Army kettle every yuletide.

You smile and wink at the cranky child in the checkout line at the grocery store so the kid stops fussing at the frazzled mom. She never knows you tried to help her out. The kid thinks your antics are odd and stops crying while watching you. Small things of course, but there are many ways we can be kind to our fellow humans if we are willing to do so without grabbing the credit.

The 12th house is the house of all the things that have ever annoyed us, hurt us or shamed us. We can always choose whether to bandage up our own injured selves but some people instead decide to get even with the world by spreading the misery around. People with malefics in House 12 are often secretly angry and vengeful over real as well as imaginary slights and may work behind the scenes to "get even" with others in petty ways where they won't be caught. It's identical to the first scenario, but not nearly as nice. They, too, seek people on whom they can practice. They may even marry them. They do sneaky, petty things to each other trying to get even and just as in the eye-for-an-eye scenario, both may go blind in the process.

We can all choose to be what we wish, but once we realize when our behavior is secretly "helpful" or "hurtful" we can tell which we have chosen to be—secret friend or secret enemy. In practice, it may not be so clear cut as I am describing, of course. But if we really want the truth about ourselves and we really want to become the best self we are capable of, we will recognize the difference. Acting on it is up to each of us. But this is why people with 12th house benefics often receive aid in unlooked-for ways when they need it and people with 12th house malefics often get a punch in the snoot "for nothing."

In a metaphysical sense you could say you sent out a certain type of energy into the universe and it sent it back. You cast your bread on the waters of life, so to speak, and you reaped what you sowed.

Does that mean benefics in 12 are always good? Nope. Some people are happy to grab the goodies of having such a position but don't give anything back. And some people with malefics there humbly deal with the punches in the snoot and keep trying to do right by others. Pretty soon the universe notices. Meanwhile we can have a lot of happy or unhappy relationships until we figure it all out.

Sometimes when we come to the end of life, when all that is left is the limitation imposed on us by failing physical abilities, memories and their richness truly become our refuge. We look back on the past fondly and enjoy once more all the good things we once loved, and maybe still do. All that we have stored in a long and varied life is still there, like old photo albums and souvenir books of memories. It is the juice of our living, squeezed out to nourish our last days. It is our final gift to ourselves.

Chapter 24

Interpreting the Natal Chart

In order to learn astrology you have to learn how planets and signs function as if they were there all by themselves. When you learn a little more, you realize that they almost never are "all by themselves," but linked in such a way that they affect each other.

The Ascendant still determines your physical body, but now you need to know how the planets modify the basic costume. It's like describing a blue dress. The world is full of blue dresses. To describe this one individual blue dress, we need to know if its casual or dressy, two piece, long sleeve or short, a-line, empire, long, short, etc., etc. All the modifiers are like the planets and the rest of the chart. But it is still a "blue dress."

The Solar Chart

If the birth time is unknown I always put the Sun on the Ascendant and use noon positions for all the planets right out of the ephemeris for the reading, since that gives you the closest approximation for the Moon . You're within about 6 degrees either side of being correct. Over the years I've found that's the best set up to use.

Some astrologers will simply cast a noon chart to start with but I never do that since it puts the Sun in House 10 which can confuse you and make the chart appear more powerful than it may actually be.

There are other types of charts which can be used, in case a time is unavailable. One is the Johndro chart based on the locality where an event such as a murder occurs. The Johndro chart can be quite revealing. It used to be a real pain in the neck to calculate them, but now that you can do it with a computer program it's easier. I can't honestly say I ever use them, though, because I think the simple solar chart does a perfectly acceptable job. But Johndro charts were quite the thing in the 1970 and 80s.

The late Barbara Watters was a big fan of them, particularly in criminal matters, since it puts one in the center of the action in a given location on a particular date. The information on how to do them is in the Johndro books if it interests you. Watters was a Washington, D.C. astrologer who was particularly good as criminal matters. She wrote a couple of very good books I have listed in the rear of this book in the bibliography.

Location, Location, Location

Sometimes astrology is like real estate—the key is location, location, location. And, location means the places where the angles are. The "power points" in any chart are the angles—the cusps of House 1, 10, 7 and 4, in that order. In other words, a rising planet is in the best seat.

The most powerful house is the first. A planet there determines a lot of our life choices and the way we live. It's what we look like and how people first see us. It is a ticket to many of our life experiences. A planet in House 10 is in the next most dominant position if there is nothing in House 1. After that, the seventh house is the next most powerful (if there is nothing in 1 or 10), and if all other angles are empty, the 4th house can dominate the chart. Its activities and aspects show up first and most strongly, etc.

In general, the ruler of the rising sign is the chart ruler. There can be some confusion about this because sometimes other planets seem to be more significant. It may not be in the most powerful position but most of us take a back seat to many others in our lifetimes anyhow, so we can understand how this works. There are tons of classical rules that are different than the above, but these provide simple, direct answers that are surprisingly workable. It never pays to lose sight of the place a particular planet occupies. The house really does matter, particularly in terms of the planet's ability to manifest action in the life.

There are two fundamental ways people get things accomplished: push and pull. You can also call them positive and negative, or masculine/feminine or yin and yang. Those aren't jokes, they are basic ways we react. Push people are Mars types, independent, take-charge individuals who intend to get somewhere if they have to trample everything and everyone in the way. Pull people are those who smile and charm their way to their goals, getting other people to support their aims and boosting them ahead. Sounds like Venus, right?

Most of us operate toward one end of this polarity rather than the other. This does not mean you have to have Mars rising to be a "push" person, nor Venus rising to determine that you are a "pull" person, but it helps. Masculine planets such as the Sun, Jupiter and Mars enhance the "push" tendencies.

If Venus and the Moon are the only angular placements in the chart, the individual is likely to be a pull person no matter what Mars is doing. Their fundamental approach to life is congenial. If the person has a Sun/Mars linkage in addition, even though succedent or cadent, they may apply plenty of push as well. If neither seems strong, the individual may amble through life hoping to get somewhere but not accomplishing much, in any case. We have to choose our manner of action and when you aren't getting anywhere with "push," it may be time to learn "pull." If "pull" is not helping you reach your goals, it's time to find a way to apply some "push."

That sounds like a simplistic answer, but you'd be surprised at how often it proves to be a key to the choices people make and how successful they are. Mars and Venus, the two planets closest to the earth (excepting the Moon, of course) really have a great deal of power. Modern astrologers tend to get too hung up on the outer planets and lose sight of this.

Drawing a Blank

It takes time to get the knack of putting a chart together concisely, and sometimes I fail after nearly 50 years of doing it. We all have off days even when we know better. I pick up a chart and look at it and I haven't a clue as to what in the heck it means. When that happens and I draw a complete blank, I go back to the basics of 1, 2, 3—Sun, Moon, Ascendant—and this steadies me on the way. If you have the 1,2,3 always tucked in your back pocket, it's like money in the bank, something for the rainy days and Mondays.

We are rather like onions. The outer layer is always the Ascendant which describes our height, weight and coloring. It is the gateway we enter at birth. The "stage" on which we will choose to operate will be heavily influenced by it. Aquarius rising will always seek "the group" in one way or another. Aries seeks independence. Gemini rising focuses on information, Leo on children or recreation. Libra needs a partner and so on. These are clear definitions.

The next layer inward is the Moon and it will be our emotional responses to everything around us and all our sense reactions. It will be our eyesight and our temper or lack of it, our enthusiasms and the way we want to live. It is our families and our habits.

The final core is the Sun, and that is the inner self we aspire to become as well as the person we know ourselves to be. We grow in life from the characteristics of the Moon to those of the Sun. The younger we are the more we are creatures of the Moon, under the influence of our mother and family. The older we get the more individualized we become, gradually asserting our own unique self-hood, and that's the Sun. The skilled astrologer will always keep an eye on the age of the client.

With the Sun one should also be aware that the polarity of Sun and earth will be operational. The Sun will always be in the sign opposite the one the earth actually occupies. That's why Virgos often seem like creative Pisces types and Leos become inventors. Taureans can have a strong streak of militarism like Scorpio and Scorpios sing and entertain like Taurus. This only works with the Sun, by the way. There is no polarity operating with the Moon or the other planets. The Ascendant doesn't operate that way, either. Why does it work this way? Well, imagine a dance done in a circle around a chair. The chair can be the Sun. If you are in the dance you can see the person opposite you on the other side of the chair. When the earth is "you" then the position opposite you is like that person. The zodiac is imagined as being marked off in 30-degree chunks and the one opposite you looks like the one who occupies the "chair." So, because of the angle of vision, you are said to have the Sun in Virgo when you are actually moving in the Pisces sector.

There really are such single factors that mean things on their own. They may be modified by other things, but their intrinsic meanings must be kept in mind for good interpretation or we make many more mistakes.

Cast in Stone?

Modern astrologers like to say that no astrological configuration indicates that anything will definitely happen, or that anything in the chart is cast in stone. I only wish that were true. Some things do seem to be "cast in stone." I am not running the universe, merely doing charts, but I see things that seem inevitable no matter how one tries to avoid them. (Some have happened to me.) Many other things are optional. And for the record, how we respond to any particular thing always seems to be under our control.

Astrology cannot predict what a person does with his/her natal potentials, but one can have a very good idea, based on the pattern. Once we have gone that far, there is still always a small remainder of events clearly marked in our charts that are "inevitable." Such things as the deaths of our parents, for instance, are out of our hands. Accepting that we cannot control everything that happens is something people in general need to learn. Astrologers should keep it in mind, too.

The "Esoteric" Questions

Over the years, I never taught students to use any esoteric idea to explain anything in the chart. I have been asked about this many times, but the key to me is this: anything in the birth chart can be quite adequately understood in terms of this lifetime alone. Anything in the chart can refer to events from the here and now.

I don't discount the notion of reincarnation at all. I don't discount the idea of karma, or dharma or any other Buddhist, Hindu or New Age ideas. I just don't use them to explain astrology. Astrology can stand on its own, thank you very much.

Take the nodes, for instance. I hear people talk about their aspects as referring to spiritual or destiny stuff from past lives. To this I can only say, "well, maybe." But what is absolutely sure about the nodes is how they work in this life to explain relationships, their quality and stresses and enduring possibilities. And relationships may or may not come out of the past. I just use what is in the here and now and leave the rest out of my analyses. It's a lot more useful, I think. Besides, it forces us to learn how things work now, not in some (maybe true but impossible to prove) past.

I have a chapter on the nodes called "Tale of the Dragon" elsewhere in this book. The nodes will always tell you something about the future of whatever you get yourself into, such as marriage, or a job. One woman whose marriage was falling apart asked me why and when I looked at her chart and that of her husband I saw no nodal ties between them at all. I was a little stunned that they got married in the first place, but I suspect it was a hasty choice, perhaps made under the influence of progressions or whatever drug they were using at the time. Both were active in the drug scene then. They eventually divorced and lost all contact with each other. They were simply indifferent to each other.

Strong, enduring relationships always show nodal ties in the charts of the two people involved. One of the strongest is the nodes of one on the angles of the other, or to their Sun or Moon. When both people have them to each other's charts they are relationships of a lifetime. **A planet conjunct one of the Moon's nodes in your chart is important. Period.**

Getting into the chart

Once you have gotten past the ABCs of the chart (Sun, Moon and Ascendant) it is time to examine the aspect pattern. The work of Marc Edmund Jones was a landmark in this area. He saw "bucket" and "bowl" arrangements and helped us understand how these formed personality. He examined the "seesaw" pattern based on several oppositions and said it was a person whose life would be heavily affected by the need to compromise, conciliate and learn to see the viewpoints of others. He saw the "handle" of the bucket arrangement as the determining factor in choosing ways to operate and said that the grand trines and fixed cross patterns also worked in specific ways.

His book on this is worth reading, studying and having in one's library. Some authors are simply too good to ignore and their ideas are so important that it pays to give them the attention they deserve. Jones is one of them.

The Sun

Almost any good astrology text book will tell you how important the Sun is and how it works as the key planet in every chart. It naturally seeks a stage where its light can shine. The stage is the house where it falls in the natal pattern. In the case of Virgo, it won't make you into a person who wants the limelight, but you will be attracted to those who do—or those who take the lead role by some sort of "divine right." I knew a Virgo who told me he didn't ever want to be the top dog, but he wanted to be No. 2 to the best top dog around.

When a woman's Sun is very powerful and she has no career, her Sun refers to the man in her life, and he often becomes her career. This was more common in previous generations, and women's charts were often examined to see how well they fit the "company wife" profile which supposedly helped men get ahead. A company wife entertained beautifully, always was so well organized she could host the boss for dinner on a minute's notice and charmed all the important men who could help her husband. Nowadays, if she has a career, the Sun indicates her own work. In the case of a queen, she is a power by virtue of who she is and her power is inborn, not provided by anyone else in her life—she's a solar figure.

In a man's chart, Sun reveals his health, ego and career. It is his personal power and his ability to affect the factors in his environment that he wants to change. The Sun for both sexes reveals the strength and vitality of the genetic heritage. It is the package we got at birth.

The Sun also always refers generally to all the men in our lives, father, husband, grandfather and boss (if male). In a mundane chart it can refer to the ruler or the president, the mayor or governor or the like as well. It is always the power point.

In a broad sense the Sun also refers to our sense of what is right and wrong. The Sun is the noblest aspirations we have as well as the dream of the ideal in our own lives. Being "the best that we can be" is always a matter of the Sun. Being less than that is letting our Sun sign down.

The Moon

The Moon has a great deal to do with sense impressions—all of the senses. It is the senses that allow us to perceive what is going on. Defective vision, for instance, can affect learning. Ask any child who can't see the blackboard in class.

Both the Sun and the Moon rule the eyesight. In a man, the Sun rules the right and the Moon, the left. In a woman the rule is reversed, the Moon rules the right and the Sun, the left. For both sexes the Moon reveals how well the body works. It is the efficiency of the machinery. One can have a weak Sun but a well-aspected Moon and sail through life without difficulty. But a strong Sun and a poorly functioning Moon may send one to the medical profession for help over and over. Recovery may be assured, but it is a constant process of repair and renewal.

A good comparison is a car. You can have a marvelously designed race car, such as a Ferrari (Sun), which is always in the shop (Moon) and requires endless tinkering (Moon) to show off its innate quality (Sun). Or, you can have a poorly or very simply designed car (Sun) like the old Volkswagen "beetle" which just keeps operating no matter what happens (Moon). In both cases the aspects will tell you which one you are dealing with.

The Moon's monthly cycle has some specific effects on one's life that were elucidated in the book *The Lunation Cycle*, by Dane Rudhyar. He discovered that the eight phases of the Moon put emphasis on different planets in the natal pattern and could also alter the way one functioned. He found that the first 45 degrees of the Moon's travel after the New Moon (New Moon Phase) are affected by the Sun in a sort of subset. The 2nd 45 degrees, the Crescent Phase, shows emphasis on the Moon.

The First Quarter phase, from 90 to 135 degrees, belongs to Saturn and the Gibbous phase, from 135 to 180 degrees shows the emphasis on Jupiter. The Full Moon phase from 180 degrees to 225 is for Mercury and the second gibbous phase which Rudhyar calls the Disseminating Phase, belongs to Venus. That's from 225 to 270 degrees. Last quarter, from 270 to 315 degrees is for Uranus and the final 45-degree phase, the Balsamic, is for Mars. When the Moon is in specific signs or making certain types of aspects, the effects can be quite strong. Like all of Rudhyar's books, this one pinpoints things good astrologers should know about. He's an important influence in modern astrology and his book on the lunation cycle also belongs on an astrologer's shelf. Some of his other books are more theoretical but it's part of an astrologer's education to look at our craft from many other viewpoints.

A Moon/Saturn conjunction gives a child a heavy sense of duty and responsibility for and to her parents. Any Moon/Saturn tie at all gives one a strong sense of responsibility. These are the people who never make a promise they don't plan to keep. You may have a hard time getting a Moon/Saturn person to agree to do something but once they agree, they'll do it. If the Moon/Saturn linkage at birth is weak or non-existent, a promise doesn't matter. Promises and agreements are simply the individual's way to get you to quit bothering them. Such a person will promise you anything but may never produce. Look at the charts of many politicians and you will see how many have very little sense of obligation when it comes to a promise.

The sign the Moon occupies matters greatly. When the Moon is in Scorpio a woman will have gynecological difficulties. Guaranteed. The delivery of a baby is often difficult, and sometimes dangerous to the mother. It will often mean additional medical care for one reason or another. Never overlook annual GYN exams! The Moon deals with the reproductive function and women born with that Moon position can have things like toxemia, placenta previa, breech birth, a tubal pregnancy and tons of other major and minor difficulties. It may include Caesarian sections if there is a Mars aspect to the Moon. A poorly aspected Moon can mean miscarriages, for instance. The Moon debilitated in Capricorn can provide some of the same problems. Capricorn also seems to provide lactose intolerance for milk and dairy products. Aries and Aquarian Moons seem to have this problem, too.

Fears show up quickly in Capricorn Moon children. They need a lot of simple reassurance and demonstrations that there really is no monster under the bed in order to grow up as confident, secure adults.

Aquarian Moons are people with lots of theories about how to make things work better. You find them everywhere in scientific and mechanical arenas where their inventive streak turns practical as well as in politics and charitable organizations. Both Virgo and Aquarius Suns think other people need fixing. Virgo does it one person at a time and Aquarius will try to do it wholesale with society at large. Both can be tiresome when this is carried too far.

The Taurus Moon is remarkably easy going in life and seldom gets upset at what others do. It's their business, this person thinks. Sometimes there is an ability to handle money well or an interest in music. Sometimes a parent is an important musician. Life tends to take care of Taurus Moon people.

The Cancer Moon can often be a moody person, going up and down with the way the wind blows. This is a highly sensititve, intuitive child who needs plenty of babying from mom and in adulthood will fuss over the home and kitchen. They like to cook as a rule, and it sometimes becomes a career. Family is highly important in their lives.

The Pisces Moon is blessed with imagination and creativity. The Leo Moon gets management skills and Sagittarius Moons often have a major case of wander lust. (So does the Sun in that sign.)

Gemini Moons have wide interests and like to talk about them. Like all the air signs they have a hefty streak of sociability. The Virgo Moon person needs careful tending, because he or she develops allergies and environmental sensitivities as fast as you can count. It's also one of the best positions for the conscientious worker.

In a broad sense, the Moon is all the women in our lives, starting with mom and her nurturing qualities. It's a man's wife and what kind of home he wants. In a woman's chart it tells a lot about how many children she'll have or how strong her interest in them is. In all cases, it is the empathic qualities that give us insight into the "feelings" of others. It's also our personal habits and the strength of the tie to our families.

Mercury

Mercury rules the mind generally and its faculties particularly. Mercury processes the information we absorb. It does not tell us what we process. People with stationary Mercury at birth process the data with lightning speed and are often very witty as a result. They love puns and see double meanings everywhere, and not necessarily only sexual ones. Mercury retrogrades process information more slowly than Mercury direct types, but they seem to do it more deeply and thoughtfully. During a lifetime, many of us experience periods when progressed Mercury changes direction and we may begin or end times of intense study, for instance, that last many years.

The sign of Mercury, the aspects it receives, the ruler of House 3, any planet in it and Moon therefore are ALL needed to assess learning abilities. Mercury alone does not tell all.

Mercury in air signs is the most logical and processes information gained from others the most readily. Mercury in the fire signs likes direct experience (they're the hands-on types). They like to learn from doing. Earth sign Mercurys are the most orderly and structured. Give them a manual of instruction. Water sign Mercurys take all kinds of mental leaps and make intuitive connections. They absorb information from the air sometimes, it seems. These are the children who get the math answers without seeing any need to account for all the intermediate steps. They drive teachers mad and the children miss the point entirely.

These general ways of functioning can be sharply modified by the third house and or other factors. If you have a Gemini Sun, you will always have some mental quickness even if the Mercury is afflicted by slow-boat Saturn and located in matter-of-fact Taurus. Virgo Moons will always exhibit some type of orderly mental process. A lot of air in the chart is mental, no matter what else is going on. An active third house is an active mind.

Capricorn Mercury wants information that is true, reliable and can be proven. It does not like wishy-washy stuff that floats around in the air (spoken or heard). It likes a manual or a book. It wants to be able to find the same information again in the same words on the same page and be able to make sure it's still there. It's all part of the cautious nature of the sign.

Venus and Mars

One night I was watching the televised story of the Hillside Stranglers case where two men with twisted attitudes toward women would use their victims for sexual experimentation and then torture them in various ways before killing them. The psychologist on the show talked about the dominance issue getting out of hand—in other words, strangling a woman gave these two weirdos the ultimate feeling of dominance over the female.—Mars damaging Venus, for sure. One of the traditional stances on Mars and Venus is that Venus never benefits from too much Mars. The niceness of Venus gets overwhelmed by Mars crudity.

I seldom work on the charts of criminals. For one thing, crimes upset me and I just can't feel interested in delving into the minds of the perpetrators, particularly those of sex criminals or those who torture others. But I would expect to find perversions of the normal Mars and Venus drives in such charts.

Others who have studied them say parental houses should be examined as anger and violence are learned young, certainly in the home. Every chart should be looked at that way, to my mind. What we are is shaped so powerfully in childhood that the adult can never be fully understood without this knowledge.

Personally I find it difficult to understand such twisted attitudes. Part of the need to understand some of the more violent patterns is plenty of experience. I think I would need access to a lot of bad charts before I could pinpoint the precise mechanisms involved. I know there are many astrologers who like to dig and pry at the charts of criminals to see how they function. I'm not one of them. Creepy people just give me a great distaste for such work. I'm glad somebody does it, but I don't want to be the one.

The reason the conjunction of Mars and Venus damages Venus—the planet of love and harmony—is because Mars is simply stronger and physical urges are mighty tough to rein in. It takes some good aspects –trines and sextiles, for instance— to bring out the gentleness of Venus without squelching Mars. But it certainly gives the individual sex appeal. And, interest in sex, for that matter.

The late, great Marilyn Monroe, considered one of the world's "sex goddesses" also had a pretty large number of men with whom she had love affairs. It would be ridiculous to think they were all platonic. I've included her chart so you can see how well she parlayed her Venus and Mars into fame and fortune. (See her chart on the next page.)

I would not go so far as the late Rheinhold Ebertin does in one of his books, flatly saying aspects of Venus and Mars to the outer planets leads to perversion, but I think any contact by Venus or Mars to the outer planets can encourage a "twisting" of the norm. It can get out of hand in a hurry. Mix in a little Uranus or Pluto and it can all get very, very murky. This is where other areas of the chart need to be studied for ethical considerations.

On the other hand, contacts to the outer planets can also make people more interesting and exciting. If the rest of the chart is that of a stable personality, the seasoning of such aspects is delightful. Venus gets creative with contacts to Neptune. Mars is full of surprises and invents interesting things to do and see with aspects to Uranus. A Saturn contact can be stabilizing, and a Jupiter one can give a sizeable push toward goals in life.

One of the more interesting progressed aspects in a chart is when Venus comes to natal Mars or Mars progresses to natal Venus. In both cases the individual seems to face a decision: The spirit or the flesh. It may be disguised as something else, but often it is a quite clear choice to make. If either planet rules the house of marriage it can be the time when the partner is first met or when the marriage occurs. Or, it can be when the marriage takes a turn and deepens or even ends, sometimes because a third party enters the picture. It is never a wishy-washy contact.

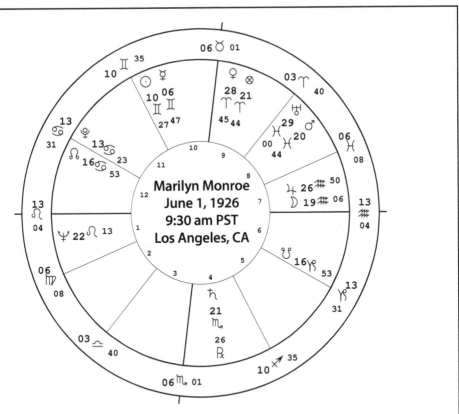

Marilyn Monroe was born Norma Jean Mortenson, and became a worldwide icon of sexuality in the movies. Her angular fixed T-square with its outlet in House 10 shows the drive to succeed. The Mars/Uranus conjunction in the 8th house shows the mysterious nature of her death and the suspicions surrounding it. She remains an iconic image of sexuality long years after her death. Chart is AA from Clifford Data Compendium.

Jupiter

Jupiter is a planet with a mission. It wants to improve everything, make it bigger or better and save it for tomorrow. It deals with the principle of expansion and is one of the two planets aimed at society in general and how we function in that area of our lives.

The expansion can be in the waistline or time spent in the soup kitchen that one's church operates for the poor. It can propel us to find a wider arena for our professional lives as well as helping us improve our education to fit that bigger role. It brings opportunity and important people who can help us reach our goals. It inspires us to benefit others in society. It preserves us at our peak, or tries to. This is why it is often credited with helping us recover from illness or accident. It is the "lucky" planet, so many people believe, though Venus is the ruler of money. Jupiter opens the way to make money.

The principle of preservation can be seen in the humble can of peas in the kitchen cupboard. The earliest and most successful canning method which preserved food was the tin can and tin is Jupiter's metal.

Laughter belongs to Jupiter, as do parties and all convivial get-togethers. These things preserve our mental balance and help us through the rigors of daily life. Jupiter deals with hope and belief.

Any activity which expands or stretches mind or spirit comes under Jupiter. Education, political ideas and philosophy, religious beliefs and practices belong to Jupiter. So does foreign travel. People from places different from our own experience are said to "broaden" our horizons as they force us to think or behave in different ways. All the activity which prompts us to think out of the box or over the hill to the next place is Jupiterian.

Philanthropy, the providing of benefits for the common good, comes under Jupiter. Thus, foundations operated by the wealthy, as well as grants and awards in general are part of the Jupiter package. Honors of any sort always come under Jupiter, whether it's a simple certificate of accomplishment or a Nobel Prize.

Jupiter is one of the two planets which rule travel and how we do it. The other is its natural partner, Mercury. While Mercury takes us next door, Jupiter takes us to a new country. When man lives on the Moon routinely, Mercury might eventually rule such travel. But for now, it's a far trip and very few people ever reach the Moon, so that level of travel comes under Jupiter. All the vehicles which enable us to travel belong to one of those two planets. A big cruise ship is Jupiter. A ferry across the harbor to get to work (which we use every day) is Mercury.

While Mercury helps us take in information, Jupiter is the planet that helps us use it to form cohesive patterns. It deals with belief systems and comprehension. Jupiter rules politics and philosophy as well as the principles of law and opinion.

When in doubt about whether Jupiter rules a particular thing, the simple word "big" can be a key indicator. Jupiter also shows the drive in a person's life for a professional standing of some sort and many people with strong Jupiter positions acquire job titles, such as Manager or Doctor or Editor, or ones that refer to rank such as Detective, Vice-chairman or Envoy.

Saturn

Saturn's children—those born under Capricorn Sun, Moon or Ascendants—tend to have their problems early in life. Their old age is likely to be considerably easier as they realize they are in control of their lives and have already dealt (successfully, by then) with most of their issues. A wise astrologer always keeps an eye on the age of a client.

Saturn is Jupiter's partner in the social arena. But it is also Jupiter's opposite in many ways, as partners always seem to be. Saturn's principle is contraction. That means shrinkage. It means less, rather than more and smaller, rather than bigger. Saturn rules pessimism and realism and one way people deal with difficult things is often through humor. Many professional comedians have a strong Saturn in their charts. Jupiter may rule laughter, but it is Saturn that finds the true pathos and humor in life. Saturn crafts the joke.

Saturn is considered the greater malefic in astrology because its lessons are always about patience, endurance, persistence, organization and justice. It can do permanent damage in life. A wise man once said we should never pray for Justice (Saturn) but rather Mercy (Jupiter) since humans are all so flawed. Saturn deals with judgment and the power to impose penalties. Perhaps if our prayers were answered with true Justice we would find it a hard bread to swallow.

Saturn is always at work when we labor, whether at a job or a marriage or a human relationship that is difficult to deal with. The process of learning is Saturn's function. Jupiter deals with life's trines, but Saturn with life's squares. In order for us to learn, there is always a lesson plan. Each chart contains the one ideally suited to the person who gets it. Saturn deals with rigor and toughness and its transits are always a testing process to see what we have learned and how well we can apply it.

One of Aesop's tales is a perfect illustration. It is about the grasshopper and the ant. It is the ant that works all summer storing food for the winter and the grasshopper which sings and plays the summer away. When the cold winds blow, it is the ant which survives until the next spring. Aesop was very good at illustrating important truths with his tales. Another very Saturn tale is *The Tortoise and the Hare*. The race is won, not by the speedy rabbit who overestimates his ability to run hard when the time comes, but by the slow, determined tortoise who just keeps on going.

Saturn deals with cold and old age, with the bones, the teeth and the skin. Its metal is lead, which protects against unknown dangers (such as radiation) but is not a healthy metal for people to take into their bodies. It is the heaviest element and the slowest to change.

Uranus

In a culture where "fitting in" is important, people who "stand out" are seen as a threat. In other words, Saturn is safe, Uranus is not. Uranus is strong in the charts of astrologers, and of course it takes a lot of independence and refusal to follow the crowd to be an astrologer.

But remember, we all grow in life. The Moon is our past, our childhood. The Sun is our future and our adulthood. We grow from the Moon to the Sun, in a sense.

You may have learned HOW to fit in as a child (Taurus Moon) , but doing it as an adult (Aquarian Sun) can be a mighty uncomfortable fit. Yet nevertheless, Uranus is active all through life and often upsets us in order to force us to grow.

When the planet rises or has too many stresses in the natal package you have the born rebel, an iconoclast and one whose own urges sometimes take priority over issues of responsibility or social obligation.

I think natal Uranus in 12 is not always the mark of the person who rises to governance—at least I haven't seen it very frequently. Uranus in 11 or even 10 is more common, certainly in the U.S. Many charts of legislators and political figures have this planet high in the chart. It's a bit more difficult to manage for some people. The political arena suits it.

Transiting Uranus is in a sign for 7 years. However, it's sneaky and any time it throws an aspect to a natal planet, or receives one, it means turmoil going on. Neptune is worse, spending 14 years per sign. And Neptune can be a continuing confusion if it hits too many natal placements all at once in its travel. These long transits form the background of affairs relating to their house position. Things are simply happening where they are, or focused in those areas. It all goes back to the natal. But doesn't it always?

Neptune

People with Neptune in the first house don't know who they are. Neither does anybody else. It's a lifelong job to figure that out and meanwhile, they are walking antennae, picking up on everybody else's emotional reactions to them.

They modify their behavior depending on who they're with. If they grow up with people who love them and approve of them, they will have a much more constructive development of their personality than if they learn to hide themselves from the harshness of others. If that happens, you still get the innocent look on the outside but the scared kid on the inside may never come out to play. That's quite common. Sometimes, Neptune in the 4th points to a big family secret or a parent who was invalided or seriously handicapped. A lot of the time it's alcoholism or even mental illness in one of the parents or in the family heritage. It's one of the best indicators of adoption. But sometimes, it's just a very murky situation.

Pluto

Pluto direct in the fourth house can be a possessive or domineering parent. Retrograde, it tends to be an isolationist parent who doesn't relate to very many people—and none in the home. Pluto—like all the outer planets—can be heavily affected by its retrograde position.

Sometimes it's a parent who withdraws completely to avoid dealing with the other parent. The result is that Pluto in House 4 people like to live alone to avoid dealing with bossy or dictatorial people. Sometimes —if Pluto is direct— they get bossy themselves, but if Pluto is retrograde, its behavior is usually withdrawal and avoidance.

I find Pluto involved in both birth and death issues, or beginnings and endings. Times when doors close and doors open. Things that arrive (like pregnancy) and depart.

Some years ago I read an article by a man who said that Pluto represents a profound challenge by the soul to deal with things that have been kept hidden. That says it, too, to me.

The Nodes of the Moon

In almost every chart I have ever done with the nodes in the same degree as a planet, that planet points to special needs—trouble, if you want to use that word—for the individual. The degree can be in any sign, what counts is simply the degree. A man I know with the Moon in that condition married twice, left both wives and the children and his birth home behind and never seems to have found a place of his own. He is constantly living with someone else whom he then leaves behind in a restless progression onward. He's always "looking" for home and always "leaving" it behind. It's curious.

Pay attention to any chart you get with this contact and give the planet extra notice. You'll be amazed by how many problems are linked to it. Jupiter for instance: trouble with education, or travel, or opportunities that never quite pan out and promotions that lead to firing, (the principle of being promoted to one's highest level of incompetence) and etc.

Ivy Goldstein Jacobson was the one who steered me in this direction and I find it amazingly accurate. A word here on Ivy's books. She is a gold mine of information and every one of her books is worth whatever you pay for it. I own them all and have for many years. If you are looking for the psychology of astrology, she's not it. But if you want to know how things really work, Ivy can tell you.

Aspects

Sorry, but nothing ever "cancels out" or negates anything else in the chart. Everything always exists side by side. The sextiles don't soften squares—only allow other options for dealing with the problems implied by the squares.

But squares are not bad in themselves. Charts with no squares or stresses are weak charts and people don't develop much inner toughness. The effort it takes to solve square problems develops grit, stick-to-it-ivity and muscle.

Sextiles are opportunity aspects—you can use them or not. Squares don't give you an option—it's do it or else with a square.

When 3 or more planets occupy the same sign of the zodiac, it is called a stellium. For most purposes, I don't use just Sun, Mercury and Venus. Mercury and Venus are always close to the Sun. I think a true stellium needs other planets—or at least one, in addition to those three. When three or more planets occupy the same house, they have some of the same effect as the stellium in one sign.

The house with the stellium has importance. A lot of the life focus will be there, in one way or another. BUT—and this is a big BUT—a lot of the energy "explodes" into the opposite direction. It is like setting off a firecracker. You light one end, but the thing shoots up into the sky in the direction of the other end. This creates tensions and stresses, because opposite signs or houses have different needs and requirements in our lives.

Example: People with 10th house packages need a stable, secure home and family life if they are going to accomplish their mission to the world. But it's a case of how much work vs. how much time at home for that person. If the north node is part of the stellium, the job will get top priority, with home just fueling the focus. If the south node is uppermost, the family will get it and the job will be "merely" a way to take care of matters in 4. In order to tell which is which, you really need to look at the whole chart, of course.

Stelliums have power—they involve conjunctions of potent energies that are more complex than merely having two planets in the same space. Sometimes people with too much power are like teens with big cars—they wreck the car the first time out and spend their life in driver's ed. Other times such a stellium can fuel a life of accomplishment. Each planet can contribute different coloring.

Jupiter is the professional person —Saturn is the authority figure—Uranus is the artsy weirdoes you keep attracting into your life, and Neptune can be the losers. But Jupiter can also deal with fat friends, Saturn can be poor relatives, Uranus can be the family's wealthy eccentric and Neptune the fiddle player for the harmonic orchestra. A lot of interpretation is fairly ordinary and there can be a wide range of things to explore.

Nothing in astrology operates alone. **My Rule No. 1 is: Everything Modifies Everything Else.** We give simplistic rules and then start piling on the exceptions, the expansions, the modifiers and addendums until you feel like screaming.

The rule sounds simple, but I know that when you are learning astrology it gets frustrating. But that's just the way it works.

Orbs

I think we have to recognize that the Sun and Moon have larger orbs of influence than the planets. Their sphere extends nearly 10 to 12 degrees and when angular, they have much greater impact than when cadent or even succedent. Anyone with planets in potent positions will express the qualities of those planets. Sometimes it's from a dignified position, sometimes a debilitated one.

Angularity is a big factor in interpretation. Angular planets are going to be more "obvious" in their expression and it really doesn't have much to do with the tightness of orb. Anyone with Mars in an angle, for instance, is going to express some Mars qualities even if all the Mars aspects to other planets are wide. I think this is what makes for confusion on the orbs.

The longer I look at charts the more I think that some rules are too loose and some rules should be ignored. Figuring out which is which is what takes 50 years or so. I'm still working on it. When I finalize my opinion, I'll let you know.

Fine Tuning

Dispositing is a simple principle. The Moon rules or "owns" Cancer. Any other planet there is either a guest (like Mercury) or an honored visitor (Jupiter) or an undesirable visitor (Mars or Saturn). Therefore the Moon, just like a landlord, is said to disposit (outrank) any visitor at all. The Moon owns the property. This is why rulership is important. It establishes rank.

Jupiter is "exalted" in Cancer (honored visitor—drag out the best china and chill that $50 bottle of wine.) Saturn is debilitated there (it rules the opposite sign, Capricorn) and Mars is in its fall there (it is said to be exalted in Capricorn). Therefore, serve hot dogs and beans and use paper plates and hope the heck they leave soon, right?

These things are pretty simple when you understand the principle.

Rulership

Now, one of the big problems in our high-tech era, where new asteroids and comets and planets are coming out of the woodwork every other week, is to figure out where they all "belong." We have had Uranus around since the start of the Industrial Revolution. It wasn't too hard to give it a high tech slant and see that it "obviously" belongs to Aquarius, the sign of inventions and science. So, there is a lot of general acceptance of this one.

Neptune came along quite a bit later, but as soon as Neptune showed up the world was full of "mystic wonders" and spiritualism and was quickly assumed to belong to Pisces, which everybody knows is the only place for a ditzy planet, right? It's been studied for well more than 100 years.

Now Pluto pops up—in Cancer, yet—in the '30s and women marched off to the factories en masse, simultaneously altering the balance of family power, as the world launched WWII and eventually the nuclear age. There is pretty much agreement that nuclear energy is Pluto's department (hence the Power business—the first folks with "the bomb" held the clout in world affairs.). Wasn't too long after all that before the feminist movement exploded as women refused to surrender their own power, heading off to the job market again and the power of the paycheck, along with independence and personal determination.

So we had two signs suggested—Aries and Pluto. While some few may still try to attribute Pluto to Aries, most of us in the last 45 years have concluded that Aries is too simplistic for the kind of power/control issues that Scorpio can manage quite well. We shoved Pluto's general rulership into Scorpio's hands.

Along come asteroids. We get Juno, Vesta, Pallas, Ceres. The rush is on to find them a slot. Virgo? Libra? Oops, now we've got Chiron. Where in blazes does that one go? This thing is getting out hand. We are naming asteroids right and left. We have comets roaring into the system. (Gee, what sign rules comets?)

Astrologers are creatures of custom like everybody else. We want to put things where we think they belong so we can get a handle on them. But the big question is, are we right? I don't know, to tell you the truth. Personally, I use the so-called "old rulers" far more than the outer planets in the vast majority of my work. I get straighter answers.

Yes, there are times when a question or a topic obviously belongs to Uranus or Neptune or Pluto, but does that mean they "rule" a sign or just "rule" certain affairs only? Are they outside the whole rulership business? Acting more like traveling meter readers to all the signs? Beats me. I still have an open mind on the question, though I tend to go along with the majority on the Scorpio/Aquarius/Pisces co-rulership idea. But just because you renovate the upstairs and rent it out to a new tenant doesn't mean you are any less the owner. I still use Mars, Saturn and Jupiter for Scorpio, Aquarius and Pisces.

The Nonagesimal

The correct term for the point 90 degrees from the Ascendant is the nonagesimal—instead of confusing it with the MC, which is correctly called the Midheaven. The nonagesimal has some very interesting properties all its own. It can be looked at in a similar way to a last quarter phase Moon but in regard to the Ascendant. I think the nonagesimal is more a personal point of accomplishment than the MC, which has to do with how we fit into the broader community. For instance, when Saturn crosses the nonagesimal, one is at a peak of personal status, money making, accomplishment. It's a time of feeling good about yourself.

When Saturn crosses the MC it often brings added responsibility as the community assesses us and sees what we ought to be doing. For people who have been doing what they shouldn't, this is karma time, big time. But it can just as easily bring the Presidency to a candidate—the "responsibility" business.

Saturn across the MC usually comes when "the company" we work for is in trouble and "needs" us. The reward of doing what is needed comes later but with Saturn, it always comes. Saturn to the nonagesimal seems to say: See what you can do when you try? Aren't you proud of yourself? Look around, this is the place you worked so hard to reach. The nonagesimal point is personal ambition, desire, self-focus, which may have nothing to do with the broader, community-oriented issues of the MC.

The MC is specifically career. The nonagesimal may have to do with intensely private activity. The nonagesimal —like all equal house factors— relates directly to the ascendant, which is the one absolute point of an equal-house horoscope. It also shows what we are willing to do to reach personal goals, etc., and our hidden motivations and ambitions.

Saturn crossing that point, or its opposite, which is also in stress aspect to the ascendant says: Are you ready for a break? Getting tired? Taking care of yourself? Eating your veggies? Getting exercise?

Watch transits to the nonagesimal. See for yourself. Any major transit will have enough punch for you to register what it involves if you watch a bit. Just remember that it won't act in the same way as the MC, which dumps us out into the open for our "public persona." If they are close to each other, or in the same sign, they may appear to work alike. They don't.

The Natal Chart in Relationship to Transits

A transit in the 4th house of an older person may point to their house or members of their family needing care. Same transit of the 4th for a young person may mean deciding where to live and how they deal with moving out of the parental home. It may involve dealing with the health of parents. The transit of the 5th is different—putting focus on children OR love affairs, perhaps, for the young OR leisure travel for the seniors, etc.

The fact that you point out long-term activities or see them gives you the framework for what is happening in the background. This is a tool for everyone to use. But like a chisel, it accomplishes more in the hands of someone who knows how to use a chisel.

I don't use planetary returns very often. It's one less thing, as Forrest Gump used to say. But when a planet aspects itself, it sets off the natal indications. Here we go again—back to the natal. If the planet was well aspected in the natal, events are seen as interesting and favorable. If the planet was under stress in the natal, the events are seen as stressful.

I think people look at the transiting aspects Uranus makes and gets and forget about what Uranus was doing in the natal, for instance. Personal example here, if you will forgive me. Uranus transiting my 3rd was conjunct my natal 3rd house Saturn off and on for a couple years. So, during that time, my neighbor the local school system, decided to use the "unneeded" woody property behind me to build 3 new elementary schools, which created a big mess and absolutely destroyed the wooded, rural aspect I treasured. But my chart tells me it will probably help my property value in the long run since I had a good natal aspect between that Saturn and Uranus.

Uranus followed that up with an aspect to my natal Moon, which echoes an opposition they form in my natal. This implies property, home and family. During the same time period my sister moved and put her car into storage at my house so she could go off to Europe.

Another sister sold her house, also put some things in storage in my house and headed off to Florida to find a new life. It was a long transit of my 3rd house. The transit over Saturn ended but the one aspecting my Moon was repeated by a later station. My sister came back from Europe and stayed with me for some months. It had other, more favorable aspects so everything was not bad, but it was definitely change, change, change for my siblings. Oh, and they did return and pick up their belongings.

The natal is the acorn out of which the oak grows. If we look at how two trees interact with each other and forget what they are doing to the third one we miss the point. If the two trees are evergreens and the third is a cherry tree, the cherry won't do well close to them no matter what kind of mulch we use. The evergreens have turned the soil too acid for the cherry and you simply can't make them compatible. You can't say that just because the two evergreens have plenty of room at the top and the cherry has room at the bottom they should get along. You need to think of what they ARE.

The evergreens are like the natal. It was there first. The Johnny-come-lately cherry just won't do well in that environment.

Chapter 25

Going Backward
The Matter of Retrogrades

The issue of natal planets retrograde is one I have found useful to include in my bag of astrological tools. While some astrologers do not make use of their subtle influences, I do, and I would like to mention some of the important things they tell me.

First of all, retrogrades frustrate the action of the houses they rule. They promise more than they deliver. Charts in which there are many planets retrograde are said to lack "vitality" in some of the old texts and supposedly are not the mark of people who live long and healthy lives. Muhammad Ali had six planets retrograde at birth and became a sports superstar, but has spent most of his adult life suffering from Parkinson's Disease.

The average number of retrogrades which most of us get is two. People with no retrogrades or only one have some unique characteristics. For one thing, they don't seem to need the approval of others before taking some action on their own behalf. It seldom occurs to them to ask for it, in fact. The result is that they seem more independent than those around them and rely less on the opinions of other people. They are often surprised when people call them selfish or inconsiderate. They were just doing what they saw needed to be done and are usually astounded by the accusation. In the first place, they didn't think they needed approval. And in the second place, they didn't have time to bother with it. And in the third place, if you don't like it, it's your own fault for not getting up and doing something about the situation yourself. And in the fourth place—forget it. It's over and done with now, anyway.

People with more than two planets retrograde need more approval for their actions. The more planets retrograde, the more time they are apt to spend getting feedback before they do anything. Is it all right with Joe? And how about Mary? What will Billy think? And Jake? Will this have an effect on something else I plan to do? I want to make sure that when I do this there won't be any surprises for anyone and nobody gets upset. You get the picture.

A lack of retrogrades is not the kind of setup for someone who chooses politics or the diplomatic corps. It's dandy for an entrepreneur or a problem-solver of course, because these are people who operate so far out on their own they don't even leave tracks.

Which is best? Neither. They are merely different. A knitting teacher I once knew said there were no errors in knitting, only techniques that didn't fit in the current pattern and were better saved and used elsewhere. That applies quite well to the retrograde/direct question, I think.

The outer planets spend a great deal of the time retrograde. We must draw a distinction between the personal planets Mercury, Venus and Mars, which spend most of their time direct in motion and the rest of the planets, which can be retrograde half of the year.

Mercury goes retrograde three times a year. Venus and Mars only go retrograde every other year. The Sun or Moon, of course, never go retrograde. Retrograde Mercury types are seldom quick with repartee. They like to think about things a while before they talk, and I have heard retrograde Mercury people moan for years that they could think of a million things to say about a subject the day after the party or a job interview or the like. However, when they do speak, it is pointed and goes right to the bone.

Example: A **retrograde Mercury** ruling house 10 goes direct at age 33 (33 days after the birthday in the ephemeris). The individual changes jobs—perhaps even careers—and there is a major change in the life of one of the parents. The mother may retire from her job, or the father will become ill or retire, etc.

Sometimes learning difficulties plague the child with Mercury Retrograde. They may have speech handicaps, or be slow to talk, or simply find school less than interesting.

The year Venus goes direct always brings an important new love into the life of an individual. One man I know used to run around on his wife until his Venus went direct. They had been married several years, but that year he had a devastating extra-marital affair and then his wife became pregnant during the period when he was experiencing a renewal of his commitment to his marriage. The birth of his daughter turned him into a person who could finally say, "I love you" to the woman in his life and softened his whole range of interpersonal relations. He quit "kicking against the goal," relaxed and accepted the love in his family circle.

Retrograde Venus children have great difficulty expressing genuine affection and the normal emotional give and take of love. They may actually distrust the expressions of love they receive from others, and prefer friendship, which they understand better, or later on, lust, with which they can cope quite comfortably, thank you very much. Or, in a contrary manifestation, they give affection which appears quite genuine to everyone but it means little to them. They have been trained that way, but it lacks a certain sincerity.

The year Venus changes direction by progression is often a very dramatic one. They "discover" love if it is going direct, or they lose an important love, if it is going retrograde. Sometimes the discovery is the birth of a child, or the year one decides on marriage, but it alters them profoundly.

I have the chart of a woman with Gemini rising and a retrograde Jupiter in Cancer. It rules her 7th and such a dignified position usually promises a comfortable home and a generous spouse who makes a good living. The retrograde condition spoils that. In her case, she supported two husbands. The first was a drinker, the second simply unsuccessful. She had many lovely homes but worked too hard to enjoy them as much as one would think and was forced to leave each one behind by a job change or transfer almost as soon as she had it decorated.

A **retrograde Saturn** seems to show that the father's influence was missing in the early life. It may have been due to the father working two jobs, or having a traveling job or illness or just simply failing to give enough time to the child in the early years, but in any case, the child never gets enough of the father's attention/approval. Sometimes it was an extended period of absence or absence at a critical time rather than during the entire childhood, but it always has an important effect. The individual must work to find inner security as an adult and learn to give themselves the approval they crave. In effect, they have to learn how to be their own parent. Sometimes this makes them highly reluctant to be bossed or accept "the word" as law from anyone without proving it out to their own satisfaction. It also gives a certain lack of regard for authority, though a willingness to abide by it.

There is a very old rule in astrology that Saturn is less trouble retrograde and Mars is more trouble retrograde. It's worth keeping in mind if you are dealing with people who have such positions. Retrograde Saturn eventually grows up but retrograde Mars has a lifetime of learning to do on how to control temper.

A **retrograde Mars** in a woman's chart can often show she has fears of men and sexuality. She sometimes fears the whole notion of having a child (the physical delivery), as well. In a man's chart, there is usually early doubt of one's masculinity when one is quite young and a compensating drive to prove it later on. In both sexes, there is an unwillingness to use physical energy for "work" and mental tasks will be chosen instead for money-making, if possible, so that the physical energy can be used for "play."

I find it fascinating that basketball superstar Michael Jordan and golf superstar Tiger Woods both had retrograde Mars positions and both became fierce competitors. Both chose sports careers that allowed them to "play." (See their charts on page, 210.)

The story about the coach who cut Michael Jordan from his high school basketball team because he just wasn't going to turn into a decent player is legendary. Of course, Jordan's Taurus ascendant would never give up, either, but a sports career is a classic case of finding a way to "play" in life.

Tiger Woods was trained by his father from childhood to succeed. A very Saturn tale about Capricornian Woods. The scandal in his private life nearly destroyed him and it is common among Capricorns when some trauma has major effect on a career. They often make surprising comebacks in later years, however.

Both men seem to have run into difficulties in their marriages over relationships with other women. Both were divorced from the mothers of their children. That natal Mars retrograde always shows in some way. Many of those with a retrograde Mars at birth will later experience a year in which the station occurs and Mars then goes direct by progression. They often leave "play" behind at that point and move into the "work" arena. This is not necessarily the year such athletes leave their sport, but it can be if they leave for a job in management, perhaps. Today many such superstars leave their sports careers so financially secure that "work" will never be a necessity for them. Thus, the retrograde Mars comes full cycle—the worth has been proven and they are free to continue playing—perhaps at another sport—indefinitely.

The years Mars goes direct changes one's attitude to the opposite sex, too. Sex can become much less threatening to women and more enjoyable (it may even be the year there is the first really hot romance, if it occurs at the right time of life) and the individual finds more physical energy available for "work." They will often take up a sport or fitness program of some sort if they have not had that in their lives before. It can also be a year when a sports fan simply doesn't find it as compelling as in the past and turns to more useful or practical pursuits.

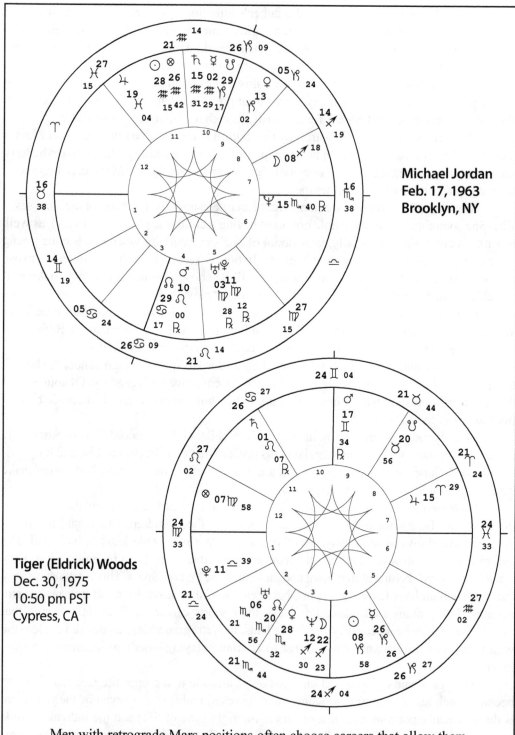

**Michael Jordan
Feb. 17, 1963
Brooklyn, NY**

Tiger (Eldrick) Woods
Dec. 30, 1975
10:50 pm PST
Cypress, CA

Men with retrograde Mars positions often choose careers that allow them to "play" with their physical energy rather than use it up on "work." Some of the best choose professional sports. Here are two world class athletes with such a position.

A **retrograde Jupiter** often shows up in areas dealing with generosity and magnanimity. These can be people who have to learn the "rules" of generosity before making gifts and who will often be found in positions where they make decisions about others. Because Jupiter has so much to do with education and religion, there are often difficulties in achieving higher education and the individual changes religious practices at least once during the lifetime.

The nodes of the Moon go back and forth continually and are retrograde so much you can ignore their motion. I do, anyway.

Retrograde Pluto is fearful of using power and will often avoid jobs and situations that incur too much authority for that reason. It does not want responsibility if it can avoid it. It fears power and will seldom accept it.

Retrograde Uranus hides its independence and will often appear to go along with the majority. If people with this position don't agree, they simply nod to acknowledge that they know what you mean. Then they go do their own thing. But quietly. Sometimes, they like to tell others what to do because they think they know better. This can sometimes be a mark of the busybody.

Retrograde Neptune has problems with issues relating to charity and giving. They can't decide how much or how little to do, and seldom seem to hit a happy medium. Their "hunches" are often untrustworthy. They may tip lavishly or not at all. They give gifts when the mood strikes them and may resent and avoid situations where giving is expected, such as Christmas or birthday parties, for instance. They are not uncharitable, just unwilling to follow other people's rules about it.

During the life, progressions will often change the status of such planets. I strongly recommend that you take a paper ephemeris, go through it for the days after birth and note when each planet will change direction. Each day after birth corresponds to a year in the life. This is vital information for the astrologer.

The year a planet goes direct marks a change in the way individuals use the energy and the way they deal with the affairs of the houses the planets rule. It will also produce events to dramatize such changes.

But what about the reverse situation, you ask. What happens when planets that were direct at birth go retrograde? Ahhh, another tale to tell. For this one, you need to be aware of what areas each planet rules in the birth pattern. A change of direction is vital in understanding subsequent events and will save you from making dumb mistakes in forecasting.

Take Mercury, for instance. One chart I did showed Mercury ruling the 7th house of marriage. The woman was born with it direct in motion. The year it went retrograde she married. The year it later turned direct again, she divorced. Since Mercury's retrograde period runs about three weeks, it is about 21 years by progression, not too many for a difficult marriage to run out of steam.

The retrograde period also marked the end of another woman's education. When Mercury went direct again, she took up a new course of study in an area which had been a hobby and turned it into a successful business not long after.

The year Venus goes retrograde can be a year of heartbreak and emotional loss. I hate to predict for anyone whose Venus is going retrograde because it marks a year when the lover finds someone else, or they lose a beloved member of their family or their spouse asks for a divorce or they are bitterly disappointed by some other deep emotional loss. Sometimes they retreat after that from situations and relationships in which they can lose. They certainly do so for a period of time while healing occurs.

Of course a prediction depends on what house Venus rules and at what stage of life the person is.. If it rules one of the job houses—6 or 10—it can be the year the career ends or the business is lost. If it rules 5, an adored child can leave home permanently and the older parent experiences a severe "empty nest" syndrome. In a younger, unmarried person, it is probably the loss of the lover, or the breaking of an engagement to be married. Because it is Venus, there can, in addition, be financial loss.

It is as well to put a comment in here about the fundamental portfolios that each of the planets has. Whenever a major anything occurs in the progressed chart, it will result in events connected with what the planet naturally rules (Venus for money, or looks, for instance) and what it rules in THIS chart (say the 9th house of education and travel).

A forecast should always include consideration of both things. Obviously there will be a loss of opportunity for travel or education when such an event relates to a 9th house Venus, but the reason may well be financial or emotional. If Venus rules the sign on the 8th, it could be a death that causes the problem, or debt.

It always goes back to rule no. 1 in astrology: Everything modifies everything else.

There is a big difference in astrology between the "always repeatable" mathematical exactitude of chart calculation and the "never repeatable" dynamics of chart interpretation. Each chart we do is unique. We have never seen it before and will never see its exact like again unless the individual has a true time twin. That means we are ALWAYS in terra incognita and we need some tools to help us find our way around. True, a measuring stick that always works would be wonderful, but until we find it, we are left with the process of using generalities to find the specific dynamic of THIS chart.

We are always learning, with every chart we do, I think. We test hypotheses and try to work our way to the truth of them.

I admire people who can be dead accurate 100 percent of the time, but I never expect that of myself. I study, I ponder, I ask questions and I search for what will help an individual find meaning in their life and what provides insight into the way they live it. I've used retrogrades and stations for years because they help me do that, and that's all there is to it.

Chapter 26

The 29th degree

I like to think of the 29th degree as the end of the sidewalk and the beginning of the steps up to a new place. It's not the end of the world, merely the end of one phase of experience.

The 29th degree is probably mis-named. It should be called the 30th degree. After all, the first degree is all the minutes up until you have a total of one degree. The second degree is 1 degree plus so many minutes until it has filled up two degrees.

Nevertheless, we'll stick with the 29th degree title so we all know what we're talking about. This means a planet or angle at 29 degrees and change, just before it enters another sign. It has a number of interesting effects when planets are found there in any sign in the chart. Some people like to say it means the individual is an "old soul" wrapping up "karmic obligations" in this lifetime. I don't use such explanations in my interpretations because, frankly, I don't think we can be sure of that and I don't want to give out misinformation.

What I think it means is that such people have major shifts that happen in their life-times in the areas ruled by the planets in those last degrees. I think the 29th degree always points to an element of difficulty. Sometimes it is the key factor in understanding a chart. If either the Sun or Moon is there it has some very specific meanings.

The 29th degree is a degree of being "worn out" or sometimes shows a planet there lacking in ability to manifest smoothly. It can show difficulties in functioning in the normal way. It is similar to both the group of Pleiades star positions (which mean something to weep about) at the end of Taurus (one of the group, Alcyone, has just entered Gemini) and Regulus (the king maker) star at the end of Leo, which will soon enter Virgo. There can be dramatic climbs to the top and sudden falls. A hundred years from now our perceptions of their functions in Taurus and Leo may seem quaint to those whose experience with them is different. It's as if the 29th degree is the last straw of the old and the individual looks forward to the new sign and planets which often express something new from the oncoming sign far more openly than the previous one. It is never a good position to overlook. Some-times there are similar effects at any of the last 3 degrees of a sign, but generally, it is easiest to see in the last degree. It's obviously the source of the "cusp position" dynamics.

Let's start with the Sun. In a man's chart it is his identity, his career and his health. The 29th degree shows at some point there will be a major decision which will alter his career path. It will not be merely a new job but a whole new direction and an actual change of career. It's like a stockbroker quitting to become a school teacher, or a businessman turning to carpentry.

Occasionally that happens quite young and the individual, who has, for instance, gotten a medical degree decides to become an administrator and never practices medicine at all. Such a one never really identified with it and never became known as a physician. The career is in administration. Other people who don't have their Suns at 29 degrees or even close to it may also do this, but if the Sun is at a 29th degree, there is a strong likelihood of such a thing.

It may also imply poor decision making. Or poor timing. Particularly this is true among those who resist change and stick to the old patterns. These are the kind of people who started buggy whip businesses at the dawn of the automobile age.

It's a good idea to think of the beginning of the sign as the strongest area of it—or the place where its qualities manifest the most purely. Each subsequent decanate is a blend with the qualities of the second sign in the quadruplicity. For instance, the first ten degrees is Aries-Aries, the second ten degrees is Aries-Leo, and the third decanate is Aries-Sagittarius. 29 degrees is the last straw—the last gasp, as it were, and the least "pure" point of the sign. Planets at 28 are not as far gone. Any planet in the 29th degree in my opinion acts weakly in terms of the sign's qualities and presents the chart with a fuzzy image of that area of the life or the people it represents.

Example: Women with Suns in 29 degrees plus minutes often marry men who mean well but who are—in some way—somewhat ineffectual. They may have trouble keeping a good job, or their parenting skills are non-existent, or they are born followers, or too passive, or have emotional problems or something. Maybe they just can't manage money and screw up the budget until you take it away from them, but they lack something noticeably. They may actually have a power drive as a substitute for human interaction, or use aggression rather than sympathy in their family relationships.

Many women with Suns at 29 degrees marry men who have those career changes I mentioned. A lot of them also have major health crises in their lives. Sometimes those crises prompt the career change. This is a degree of weakness, which is probably what spurs the change. There is a weak commitment to the first career choice or weakness of the body, which can't sustain the first choice. Sometimes there is another compelling reason.

In today's world, women also have careers and this happens to women as well. A nurse for whom I have verified birth data has her Sun in the 29th degree. She left the hospital scene and went into sales. (See her chart in the Mars chapter on page 55.) Also, I already mentioned the woman who got her MD degree but never practiced medicine. She told me she had found out she didn't really like dealing with sick people. I laughed, but she was serious. There was a pretty weak commitment to medicine, obviously.

When it comes to the health issues, the "weakness" theme continues. Sometimes it is an inability to deal well with stress or frustration and the individual develops a reputation as a bad-tempered person. Other times the weakness shows up in a lack of common sense or an inclination to make poor health choices and the like. But with any corroborating aspects tied to the sixth house, there can be a major shift in the health pattern. An accident leaves a person paralyzed or unable to do the previous job. Or perhaps they have mental issues that affect the job. Bodily health and mental health can be two different things. The weakness can show up in either.

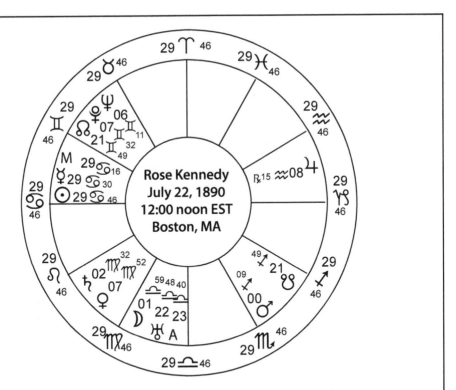

This is a solar chart, noon positions, for Rose Kennedy, the mother of President John F. Kennedy. She was the wife of Joseph P. Kennedy, who was both hugely successful in business and heavily involved in politics. He also served as ambassador to Great Britian and had a notorious liaison with movie star Gloria Swanson when he moved to Hollywood to restructure the movie industry. He was chairman of the SEC and reportedly had his fingers in the illicit liquor industry during Prohibition.

I mentioned that women with the Sun in 29th degree may have passive or ineffectual husbands I used those terms as examples of possible problems —not the only ones. I would not have wanted the man Rose Kennedy married no matter how rich and powerful he was—he was apparently not a very nice man and made her life miserable, according to stories written about him. Her Sun was in 29 degrees. (See chart above.) She was the mother of former U.S. President John F. Kennedy. Powerful men are not always comfortable at close quarters.

There are a surprising number of famous people with 29 degree Suns. Actress Goldie Hawn's "husband" isn't. She and Kurt Russell have yet to formalize a life situation of many years that leaves all their grown children technically bastards. And yes, I know, I know—it's fashionable nowadays to have children out of wedlock, but who doesn't love who enough in these deals?

As to the men, take Raymond Burr—his health problems were well known and cut short his very successful television career. Comedian George Burns (see chart on page 216) lost Gracie Allen, his wife and lifelong comedy partner. She was the one who said the funny things and made the jokes work. He had to restructure his career late in life to become the funny one. His roles as God in two movies in his very old age are classics and he didn't die

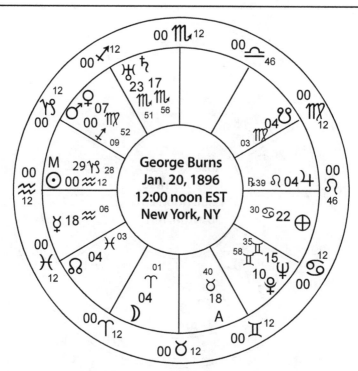

This is a solar chart, noon positions, for George Burns, born on the Capricorn/Aquarius cusp, birth time unknown. However, his life suggests a 29th degree influence possibility, which would give him a birth time earlier in the day. He and his wife, Gracie Allen, were enormously successful for decades in stage, radio and television. After her death, he had to resturcture his act to become the humorous one, since he had always played straight man for her. He also turned to acting and became highly successful.

until he was 100 years old. Many younger people never realized he had become famous originally as Gracie's straight man.

Famed author Edgar Allan Poe was thought to be a near lunatic, even if a wonderful poet. His fiction dwells on the horrifying and there are still questions about his mental stability. (See his chart on the next page.)

The three charts shown here are solar charts, birth time unknown. **For an example of a 29th degree Sun in chart based on recorded birth time, see the Nurse on page 55.**

The 29th degree does not prevent success, but it may come as a result of change imposed by someone else or be less than it otherwise might be due to some flaw. Those are more possibilities. If the 29th degree is the Moon, we have another whole set of problems. First, there will be some major difficulty with the wife and the domestic arrangements if it is a man's chart. One man I know never actually wed his wife but they have a 30-year common-law marriage. She rules the roost, however. He's not happy but very unlikely to ever change that arrangement. He told me he was too old to change. He had just turned 60 and decided facing old age alone would not be fun.

Some men marry women who have health difficulties or who later develop some. This may not show until menopause, for instance, when the woman loses all interest in sex-

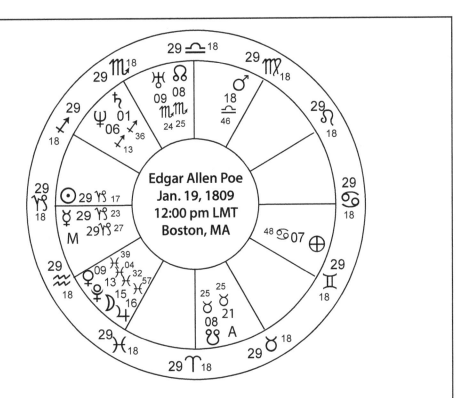

From an unfortunate childhood to his death at 40, Poe's life was full of struggle and difficulty. He was considered somewhat disturbed by many, even as his poetry and stories became hugely successful. For his most famous poem, *The Raven,* he earned only $9. He drank heavily after the death of his young wife from tuberculosis, and the cause of his own death is unknown. (Solar Chart, noon positions, birthtime unknown.)

ual activity. While the woman may not consider it a health problem her husband probably does. There is new research being done on this fairly common development and a medication is out to increase female interest in sex. There are men who would be thrilled to have their wives try this.

The Moon rules the mother, of course, and can show either a weak set of parenting skills on the mother's side or a problem having time to do much of it. Sometimes there was a necessity for the mother to work long hours to support the child, or there was a health problem in the family, perhaps with an elderly female relative. That can force care giving of a different type, which may mean the child gets left out in the process.

The 29th degree usually implies a Void of Course problem with the Moon, which hampers the emotional development. One VOC Moon woman client was devastated by the death of her father when she thought ahead of time during his gradual decline that she could deal with it fairly rationally. She didn't. Such people often kid themselves about their own emotional reaction and then are surprised when their rationalizations prove untrue.

The 29th degree Moon in a woman's chart may show her own weak parenting skills, of course. Sometimes it points to a woman whose thinking becomes more rigid with the years and who refuses to try new things until some major difficulty forces her to do so.

It also shows difficulties in child bearing if there are any supporting aspects. It is not a good position for having many children. One or two is usually the limit and sometimes there is surgery to solve health problems which may involve a hysterectomy. In a man's chart, it points to his wife and her problems. It may be just dissatisfaction with her but not enough to end the relationship, as I said.

In both sexes it can produce stomach problems or breast problems. It is best to be aware of this and not ignore symptoms in those areas.

Some years back I had a client with her Moon in the 29th degree who wanted my opinion on everything and then wanted to argue about it and couldn't make up her mind about anything. I once discussed both sides of an issue with her (some property sale, as I recall) and she insisted I was wrong on both sides (to sell or not to sell). But she couldn't figure out which side she wanted, either, and she was convinced there was a third side to argue about. There are other ways the 29th degree can show up, on the angles or with other planets.

I have said the qualities of the sign weaken as the decanates go on. This does not mean to imply that the people of those subsequent decanates are "weak" in the qualities of the sign, but rather that the sign itself began to become more mixed in the qualities it gives to planets in its area. The 29th degree can have a raft of effects when one of the inner planets Mercury or Venus occupy it. Mercury is often more active than one would expect and Venus may get less satisfaction in a number of ways. Mars may prompt some type of unusual sexual preference, for instance. It only makes love in the morning, or only under the kitchen table, etc. There are as many likes and dislikes as there are people when it comes to sexual activity but the 29th degree Mars person manages a few extras.

Venus at 29 may have trouble with money or a tin ear or actively dislike music. It could also have a complete lack of taste in color or design and no manners at all. Or, it goes to the other extreme and overdoes it. Mercury may end up in sales or may hate sales as a career. It may give someone the desire to write and plenty of good ideas but absolutely no talent. Or the reverse. Talent, but no interest in doing such work at all.

The outer planets are less affected by this position on a personal level. Jupiter is the planet that produces opportunities and fewer may come around when it is in the 29th degree. Saturn may show a complete lack of responsibility. But these flaws can be attributed to other things in the chart and perhaps they are, but the 29th degree's influence will always show up somehow.

Would an aspect to the 29th degree draw another planet into the same type of interpretation? For example with Pluto at 29 opposite Venus at 28, does Venus act in the same way? No. Only Pluto, looking beyond the present and into the future for its goals, does so. It develops a new vision for loving perhaps, but the individual does not "suffer" the same as a 29th degree Venus does. Perhaps it isn't necessary. Besides, Pluto will drag Venus into the future anyway.

Not everything in the chart is caused by a single aspect but when the 29th degree appears it may reinforce something showing up elsewhere and is worth keeping your eye on. And yes, there is some of the same effect apt to manifest in progressions. The 29th degree also seems to have a kind of "universal" influence that I think sometimes operates outside the sign altogether and might even be symbolized by Janus, the two-headed god of the Romans, who looked both back into the past and forward into the future.

Above all else, it shows change is in the wind and the life will reflect this. When the sidewalk runs out, we step onto a new path.

Chapter 27

Critical degrees
(and other things)

The reason 0 degrees is strong is particularly true of the cardinal signs because the solstices and the equinoxes occur at those degrees. They are called the cardinal points of the zodiac. 0 Aries is spring, 0 Cancer is summer, etc.

Then we come to what are called "critical" degrees, which are based on the ancient use of the first degrees of the "mansions of the Moon," which are roughly every 13 degrees through the zodiac. It's actually not exactly 13 degrees, of course, but 12 and change. Those who use them say these are sensitive areas. This is primarily a sidereal technique, not geocentric. Those of us who do tropical astrology use them only occasionally or perhaps not at all.

The Arabic astrologers of old put a great emphasis on the Moon. So did many ancient peoples who used the lunar calendar more than the solar one. We don't use the Moon quite that way today. But they did and it is important in Hindu astrology (Vedic or Jyotish, as it is termed today).

Anyway, they divvied up the zodiac roughly every 13 degrees, which is near to the Moon's average daily motion, starting at 0 Aries and went around it this way.

0—13—26 in Aries

9—22 in Taurus

4—17 in Gemini

Repeat

You can, of course, calculate more exactly and if you have questions, I would recommend Mohan Koparkar's book "The Lunar Mansions" for more details on how to use them.

In certain types of astrological work—particularly sidereal and Vedic—the general areas of each 13 degree "mansion" are used to explain differences in planetary function. Planets that fall on those first degrees are said to be highlighted and more important in the way they function.

The actual USE of the critical degrees is really almost in the horary domain, following many of those rules. In practice, I think the critical degree business accentuates the energy of whatever planet is there. Sort of like adding color to your interpretations, or exclamation points!!!!!! A planet in these areas seems to have more latitude to act than otherwise.

There are other ways to divide the zodiac. Harmonics are simply dividing the 360 degrees of the zodiac by some factor. The 2nd harmonic is 180 degrees (the opposition); the 3rd harmonic divides by 120 degrees (trine) and so on. This is a very valid system and many use it. The actual degrees are not termed critical. "Critical degrees" represent a different type of division. The "critical degree" term in this case is more like "cusp," showing the borders between the lunar mansions.

There are some well known fixed stars which may have an important function in the chart (the Pleiades at 29 Taurus which are moving into Gemini these days, for instance) but which are not technically "critical degrees" in the commonly accepted term. Once you know WHY the areas are said to be important or special you can begin to see how they work.

The 15th degree, while not a true critical degree, is nevertheless a powerful degree area which only applies to the fixed signs. And here's why. Any planet in 15 degrees of a fixed sign automatically acts as if it were also in the 15th degree of another fixed sign as well, by solstice point or "reflex point." It creates a reverberation or echo across the four fixed signs that intensifies rather than being dissipated readily as the energy is in other areas of the zodiac. The reason 15 degrees of the fixed is considered the "most" fixed is because of this effect. 15 Aquarius is square to its solstice point of 15 Scorpio. 15 Leo is square its solstice point at 15 Taurus.. It's like too many men tromping across a bridge in unison. The reverberations build and can bring the bridge down. That's why they never march in step across one. Fixed signs are tough but that echo effect of the solstice points intensifies anything in its range.

Chart Ruler

I use the ruler of the 1st as the chart ruler simply because the first house represents the "me-ness" or individual in question. Things that happen to that planet happen to that person in a very direct way and because it rules the first house has special significance in terms of health and vitality.

However, it may not be the strongest planet in the chart. Most of us are not the strongest and/or most dynamic or influential person in our circle. But that's life. Just because we have a Leo ascendant doesn't mean we rule the world.

But it does mean that our Sun position, sign and aspects are extremely important in analyzing who we are and what we're doing here and what is happening to us at any given time. It does that quite well, I think.

A woman, for instance, with Cancer rising and a powerhouse Moon will zero in on the lunar area and her significant life's focus may be directed toward the lunar activities, the house it's in, and the sign it's in. There will be a strong emphasis on the 4th House and its activities.

We are continually balancing the factors of personality in chart interpretation. The ruler of the Sun sign can often rank as high as the ruler of the ascendant. Add in the most potent planet and wham bang, you have a mixture. Tra la!

I try not to mix up my terms in astrology lest confusion reign. So, I always call the ruler of the ascendant the chart ruler even if other factors show that it is more like the court jester than the ruler because the power in the chart belongs to other planets (which may even signify other people in the individual's life). But that's life.

Dispositors

This is the simple principle of rank. The Moon rules or "owns" Cancer. Any other planet there is either a guest, like Mercury, or an honored visitor (Jupiter) or an undesirable visitor (Mars or Saturn). Therefore the Moon, just like a landlord, is said to disposit or outrank any visitor at all. The Moon owns the property.

Jupiter is "exalted" in Cancer (honored visitor—drag out the best china and chill that $50 bottle of wine.). Saturn is debilitated there because it rules the opposite sign, Capricorn and Mars is in its fall there since it is said to exalted in Capricorn. Therefore, serve hot dogs and beans and use paper plates and hope the company leaves soon, right?

These things are pretty simple when you understand the principle. By seeking the "final" dispositor one theoretically locates the strongest planet. However, any planet in its own sign can't be disposited unless one uses increasingly obscure rules and in a chart with several planets in that condition the whole thing becomes unwieldy.

Now, one of the big problems in our high-tech era, where new asteroids and comets and planets are coming out of the woodwork every other week, is to figure out where they all "belong" so that dispositorship can begin. We have had Uranus around since the start of the Industrial Revolution. It wasn't too hard to give it a high tech slant and see that it "obviously" belonged to Aquarius, the sign of inventions and science. There is a lot of general acceptance of this one.

Neptune's discovery came along in the late 19th century, and as soon as it showed up the world was full of "mystic wonders" and spiritualism and so it was quickly assumed to belong to Pisces, which everybody knows is the only place for a ditzy planet, right? It's been studied pretty intensely since then.

Then Pluto pops up—in Cancer, yet—in the 1930s and women march off to the factories en masse, simultaneously altering the balance of family power, as the world launches WWII and eventually the nuclear age. There is pretty much agreement today that nuclear energy is Pluto's department. Hence the Power business—the first folks with "the bomb" held the clout in world affairs for several decades and the U.S. was spied on relentlessly by those who also wanted it. It wasn't too long after that before the feminist movement exploded, as women refused to surrender their own power, heading off to the job market again and the power of the paycheck, along with independence and personal determination.

We had two signs suggested for the rulership: Aries and Scorpio. While some still try to attribute Pluto to Aries, most astrologers in the last 60 years have concluded that Aries is too simplistic for the kind of power/control issues that Scorpio can manage quite well. We shove Pluto's rulership into Scorpio's hands.

Along come asteroids. We get Juno, Vesta, Pallas, Ceres. The rush is on to find them a slot. Virgo? Libra? Oops, now we've got Chiron. Where does that one go? This thing is getting out of hand. We are naming asteroids right and left. We have comets roaring into the system. (Gee, what sign rules comets?)

Astrologers are creatures of custom like everybody else. We want to put things where we think they belong so we can get a handle on them. But the big question is, are we right?

I don't know, to tell you the truth but I have strong opinions. Dispositorship only works when there are clear rulers of the signs and I think that means the classic rulers. I use the so-called "old rulers" far more than the outer planets in the vast majority of my work. I get straighter answers.

Yes, there are times when a question or a topic obviously belongs to Uranus, Neptune or Pluto, but does that mean they "rule" a sign or just "rule" certain affairs only? Are they outside the whole rulership business, acting more like traveling meter readers to all the signs? But just because you get married and the new spouse moves in doesn't mean you are any less the owner. I still use Mars, Saturn and Jupiter for Scorpio, Aquarius and Pisces.

I have never used the final dispositor business much for a couple of reasons: First of all, there is that serious dispute about modern mutual receptions. Do we set those aside and find a dispositor or do we admit there can't be one? This can happen when several planets are in signs they rule or in which they are exalted.

Secondly, if this is not a valid technique (and there is some dispute on whether it's even worth bothering with) why are we using it? Wouldn't it be more practical to work on techniques that have some history and a better track record? I don't bother with it, as I said, but I know a lot of people do and they seem to find it useful.

I think information about the most powerful planet is available in the chart in other ways, such as angularity, sign and house position, aspects, etc. Mutual reception is a horary technique which translates fairly well to natal work and dispositorship is simply another coloration factor.

Gender

Gender is traditionally part of the attributes of the planets and helps explain their function in many ways. Jupiter is masculine and warm; Saturn is feminine and cold, etc. I find it a vital component when it comes to horary. The "people" of the houses are thus described.

As to Neptune, Uranus and Pluto, I think we almost have to go back to the old gods on some of it. Neptune or Poseidon, was lord of the sea, Uranus was the father of the gods and Pluto was lord of the underworld. All masculine, of course. Uranus is so "airy" I think he's like Mercury—a switch hitter. Ganymede and Genevieve all at the same time, but mostly reverting to the masculine. I have Shakespeare's plays in mind. He loved to have a girl dress up as a boy or vice versa and have everyone get all gender scrambled romantically.

I think there is a strong bi-sexual component in Mercury—and by that I mean being either male or female or having both genders handy for temporary use. It may be swing both ways in technical terms, but in practice, I think it "makes use" of gender. Ever read any science fiction about one-gender worlds? The people are usually very confusing to those of us from little ole earth, because they give us both kinds of gender "signals." In such imaginary worlds, of course, the people are both, not "neither." Mercury, of course, is the "neither." How's that for confusing?

It's interesting that the Greeks said Diana the Huntress was goddess of the Moon, but in some more male-dominated societies, you find the "man" in the Moon. I think this man-in-the-Moon legacy is why there seems to be so much emphasis on the "positive" qualities of the air and fire masculine signs in some astrological tradition and less respect for the so-called "negative" qualities of the feminine earth and water signs. Notice the verbal use of "positive" and "negative" as if they were interchangeable terms with "good" and "bad."

The entire non-astrological Christian tradition, for instance, is stuffed full of the notion of the virtuous male being tempted by the weak, non-virtuous female. (Read the lives of the saints and how the poor boys were always being tempted by women.) We say violence and killing is OK (male territory) but sexuality leading to reproduction of human life (female territory) is "dirty" and words about it are "bad."

Sounds like I took a big leap here, didn't I? But truly, this gender business pervades society, not just astrological tradition. There is too much tendency to read Mars as "good" because it has strength and Venus as "not as good" because it's soft, therefore weak, therefore not as respectable.

For every action there has to be an equal reaction or the action just gets dumped down a dark hole and nothing happens. Action rightly belongs to the fire and air but there has to be something acted ON to create the reaction, and that's earth and water. The ying/yang notion of equal billing is one we need to keep in mind in astrology as well as life, I suspect.

Elevated Planets

When it comes to elevation, the high point in the chart is the MC—the planet closest to the MC is the most elevated. It can be on either side of the MC. It's easy to see. It often becomes one's public image and a focus of one's goals. The most elevated planet is like being King of the Hill—top dog, holder of the high ground, etc. It's just like real estate. The number one rule in real estate is the same as it is in astrology: Location, location, location.

Whichever planet is closest to the MC is the key—but if there is a toss-up, the 10th house side is more powerful by virtue of angularity than anything in the 9th. The ancients allowed about 10 degrees on the 9th house side to count, however.

Suppose you have a 24 Leo MC with the Sun at at 0 Virgo square Mars in Gemini. The Sun is "the boss," and one should not make any mistake about that. However, it will show off its best nature there and is not particularly defensive about it.

It's quite different if Mars is in Gemini and throwing a square to it. In that case the Sun is getting its energy modified by an extremely quick-reacting and somewhat cantankerous Mars. The picky energy of Virgo can be intensified and while the drive to succeed is powerful, it can be expressed in rather harsh ways.

Void of Course

The key thing is that routine, everyday life goes on during every void period. These are times when the Moon is done making all aspects before it leaves the sign it is in. You can't escape the dirty dishes or the lawn mowing just because the Moon is void of course. They'll have to be done again tomorrow or next week anyway, void or no void.

But starting something new is what is problematic. Picking a new optometrist is a waste of time. Seeing the old one for a routine check is another matter. I have seen the void of course Moon in operation for decades, ever since the late Al Morrison popularized it by sending out little cards for the pocket or purse with the periods listed on them. He bore much of the expense of printing them by himself but did accept contributions. I got a few every year for years and years until the positions started being noted in ephemerides. He had succeeded in making the world aware of Void of Course.

When things start under this period, they are seldom of importance because they don't "do anything new." They are sort of eviscerated energies. Most of the U.S. Moon shots were done in the void of course periods. Oddly enough, they, too, ended up in Limbo, going nowhere after we had gotten to the Moon. I mean, we just turned around and came home and that was that.

Candidate debates are usually not really important to the voters because they usually don't "do anything new." Or they won't "do anything new" to alter the course of the race.

However, back when Ronald Reagan was debating Walter Mondale he did not appear at his best in his first debate during a void of course Moon period, but the second one is generally credited with turning his campaign around and giving him the presidency. His "There you go, again" humor won the voters.

Some of these things get to be cliches precisely because they really do work so well. VOC Moon is one of them.

Out of Bounds

A word on Pluto and Out of Bounds (OOB) is in order, I think.

Only the planets which are normally on the ecliptic technically ever go out of bounds, which is past the Sun's maximum declination of 23 degrees, 28 minutes. Pluto is not on the ecliptic—it starts out at a high angle to ecliptic and swoops down past it—sort of diagonally. Being OOB is irrelevant to the whole idea for Pluto. It just doesn't deal with the plane of the ecliptic the way other planets do.

The late Kt Boehrer, whom I knew, wrote an outstanding book on the out of bounds planets, and coined the phrase "out of bounds" itself. Her book is not in print but may be obtainable in the used book markets and is very worth having on one's shelves.

Kt's research found that just the out of bounds Moon, when not accompanied by any other OOB planets, usually indicated a troublesome mother, with abuse and cruelty often inflicted on the child. More than one OOB planet in a natal pattern often nullified some of the possibilities, rather than increasing them.

Her extensive work on converting the declinations into longitudinal positions for secondary analysis of the planets is quite interesting.

Chapter 28

A Tool to Fit Each Job
The Benefics and Malefics and How They Work

The benefic/malefic thing is as old as astrology. Modern astrologers didn't invent the terms, which are found in every astrological system worldwide and are many hundreds—and thousands—of years old. If you don't know the terms and haven't learned why they have the names, you are handicapping yourself in astrology, in my humble opinion. Just because a few people don't care for the labels does not invalidate the tradition. It simply means we have to look carefully at each chart to see what is truly helpful or not-so-helpful in a particular situation.

Take the whole notion of malefic for instance. Suppose I want to hire an exterminator for an infestation of termites. On the day I choose I do not want to do it with the Moon in good aspect to Venus. If you want to go socialize with the wee buggies, be my guest. I'll skip Venus, thank you very much. But I do want Saturn strong. I want to get rid of them permanently—Saturn is a malefic—in this case to the bugs, but a benefic to me. Pick a time when the Moon is aspecting Saturn closely.

For those who want to do effective electional work and find clearer interpretations of horary charts or natal patterns, these distinctions become significant. Planets have functions that are also traditional and based on age-old experience. Malefics Saturn and Mars each carry a portfolio of functions. So do the two benefics, Jupiter and Venus. They haul out the tools needed for different jobs. They do not carry the same tools, and this is something we have to keep in mind.

Years ago I was metro editor for my newspaper and had to assign reporters to various stories. There were reporters who were great —I mean great— in a crisis situation but others who were intimidated when they had to talk to people in traumatic circumstances. They functioned best with research to do and records to find. It was my job to send the right reporter to the right story if I could do so. The man I might send out when there was a plane crash was as scratchy as a steel brush but always came back with the information. Not much got in his way. I would never willingly send him to talk to the family of a victim. A gentler type—perhaps a sympathetic Cancer or tactful Libra —was a better fit. This is only common sense, right?

So are the ways of benefics and malefics. It is up to us to find out what tools are in the portfolios of each planet and how to make the wisest use of them. They will function in their own ways. That doesn't mean any is always more effective than the others or always to be preferred. It means there are a lot of roads one can take to get to Toledo. What counts is not the scenery along the road or the driving time, but the fact that you get to Toledo.

Take Venus, for instance. It is the planet of sweetness and light, courtesy and social grace, manners and music, poetry and conversation. But it also deals with money and stability, the dirt out of which roses grow and the practical ways we deal with problems. Mars is rough, coarse, rude and hasty, cutting through what it considers as extraneous detail and impatient with distractions. It is antagonistic and independent. It likes to hit things, throw things and cut things. A Venus road can take you through lush scenery and fields of flowers, with plenty of places to stop and chat with the locals or have a nice lunch with a harpist for entertainment. There are some nifty shops to explore and one has a small fashion show going on that you may sit and watch. It may take a couple of hours longer than other trips but some people think it's the only way to go.

Mars, on other hand, says "Let's get there as fast as we can and not stop to dawdle." Get a hot car with a fast engine, put the pedal to the metal and roar down the road. Anybody foolish enough to get in the way or challenge your right to use the road will get an earful of horn and exhaust as you roar by. If you are in a big hurry to get to Toledo, this could be your vehicle of choice. Everyone knows there are times when a fast trip is more important than a pleasant one. This, too, is simply common sense. Sometimes in astrology we forget common sense.

If I have a newly diagnosed cancer, which should I choose in an election chart as the planet to rule my treatment? A nice neat surgery which will cut the nasty thing out (Mars) or should I spend a few months going from doctor to doctor talking about it looking for the most congenial bedside manner (Venus)? If I had to choose I would pick an arrogant, grumpy surgeon with a great reputation over a much nicer one whose bedside manner made him popular at the country club. Qualification and speed, in this case, are of greater value to me. You just want a good "cutter" and that's a Mars task.

But perhaps one is concerned about a tonsillectomy for a child. A Venus-ruled doctor or nurse might be what you want to find, one whose gentle presence can reassure the child and parent and make the experience the least traumatic possible. Venus is the planet of comfort, warm blankets and soft lights. For a child's tonsillectomy, it's worth the time to get a nurse who thinks popsicles in many colors are good medicine.

Venus is the planet to select for a great party. You want Venus on your side for vacations and in the paycheck. We all want a good Venus-blessed bank account. When you marry you want a happy and loving relationship. We often assess the quality of our life by its Venus components: Love, money and pleasure. All types of physical pleasure, from a backrub to hot chocolate on a cold winter day or perfume with power and our favorite music come under Venus. Sexual pleasure occupies a slightly different niche and is ruled by Mars, but the satisfaction afterwards that one achieves (hopefully) belongs to Venus. Thus, we call Venus a benefic and Mars a malefic. It sorts their functions handily for us.

Mae West, famous movie star of Hollywood's Golden Era, once cracked "too much of a good thing is wonderful." Most of the world agrees, but a strong contingent believes balance works better. Too many sweets in life are cloying or make you fat. On the other hand, callous disregard of other's needs and opinions can make you an unpopular person.

When Venus and Mars are too closely connected in a natal pattern it shows intense (sometimes almost obsessive) interest in the pleasures of sexuality. There's nothing wrong with sex, of course. None of my readers would be here without it. But like all joys of life, there is a time and a place for it. Venus and Mars both do best work when under some restraint.

Enter Saturn, the greater malefic and the planet of restraint and discipline. Saturn's qualities of permanence, contraction and solitude are often seen as less than lovable. It rules heavy things, time and a slow buildup to achieve goals. It reins in the impatient and puts high walls around the undisciplined and the childish. Yet Saturn also favors the disciplined athlete who spends hours alone in the gym and who is apt to succeed on the floor during the game. It is the golfer who lifts weights in private and whose muscles drive the ball farther than anyone else. Here the greater malefic is at work helping the athletes who function under the lesser malefic, Mars.

To be fair, Saturn and Mars also deal with the injuries those athletes may run into. Saturn's pervue is bones, particularly the knees, and those are vulnerable. Mars is injury and breakages of all kinds.. But some research suggests that athletes who take the time to stretch their muscles and warm their bodies up before strenuous efforts are less likely to incur injuries. It is the slow years of disciplined eating and excercise that keeps a movie star on top of her game and her beauty unmarred. Again, the greater malefic's tools work to make Venus even more spectacular.

Jupiter is the greater benefic and Venus the lesser. There's a reason for that. Venus tends to work on the personal level, with human relations and day-to-day living. It is the "quality of life" planet. Jupiter on the other hand is a social planet and its function benefits society at large and brings social opportunities to the individual. Jupiter opens doors and acts as a sort of card file of people. It allows one to build a network of friends and acquaintances at all levels where favors and social contacts are exchanged. It is the planet of education and religion and foreign things. It deals with colleges, publications and travel as well as politics, philosophy and the synthesizing of information into meaning. It is the opinion maker. As the planet symbolizing the principles of expansion, Jupiter rules a wide array of human endeavor. It is the far horizon and the big opportunity. It is important people. It is "who you know." And we have all heard the old adage that success is more a matter of who you know rather than what you know.

All organized giving is called philanthropy. The giving of most gifts—say for birthdays, or holidays—comes under Venus. But the big grants are Jupiter and that's philanthropy. Since Jupiter deals with philanthropy you will be quite happy to know that much of it supports higher education and various religious organizations. There is also an abundance of social programs to help the sick and the poor. Very Sagittarian and Piscean, eh?

Often scholarships are given or "won" by students intending to learn something. This is almost always Jupiterian because the learning will broaden our horizons and make us better citizens of our community. Grants for merit or need are common in our society and often seem to go to those already marked with potential for future contributions to the general welfare. Some are actually for travel, or study abroad.

It's important to keep in mind that Jupiter and Saturn are both social planets and intended to improve society at large, not merely a single person. Saturn deals with the obligations we have as citizens of our community and members of our social class or milieu. It has to do with the position we earn or occupy and the tasks that go along with maintaining order and structure in both the individual life and that of society at large. It is often considered to be the planet dealing with the power structure, the "establishment" that makes the decisions and those who assume leadership roles. Oddly enough, Saturn is often very strong in the charts of those who become truly wealthy. Great wealth is far more than simply money earned at a job and needs both discipline and strength of purpose to achieve. True, it can produce the miser and the Scrooge, but that is a misuse of its potential.

There is a vast difference between how the planets work in a natal pattern or a horary question and how they can be used in electional or mundane work. In any pattern, so many things affect positive or negative manifestations. Squares almost always imply problems to solve and hindrances. They don't always deny success, but if Saturn is involved, success is either a reward after a very long period of effort or comes only after serious obstacles have been faced. A square between Venus and Saturn can prove sharply limiting in the emotional life and very discouraging in the financial one. But unselfishness and faithfulness can bring deep happiness and careful budgeting and fair play can be rewarded with financial security. It's all in the point of view. Saturn just says it has to come the hard way. The problem of selfishness (that Venus-Saturn square) has to be overcome first.

Many Jupiter aspects are nice, but some are also squares which hamper Jupiter's more constructive appeal. A Jupiter square to the Sun, for instance, can make one quite pompous and proud of one's opinions. A square to Venus is often extravagance and one can develop intolerance of those whose charts do not provide the easy benefits in life. The trines imply you had such goodies at birth. We won't all get them. People who have them can develop blind spots about the lives of others. Marie Antoinette is credited with the classic Jupiter/Venus/trine response when she was told the poor had no bread. "Tell them to eat cake," she is reported to have said. She was young and royal and had never known want. It was obvious ignorance on her part but that didn't make it any less outrageous a remark.

Mars-Jupiter squares and oppositions are fighters, and not always for the right, although they like to think so. Many times they poke holes in the egos of the self-satisfied, but sometimes they pick their targets erroneously. They are like attack dogs—very good with intruders but you don't always want them in the house. Mars's temper is famous, but combine it with a stress aspect to Saturn and you can have envy, jealousy, spitefulness and vindictiveness. Sometimes the applying aspects show the individual has those qualities. The separating ones can show the individual suffering from those qualities in others.

Saturn's best side is one we all admire. It gives patience, loyalty, common sense and the ability to do careful planning that pays off in the long run. Above all, it is the willingness to accept responsibility. Most of us have to learn those things in life. Few of us are born knowing all the Saturn lessons.

Combinations of the other planets can alter the ways the benefics and malefics function. Mars-Neptune squares show problems with reality. These are the folks who head off into bottles and pipe-dreams to avoid life's problems. In a man's chart it's a great deal of self-doubt, often of his masculinity. In a woman's chart, especially linked to the 7th house, it can show the man in her life, and it can be pretty dreary married to an alcoholic or drug abuser. It often takes some active intervention by Saturn to lead to a solution. The alcoholic must learn to deal with reality and achieve honesty before a turnaround happens in life. That's pretty definitely Saturn stuff.

The Sun, Moon and Mercury all have contributions to make to our life experience, as well. The benefics and malefics have dramatic differences when involved with them. Take Mercury for instance. It is classed as a cold, changeable influence, drastically altered in manifestation by the planets that aspect it. It is either the juvenile delinquent or the youth with a sense of fun and humor. Sometimes it is both. It always deals with the intelligence we have and how we use it. When there is some tie to a benefic, it shows its best side. Any Saturn aspect will give it practicality, a certain canny approach to problems and a deep fund of common sense. The aspects also give it a tendency to depression (too big a dose of reality, sometimes) but there is usually skill with numbers and order in the mental processes as well.

Unfortunately, the stress aspects can also bring less desirable qualities. Saturn can trigger fear or meanness. Linked to Mercury, it can prompt one to adopt lying as a way to avoid dealing with harsh truth. Throw in emotional Moon and it's a good bet that one uses too many fibs to get around unpleasant situations. Mars can mean too much energy for Mercury. It's the classic "motor mouth" or the mean mouth, the cutting remark, the snide comment.

The Moon is involved in all of our affairs. In every chart, the Moon is important because it translates all the energies of the other planets into our lives. In every single electional or horary chart it rules ALL the forward action and tells where the situation will go in the future. In every human natal chart it deals with the emotional package we inherited and how we use that emotional package to deal with life in the broadest sense. The benefics and malefics alter the expression of that emotion and suggest roads for us to take which are the "easiest" because they fit our natural tendencies.

The Sun is the fundamental ego. It can be disciplined and toughened by Saturn and made more generous and upright by Jupiter. It can also be self-centered and greedy when Saturn is operating in a malefic sense with a bad aspect. A square from Jupiter can produce a smug, egotistical know-it-all who thinks the opinions of others don't matter.

There are a few simple rules to keep in mind with the benefics and malefics.

1—Sign matters. Planets in their own signs or in the signs of their exaltation tend to express their better side. It takes stress, such as being retrograde or harsh aspects to spoil all the goodness. Planets in signs of debility and fall tend to express their less perfect side. It takes good aspects to bring out the best in them.

2—Aspects matter. Good aspects open doorways to good manifestations of the energy. The reverse is true when the aspects are squares or oppositions.

3—Retrograde planets promise more than they deliver. They also frustrate the intended effect, and may send matters in exactly the opposite direction from the one we would prefer.

4—Stationary planets are always at maximum power. Consider that planet at least twice as potent in its effects as one that is not at station.

Having all the rules down doesn't mean you will always be right, though. Many people with harsh aspects take steps to solve their difficulties and find constructive ways to deal with their problems in life. They grow into people worth knowing, using the stress to provide grit and strength to accomplish their goals. Too many good aspects can provide one with such a "soft" life that one never accomplishes anything of value. When the clouds in life gather, these people may sit back and wait for the problems to go away, or seek the easy ways out and become criminals. In the end, we all have to make choices. Our life's harvest depends on which seeds we water.

Chapter 29

At Home and Away
The Dignity and Debility of the Planets

A few thousand years ago astrologers of the western tradition established the rulerships of the signs of the zodiac. And while they were at it, they decided where the various planets manifested in the best way and where they did so in the worst way in the sense of expressing their innate quality.

Nowadays with the discovery of the so-called "outer" planets and the naming of every asteroid, comet and dust fuzzy around, astrologers are continuing an effort to find out exactly where everything "belongs." It isn't easy. Maybe it isn't even wise, but astrologers have no corner on the wisdom business.

First of all, the old-timers established a ranking with the Sun and the Moon side by side owning, or "ruling" Cancer and Leo. Then they put Gemini beside Cancer and Virgo beside Leo and said each of those two was ruled or owned by Mercury. Next on either side were Libra and Taurus, ruled by Venus, and then on either side were Aries and Scorpio, ruled by Mars. After that on each side came Sagittarius and Pisces, with Jupiter rulerships and finally, Capricorn and Aquarius, both Saturn ruled. It was a very orderly system.

Everybody got a planet and the ancients said that the feminine signs (the water and earth signs) would be the "night" houses of the planets and masculine signs (air and fire) would be the "day houses." Sun and Moon, being lights not planets, only got one sign each, since the Sun didn't shine at night and the Moon didn't shine in the daytime. (Yes, yes, I know you can see it in the sky in the daytime sometimes, but that doesn't count.)

Then they decided that the planets in signs opposite ones they ruled would be considered "debilitated" or handicapped. They would be out of their true neighborhood, so to speak. So far, so good. The rules of planet ownership and "guest-ship" were established and helped make techniques like horary astrology workable. Astrologers who study such things as the weather are finding this a powerful influence in their work, by the way.

Next they looked at where the planets would be most exalted, where their energy would manifest at its very best or the most easily. Even as we sometimes show our best sides away from home, so do the planets. The Sun would be exalted in Aries, the sign of new beginnings and the spark of life. The Moon would be exalted in Taurus, the sign that gives form to life. Mercury then would be exalted in Virgo, where the mind seeks to impose order on information. Venus would have to be exalted in Pisces, where love reaches down to the least lovable in humanity and includes all that lives. The exaltation of Mars would go to Capricorn, the sign of discipline and hard work and Jupiter would be exalted in Cancer, where its generosity and optimistic outlook could make domestic life rich and worthwhile. Saturn would be exalted in Libra, the sign of justice and fairness in human relationships.

Now, you may have noticed a curious fact—Mercury is exalted in its own sign of Virgo. I didn't invent the system, you know, but a lot of modern astrologers would like to reorder it by changing that and giving Mercury an Aquarian exaltation, but it won't wash. The dignity and debility business is thousands of years old and has suffered pragmatic use and analysis by generations of astrologers. It really isn't debatable, in my opinion. It's old knowledge, not old opinion.

Now Poryphyry, (233-303 AD) noted in his commentary on Ptolemy's Tetrabiblos, that the diurnal (daytime) planets were exalted backwards by trine (the Sun to Aries from Leo, Saturn from Aquarius to Libra) and the nocturnal (night time) planets were exalted backwards by sextile (the Moon from Cancer to Taurus, Venus from Taurus to Pisces). A curious fact. Of course Mercury, which could be either masculine or feminine, a diurnal or nocturnal planet, was probably worn out with all its risings and settings and so Poryphyry thought it was tired and sought refuge in Virgo, hence was exalted there.

The exact degrees of exaltation are: the Sun at 19 Aries, the Moon at 3 Taurus, Mercury at 15 Virgo, Venus at 27 Pisces, Mars at 28 Capricorn, Jupiter at 15 Cancer, Saturn at 21 Libra and the Moon's north node at 3 Gemini.

The signs and degrees opposite those of exaltation are the signs and degrees of "fall." These are where the planets show their worst side, according to tradition .

As I say, it all worked very well until the fairly modern discovery of Uranus. And then the stuff hit the fan, astrologically speaking. Ever since, astrologers have been trying to assign places to the newer planets. Logic said the old planets didn't need BOTH a day and a night house. So, the thinking went, let's take one of them for the new kid on the block. So, Saturn's day house, Aquarius, became pretty much the consensus home of Uranus, which was the first of the outer planets to be discovered and came at the dawn of the Industrial Revolution. Its link to technology, invention and forward thinking was probably inevitable.

Neptune's arrival on the scene occurred just as interest in spiritualism and the psychic realms were finding a place in cultural awareness. It seemed to have a pretty good tie to Pisces, Jupiter's night house. Soon after came the development of movies, which were shadows created by light and that seemed to clinch the subject.

And then Pluto was moving in on Scorpio, the night house of Mars. Its discovery came at the time just before World War II, which launched the Nuclear Age. There was a big fight about that for a while as some very good astrologers tried to put Pluto into Aries, the day house of Mars, but they seem to have essentially lost that battle. Pluto's qualities as they were studied seemed more and more obviously akin to those of Scorpio.

Some have also assigned the four largest asteroids, Ceres[1], Juno, Pallas and Vesta to Virgo, or occasionally to Libra, where they don't seem to fit very well. We also have Chiron in the system now, which is seen as a transition body[2] between the energies of Saturn and Uranus, and a number of smaller asteroids to consider as well. There is still the possibility of other, still smaller or yet more distant bodies within our solar system which may affect human behavior. Some may achieve planetary status.

Now the question becomes: do all those newer planets really belong in the signs we have given them? Well, I have a suggestion. This is it: I think we should leave the old system alone. And having said that, I have a couple other suggestions, too, which will contradict that a bit.

Uranus, Neptune and Pluto certainly seem to have affinity with the signs Aquarius, Pisces and Scorpio. Perhaps their relationship to those sign rulers is more like that of new partners or tenants. The old owners still have title to the property, but they have adopted some new members into the family who may—I say may—inherit full rights down the road.

With the rise of feminine power in recent years it is very obvious (to me, anyway) that the importance of asteroids with feminine attributes, such as Ceres, Juno, Vesta and Pallas, is growing. They seem ripe to move in on Virgo. You may have noticed that in the original lineup, most of the rulers were male gods. Eight, in fact. Androgynous Mercury got two signs and Venus was given two, but the Moon only one. Perhaps this is the reason things are changing nowadays as society moves away from the exclusively male-dominated cultures in the direction of more equality.

Ceres the earth mother, whose symbol is the sheaf of wheat, is suitable to the harvesting sign of Virgo. Vesta was the vestal virgin of ancient times whose single-minded devotion to her work kept the religious observances on track. Hard work is a Virgo trait. Juno or Hera was goddess of marital fidelity who was also the patroness of safe childbirth. Virgo is one of the medical signs particularly involved in nursing and midwifery. Finally, Pallas Athena was the feminine warrior who taught the domestic skills of spinning and weaving to women. Virgo also deals with most of the hand crafts and fiber crafts. It all sounds very Virgo-ish to me. At this rate Virgo could have a whole harem, perhaps displacing Mercury as ruler.[1]

There's a move on to give Chiron a spot. What about Chiron? I haven't a clue. Some of the characteristics strike me as potentially Libran. And Libra, a masculine sign, has a feminine ruler, Venus. Perhaps it needs a masculine co-ruler to keep things balanced. Others have other ideas, of course. And some see Chiron as a mediator between Saturn and the outer planets. Some advocate putting Chiron under Sagittarius since Chiron was a centaur in ancient lore. The astronomers have specifically designated Chiron as a Centaur, the first of a new category that now has many others found since Chiron's discovery. [2]

The feminine signs are Taurus, Cancer, Virgo, Scorpio, Capricorn and Pisces. They should have feminine rulers or certainly some feminine co-rulers. We have a problem with Pisces, however. Neptune was a male god. He and Jupiter were brothers in the old pantheon. Neptune ruled the sea and had the power to shake the earth (earthquakes). Jupiter ruled the heavens and earth and had the power to shake the heavens (thunder and lightning, and so forth). Their tenancy makes for a comfortable relationship in Pisces, but it leaves us with a feminine sign without a feminine ruler or co-ruler.

Consider Saturn and Pluto. They both seem to be on the same wave-length as the Moon. The Moon takes 28 ½ days to circle the earth and Saturn does it in 28 ½ years. Pluto's rotational period is surprisingly close to 285 years. This strikes me as a common linkage, and a feminine one at that, thus providing a tie to the feminine signs Cancer, Capricorn and Scorpio.

Besides, at least one ancient rule called Saturn feminine and cold in nature. Not an old man but an old woman. This is, of course, a subject that will be contradicted by many and some of them for quite traditional reasons. I merely throw out the idea as offering a satisfactory linkage to the feminine sign of Capricorn.

Now, how do we use these assignments? Are they just a nice little arrangement to help students learn astrology or they do really mean something? In a word, they mean something. Here are some things to consider.

1—A planet is apt to manifest its best side in its own house or exaltation in a person's birth chart. It takes really bad aspects to destroy ALL the good. Everyone who met Hitler socially in person considered him charming. He had Venus in Taurus and a little of the Venus in Taurus niceness came through despite the mess in the rest of his chart which made him such a bloody murderer.

2—A planet is apt to manifest its less desirable qualities in signs of its debility and fall. It takes good aspects to bring out the best. Some smidgen of its unpleasant side always sneaks out—often in a health problem or something. Any woman with a Scorpio Moon, for instance, will tend to have problems with the female reproductive system. Some will have a gynecological history of things going wrong that's as long as your arm. Learning disabilities can show up with a debilitated Mercury, or even outright retardation. Or maybe just a mean tongue. Debilitated Venus may have trouble with color sense and emotional responsiveness. Perhaps a complete lack of fashion sense or a tin ear, if nothing else. Mars in debility can have problems with the male energy, nasty temperament or laziness.

On the other hand, in some charts those qualities seem to be sharply reversed and we find the other extreme manifesting. Mercury becomes a genius, Mars a mighty warrior or athlete and Venus a sex goddess, for instance. Nevertheless, in debility those roles express some of the less desirable qualities of the planets. Mars may have a streak of cruelty or temper, Mercury too much cold-bloodedness and Venus becomes promiscuous.

3—In charts with two or more debilitated planets and none in dignities or exaltations, I expect to find problems. There are usually difficulties in dealing with society and its norms. Sometimes there is a lack of ethics or standards, a certain expediency of approach to life.

4—In charts where there are two or more planets in their own signs or exaltations, the individual functions very well in society. There is usually a high set of standards and the individual is someone you can rely on to do what they say they will.

5—In charts where you have a lot of dignities and ONE sharp debility, the debility often becomes a focal point and a powerful pivot of the life. If it has a lot of good aspects, the person makes superb lemonade out of their lemon, and seems to derive more strength from the debility than they might from a planet in its own sign. It's as if the strength of the sign was somehow needed in their package even if it meant putting a planet there that would normally be a debility.

6—In charts where you see one dignity and one debility, you see both sides of the dignity/debility issue express very well in the life. It poses continuing ethical or social problems to the individual.

I have watched these rules reaffirm themselves over years of practice and while I don't consider Mercury in Sagittarius the "moron" position, I look carefully at house and aspects to see how well it will function, just as I do if it is in Virgo or Aquarius or anywhere else. A well-aspected Mercury is one of the indicators of intelligence, no matter what sign it is in. In Sagittarius or Pisces, it has to work harder and there may be some other Mercury handicap expressed in the life.

If I see a poorly aspected Moon in Scorpio or Capricorn I know what to expect. The emotions which the Moon represents become more intense and aggressive in Scorpio and more fearful and cramped in Capricorn. Does this mean ALL those with the Moon in Scorpio or Capricorn will express such tendencies? No, but the likelihood does exist and we must recognize it when aspects from other planets act to enhance the good or the bad sides.

These principles are valid with all the old planets in dignity and debility. I disagree entirely that there is any—and I do mean any—dignity or debility business that's valid for the planets Uranus, Neptune and Pluto. A number of astrologers have opinions on this and will try to assign them places. When we've studied them a few hundred years more maybe we'll have a valid case, but at this point, I think not. We still aren't sure they should even be used as true "rulers" of Aquarius, Pisces and Scorpio, or co-rulers, or merely as planets with "affinity" to those signs. Personally, I tend to straddle the fence and give them co-ruler status. I guess it's sort of like a common-law marriage. There may not have been any vows but they seem to make a lot of decisions in the partnership anyway.

Forecasting and horary techniques work much better using the old rulers unless the issue in question is one which truly seems linked to one of the three outer planets. Such things might be aeronautics and aviation for Uranus, recycling efforts or organ transplants for Pluto and chemicals, oil and the paranormal for Neptune.

One other thing that the dignity/debility business does is allow for what is known as "mutual reception." This is a horary function which nevertheless has some validity in all astrological work. Mutual reception occurs when two planets swap signs of their own rulership or exaltation. Saturn in Cancer and the Moon in Capricorn are each in each other's special place and thus can—in effect—agree to switch places. It allows for a way out of difficult situations and provides flexibility when times are bad. It implies that one is not locked into troublesome situations.

This can also work with the planets in exaltation, such as a combination of Mars in Pisces and Venus in Capricorn. Planets in mutual reception do keep the same degree, however. Mars in 16 Pisces can be read as if it were at 16 Capricorn and Venus at 2 Capricorn moves to 2 Pisces for a secondary reading in the chart.

This little trick comes in handy when choosing an electional chart for a time when the planets won't arrange themselves to suit your needs. If you can find a time with a mutual reception it can provide (with the secondary reading) a way to accomplish your goals.

In natal charts mutual reception explains much that is otherwise puzzling. A truly great entertainer who adores attention is not usually signified by a debilitated Saturn rising in Cancer. However, the singer Cher, who has been outstanding in four different careers (television, movies, music and publishing) in four decades has it, and also the Moon in Capricorn in the seventh, providing the mutual reception that allows the Moon to give her the ability to dramatize herself quite well. One of her trademarks has always been outstanding costumes and wildly dramatic clothing.

Debility can also become significant when natal planets by progression shift signs. For instance, when someone has Venus in Virgo natally and it moves into Libra by secondary progression, all matters ruled by Venus improve. Venus was hampered in Virgo but goes "home" when it gets to Libra and can shine more fully there, and the individual has better Venus experiences. It can improve the affairs of the houses Venus rules natally. Of course, when Mars has been in Aries for one's early years and then moves into Taurus, the reverse will be the case, as Mars leaves a sign where it has been happy and shifts into a sign where it is debilitated.

Events linked to Mars have less happy outcomes and can become more problematic. Things seem to take more energy and hard work to accomplish, with results that are sometimes less than was hoped.

These are fundamental principles which can be applied to all of the traditional rulers. They give a great many clues to events in mundane work and are of consistent help in forecasting changes in the life during the year a planet moves to a new sign of better or worse outlook.

Sometimes the Universe can be very literal, as one learns when watching how debilities and dignities work.

[1] Ceres, following 2006 decisions of International Astronomical Union, is no longer officially designated as an asteroid, even though a great many astrologers continue work with her primarilly as one of the four "major asteroids." The change took place in 2006 after a new planet beyond Pluto and larger than Pluto was discovered orbiting our Sun. In the controversy among the astronomers about what to do about this new discovery, the IAU then voted to create a new category of "dwarf planet." The new and larger-than-Pluto planet was named Eris, for a goddess of discord, as symbol of their discord over what to do about her. Pluto was demoted to "dwarf planet" status, and then IAU also decided to promote Ceres from asteroid to become the third "dwarf planet." Since then they have discovered two others to add to their new category and named them Makemake and Haumea.

The main distinction between planets and dwarf planets is that planets entirely clear their orbit around Sun, but dwarf planets orbit in zones of similar objects that can cross their path, such as happens within the asteroid belt and the Kuiper belt.

More recently, the IAU "threw a bone" to Pluto as (perhaps) an apology for his lost status, by deciding that all new planets to be discovered orbiting the Sun beyond Neptune will be called Plutoids. Thus Pluto and Eris are defined as plutoids, while Ceres remains just a dwarf planet.

The specific definition for the new category (whether one calls it "dwarf" or "plutoid,") is that it must orbit Earth's sun, have enough mass to assume a nearly round shape, but has not cleared the neighborhood around its orbit, and is not a moon..
Ref: *http://solarsystem.nasa.gov/planets/profile.cfm?Object=Dwarf&Display=Moons*

[2] The official astronomical designation for Chiron remains controversial, although most recent sources give the designation of Centaur. Chiron, discovered in 1977, is considered the first of a Centaur category that now has many hundreds of other bodies added to it. Centaurs are small bodies only around 160 miles in diameter or less, that are thought to have originated in the Kuiper belt and now travel in unstable orbits that cross the paths of the giant planets, and could collide with them.
Ref: *http://www.britannica.com/EBchecked/topic/1075823/Centaur-object*

Chapter 30

Asteroids and Some Archetypes

These bodies in the heavens located in a belt that orbits between Mars and Jupiter have occupied a great deal of astrological interest since their size and movement have become so well documented. The largest four are Ceres, Pallas, Juno and Vesta, named after Greco-Roman goddesses with important functions.

Chiron, a masculine-named asteroid, now classified as one of the "centaurs," has lately come under study as well and the late Zipporah Dobyns did an extensive research of a great many asteroids. Many of the larger ones seem to occupy prominent positions in the charts of those who are interested in their functions. For those interested in studying the asteroids, her lists are available online.

Venus, which the Romans considered a sex symbol, had many important functions in traditional times. She was responsible for fertility and the continuation of the species because she ruled the attraction between men and women. Her job was more than simply a pleasure creator. It was also to spur pregnancies. Those were years before every pregnancy produced enough healthy babies to keep the populations levels up.

The Moon, with her ruler Diana, the huntress, was seen as night's arbiter and in charge of the mysterious and hidden in the world. And yet, the Moon also dealt with the home fires, the comfort of a good bed and decent cooking and the domestic pleasures that give life its sense of fulfillment to most of us. The Moon deals with the everyday stream of activity and events.

Pallas Athena, the warrior goddess, was supposedly born as an adult in a full suit of armor from the forehead of her father, Zeus, ruler of the gods. It obviously must have given him a headache but then women have been giving men headaches for a long time. She was the original uppity broad and the goddess of wisdom and military strategy. Her brother (half-brother? Sort-of brother?) Mars could handle a sword but he was no strategist. The Greeks called him Ares and the Romans renamed Pallas as Minerva.

In addition to being the warrior goddess, Pallas Athena also supposedly taught women the domestic arts that enabled them to feed and clothe their families better. She was the patroness of spinning and weaving as well as other domestic skills like cooking and growing herbs for flavor.

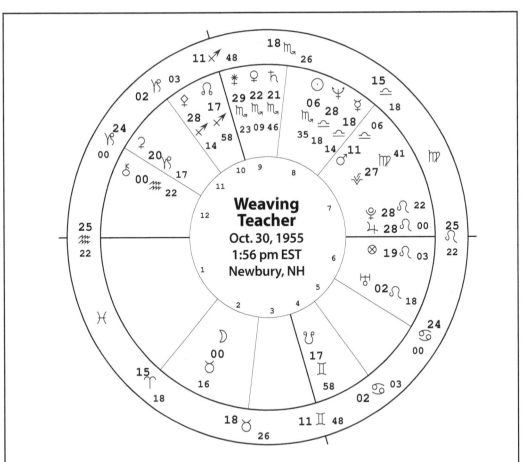

This woman weaver is also a teacher of weaving at the college level. Uranus in the 6th house is part of a T-square with Sun and Moon. Moon rules both the 5th house of hobbies and creativity, and the 6th house of fiber work and jobs. It is a tight, out-of-sign trine to the 7th house Jupiter and Pluto. The asteroids Vesta and Juno all form aspects to Jupiter, as well. Jupiter, the teacher rules the 10th house and Pallas at 28 Sagittarius is exactly trine it from the 10th house. All of the clothing arts are part of the 6th house of domestic skills. Chart AA from baby book.

There is a famous tale of a young weaver named Arachne who bragged she was as good as Pallas Athena and after a demonstration annoyed the goddess so much she was turned into a spider for her temerity. It also was a good way to insure she could spin forever and catch the bugs in the house that irked housekeepers so much. Of course, biologists have called the class of spiders Arachnids ever after.

She was known for being testy with men who couldn't see beyond a good set of boobs which she probably had and was supposedly heavily involved in the Trojan War behind the scenes. She was a good friend to those who appreciated her but a bad enemy to those who didn't. She was not reputed to be one of those who took fools lightly.

Devoted Vesta, who kept the fires burning in home and temple, also kept the place clean and meals prepared. She was known for her work skills. She was also the ancient equivalent of a sex therapist—though classicists will probably throw something at me for saying so. There are sources which explain this and the likelihood that she would not serve many years in the role before leaving the temple.

Demeter or Ceres to the Romans, who ruled the fertility of the earth and sponsored the growing of vegetables, fruit and grain, made sure there was food for Vesta to cook on the fire. Obviously, hers was a much more important role than astrological tradition has given it. Things made from natural substances, such as dyes, were also her bailiwick.

Ceres, by her very size, has been considered the most influential of the asteroids. She was actually promoted to planetary status (or some say "planetoid") by modern science at the 2006 convention of the International Astronomical Union. There is still some dispute about exactly how big a planetoid (which is how they earlier decided to classify Pluto) must be to be to graduate to planet status. The uproar over that is undiminished, however, and astrologers are beginning to grant both Ceres and Pluto status as planets.

Hera, called Juno by the Romans, was the wife of Zeus and the patroness of marriage and childbirth. In eras before modern medicine it was not easy to produce a healthy child and a healthy mother after the trauma of childbirth. (Of course, it would have improved the odds had midwives known anything about simple cleanliness and washed their hands more often and more thoroughly.) She was also the goddess for women who had a problem with their men, and since Zeus was a notorious rake, women believed they were apt to get a sympathetic ear from her. There are many tales of Zeus pursuing young women.

They seem to be Virgo and Libra prototypes according to some writers, and I must agree. These goddesses all occupied extremely important roles in the Greek pantheon but were rather downplayed by the more macho Romans. We have 6 feminine zodiac signs but only two truly powerful goddesses assigned to them as rulers: Venus, or Aphrodite, a clear sex symbol to the Romans, and Diana, huntress of Moon, who refused male attentions. Perhaps the modern emphasis on asteroids might correct this, and they will become co-rulers in the future.

Why is it that decent food, clean underwear and clothing that fits and keeps one warm or comfortable was so thoroughly ignored in importance by historians who would themselves go absolutely nuts without it? Obviously, many men took it for granted in eras when women were the custodians of such things.

Had they not been available, however, perhaps enthusiasm over warfare and conquest would have taken a back seat to obtaining warm socks and real shoes for winter. To say nothing of a soft bed with ample blankets and the easy chair year 'round. Perhaps that's why Pallas Athena's work was so important.

Ordinary day-to-day comfort is one of the things we take for granted in modern times. But we live better than royalty in the old days. It's been calculated that it took the labor of more than 150 people working full time to support a single knight in armor in the medieval era. Too bad we invented ways for fewer people to support fighters so they had more time to think up better weapons.

One of the interesting things about warfare in early times was the recorded number of slaves that were taken as prisoners and sometimes exchanged by rulers. They were not merely anonymous bodies, as moderns might think. A great majority of them were fiber specialists, spinners, weavers and those who could sew, according to old lists. It was the recognition of the importance of those products to society and rulers were not slow about things that kept the populace happy.

When you think about it, the use of spun fibers and woven cloth was a vast improvement over animal skins and the work symbolized by Pallas Athena's mandate plays a large role in society. In eras before mechanization the family contribution by the weaver/spinner/sewer was easily equal to that of farming and animal care. For that matter, the growing of vegetables which keep us healthy made Ceres' work significant, too. Agriculture around the world keeps people alive and can hardly be considered a lesser job.

There seems to be an interesting divide between spinners and weavers of fiber and cloth as well as between those who use sharp pointed needles for sewing and embroidery and the dull ones used for knitting and crochet work. These may be due to the influence of other planets in the chart, or perhaps other asteroids yet unstudied.

I notice that what I call "sharp needle" arts—embroidery, quilting, sewing—seem to be beloved by those with a Mars tilt to the personality. One woman who lectured me on the difference between owning "real" tools and my scissors, loves the sharp needle skills and once worked as a tailor. She has Mars in her 5th house of hobbies. She needlepoints furniture and makes wonderful quilts. I know a Scorpio man who does gorgeous needlepoint. Many men are career tailors, too, adding to my curiosity about the Mars link.

Not all spinners are good weavers. I have tried it but I never will be a weaver. I don't really enjoy it. I just like the finished product. I know some superb weavers who have tried spinning. Mostly they don't seem to enjoy it either and leave it to those of us who do.

I think the Moon strongly influences spinning. Both the Moon and a spinning wheel go round and round. Weaving is more akin to music than anything else—the harmonies, the numerical sequences, the rhythm, etc. It's a far more complex craft and many of the weavers I know play a musical instrument.

It was weaving which inspired the first computer program and to this day many computer terms are from the weaving vocabulary. Some of it obviously belongs to Mercury but perhaps the influence of Pallas Athena lingers. A modern development, of course.

I get crotchety when people ignore the contributions symbolized by the feminine archetypes and act like dates of conquest and battles are the sum total of human history. Tell me why we can exalt the man who designed a better gun but the designer of the loom is "anonymous."

Chiron was named for a centaur who was a "wounded healer." He is said to rule healing and those who live with handicaps in life. Chiron is seen by some astrologers as a transition body between Saturn, ruling the old, and Uranus, the planet of the future. Because he was a centaur, some think he belongs in Sagittarius, perhaps subordinate to Jupiter.

In any case, asteroids will well repay a bit of study.

Chapter 31

What About My Sister's Dog?
Derived Houses

The system that lets the astrologer answer a wide range of questions about matters that may have nothing to do with the client is called the Derived House system. This is a tool that every astrologer simply must know how to use or be forever half blind when looking at a chart. What is it and how does it work? It is a simple method that allows an astrologer to mentally turn the chart so that matters of another house are rising. Then the events are revealed as one counts around the circle to the necessary area for judgment.

An example helps clarify things. If a woman wants to know about her husband's job, you use the 7th house as the husband's 1st and count around the chart until the 10th house is reached. (This is actually the client's 4th house, of course.) The 8th is thus the husband's 2nd house, the 9th is his 3rd house, the 10th is his 4th house and so on.

A Neptune transit about to hit the client's 4th cusp? That's the husband's 10th house of career. There is probably a layoff in the works, or perhaps a buyout. In any case the company is in trouble and his job is about to go. Maybe instead your client has a Jupiter transit in her 4th. It's a very favorable indicator for the husband's job. In either case, the client is probably aware that matters are in the works and you can help her get a clear answer to events concerning her husband's job. That may be a critical matter if the client herself is not employed.

No house in the birth chart is limited to a single matter. The 4th and 10th traditionally belong to one's parents. They are also one's career and one's home or real estate. After one marries, they are the spouse's parental axis as well. By making use of the derived house system you can see that your 10th is also your brother-in-law's spending habits because it rules the 2nd house of the brother-in-law (brothers-in-law come under the 9th house), your co-worker's vacation time (5th house from the co-worker 6th house) and a wide range of other things. If your husband has several siblings, you will have to figure which one is involved. The 9th is the oldest of them, the 11th is the next oldest one and so on around the chart, skipping a house for each one. (Your husband is not in the lineup, of course—he's your 7th.)

The use of the derived house system multiplies the house meanings almost exponentially. For example, suppose you are looking for an answer to the health of your mother. I use the 10th house for the mother, but there are some charts where the mother is clearly the 4th house parent. Count ahead 6 houses and you find that the mother's house of health will be your 3rd house (or 9th in the case of a 4th house mother).

A word here on this topic which I have discussed elsewhere in the book. There are good reasons for using either house for either parent and I suspect it is less an astrological cast-in-stone law than merely the way each child responds to parenting. Where there is a single parent doing the rearing you can often see quite quickly which house is the key parent.

How about a brother-in-law's current romance? Will he wed? He's signified by the 9th house. His 5th house of romance is your 1st. A wife is your 3rd (his 7th). A favorable transit of Jupiter in your 3rd this year could prompt a wedding. If you only have one sibling, he or she is the third house. The next one in order of birth would be your fifth house.

If there are 6 children in the family, you take the client out of the rotation and give the siblings numbers to make it easier. Oldest sibling gets house 3, number two gets house 5 etc. Once you know that Charlie is house 7 you can start looking at Charlie's children. Suppose the fifth from the 7th, which is 11, is getting a Saturn transit. Then Charlie is the one whose kids are worries right now. Maybe one of them broke a window at school playing baseball in the parking lot on Saturday. Or there are problems with health, etc.

Perhaps the Saturn transit is in the client's 10th. That's Charlie's fourth, so he's got problems with an elderly parent or perhaps with his house. It only sounds cumbersome when you first try it. If you can do astrology you can count to 12 so you can count around the chart. That's really all there is to it.

The reason it works so well is that these people are part of your life and all of your life is reflected in your chart. When people sit down to talk to an astrologer they always want to know about their families and their children. The houses to use depend on whether your client is a man or woman. A woman's oldest child is ruled by the 4th house. Her 5th house is all her children generally, of course. Her 6th house is the 2nd child and so on. In a man's chart, the 5th house is the oldest child and the 7th is the no. 2 child. Men often refer to their first child as a "chip off the old block," or use some other euphemism to say the child is "like me," or reflects something of "my" nature.

You don't hear women referring to their children as expressing "my" qualities or being "like me." On the contrary, they see their kids as adorable because they are different and unique specimens in their own right. They also see them as personal responsibilities and their care and protection becomes a 24-hour job.

Women don't make crucial decisions without considering their children as a rule. "If I leave my job at the grocery store around the corner, how will Jimmy find me when he needs to get in the house after school? If I take the job at the store across town, he's going to be upset and what if something happens and he needs me and I'll be worried sick if he doesn't call me and and and..." This is typical female thinking but men usually don't do it. They think about the job first ("Gee, I'd make a lot more money over there.") and only later—"Oh well, we'll figure something out for Jimmy."

Only live births get a house. Some astrologers may try to include still born children or miscarriages but they aren't "children." They were merely "fetuses," the unborn. A "child" must take at least one independent breath. It may die later, of course, but we have to be clear about this. Until true separate life exists you do not yet have a "child." This is not my rule, by the way. You will find it in Bills' *The Rulership Book* and other much older texts. The reason why a woman's 4th house is her first child is that a child alters her entire life and she is never the same afterwards. The 4th is the foundation of her life. A man can have a child and not even know it. Even in nature, the mother defending her young is a far different opponent than a father defending the family. Large animals will back down from very small moms rather than take the grief.

Here's an example on how the 5th house works. Anyone with natal Uranus in 5 is going to have uppity kids, bright, stubborn, independent. Most parents with Uranus in 5 are going to get a big kick out of seeing that element of their personalities manifest. So, within the framework of bright, stubborn, independent, uppity kids you will see the mother's 4th house indications for the oldest child, the 6th house indications for the next child and so on. For the father, child number 1 starts in House 5 and then child no. 2 is reflected by House 7.

Women with Saturn in House 5 are going to have children who are all serious about life. The specific ways they are serious will be shown by Houses 4, 6, 8, etc. If you have Mercury there, all the children are going to be cerebral, adept at doing more than one thing at a time, verbal, etc. Their key focus in life is going to be in the mental areas—the thinking process. Now obviously if you have more than six children you have to give the same house to the 1st child and the 7th child. No problem. It's amazing how well they will both fit.

If you have more than six marriages, the same thing happens. This doesn't affect most of us but there ARE people who just marry everybody in sight. Movie star Elizabeth-Taylor comes to mind. Movie star Mickey Rooney was another one. They went well past 6 trips to the altar.

If one asks an astrologer about whether she will lose her cleaning lady whose husband is quite ill, you can see it. The 6th house is the house of servants and rules the cleaning lady. The 12th house is thus her husband and his health is his 6th house, or the client's 5th.

Deaths in the family come under the 11th house. The family in the broad sense is the 4th house. The 8th from the 4th house is the 11th house, so stress in that house can often show a death. It may be an elderly aunt or a cousin who lives far away, but activity in that house will show.

Stepchildren are another thing that is quite common today with all the shifting patterns taking place in family affairs. The oldest child of one's spouse is the 11th, the next oldest is the 1st and so on. Many people marry spouses that come with baggage and it may have some problems attached. Sorting out which house to look to for answers is the astrologer's job.

For example you have a stepson and a younger stepdaughter. The son would be your 11th, and the daughter (assuming you have no older step children) would be your 1st. But if their father was your second husband the daughter would be your 3rd!! Second husband is the 9th, so his second child would be 7th from the 9th which is the 3rd. The 11th is also marriage for one's children. It is the 7th from the 5th and pleasant transits there often mean weddings when adult children reach the proper age.

All of one's pets come under the 6th house. This house refers to small animals. A person who raises horses uses the 12th house, which rules large animals. In today's rather silly world, some doting pet owners treat their dogs like they were children, sometimes even calling themselves their pet's "mommy" or "daddy." It doesn't matter a whit how well they treat them. Dogs are not one's children and they are still ruled by the 6th house. Any thing that gives us comfort or provides for our comfort comes under the 6th house. Our animals comfort us. The 6th house also rules the fancy chickens a friend of mine raises in her back yard as well as the sheep she and her husband show at fairs around the country. They have a number of cats in the barn which keep down the mouse population and dogs which come into the house with them. All are 6th house. When the 6th house shows stress in the chart of someone like this, it can mean a pet is lost or ill or requires care. In the case of my friend with the sheep, it could be the loss of one of her animals.

If the client is worried about a surgery for his brother, you need to see if he has more than one sibling and whether this is the oldest of them, or the 2nd or which. If it is the 3rd sibling you count from the 3rd house, skipping a house for each one until you get to the 7th house. That brother's 8th house of surgery is the client's 2nd.

Grandchildren come under the 9th house and their needs are read in the same way. The oldest grandchild is house 9. The next one is house 11 and so down the age range. As they grow, each may also have a spouse which is the house opposite the one that rules the grandchild in question. Their careers are ruled by their 10th houses.

Just as the 5th house describes all one's children generally, the 7th describes all one's spouses. We always choose to wed one who fits the image of the 7th house. The 2nd "person" we wed may be the 9th house and the 3rd marriage come under the 11th, but once wed, the 7th house is applicable. And ex-spouses? They go into the 12th house of the past, as do all our old lovers, friends we have long since left behind in the years and other people we may remember but who are no longer part of our lives. Friends are never lovers. If a sexual relationship begins with a friend, the relationship shifts to that of a 5th house "lover." When the relationship is over, it goes into the 12th house unless it is resumed. In which case, it does not start over in the "friend" house but in the "lover" house, the 5th.

Of course if you have the person's chart, you don't need to use the derived house system in your client's chart, but it's good practice to be able to whip this stuff out. In addition, it's confirming information, which can help give you confidence. It only sounds cumbersome when you first try it. That's really all there is to it.

Some years ago I did my first lecture on this topic called "What About My Sister's Dog?" I asked anyone in the audience who had a sister with a dog to share his or her own birth chart and got a great lecture out of it. The woman who loaned her chart just sat and smiled until I described the dog as menacing and hard to control. I showed how it looked like the family was worried about it biting someone. She about fell off her chair because they were considering putting it down for just that reason.

In a general way every house is the 12th house to the next one, so the first house is the house which forms our ideas about money, the 2nd house is the one that expresses how we really feel about our siblings, and the 4th house shows us important information about our lovers or children.

Each house is also the 4th house of endings to matters 4 houses back or the 7th house to the one opposite. The more often you use this system the faster and easier it becomes. Not only is it helpful to the client to be able to do this but it makes us better astrologers. The reason it works so well is that other people are part of your life and all of your life is reflected in your chart. The derived house system is like a good Phillips screwdriver. You mostly use the other kind but when you need it, a Phillips is worth its keep. I adore good reliable things that work when I need them and the derived house system is one such tool.

There are a lot of times when an astrologer does the chart of a client who has questions about their children. People want to know about their fourth grandchild who's in the hospital, or the third brother-in-law who just lost his job, etc. Somebody's worried about an aunt who's developing Alzheimer's or whether their dad is retiring this year..

When that happens to you you'll be very happy you know how to use derived houses.

Chapter 32

The Stars in Their Courses
Fixed Stars

While most modern western astrology is based on the tropical system, the stars which play such a big role in the sidereal or Hindu (Jyotish) systems are highly significant. They can exhibit important roles, particularly in the charts of those whose actions can affect the lives of millions of others or events with vast, far-reaching effects.Some are critical in horary astrology. Others seem to show strongly in the charts of rulers, presidents and the like. For good or for bad, they are powerful.

Aldeberan, at 8 degrees Gemini, marks a very strong fixed star that is fairly close to the earth, astronomicly speaking and which is a star of violence. When a birth chart shows a planet such as Mars, itself a possible indicator of violence, linked to it, violence is bound to show sooner or later. It is opposite Antares at 8 Sagittarius, and both were two of the royal stars of the ancient Egyptians. If you look at the charts of Jack and Bobby Kennedy, who both died by violence, you find many contacts to fixed stars which were apparently signatures of charm, fame, wealth and violence.

If you want to use a star on the MC in an election chart, it can have a dominant effect on the event. Be sure you choose wisely. Vivian Robson's book is helpful. Diana Rosenberg's book is superb if you have access to a copy. But if you want conjunctions to the Ascendant, you must correct for them since longitude is strongly affected by latitude on the earth. Use the tables in the Tables of Houses if you do. Or, alternatively, use Bernadette Brady's "Starlight" program.

Those stars which never rise or set in our northern latitude, for instance, can never actually contact the Ascendant, only the MC. The same is true of southern latitudes south of the equator. This is why I am very leery about orb and position when someone claims a star is "on the Ascendant." Just because the apparent "degree" of a fixed star is said to be rising, this doesn't mean anything if it's never going to actually be there. I see a lot of articles saying this or that star is conjunct this or that point when it isn't and can't be. Many astrologers do not have a sufficient background in simple astronomy to realize this.

Stars have practically no orb of influence. I would not use 3 degrees at all. I would use no degrees. If a star is farther than 60 minutes away, it's too far from a natal point, in my opinion. These stars are light years away and have a very narrow focus. Generally speaking, I think we have to use VERY tight correspondences with them. They aren't planets, like fat old Jupiter with its honkin' orb.

Part of the problem, which is poorly understood by many astrologers, is that the stars, unlike the planets, are not all on the ecliptic plane and thus have an added factor to account for—their distance above or below it. Algol's longitudinal position at 25 Taurus, therefore, is ONLY exact when it occupies the MC of a chart. For it to occupy the Ascendant, that distance from the ecliptic must be accounted for (remember, we are on a curved surface, too), so it really is not going to be there at the same degree. It will be appear to be "off" somewhat. Same thing occurs with all the planets except the Sun. The stars are a much bigger problem.

So, if you think your rising Venus is conjunct Algol, you will have to calculate the variation to be accurate. It's no wonder so many people don't think the fixed stars "work." They aren't calculating the position accurately and fixed stars so accuracy is doubly important.

The "Starlight" computer program designed by Bernadette Brady can do a lot of this work for you. Those interested in adding fixed star information to the charts should definitely examine her program.

The stars also move, even though very slowly, and occupy different locations than they did in ancient times. The Pleiades, for instance, a group of stars called the Weeping Sisters once at 29 degrees of Taurus, is now actually moving into the first degree of Gemini. The star Alcyone is there now. Since Taurus and Gemini are different in their effects, we may, in future, have to modify our interpretations of what this position means in practical terms.

I think a new Moon conjunct Spica, the star of sweetness at 23 Libra is probably very good for the candy business and when Halloween comes, I'll bet candy companies love it, too Other big holidays when candy plays a prominent role could be Valentine's Day and Easter, so any contact by a planet to Spica then would boost sales. New Moons and transits, particularly stations, that conjunct any fixed star affect mundane events and are useful in predictive work. Sweetness is a Venus characteristic and contacts to Spica can prompt many events ruled by Venus. It has traditionally been labeled as the only "safe" place for planets in the Via Combust, the Latin name for the "fiery pathway" of stars between 15 Libra and 15 Scorpio.

Spica indicates increase in the happiness of weddings, romanticism and reconciliations. In a mundane or legal sense, it is good for peace negotiations and agreements and settlements of law suits and disputes. Do I think it will single-handedly stop military attacks or wars? No, but I do think a few olive branches will start waving from one side or the other when Spica is contacted by a planet important in the affairs. Any war may develop some financial teeth since Venus rules money and there should be—at the very least—some story about plugging some money holes as armed events get underway.

Look for the stock market to improve, too, when Spica is involved in any planetary action. You are also likely to hear about banking and currency issues, though these are more often triggered by transits or lunations involving Taurus stars such as Algol at 25 Taurus. Algol is not a happy position, though, and it's more apt to show up in events where there is violence and death.

If you do charts long enough you will find Vindemiatrix at about 8 degrees of Libra works just fine as the star of widowhood. Sometimes it is loss of the husband's companionship through his traveling job, or divorces (the modern widowhood) or obsessive hobbies that consume too much time, etc. Sometimes it is just plain widowhood, of course. Occasionally it refers to a divorced or widowed woman in one's own chart. (In 10 in could be a boss, in 11, a friend, etc.) It is a very handy star to remember in horary charts.

I think careful thinking in astrology is very important and it would be wonderful if we could have researchers line up thousands of cases where similar events are linked to specific stars, but meantime we rely on astrological traditions which are reports that go back many hundreds or thousands of years. Modern scientific thinking would call such reports unproven but astrologers have been studying this stuff as long as we have any record and most were quite savvy about cause and effect. I tend to take their word for it.

Diana Rosenberg's books are a massive compilation of tradition and cultural references to the stars which can enrich anyone's interpretation. She is also the most current source for information on exactly where the stars are now, aside from the Brady computer program. There are valid reasons for keeping those designations which have history behind them and the experience of countless astrologers. I've done consulting for nearly 45 years and the simple fact is that Vindemiatrix does seem to signify the state known as widowhood.

I have also seen it triggered when divorce occurs. The key factor seems to be an event that leaves one spouse to continue on without the other.

For a truly comprehensive look at the fixed stars I strongly recommend the works of lifelong researcher Diana Rosenberg and Bernadette Brady, who have spurred astrologers to look at the sky and understand the movements of star and planets. Vivian Robson's book is also a good one to have on the shelf.

Chapter 33

A Bird's Eye View
The One-Degree Method

This is a modified solar arc predictive technique. It has been called the simple "age arc." In the true solar arc you use the actual motion of the Sun so many days after birth for a forecast. True solar arc is actually the basis of the secondary system of progression. In other words, if you are 16, you count ahead 16 days to see how far the Sun has actually moved in 16 full days from its exact natal position. (You use the actual positions of the planets on that day for the "progressed" chart.) If you were born under Cancer, when the Sun is moving less than a degree per day, the increment might be—when you are 16, for instance—15 degrees and 48 minutes. If you were born under Capricorn, when the Sun moves a tad more than a degree a day, the increment could be 16 degrees 11 or more minutes. Then this increment is added to each different position in the chart one at a time to see where things fall.

The one degree system skips all that. The one degree system is a symbolic system and was laid out in the work of C.E.O. Carter. It, too, is based on solar motion, but an average motion. The Sun's average motion is one degree a day. Dirt simple. If you are 33, you add 33 degrees to the Ascendant and see what it would aspect in the natal chart at that point. (You only move one factor at a time, leaving everything else alone so you can see aspects that occur.) You can add 33 degrees to the Moon and see what it would aspect from the new location. Maybe it trines a natal 5th house Mercury. Well, guess what—you'll have a pregnancy, or, if you're a married male, a child. Maybe only a love affair, but 5th house affairs will be in the spotlight..

Carter's system does not—repeat not—interact with any other system at all. You can't say "my one-degree-Mars is on my progressed Moon." It doesn't work that way. These aspects only work on natal positions. To calculate any event during the life, all you need is the natal chart and paper and pencil. If you're good you can do the addition in your head. Any year in which a lot of these ODs (One Degrees) culminate is important. They pinpoint major life events. Planets can come to angles or angles can come to planets in this symbolic movement. Yes, you should use the nodes and the part of fortune, too.

Carter, in his book *Symbolic Directions,* tried to get it down to month and week with his calculation. I do not use it that way, but more as a "bird's eye view" of the whole year's influence. I don't find exact calculations particularly reliable, though he worked them in tinier and tinier increments trying to make them so. (Carter's book is sometimes out of print but can be obtained—do an online search for it.)

My system is similar to the true solar arc system and if you learn to use solar arcs and like them, I have no quarrel with you. I'm a down-and-dirty astrologer and my one-degree method is just faster and quite dependable. However, there is a good "whatever" to keep in mind—events occur **after** the aspect is exact for those whose natal Sun is in Gemini, Cancer and Leo and **before** the event is exact for Sagittarius, Capricorn and Aquarius. It is dead exact to the year for all other signs. Obviously, you will say, this reflects the true motion of the Sun. And I will say, "Yes it does." So why not use exact solar arcs? No reason at all. This is just handier and quicker and Lord knows we sometimes need handy and quick in our lives.

Another measure is the Naibod measure of 59'8" per year, as C.E.O. Carter explained in his book first published in 1929. He cited Sepharial in the *British Journal of Astrology* as having first written about it. It was particularly intended to be used in right ascension, as a type of primary directing, although it came to be used with longitude later.

The one-degree method has as its particular charm and virtue its simplicity and its usefulness in pinpointing important years and major events in the life. I use this method relentlessly with every chart I do. I consider it one of my indispensable tools.

How do the aspects work? In terms of the natural rulers of various topics (Venus for money and marriage, Mars for trouble and falls, etc.) and in accord with their position in the natal chart. Natal Venus in House 4 also means family matters and/or real estate and/or money related to those things. If it gets a conjunction from OD (One Degree) Saturn, it means trouble, restriction or limitation and delay. Simple and straightforward.

The type of aspect the OD planet or angle makes is less important than you think. What it aspects is the key. If the MC comes to a Moon that is getting a natal trine from Jupiter it will bring benefit. If the MC squares a Moon that is getting a natal trine from Jupiter it will bring benefit. If the MC conjuncts a Moon getting a natal square from Mars, it will not bring as happy an event. That's all there is to this. The rest takes practice. Just keep in mind that you need to use the intrinsic meaning of the planet or point involved as well as what that planet refers to in a particular chart to get the full interpretation.

This is a very effective method for showing accidents in childhood if there is a planet rising in the first house. The year the Ascendant comes to a rising Saturn there is breakage of bones or teeth or an injury to the face. If the Ascendant comes to the opposition to Mars there will be an injury or surgery which will leave a scar. With a rising Saturn in Aquarius, say 10 degrees from the Ascendant, you can ask your client if he broke an ankle at 10, or the leg itself. In Capricorn, sometimes it's a broken tooth. Any rising planet getting an aspect from Mars of accidents or Saturn of bones shows the likelihood of damage leaving a scar.

There is nothing so worrisome for the astrologer as sitting down to talk to a client who supposedly has Leo rising, and after taking one look, recognizes immediately that this is no Leo-rising type. Then what? Obviously, a few questions on timing are in order. If the body is top heavy and the face round, I would start working back toward Cancer. If the body is neat and the feet small and the hair curly, I'd look to Virgo. The one-degree method of confirming years in which events occurred is a Godsend to the busy astrologer. It also tells the client we can "see" their lives.

ODs show changes in the home quite clearly when the MC conjuncts or opposes a planet. It may be a physical move to a new location. To Uranus it can show a split between the parents (if the natal chart suggests this) or a change in the dominant parent's career. I say dominant parent because sometimes that's the mother in the case of a single parent. In a traditional family, it may be the father. Later in life such aspects show changes in one's own career. The 4th house cusp coming to an aspect to Fortuna can show the purchase of property. A 12th house planet moving to the Ascendant can show a serious illness. A 3rd house planet being aspected in early life often indicates the birth of a sibling. The OD position can give and receive aspects other than just the conjunction.

This is a handy tool for rectification. Every astrologer should use it routinely to check the veracity of a chart. A simple query about the years when major events have happened is usually enough to prove whether the chart works well. The first marriage is one of the easiest to use. It will be the year when the 7th house cusp, its ruler or a planet in that house forms or receives an aspect to or from Venus. If Venus does not receive or form an aspect during the time period most likely for it, occasionally the aspect will be to or from the MC. The MC is less likely, of course, but there are some charts that work that way. I was highly annoyed by the exception, but there it was.

There will also be aspects to the Sun or Moon or—usually—both, Mars, the nodes and Fortuna. Fortuna indicates the change of fortune, the nodes show the "knots and ties" of life and Mars is sexual activity. The Moon is the residential alteration and the Sun is the change in status from single to married. Be extremely wary of marriage indications where is no Mars aspect. Something else is at work, other than the normal physical attraction.

Sometimes a chart will show only some of these linkages and marriage is planned and desired but does not occur. An example might be Venus forming an aspect to the Ascendant at 14, but nothing else happening. In modern society age 14 is considered too young, and in some places actually illegal, for marriage. In primitive societies or among high-born families in olden times, children were once wed by proxy as early as 6 or 7. Such a practice occurred many times in history. Now, an aspect at age 14 might very rarely show an attempted elopement, but mostly it will mean an intense love affair that goes nowhere. In a suitable year—say at 21 or 22—it can reflect a broken engagement.

Second and third marriages may also fail to involve all the various planets. Sometimes the parties are already living together and the Moon is not aspected since there is no change expected in the domestic arrangements. Mars may be absent because they are already sexually involved with each other so no "new" development is expected in this regard, either. In some charts the first marriage is so brief and forgettable that the second marriage may have all the strong indications the first one did not. I have had charts like this. Occasionally under-age teens elope and try to "marry" or simply move in together but the parents get it annulled or otherwise dissolved.

Also, charts of senior citizens may have fewer ties apparent. Sometimes they have no intention of forming a household together or having children (and are past the age of conception anyway) or accepting responsibility of them for a lifetime. Occasionally there will be no sexual relationship, though that is unlikely. Sex comes in all forms and varieties at all ages in human affairs. But almost always Venus will be aspected or form an aspect if any union is accomplished. I should warn that this may reflect the years of actual union, when a couple assumes residence together, rather than the year in which a formal legal marriage contract is made.

If in doubt as to whether a particular union qualifies as a marriage, apply the 3B rule—bed, board and the bills. Once a couple is actually sharing all three, it's a marriage, with or without legal sanction, and the chart reflects that. If one is seeing such a chart later in the life of the person involved when it is actually a second marriage that has been made, errors in interpretation can come from overlooking the first "marriage." That was the one which had the 3 B's but may not have lasted long enough to invoke the "common law" rule which declares a marriage legally exists after so many years of cohabitation.

In today's world astrologers can make major mistakes talking about marriage when the client has had one or more "live-in" affairs over the years without benefit of legal arrangements. Looked at from this perspective, the client may be forming the 3rd or 4th "marriage." It is always wise to simply ask if the client has ever had a live-in relationship before discussing matters of the 7th house.

The years of accidents that threaten the life, or major surgeries, or retirement, or the birth of children and deaths in the family can readily be seen using this One-Degree technique. It is one of the most reliable tools in one's bag of tricks. If it doesn't work during times of major events, the chart should be eyed with great suspicion. A full rectification is probably indicated. One of two or three things may be happening here. The first is the client has given a false date of birth, thinking it didn't really matter and she doesn't want her true age known. The second could be an adopted child mistaken on the actual day or year. And don't overlook the possibility of astrologer error. Writing down an incorrect year or date, or misreading what one wrote when accepting the appointment happens at least once to everyone. A rare fourth possibility is that the client is testing the astrologer to see if the error can be spotted. This may happen with clients from a culture where astrology is common and they are trying to see if the astrologer is reliable. What this shows the astrologer is the extreme value of a quick, dependable way to check the chart's validity. And for that, the One Degree method is superb.

In years when no or very few aspects are forming, little of major note occurs in life, unless the few aspects involve the angles. In years when everything in the chart is involved by either making or receiving an aspect, expect some of the biggest events of the life to occur. Should one such come early in life, examine the chart carefully for longevity, paying particular attention to the ascendant and its ruler. After one has reached old age, it can mark the year of serious illness, or even death. At the very least, it is life-changing events.

Carter's book also uses other symbolic measurements in ascertaining the main events in life and if one is interested, should be consulted for them. One of his techniques uses 4 degrees per year and another ¼ degree per year. Those always struck me as excessively finicky, but there are many people who like to try as many different techniques as possible and confirmation is always helpful.

I often use simple OD arcs for rectification. I call it thumbnail rectification because you can mostly do it in your head. Once you get in the correct ball park you can refine. The point being affected and the planet doing the deed are key factors.

In all judgment matters you want to see how these two things are linked at birth —if at all—and how they are natally aspected to other planets. For instance—is the Ascendant unafflicted or does it have a square from say, Mars? That might mean a Pluto contact could set off a need for surgery. What kind of shape is Pluto in natally? What will it bring to the point it touches?

Or, for another example, a Pluto with a Venus trine natally will bring the urge to beautify to the Ascendant and the trine says the changes will be beneficial, profitable in some way and may involve love relationships or the arts. If you have Pluto in 10, it could be a job change involving those things. Of course, it could also be a face lift, particularly if Mars indicates surgery likely that year. If the ruler of Ascendant is in 3, perhaps the change involves communication or travel, if it receives any aspect from the Pluto contact. That implies that it aspected Ascendant or Pluto natally.

Chapter 34

The Ages of Life

Here is an odd little symbolic tool to play with that works surprisingly well. I read something about it years ago and have found it useful, but I have long since forgotten which author first noticed it. You count the number of degrees from the ascendant to the 2nd house and 3rd house cusps. The houses of the first quadrant measure the three stages of life—youth, maturity and old age and how long they last in each chart. Each degree is a year of life.

I use Placidian houses as a general rule, but feel free to see how it works with Koch or any other house system. Different people seem to respond best to different house systems. Odd, but I've seen it work that way. Equal house is not satisfactory of course, because it doesn't allow for individual variation. It just assigns every stage 30 degrees and that invalidates the whole point.

The three stages of life correspond only very roughly to the three traditional ages of humankind—youth, maturity and old age—and are vaguely linked to Saturn, I suspect.

The first house I generally think of as the time we are exploring who we are and what we want to be when we "grow up" by whatever standard we use. This is, after all, a highly subjective and symbolic way of looking at your life. Only you can decide for you what that is. There is a rule in life that you have to get older but you don't have to "grow up." Most of us do have a sense of that after getting to house 2, however. The first house is our playful period, time to explore the world. It is like our first Saturn cycle of life, but sometimes does not quite match the Saturn period.

The second house moves us into the productive years where we struggle to achieve success or fulfill our mission in life or reach our goals, etc. It is these mature years, the adult stage of development, in which we produce whatever we are meant to produce in our life.

The "latter years" are when you shift gears and say, OK, been there and done that, it's time to find new things in my life and see what else there is around. It's when we enter the third house, drop the old image of ourselves we've been carrying, or the old role we've functioned in or the lifetime obligations and responsibilities and say, "time for me."

Sometimes entry into the third zone is marked by a clear event—one client told me her only child married that year and left home, when by symbolic measure she "entered" the third house. It was definitely the end of her role as "mom" and the responsibilities that implied. Now it was time to feel lighter for having set down the load.

All of astrology is a way of looking at ourselves and seeing who we are, where we came from, what we want, how we get it and what we want to be. This is just another such tool. Note the years when the actual shift into each new house occurs. There are often defining times.

Some people may want to know what happens if they live beyond the measure of the third house and enter the 4th house. This is extended time, I think, sort of like overtime in a ball game. It's when the final innings are run and the last details of living are completed. Not everyone gets to this stage. But then, not every ball game goes into overtime, either.

If you get into your overtime, make the most of it. It's life's bonus to you.

Chapter 35

As Time Goes By
Transits

This is where I remind the reader that I am not writing a complete textbook on any subject. If you want more information on any of the topics I have brought up, sample other authors' works. This chapter on Transits is not going to be complete by any means so if what I have written doesn't help you, try another book.

Transits to the natal angles are quite reliable indicators of events. If you want to know how yours work, the best thing is to keep a small diary and note when planets cross your angles or form squares to them. You can learn things quicker that way then any other, I think.

If you are looking at a particular day, especially if you are using a diurnal chart, then the transits of the MC and Asc are important. What is a diurnal chart? It is a chart cast for any day at the exact time and place of your natal chart. Suppose you were born at 2 p.m. in Chicago. Tomorrow you cast a chart for Chicago at 2 p.m. and it is your diurnal chart (meaning "daily") for tomorrow and events in it manifest after 2 p.m. You can do this every day. You can keep a notebook with the charts and make forecasts. It's fun and educational.

When the transits show a crossing of your natal angles or if the natal angles contact diurnal planets, important events are likely to manifest. This is a fairly simple technique which can also help you forecast events to the day. If your chart is consistently off a couple of days on this, it probably means your natal time is off a tad.

If you aren't using a diurnal chart but just following the transits day by day, angles are unimportant, because they keep changing all day. The diurnal chart provides angles.

Say you want to know about a job interview but you aren't working with a diurnal chart and actually cast a chart for the time and place. Those angles are significant. If you meet someone and happen to note the time, angles will tell you how important the relationship is likely to be and where it's going. But if you're just watching how Saturn moves along day after day, you aren't using angles because you don't have any time and place which give angles. That's what the diurnal chart provides.

The rule is that the transiting planet activates the basic meaning of the natal chart. Mars to the natal Ascendant is usually a reliable indicator of heavy activity or physical demands because you have a lot going on. The Ascendant rules your physical body. Mars on the MC or in House 10 activates things having to do with your career, or your standing in the world. And so on.

If you have Mars natally aspecting an angle, it triggers the natal indicator and its effect increases. Mars in Gemini, for instance, opposed the Ascendant? Broken fingernails every time Mars transits the Ascendant or the Descendant. Sometimes other things, too, of course, but the broken fingernails are a small but reliable event. A single transit alone will not provide major events, however. Those are always a combination of things.

Suppose you have a Venus trine your natal MC from your 2nd house. A transit of Venus over that MC could bring a raise, or an improvement of your business (if you have your own business) or be an opportunity to make money. It might be a job offer. It's a case of the natal indicator getting a boost from the transit.

But waiting for "your ship to come in," by watching transits is futile unless your chart promises such a thing. If your chart does not offer windfalls, then you'll have to work for your financial security one step at a time just like the rest of us. If it warns of financial difficulties in life, you'll have them but you can anticipate some of the worst and soften the blows.

Maybe this is the lifetime when you have to sort out your Venus priorities and decide whether you really need 40 pairs of shoes, or whether it would be better to have some money in the bank for emergencies instead.

We all make tradeoffs, and transits that look like disasters for some people can bring good things for others, depending on how their individual chart is arranged. Or transits that look like they will produce those financial windfalls happen and you get no financial windfall because your chart has nothing to create an echo and draw it in. Nobody gets all the goodies. The sad truth is that we can't always get what we want in life. And for most of us, that's a very good thing.

Personally, I think the universe gives us what we ought to have instead, which is a whole other kettle of chicken soup.

Transits to Intermediate House Cusps

Some astrologers make heavy use of intermediate house cusps. I never have for this reason. One day I sat down with all the different house systems and calculated all the intermediate cusps for one natal chart. The range was very wide. It was ten degrees or more. The only reliable cusps were the angles, which are the same in all systems. So which house cusp could I possibly use? I didn't know so decided to use none of them. You may disagree and use them. I hope it's reliable for you.

One astrologer I know who lives far south of me uses the Placidean system exclusively and accurately predicted imprisonment years in advance for a client using his 12th house cusp. That method simply isn't that workable for northern latitudes, in my experience.

I know astrologers who favor the Koch system in this northern U.S. area. Many British astrologers who are higher yet in latititude scrap them all and use equal house. Margaret Hone, A Brit who authored a classic textbook on astrology, was a big fan of that system.

As for me, I stick to the ruler of the house and sidestep the whole controversy. And, since I strongly urge that the simple solar chart (Sun on Ascendant) be kept in mind for every forecast, I think I'm covered. There's a chapter in this book on it which you may want to read.

Parents often ask about their children and how the child will do in school. Rather than using the house cusps, I use the rulers and the planets which may be in the child's 3rd house natally. Generally speaking, the third and ninth houses are reflective of schoolwork and the 10th, how the student ranks. A benefic in one of those houses is a big help since the 10th is also the teacher who judges the child's work.

For a particular (but not especially important) test, look to transits of the 3rd, since it rules tests specifically, and to the 6th as the outcome (4th from the 3rd). If the test is for something like a major fellowship or a trip abroad I would use House 9 as well. If the test determines something like beginning part of the national merit scholarship awards, I'd add the 10th house, since such a ranking is basically a "status" thing. Ditto if the test determines career track.

Where does the house start? Well, here again we are back to the problem of the intermediate cusps. I use the Placidean system for reasons which seem sensible to me but I am no fanatic on exactly where the house begins. Some people seem to be getting third house effects sooner or later than others. I can't do enough research to prove any theory so I just agree with myself that it's all very interesting and go on to the next chart.

Cop out? Absolutely. But life is full of things like that and I don't have enough years to worry about them all.

The Annual Tools

Every year when I get my new ephemeris for the coming year, I make a list of all the stations and the dates on which they occur. I note them on a 3x5 card, along with the eclipses for the year and any major planet sign changes—such as Jupiter going into Sagittarius, or Saturn into Leo. I keep that card in the ephemeris all year because it gives me the time period in which events will develop for those with planets at the sensitive degrees. It's a short cut for me, since I find that events are far more likely to cluster at the stations than they are at the time of the exact aspect.

To show you how this works, take your own chart and note the stations and compare it to a list of events that are linked to them. For instance, one year there were two stations in November. Uranus was SD at 10 Pisces Nov. 20. Mercury was SD at 9 Scorpio on the 18th. Thus, any planet at 9-10 degrees got action around the 19th of the month. If you had an MC at 10 Pisces, for instance, there was likely a status change, or career change. Because the Mercury station was in aspect to it, it had a hand in the event.

After you do this a few years you may notice something very interesting. A lot of degrees that are in for action during the year will have stations of more than one planet as well as eclipses and New or Full Moons at the same degree or nearly so. For instance, Mercury will station at 22 Aries and you notice that there is a Saturn station at 22 Libra and a solar eclipse at 21 Cancer. There is also a lunar eclipse at say 19 Cap. And both the Aries and Libra New Moons are in the late teens. Now, it doesn't require a lot of fancy math to realize that ANY CHART with placements in the 19-22 degree cardinal range is going to be affected in a pronounced way this year.

When it comes to planetary transits, the stations are powerful indicators. Every year there is some major planetary activity that dominates. One year it may be a triple conjunction of Uranus and Pluto as they go retrograde and direct, passing and re-passing each other. Another year Jupiter and Saturn repeat a series of squares, etc. Notice the degrees at which the direction changes. Those degrees should be listed on your card. They are important for that year.

Next year, do this again. Watch how the degrees of the stations are echoed by the New Moons and Full Moons close to or on those activated areas as the year goes by.

Sometimes they are all in cardinal or fixed. Occasionally they may be all in fire, or water. Watch these linkages shape up. If any chart has these areas of the zodiac occupied by planets, that chart will be in for the action. If the degrees getting emphasis are on the angles, major activity is scheduled.

I hope this is clear. The solar system is like a game of tag, and sometimes the one who is "It" changes, bouncing from person to person. Look at the chart in terms of these periods and you will have an eye opener, I think.

A Forecast to the Day

There is always a lot of talk about how to use transits to forecast to the day. That's tough. It's easier to get in the general time period by a couple weeks or so. But it can be done. I use a mix of many people's ideas. This whole field is pretty eclectic, which is good for us, I suspect. It's sort of like cooking with a dab of this and a dab of that to taste.

Here is an overview of some things I use that might be helpful.

1—First thing I ever do is choose the dominant planets/patterns/etc in the natal because they will respond most quickly. A planet near an angle is a good one to use. Anybody with strong Mars influence (Sun sign or ascendant ruler or angular placement) will react to Mars very reliably. Same thing with Venus or Mercury. A strongly Venus chart ticks off when transiting Venus starts operating. Leo Suns, or Leo rising do solar returns quite reliably. Cancers just luuuuv the Moon. And the Saturn or Jupiter-ruled react quite sharply to those transits.

2—Find transiting Saturn. I know, I know, everybody worries about it, but Saturn is the most reliable pointer to what is the main concern, focus, worry at any given time for the vast majority of us.

Just the two things above, alone will give you the flavor of almost any time period in the life. Following are more useful tips:

3—Find transiting Uranus. If the individual has a good natal Uranus, the time is generally full of favorable change. If there is no good pattern or a bad one natally, the changes caused by the transiting Uranus are stressful and unhappy. Watch for exactitude. Wide aspects are a waste of time. Either the action is not ready yet or it already happened.

4-Look at transiting Neptune for confusion and health problems and vulnerabilities. Again, check out exactitude.

5—Pluto will often provide contacts with the underside of anything. Here again, exactitude and the natal pattern is the key. Transits of the three outer planets "color" the time period.

6—Use stations of the planets. Transits—even the dead exact—are just that—transitory or passing. Stations trigger events. I rarely pay as much attention to daily transits as I do to the stations. Once a station is in range *then* I watch the daily stuff closer.

7—Keep a list of the last few big eclipses that hit this particular chart. Exactitude is the important word again. They can keep operating for a while. If the eclipse happened more than 3 or 4 degrees away from anything forget it. If a key planet nears the eclipse degree, it's important. Some eclipses hit the whole world. A good example was the Aug. 11, 1999 Millennium eclipse. I felt it would be effective for several years in various charts. (It has been, of course.) I use a Libra-rising chart for the U.S. Sure enough, transiting Venus was exact on that eclipse point on 9/11 when the twin towers filled with financial businesses were attacked in New York city.

8—Start checking out the last couple of lunations. From November to March each year they come on the same degree in each succeeding sign. Look at an ephemeris and see. If that degree is emphasized in the natal it will be an important time—stressful or otherwise.

9—Always look at Mars for activity. Pick out the day the transit is exact. Expect action the day before. Mars is the original premature operator.

10—If Venus or Mercury is stronger in this particular chart than Mars and past events have been more activated by one of them, use it instead of Mars. Keep an eye on Mars just the same. It's hard to push Mars entirely into the background no matter what your strongest planet is.

11—Watch the Moon. Watch the Moon. Watch the Moon. People often tell me they have one sure "down day" a month. Keep a log. It's usually a 12th house transit or the day the Moon passes over natal Saturn.

12—It's a good trick and really impresses somebody if you pick up the chart and note yesterday was a good shopping day for them—or a good day for getting one's hair done, etc. A simple lunar transit explains TONS of daily activities. If you practice with your own chart you'll see them coming along quite regularly.

13—When you need to forecast daily stuff you can. Here's a good example. A client who gambled regularly wanted me to make a list of her "good" times at Las Vegas so she could stretch her vacation money at the casinos. She often lost it all the first day and then had to wire home for more in order to have any money for the rest of her visit. I know—most of us would just go home, but she was a Pisces and ended up in debt all the time. She wasn't a heavy gambler, just lost her head on vacations.

She wanted a forecast that worked for the good times and the bad times. So I plotted it out with an ephemeris. She had transiting Saturn aspecting the ruler of 5 during her vacation,—not good for gambling—so any time there was ANY aspect to Saturn she was dead in the water. Any aspect to her natal Venus, POF or her Jupiter trine was good. You can go through a whole 24 hours and bracket the hot times and the dead times. I've used that trick for a lot of people visiting Vegas for years. It worked fine.

The first time I did that was the first year she stretched her money the whole vacation time. She was so pleased she came home and baked me a German chocolate cake. The cake was terrific.

14—Sometimes people will ask me about specific days and whether events will be favorable that day or how to make them favorable. You can do this list pretty quickly once you have it in mind and then go to the Moon and see what's operating and check out any exact aspects which will affect events.

One executive had to do major presentations to management on a day with tough 10th house aspects for him but good 6th house aspects. I told him to emphasize the time and labor-saving elements, which would appeal to any secretaries that would be present, and to "dress down." It worked. Management saw him as a hard working man with an eye on efficiency (all nice Virgo words) who knew how to save them money and get the most out of their people, which appealed to them.

Another time a woman had to make an appeal to a grand jury and she had everything favorable except an exact Mars/Mercury square affecting her natal Mercury, which could go either way. I told her to plan exactly what to say and not to exceed that, to speak very softly (using the Venus voice as an antidote to Mars) and slowly (to counteract the motor-mouth effect of the Mercury/Mars) and then shut up. We went over the motor-mouth business very carefully. She won her appeal and was told later that her quiet restraint impressed the panel. I was pleased to hear it. The Mercury/Mars aspect told me it was a day when her words would be the action but could also cause her to lose her approval if she got carried away.

15—A diurnal chart can be helpful. This is a chart cast every day for the current planetary positions at the natal birth time in the natal place. As transiting planets hit the angles (which are constantly moving day after day), activity occurs. I have used them from time to time and find them helpful. They are a fun way to watch events march along through the month.

As a lazy astrologer, I don't do this all the time and certainly not for every chart. But if there is a specific need to know an exact day for a specific event, you have a lot of tools to use to predict it. And we all need to know how, even if we don't do it often. It's like decorating a Christmas tree. Most of us do that one day per year, period. But we know HOW.

Stations

I use the transiting stations heavily for forecasting. I think they are among our most reliable tools because a station intensifies the energy of a planet. Think of a moving spotlight and then think of how much more impact it has when it stops and focuses on someone.

Planets that change direction after a station by progression are always significant because they mark a shift in the way the energy is used and the affairs of the houses where they occur and those that they rule.

As a general rule, I have found that if you have a retrograde planet at birth, its later transiting retrograde periods affect you much less because it's your "home place," in a way. You were born with that energy in your pattern, so later transits are comfortable for you. I wouldn't pay much attention to the outer planets in that way, though, since they tend to be generational and not personal, but changes of direction by Mercury, Mars and Venus are signficant, as are Jupiter and Saturn to some extent, but I think of them more as social planets unless one of them rules your chart.

Take Mercury, for instance. If it rules House 7 and changes direction by progression, the individual may marry. Or, it may end a marriage. But it marks a major change in the affairs of that house. The timing can depend on a transiting Mercury station. Should it fall natally in 6 (but ruling 7), it may have to do with a job as well, particularly for a woman who may decide to return to work or end a job at the time of the marital change. If the progressed chart is showing such a Mercury change every transiting station of Mercury during the year will provide action. Any that are near the progressed station by degree can set it off sharply.

ALL of the stations are of value. The Stationary Retrograde (SR) period usually has an element in it of "going back to finish something" or "fix something" or give something a fresh look, etc. Sometimes it is the development of a theme begun before, which will be concluded when the planet goes direct again. If you don't have a planet near 25 degrees of a fixed sign, you may not even notice the effect of a Saturn station at 25 Leo, for instance. But if you do, the time period will be significant.

A station on one's Moon is often related to housing or family or the women in your life. If the Moon is in or ruling natal 5, it has to do with children, or one of them. Sometimes it is another purely lunar effect, such as marking the start of menopause or a course in cooking.And it always goes back to the natal chart. Where the station occurs and on or near which planet is the key.

Somebody who has a 5th house Jupiter that gets a station of a planet could very well win at some game or other. I had a student who was ALWAYS winning a little money from the lottery. She had a somewhat favorable 5th house. But she never got the big wins and she spent tons of money on tickets. I was shocked when she told me she routinely spent more than "a couple hundred a week" on tickets but never seemed to have enough money for a fun vacation. She should have saved the money for a year. She could have gone on a cruise around the world. Her other option might have been to watch for the transiting stations near her 5th house planets and only gamble then.

Usually the retrograde period develops a situation that is concluded or which comes to a head when the stationary direct (SD) point is hit. Sometimes it doesn't arrange itself like that very nicely for us, though. Here's an example: You have a planet at the SR point which creates a strong effect, but the SD event doesn't seem to be as effective. What happens is that the planet gets back to the SR point before the situation is resolved or cuts loose. Some people refer to transits in that area as going through the "shadow." It is a good term.

Sometimes you get a minor effect at SR which finally blows up into a full-fledged event at SD. Sometimes nothing much seems to happen at SR, but SD is a corker because of course, the planet's contact is the second or third time it got hit. (It went past that point to get to SR, then came back and moved forward again.)

A lot depends on the individual chart, I think. Action always goes back to the natal. A person with a strong Uranus is going to manifest Uranian stations powerfully. If the natal Uranus aspects are difficult (like a natal square to Mars, for instance, which is very impetuous) then the person may respond impetuously to Uranus stations. Or the events are sudden and abrupt, catching one off guard. If the natal is positive then the events change circumstances but may not be as abrupt.

Also, don't forget that they may refer to events related to other people in our lives. Suppose you have Mars at 14 Sagittarius ruling the 5th. When Uranus stations at 14 Pisces it could show changes in your children's lives. Not necessarily either good or bad, just change. Maybe your youngest daughter goes off to college. A son might have career changes, or move. If your children are younger than that, the events could concern sudden interests in playing football, or taking modeling lessons, etc.

Generally, I think Mercury SDs tend to be somewhat liberating times, particularly to those with strong Mercury in their natal chart. Almost as if all the backed-up energy finally bursts out and is freed to function once Mercury stations. Over the years I have used it constructively and most of those I've taught have found it so.

However, for forecasting purposes, I use all the stations of all the planets and find that whatever trouble is in the works is released, too, at the time of the SD station Venus and Jupiter tend to release whatever benefits are coming at that SD time, too. Not every station is difficult. And sometimes even a Saturn SD ends a difficult situation, providing a real blessing to someone who has faithfully cared for a dying loved one, for instance.

I have used stations for many years because I think they are one of the most reliable of forecasting tools. However, I don't see them like eclipses with "duration." I have heard it said that a Mars station degree remains sensitive for 2 years until new Mars stations form. Well, I can't verify that because I have never used them beyond their own time frame. I think a station is too ephemeral, or transitory, for such importance. An eclipse? Yes, but eclipses are a whole other set of importance. They can remain sensitive for quite a while, sometimes. Whenever a station of a planet—any planet, any station, retrograde or direct—falls exactly on an important natal point or planet, there will be a noticeable and somewhat predictable effect. I say somewhat because each chart will respond in a different way to, say, a Mars station. We can predict in the ballpark, but there will often be some distinctive difference in the event. A transiting station is not the same thing as a progressed station, but I would certainly see that as potent.

Transits of Mercury

When you want to look at the small things in your chart, Mercury is your tool. Awaiting an important letter? Look to Mercury to see if it forms an aspect with the Moon. Want to send an important one? Look for a good aspect.

A Mercury aspect is always a good time for talk or visits or communication with people symbolized by the various houses. Going through your 8th house? How about your insurance agent or investment advisor. Sixth house? Maybe you want to discuss your personal training regimen at the gym. Third house? Time to visit the new neighbor.

There are tons of things a Mercury aspect can help you do and practice will give you some pointers on the way this can improve your life. Don't ever overlook Mercury. It has a way of boomeranging if you do.

Its retrograde phase is discussed more thoroughly elsewhere in this book.

Transits of Venus

Transiting Venus changes have the biggest effect on people who are Venus ruled in some way—Taurus or Libra Suns, for instance, or Venus rising, or Venus in an angular house and nothing else angular so that it becomes the dominant energy, etc

Venus retrograde periods are a pain in the posterior if you plan to decorate the house or buy anything that depends on fashion, style, color or comfort. You never get your money's worth, either. However, people who always have parties under good, direct Venus aspects or buy clothes at those times quickly get a reputation for being stylish. A surprising number of thrifty people have well aspected Venuses in their charts. But for all of us, when Venus is retrograde it's not a good time to buy a new wardrobe, or plan a party, or start an investment program or invest in new furniture.

Case in point on the furniture business: Years ago my son, who was then a teenager, wanted to get rid of his bed and get a sofa bed so his room was more suitable for having friends over to hang out, watch TV etc. So, we went off to buy a sofa bed. We found one of a rather unusual tweedy fabric and since it was on sale, bought it, but forgot to check on Venus. Venus was retrograde. Until the day my son got rid of that sofa 20 years later, that fabric never went with any other color or fabric on God's green earth. It was a decorating disaster. It didn't go *anywhere* gracefully. Worse yet, it was never comfortable either.

When my son got married his wife asked me what colors I used to go with the sofa, since it was stashed in their spare bedroom and she wanted to improve the appearance of the room. (Another problem—it wouldn't die gracefully so she could feel justified in throwing it away.) I started to laugh and told her that if she ever found anything to let me know. I think she finally gave up and sent it to the Salvation Army. With my blessing.

Comfort is a Venus function. When we want to have comfort in our lives we often think of smooth sheets, soft towels, thick carpets and cozy chairs. We may like our music at a certain level and sweet rolls with our (sweetened) coffee. People with a strong Venus usually take steps to provide their homes and their lives with these things. But there are other types of Venus comforts in life. The comfort of a kind word or a helping hand at a crucial time, the neighbor who sees your trash can in the street and brings it back for you and a million other small courtesies. Courtesy itself comes under Venus and manners are the small bits of grease in the social wheels of life.

Money is a Venus consideration as well and so is the birthday gift you plan or buy or make for someone. If it's important then it's worth taking the time to find a good aspect to Venus for a beginning time. It's doubly important when launching a financial project of any sort.

Mars Retrograde

When Mars goes retrograde, it's time to learn to keep quiet when annoyed. People who start trouble at this time always lose. Whichever nation launches war under Mars ℞ always suffers from the action. The Falklands war broke out when Argentina tried to annex the nearby small British islands and it aroused huge ire back in England. Ships sailed thousands of miles to the Falklands, which are primarily sheep-grazing lands just off the southern coast of Argentina and not worth much for anything else. But the angry Brits stormed down and took back their islands.

Argentina, a large nearby country with lots of armaments at the time, lost that one even in the court of world opinion. It was rather humiliating for them, but the Brits were fired up.

This was not the first war the British have fought under similar circumstances. World War II was marked by Hitler's use of astrologers who were rounded up and told to tell him when the "best" times would be for his actions. It's always amused me that people actually think smart astrologers would be fooled by a man like Hitler. The time period he was given to launch his war with the Soviet Union was disastrous and starred a retrograde Mars.

Britain, terribly weakened by the battle of Dunkirk and the battles of the early war looked plainly like losers. So, in fact, did most of the European nations Hitler targeted (to say nothing of poor Poland and Russia). But nevertheless, the man with the war machine lost badly in the end. It's true that the US entry into the war turned it around, but the end was written in the stars long before that happened. Hitler's invasion of Russia was a mistake which cost him vast quantities of armaments and irreplaceable soldiers.

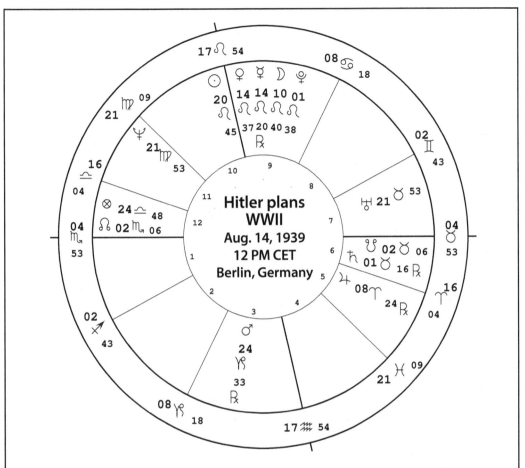

Hitler began his war with most of Europe during the sumer of 1939, and Mars was retrograde from June 22 to August 14. On that August day Stalin received a letter from him promising eternal friendship. Shortly afterwards his troops arrived in Russia where they died by the scores, much of the carnage caused by the Russian winter. The Saturn/Pluto square in this chart is a particularly vicious aspect of coming violence.

Transits of Jupiter

Jupiter is a mighty nice planet to have working on your behalf. It opens doors and brings outsize rewards when you do well. It is the planet of honors and recognition. It is the chance to travel and the good education. People once said that the lucky individual was born "with a silver spoon in his mouth." He had well-to-parents, a loving family and a happy childhood. All these are characteristic of a direct Jupiter in a compatible sign and prominence with good aspects.

When a planet that is natally direct goes retrograde by transit (or progression), it doesn't work as well as it might. It changes its focus and becomes—in a sense—more vulnerable. The squares from the other planets limit its positive expression. For example, someone born with an 8th house Jupiter often has a partner who makes a good living, or who receives an inheritance, or substantial earnings from investments. When it is limited by Sun, Saturn and Mars, it can't get going as well, and the efforts sometimes backfire. The year Jupiter goes retrograde by progression should mark a major change in the 8th house affairs—perhaps it was the year the person signed up for a first mortgage to buy a house, or an investment failed to do as well as it was supposed to, or an inheritance was not as good as it originally promised to be. Any retrograde transit would have emphasized that. Look at the houses (Pisces and Sagittarius) Jupiter rules in the natal chart. Affairs of those houses would also have taken a turn for the worse that year.

If you are working with a transit, and it's not "producing" for you, ask yourself if the planet is making a favorable transit. Is Jupiter going through Capricorn or Aquarius? Is it conjunct Neptune and retrograde in one of those signs? It certainly won't be helpful to anybody there. That's like starting a hike with cement boots on. It doesn't mean Jupiter has stopped being the major benefic or lost its ability to do things. It means it is temporarily handicapped. If you want to see Jupiter at its best, wait until it gets into Pisces or Cancer.

When transiting Jupiter is ℞, any new job you take or seek is not apt to advance your career—they end up almost as lateral changes, rather than promotions. Any time a client is looking for a job to provide the next step up and Jupiter is ℞, you can be pretty sure "now" is not the time to do it—unless they have natal Jupiter ℞, of course. The natal chart always has priority and transits that echo it, as a rule, do so favorably.

Transits of Saturn

Sometimes the Saturn limitation in one's chart shows as a long delay in reaping a Jupiter promise, and the Sun and Mars can sometimes symbolize men who frustrate the action.

About the only good thing Saturn crossing the Ascendant brings is an opportunity to lose weight if you need to. Unfortunately, it usually comes because you have taken on more work or a bigger challenge than you thought and you are just plain worn out during the entire transit of your first house. You may also feel unloved and unappreciated, and sometimes isolated, as well. Nevertheless, many people do accept the challenge of this time and look back on their struggle as one of the most important periods of their life. It seldom passes unnoticed.

If it isn't your own health that's of concern now, it's someone else's you are worrying about. Get a good physical before it happens and don't expect to look younger when its over. This is the classic "aging" transit. If you don't actually look older when it's done you'll certainly feel that way. Get plenty of vitamins and rest. You'll have to learn priorities for your energy in any case, and if you don't you'll get sick—even if that is just a cold. Colds are the body's way of letting us "mourn" for something or someone, according to the psychologists. Sometimes we just feel sorry for ourselves. Heavy emotional disappointments are often said to trigger colds, also. All are very Saturnian. Even the name "cold" is Saturnian.

Transits of Saturn may involve an ending of something, or a disappointment or a pain or grief. If you watch the transits of Saturn and transits to your natal Saturn you can see the pattern for yourself. It's always easiest to watch one's own chart. For one thing, it's the chart that most interests each of us and we are the most likely to continue the work on it without getting bored.

Since the 6th house can be both co-workers and employees, Saturn crossing a planet in the 6th can refer to any of those things. It can also be about pets, and often people with aging pets will lose them under such aspects. Saturn/Mars transits can often mean falls, accidents, breakages or temper tantrums. It can be limited energy, skin problems, fevers that come and go with great speed, periods of confusion or teeth that suddenly need attention.

What about Saturn's transit over the south node in the 8th? Yep—bills will need to be paid. Maybe sooner than you think. Don't go into debt under this aspect. Perish the thought!

Saturn transiting in House 9 can be a warning of problems with in-laws. It is specifically a problem with a brother or sister-in-law, but it has some general connotations for all siblings of one's spouse. House 9 is the house of health and limitations for parents and parents-in-law. (6th from the 4th) When a client asks you about the health of one of their parents or their spouse's parent, it will tell you quite clearly what difficulties are in order during the time period. It may mean a nursing home or worry and concern over hospitalization.

Saturn in House 9 may also point to difficulties with one's church or church officials. This can involve ending the relationship with your local church, fighting with your pastor or having a dispute on doctrine or simply ending your affiliation with the entire denomination. It may leave you hunting for a new spiritual "home" for a while. Sometimes it sends you back to a church you left years before. This may or may not convince you that you did the right thing leaving it in the first place.

This transit of Saturn in the 9th is not an easy time to start a course of study in higher education. You may have selected a program or school much more difficult than you expected which will force you to take on a serious burden of study. However, what you learn will be embedded in your brain cells forever. Or it may prompt older people to return to finish education left incomplete before to get a degree they never got around to when young.

This is also the house of grandchildren, and a grandchild born while Saturn is in your 9th can have a problem connected to him or her—perhaps health, or a learning disability or a physical handicap. Or perhaps the child will become YOUR burden because the parents are inadequate or unable to care for the child in some way. Or maybe the mom wants to go back to work and you end up doing some long term child care.

And , of course, the 9th is also the house dealing with foreigners. Never go on a trip abroad and get involved in a romantic fling without being VERY aware that your new lover may not be all he/she is cracked up to be. This is not a time to send off traveling money to get a foreign bride or the like. What you get could be trouble. Places you go during this time can snare you with their beauty and make you want to move there. You'll probably have some problems doing this. On the other hand, if you are returning to an idyllic place you found years before as a retirement location, it is likely to be a permanent residency.

If you travel or buy a car, keep in mind that this is on the 3/9 polarity and Saturn can bring you problems with the seller or the dealer or the paperwork. It may take a while to unscramble. I learned this one the hard way—when I bought a car with Saturn in House 9, the bank accidentally issued TWO LOANS. I about had a heart attack. They canceled one, luckily. I was greatly relieved. However the dealer had lost the original loan application in the meantime. We worked it out but it was a nuisance. Just because you know how things work doesn't always mean you escape trouble. It's sort of like looking backwards at the broken highway sign after you've hit it.

If you take a job with Saturn in your 9th and it is a job involving travel, the travel itself may be terribly burdensome, may lead to health problems or create problems of severe fatigue, especially if it squares anything in House 6. In general, watch the aspects Saturn has on planets in the 3rd, 6th or 12th houses for information that will help you time the who-what- when-where- or why.

Transits of Uranus

When this planet goes across the Ascendant, most people get itchy feet and head out of town. One is prompted to move or to overturn the lifestyle in a dramatic way. Women may get the urge to dye their hair or get a boob job or face lift or do else something drastic with their appearance. Men get romantic with the girl at the lunch counter or change wives. Major diets and tattooing also come to mind.

The most important thing about Uranus transits is they often bring new things into our lives that may not last. It's almost as if it's a kind of "let's try this out and see" period. One may take up skydiving or buy a motorcycle. Unless you have a powerful Uranus this is a rather unreliable transit. If you do have a strong Uranus, this period can lead you into a whole new life experience. Many astrologers start their studies under a strong Uranus transit of one of their angles.

Uranus transiting House 2 is easy—money will be a mess for a while. Depending on whether Uranus hits anything important in the chart, it can bring it in erratically, there may be unexpected expenses which dispose of it entirely, or one may just throw up one's hands at the whole notion of budgeting and spend away, to be followed at a decent interval by financial problems or even bankruptcy.

Uranus in the 3rd is a good time to buy a new car—something may happen to the old one anyway. Or your oldest sibling gets a divorce or goes through major disruption of some other kind. Your own mind is highly changeable. Don't back yourself into any corners and don't burn any bridges. It's a long swim home if you do.

A 4th house transit brings family changes. Parents get new jobs or retire or remarry or do any number of other unexpected things. People move in or out of your house and aren't particularly reliable with their schedules while they're at it. You never know where they are, when they're coming home or if you ought to cook for yourself or 16 people. The best advice is to keep to your own schedule and if all else fails and the 16 show up, order pizza. You'll probably be redecorating the house instead. It's a good time to paint or check on your electrical wiring.

5th house transits can be lovers and /or unexpected pregnancies. One married student of mine who was using birth control had two children anyway during this seven-year transit. She could hardly believe it. Children are permanent, but lovers may not be. It's something to keep in mind. This transit also can bring vacations completely different than anything you ever did before or are likely to do again. You may take up new hobbies and new sports. Try not to spend too much money on it all because once the transit is over, you may have a garage full of unwanted equipment and you'll never get your money out of it, of course.

When Uranus transits the 6th house you may change your pets. Your old dog dies or somebody gives you an adorable puppy and your cat moves out. Also, this is an unreliable transit for your health and odd ailments may show up. It's a good time to change your unhealthy habits and start seeing your dentist twice a year. Quit smoking, start a walking program or find a good exercise buddy and you'll reap the benefits of the transit.

Or, this transit may hit the work environment and if you are an employer you may be tearing your hair out before it is over. Employees just come and go and it may not even be their fault. If you are not in management co-workers may still change rapidly. It's also a time you may change jobs or assignments within your job description. Uranus is a planet of government so this is a good time to seek a government job of some sort (postal service or the like) and if you are seeking volunteer work you may end up in some situation with political ties or implications, much to your surprise. One woman ended up on her city's board of elections. She was never quite sure how she got there. But she said it was interesting.

7th house Uranian transits are known for being "divorce" transits. Not everyone will get a divorce of course. Sometimes it just means your spouse does something unexpected or changes some important element in his or her life. Job change is one thing that often happens. Other times it can mean an alteration in the quality of your relationship.

One client of mine had a marriage that had gone sour over long years. Each partner had a "lover," and she sought my advice when her latest affair ended. She asked if I saw divorce in her chart. I told her sure, but it didn't have to be that way. Her husband wasn't happy with their life together either, so they locked the door one weekend, turned off the phone and talked for hours. At the end of it they decided they already had partners they liked better than anyone else and they wanted to work on their marriage.

A big problem had been communication. Neither was very good at it so they decided to force themselves to talk to each other and stay together. They are still together as far as I know and that was many years ago. As I told her, the Uranus transit said the road they were on was coming to an end. They had to change direction if they wanted to continue together because the old way wasn't working. So they did.

Everybody prays that the **8th house transit of Uranus** will produce a surprise inheritance. Not many of us get those. Mostly we get unexpected taxes or we forget to pay our insurance policy on time just before a thief breaks into the house. This is a time when settlements in law suits may be much less—or much more—than expected and spouses get some news about their income. Change will come whether we will it to or not, so go over your portfolio carefully no matter how small it is and make sure your money is safe. Check those insurance policies.

Also, give yourself extra time to decide on going into any kind of debt. This transit and Saturn's transit of House 8 are warnings to be very careful with debt. Borrow less than you could and pay it off promptly or something will be certain to cost you more later on. People who mortgage themselves to the hilt—or who already have—are apt to lose one of the two salaries they were counting on because the spouse became ill or pregnant. Then the fat's in the fire.

Ninth house transits of Uranus often relate to the affairs of relatives unless we are in a 9th house occupation or are at the stage of life when higher education is in the works. One client of mine resisted strongly my forecast that her son would change college before he finished his education. He had a lovely football scholarship to a Michigan school along with the Uranus transit and she didn't want him to lose it. But sure enough, he did change and he got his degree from an Ohio school. She grumped a lot over that one.

Another word here on all the various meanings of the houses is probably in order. Predictions are never dead easy. It doesn't work that way. The house –any house—has a lot of things it deals with and the prediction may end up perfectly accurate about something that didn't occur to you. The 9th can deal with your husband's siblings, a parent's illness, foreign travel and a whole range of things. This is one reason it pays to forecast conservatively.

A story is in order here. One client of mine was considering going back to work. She was a nurse with several children. When I looked at her chart the pattern for a working nurse was there: disruption in the family, heavy travel, dealings with hospitals and insurance matters, and her profession as a nurse. Houses 4, 6, 8, 10, 12 and 3 were all involved. She was considering a public health nurse job which would have required extensive daily travel. I said it certainly looked like she was heading back to work.

What actually happened was that her sister, a widow in Kentucky, had a stroke. She traveled back and forth several times, took her sister's children home with her (and of course it disrupted the families and schools had to be changed and the like), handled all the details of getting her sister in and out of hospitals and finally into a permanent nursing home, the insurance matters, her sister's house, etc. etc. etc.

Every single element was covered in the forecast except one, and neither of us thought about it. She didn't make any money. But we had to agree the forecast was correct, just not in the way I thought it would work out. It taught me the importance of checking on the money house next time.

Tenth house transits of Uranus involve one's career, obviously. Sometimes they affect the business one works for. Whenever I see that I ask what company employs them. In recent years, work for local auto plants in my area was totally disrupted and unreliable, both Uranian influences. Some people would get offers to change their location (the 4th house polarity) to take a transfer to a new plant. Sometimes it's the boss who changes. Sometimes it's the client. The 10th house angle often refers to the business, a planet in the 10th can be the boss and the ruler of the 10th is the client.

Sometimes people want to change their entire career path and head off into something that stirs their heart or their spiritual goals. Be wary of these. Unless there are strong indications in the natal chart, it may not occur. With Uranus you often ALMOST get something that seems to be yanked away at the last moment, leaving you out on a limb. This happens more often than we like to think. This 10th house transit can also involve an extended period of job changes, both within a company and a change OF companies.

Eleventh house transits of Uranus are particularly good at almost giving you something you want. It's been called the "house of hopes and wishes." Well, Uranus is very unreliable there, though if you have honors coming, it can bring surprisingly important ones. Sometimes it's an invitation to join a group that interests you, but with Uranus there it may not prove to be exactly your cup of tea. It can be the income from the business, if you own one and if so, it will be a yo-yo for you.

Not enough is written about how the 11th house works but in our modern era that involves so much divorce, step children are a strong possibility for many people. Among its other functions is that of dealing with "other people's children." Strong 11th house positions incline one to either be involved in such affairs (teaching, child psychology and the like) or to marry someone with children from a previous marriage. Then the Uranian transits can bring upheaval and change. Sometimes children move in and out of the home or leave for school, or their custody is altered or they get married. This is also the house of marriage for one's own children, of course, and if they are single, they'll probably get married. Sometimes they move in together with their honeys. Other times they're already married and the Uranus transit will mean they separate or divorce. It depends on the way the natal 11th is configured.

All Uranian transits are not so fleeting of course. Some take us to places we will stay for a lifetime. Sometimes, if the natal pattern of Uranus is favorable, it will turn the life upside down and leave it in beautiful shape afterwards. Most of us dislike trauma, though, and the process may be unsettling. But as Lucy says—or maybe it was Charlie Brown—in the "Peanuts" cartoons, "all's well that ends better."

Twelfth house Uranus transits are about what you'd expect. They dredge up all the stuff we thought we had tucked away in the closet, stir it about and dump it in our faces to deal with when we're in the middle of something else. It's like your long-lost lover showing up when you're playing cards or having a cookout. Deal him in or hand him a plate of food and you'll be fine. Talk later. In a seriously afflicted chart this transit can send us into therapy of one sort or another and about time, too. It brings people out of the past to see us and old interests reawaken. It's the house of things we have earned in a way, and our past charities can pay unexpected dividends just when we need a helping hand. On the other hand, old cruelties can pull the rug out from under us just as fast.

Sometimes our miseries are very private ones. Those are tough times but luckily, with Uranus, they don't last long and few of us get the full power for more than a few months in any aspect. Most of us can hold on that long. Better days are ahead.

Transits of Neptune

Of all the major transits, I think Neptune can be the most annoying—and can bring in the most annoying people. One of the things all big transits do is bring new people into the life. When the aspect you have natally is a good one—say Neptune trine your Sun—and you get a transiting square, it can bring people who are highly creative into your circle. You meet artists, or musicians, or photographers. Sometimes they are poets or bring a gentle romanticism into your life—or maybe they watch birds and bring you feathers, or want to teach you to design your own clothes and make them into fashion statements or art objects for your fireplace or some other odd thing.

But the bad aspects are dillies. If you have a hard aspect between Sun and Neptune at birth or no aspect, and then you get the transiting square, what you get are the losers, the drinkers, the druggies and people who want to con you out of money. This is when you had better keep your pocketbook zipped, get two estimates on everything and three if the doctor wants to yank four organs at once or the dentist is quite sure all your teeth need to go. Ignore all get-rich-quick schemes and don't let your sympathies run away with you or the "poor thing" with a sad tale will move in and mooch. The next sad tale will be yours.

My very first paying client had been advised by her gynecologist that she needed a total hysterectomy. She was understandably dismayed. She was only in her mid 20s and unmarried and eventually wanted children. When I did her chart, Neptune was all over it doing dirty deeds. I recommended she get the opinions of a couple more doctors first. She did. By the time she went back to see the first doctor they all three agreed that whatever indicators had been there in the first place were illusory because they had disappeared. She was deeply grateful. She later married and had a child.

In addition to the kind of people Neptune transits may brings into your life, it also brings weird stuff out in the people you know. The Sun in a woman's chart always refers to the men in her life: father, husband, boss and her own career if she has one as opposed to a job. In a man's chart it is his own career, the men in his life and his health. It can also refer to men generally for both sexes—the brother-in-law, the guy who does your taxes, the plumber, etc. They may have, or be, Neptunian problems.This is the fog business, the confusion, deception, disillusion, dismay, depression. Yours or theirs.

Neptune stress can incline one to try recreational drugs, do more drinking at parties or in private, or develop health problems for which the treatment may be prescription drugs. With a hard aspect natally, watch this carefully—make sure you get what you are supposed to and take it only when you are supposed to. Be particularly careful with sleeping drugs and all painkillers. Use care in all situations of dealing with authority. Misjudgments can be severe.

Hard aspects can (in combination with other stuff of course) indicate ill health, loss of job or status, divorce or a case of major deception brought about by your own fault. All con artists appeal to one of two things: ego or greed. The Sun deals with ego, and when a Neptunian square is involved, it can get you into plenty of trouble because you thought you were above it all and that stuff didn't touch you, or you could handle the liquor etc., etc.

Whenever Neptune makes a powerful aspect to a power point in one's chart, the rule for survival is this: Hang on to what you know is right and good, rely on the tried and true, and wait it out. This, too, shall pass.

I still shudder remembering Neptune on my Ascendant. It is natally in square to that point from the 9th so the transit was difficult for me. I consider it the hardest of my life in some ways. For me, it put my entire ethical stance about everything into a cloud and left me unsure about my decision making. I was coping with a major decision in my life and continually in doubt as to whether I was doing the "right" thing. I felt like I was in a fog with no place solid to stand. I had always tried to make decisions on the basis of what was the "right" thing to do and suddenly I doubted what that was. Worse yet, I felt I had no resource to go to which could give me the right answer. I was on my own (or that's how it felt, anyway) with no lamp for the dark road.

I finally stumbled on an answer, however, in the writings of an old time astrologer, who said that Neptune transits were unreliable and the only way to get through them was to follow your Saturn. Make no choices based on "new" ethics, but only on the standards you had used all your life. Follow the routines you have created for yourself, accept the responsibilities that are yours without whining about it and just keep plugging. In other words, the only way through was one step at a time, refusing to veer off the road. So, I made a decision to trust that I had tried to make a good decision and not to think about it any more but to just do the job in front of me one day at a time. It really helped me get through.

Neptune is a spiritual planet and you cannot make spiritual progress without a spiritual test of some sort. That transit was a hard one but it taught me that there are times you don't get to be sure about everything. How then can you judge situations? The same way you do any other time in life. Good and bad don't change. Do the best you can, keep going and you'll get there. Just don't buy any wooden nickels

Putting drinking fountains up or a fish pond in the back yard are wonderful ways to work off the transiting Neptune energy as it crosses your 4th cusp.

I still remember an interesting story the late Barbara Cameron told after she had been living in Burma many years ago. The astrologers there foresaw "changes at the top" in the country but they liked the government and didn't want that to change. So, on a predicted day, all the roofs of the temples in the country were changed—reroofed, or re-gilded, or decorated or something to use up the "change at the top" energy. It worked—the government stayed stable. At least for several years, though it's not a very happy place now. Astrology can't solve all problems.

Whenever you do somebody's chart and there is either a Neptune transit or a Pluto transit to the 4th or a natal position of either of those two there that gets some action (Like from an eclipse) you can expect something subterranean to affect one's comfort. It may be a problem with the plumbing (Neptune and the Moon are wet) or the furnace (Mars rules hot stuff) or the air conditioning units (Saturn is cold) or the like. Malefic transits or action on natal planets in 10 may mean problems with the roof of the house.

Neptune transiting the 4th house often brings up family issues, perhaps a sickly or aging parent coming to live with you or family secrets from the past coming out.

I would be rich if I had been paid for every time I accurately forecast plumbing problems when Neptune was in and transiting somebody's 4th house or 4th house ruler. It can be water in the basement or leaky seals, or drips that cost a lot to fix, among other things. Maybe you finally get the basement resealed so it quits leaking in the rain. Maybe a new well is needed. This transit is not a position I would ever want in an election chart for work to be done in one's kitchen or basement. If you can't get a good position in the 4th for the work. at least keep Neptune away at all costs. You might also watch progressions to the natal 4th and any additional transits that might set Neptune off. (A transit of Mars might mean a broken pipe, or a Saturn aspect a frozen one, etc.) It won't take much if Neptune is already at work there.

When Neptune crosses your 7th cusp it can mean your partner is deceiving you. This is not what most people like to think it means, but it almost always does. Maybe the partner opened a bank account to save for the vacation he/she plans to spring on you as an anniversary surprise. Maybe the partner is having an affair. Not always, but sometimes.

Maybe the partner has a health problem he/she doesn't want to tell you about. Or is arranging medical counsel for one of your kids (say you are against psychological counseling but your kid needs it and the partner gets it behind your back.) There is often a medical link to a Neptunian transit and it pays to be watchful and wary with Neptune.

The 7th is the house of strangers and attacks on us, as well. Sometimes a Neptune transit is a meeting with someone who is a problem or has a major problem—like drug use, or extreme poverty or illness, etc. It can be meeting people who are divorced—a lot of them. Or, maybe you'll meet someone who tries a con on you. Be very careful of all quick money ideas with Neptune in House 7. They aren't reliable.

Now a lot of astrologers and especially young, idealistic types want to see Neptune as spiritual and artistic. It can be, but it often is not. If one is a spiritual or artistic person, one may attract that, but the vast majority of us are "just folks" and not apt to draw the highest possible types into our circle, so it pays to be careful.

It's also a warning about where we meet people. Bars are bad, swimming pools are good. Or at least, better. You need to be particularly watchful of where Neptune is in the birth pattern and the kind of aspects it makes natally. Good aspects stay good and transits trigger their benefits. Bad aspects stay bad and transits trigger trouble. **Example:** Someone with Neptune trouble in the birth pattern develops a drinking problem. Along comes stress from Neptune to the Ascendant and guess what? They go into a hospital for detox, learn they have a start of cirrhosis of the liver and meet a lot of other people with the same problem (maybe because they join Alcoholics Anonymous).

When you start thinking in terms of the most likely things to occur under a transit you are more likely to be accurate than if you just look for the most positive ones. Positive thinking is a good thing. But common sense serves us better when we read charts.

As for President George W. Bush, who had Neptune transiting House 7 during the latter days of his second term, he was more likely getting scammed—especially by those he was meeting at the time—and he was meeting people in the business of delusion or the oil or medical fields. Oil also comes under Neptune, and with his history in the oil patch, he was probably not getting the straight story from anyone involved in the oil business. It's not a good aspect for getting good advice.

Since the 7th relates broadly to ALL relationships in our life, not just our marriage partners, this transit can bring up secrets being revealed, changes in the relationships or dissolving relationships because of things hidden from us, or partners who become ill or become alcoholics, or develop other dependencies.

With Neptune transiting the 10th, the career will change. Often it can point to a lay-off. Or the company goes under, or the boss gets severely ill and the department you work for is disrupted or changed.

If you read some of the old texts, it's a good year when you don't die at least three times. Luckily, modern medicine is a whole lot better than it was back in the days when some of it was written. On the other hand, people don't always use their good aspects as well as they might, either.

Transits of Pluto

Pluto seems to be involved always in the "life and death" complex. I have found it active in pregnancy and delivery as well as in death and major change.

One client with Pluto transits in the fourth had family members continually moving in and out of her home—usually at the time of the stations—and she also did a lot of cleaning out of her home during each time period as the continual disruption forced her to make choices of things to keep in closets and drawers. I've always thought of Pluto as the Ex-Lax planet, in a way—it purges our lives of so many things.

Any time somebody asks about pregnancy, look to Pluto. It will almost always tell you what's happening. I learned that one the hard way about 25 years ago when it was sitting on the MC of a woman who asked me if she was pregnant. I kept thinking it would change her career goals. Well, yes... It did both.

Pluto transits in one's 11th seem to bring death in the family without question. Ditto angular Pluto transits. The pregnant woman lost her father about two years later as Pluto retrograded back and forth over the MC and a 10th house planet.

Pluto's transits are so slow that it takes its time but its action is pretty sure. It has a relentless quality, like a glacier. Slow sometimes, but inevitable. Saturn has the effect of ending things, too, but doesn't necessarily mean death. In combination with Pluto, though, it usually does.

Pluto's transits to the Sun can change your life, of course. To understand the effect it is important to recall the Sun's rulership over career, a man's health and ego and the men in a woman's chart. This has nothing to do with feminism but rather the normal positive/negative polarity of the planets. The Sun is dominant (important), male and rules one's fundamental strength and ability to influence the environment.

Thus, the transit can introduce a man to power and dominance, or take them away from him. And yes, like all other transits what happens has to do with the natal pattern. It's important to realize there is a dark side to Pluto, and its action can come as the result of forces from the darker side of society. In a way, it becomes a challenge to one's ethics. It can make a plunge into the depths of murky sexuality, illegal dealings and self-centered decision-making very attractive. If those things have already been part of one's life, a Pluto transit can have ugly ramifications. Life will most assuredly need to be restructured and cleaned up. Sometimes the process is painful. Other times it's a wake-up call and one hastens to get back on track.

Health, of course, needs to be watched carefully. A thorough physical is in order that includes testing of the bowels and sex organs. Pluto can affect any part of the body but its apparent linkage to Scorpio suggests those areas need extra care.

Depending on where the Sun is natally, the human relations will get a workout. Again, the process may incline one to meet people from the seamier side of life. Sometimes it is simply a change in the relationship. One can become involved with the affairs of the dead or bury people you knew were on their way out. Sometimes it is life. I think the idea of surrogate parenting came during the Scorpio transit of Pluto a few years ago. For those not familiar with the idea, it means a woman agrees to have a fertilized egg from another woman planted in her uterus and to carry it to term. Very, very Plutonian.

All of these things can be traumatic and all call for emotional stability. If you have a Pluto transit to your Sun in your future, this is something to work on. If you are a woman, these things can hit the men you care about. Expect to be involved because you probably will be, and not as a spectator. Careers can also get a drastic revamping. In the end, the changes will be apt to leave us healthier and happier but the "meanwhile" can be troublesome.

Any woman with a Scorpio Moon knows the process of producing children would have killed her off at least a couple times in the old days. This is a position that can dump the whole world of gynecological problems on the hapless female. Pluto crossing the Moon by transit often means a lot of things go. Sometimes it's menopause for the older woman or miscarriages for the younger ones. Sometimes it's another baby quicker than you wanted. It always warns you to see your doctor faithfully when you're pregnant. It's not always a positive sign for the women in your life.

When Pluto transits a Sagittarius or Pisces Ascendant or Moon it can mean a hip replacement. I suppose you could stretch the point a long way and say one is robbed of the old hip joint, but most people with a bad hip are tickled pink to see the thing go. It hurts. What Pluto does is eliminate the diseased bone and allow for a replacement part. It can replace a knee joint in Capricorn.

I have seen a Pluto transit to the 4th cusp at the time of a house robbery. Theft is when the 12th house of hidden enemies is activated in some manner, also. A thief is someone you do not know or who secretly does not have good will toward you, ergo, a hidden enemy. Occasionally you know the person and suffer openly when the person takes something from you, but cases of 7th house open enemies are rarer, I think, than the kind of theft I am talking about.

One client with a 7th cusp transit of Pluto listened carefully when I mentioned theft but she was always careless about where she put her purse. This time she lost it. A few weeks later money was taken from her desk drawer at work. She may have known the criminals but the amounts were not large enough to warrant disturbing her whole life to recover. However, she got an important lesson in personal security.

I don't get too excited over every bad transit. It takes a wide combination of things to do us in, in my opinion. Here are a few ideas for using a Pluto transit:

- Clean out your unused clothing and give it to charity.

- Sort out the books on your shelves that you've read to death and pass them on.

- Get a burglar alarm installed.

- Have your heating system cleaned before the winter.

- Check your insurance policies and make a list of things you want to know that you don't know about them. Call your agent and get some answers and make a list of them to attach to the policies.

- Buy a small, fireproof safe or security box to keep your papers in. Sort them and put them in it.

- Make up a disaster kit—candles and bottled water and matches etc. Buy a solar radio or one that you can crank up when there is no power.

- Get a box in which you keep all your hazardous cleaning supplies (ammonia, bleach, etc.) and a list of antidotes. Store them high so children can't reach.

I think Pluto's action at the last degree of a sign "introduces" change which will come later. Pluto effects only apparently come about "suddenly."

Transits through the Signs

In the last few years Aquarius has had two major transits—one was Uranus for 7 years and then Neptune, which lasted 14 years. Either planet can lead to a divorce if other things in the chart agree. Uranus wants its freedom and Neptune just dissolves ties. Of course it depends on whether the natal chart indicates the likelihood of such an event and where in the natal chart Aquarius falls. So of course we're all seeing a lot of divorce and have been for quite a while—when that sign rules the 7th in someone's chart. That means Leo rising or Leo Suns, where Aquarius rules the natural 7th. But the sign Aquarius also seems to give people the dream of finding the perfect spouse and when there is too much stress in the relationship, the Aquarian will break free. As long as the Aquarian-type partner is getting what he/she needs in the marriage, he/she will stay.

What does he/she need? A mighty loose hand on the reins, for one thing. You simply can't boss an Aquarian type. This is the classic sign which reflects the old adage that "you can lead a horse to water but you can't make him drink." They strongly resist possessiveness and jealousy as well. Aquarian types (even if not the Sun sign, the fact that a spouse is shown in the client's chart by an Aquarius planet means he/she has many of the same characteristics) make friends with everybody, and can flirt with all the opposite sex around and still go home with his/her spouse quite happily. Try to cramp their style and you can push the Aquarian right out the door.

Aquarians need lots of mental stimulation, too. Pursue your own life and interests and they'll find you interesting. Expect them to provide the entertainment and you are sure to be out of luck. Any major transit of a sign also affects the opposite one. Cancers have major change with the Pluto transit of Capricorn, for instance. That's just the way things work.

As this book is being written, Neptune is in Pisces and Uranus is in Aries where it is producing some very interesting developments on the internet. The Aquarian transit launched it, the Pisces transit brought world wide expansion and business adaptations and now the Aries transit brought Facebook and social developments. For the future, already there are concerns about privacy (Aries is as private a sign as a door knob) and talk of reining in the cowboy mentality online.

As Neptune moves through Pisces cloud computing has become *de riguer* for business as it combines many computers into a huge and powerful array to do difficult jobs. Television is full of Pisces ghosts and vampires and the world's financial mess is constantly keeping the average reader totally confused as the powers that be work to hide their machinations from the public.

But Uranus is affecting the U.S. Sun, Venus, Jupiter complex and that is bringing about the new mining technologies, including fracking, that can revolutionize the U.S. economy. Predictions are already made that the U.S. may have more oil in the soil than Saudi Arabia ever had and will not only be energy independent but exporting oil by 2020.

Neptune is sparking new creativity in society as the cookie-cutter look of manufactured goods becomes less desirable and that which is made by humans looks ever more interesting.

And as they say, we live in interesting times.

Chapter 36

When You Need a Straight Answer
Horary Astrology

A horary chart is the chart of a question and the answer is implicit in the time the question is actually born. In one sense, a horary is also a birth chart—but it is the birth of the question, not the answer. This is why getting the time of the question is so important. Every question in horary has a gestation period when you are thinking about things, trying to sort out the key elements, etc. When the astrologer actually looks at a clock to do the chart is the moment it is "born."

If you need to have an astrologer do the chart because you aren't an astrologer, then the moment it is born is when you ask the astrologer that question specifically. If you are an astrologer and want another astrologer to comment on the chart you have already done, be sure you write down the exact question. All too often people modify the question in their minds as time goes on, and sometimes think of additional things they want to know and expect that chart to tell them. It will only provide the answer to the original question. If you have forgotten the question or failed to note it exactly, you are simply out of luck as far as getting clear answers.

There are a good many astrological books out on horary. Ivy Jacobson, Alphee La-Voi, Barbara Watters and many others have written fine texts to use. My comments are not intended to provide a complete "how to" on the subject, but merely to introduce it to your thinking. I think the chart should always be set at the time the astrologer receives the question. Until then, it is germinating with the client, but the reception of it by an astrologer sets the "birth." If I'm asked to do a chart I use my location since the question has to come to me for an answer.

In horary you use the Moon's last aspect before it leaves the sign to get the final answer to the question. The only aspects that count are those that the Moon makes going forward in the sign in which it is located.

The exact wording of the horary question is always important. First of all, you may know what you want to know but you have asked the question in a particular way, so the chart will answer the question as asked, not as implied. One must also intend to ask a horary question and it must be posed clearly as one. A wishy-washy "gee-I-wish-I-knew-what- to-do" comment does not qualify. Also, there must be the specific time, date and place the question is asked of the astrologer. This is why the astrologer's location is used. Otherwise, the question is still in the questioner's mind but has not been actually asked. Horary, like all astrological techniques, has its own set of rules and limitations. If you don't follow the rules you don't get accurate answers.

Certain very specific things in a chart have a dramatic effect on the answer. Here are a few such things that have specific names and precise meanings. They are:

Cazimi

This means that a planet is very powerful—it is found in the "heart of the Sun." It refers to a planet within 17 minutes of arc from exact conjunction to the Sun. Mercury, for instance, at 10 Taurus 15 minutes is cazimi when the Sun is 10 Taurus 12 minutes. This 3-minute orb gives Mercury far MORE power than it otherwise would in conjunction with the Sun. Usually a conjunction to the Sun overwhelms the planet's influence, but when it is cazimi it becomes dominant.

Combust

This means the planet's influence is "burnt up"—unable to act for itself. That means within orb of a conjunction, but not Cazimi. The orb is 3 degrees.

Under the Sunbeams

This means a planet that refers to someone or something about the question is within 17 degrees of the Sun but its influence is being overshadowed by a stronger person, such as a partner or competitor. The condition of being "under the beams" says that whatever person or affairs ruled by the planet in question will be less free than otherwise because a large, important, or dominating force is making the decisions and running the show.

One woman once asked me about a supposedly "supercharged" planet. The term was obviously something some astrologer used who didn't know the correct term. It's difficult for anyone else to know what that meant—a conjunction, a Cazimi planet or one that merely had many strong aspects to it? It's important to use the correct terms because they affect judgment of the question.

Suppose a question is asked about buying stock in a company and the company is ruled by Mercury. If it is within 17 degrees of the Sun, it is under the Sunbeams (under the influence), but when it is within 3 degrees, it is combust, or unable to operate independently. I remember asking just this particular type of question some years back when the company that launched the laser eye operation equipment was first taken public.

Mercury combust told me that the company was either under the auspices of a more powerful entity or that its decisions would be made by that entity or that it was about to be taken over by that entity. It's exactly what happened—all of the above. A large medical equipment company recognized its value immediately and now owns it. Thus, the combust status conveyed specific information.

The words Via Combust are Latin for "road of fire," or Fiery Pathway and refer to the fact that a number of important fixed star positions fall between 15 degrees of Libra and 15 degrees of Scorpio. Poetic, isn't it? That area of the zodiac is called the Via Combust and is particularly useful in horary work. When the Moon is there, the answer can be "burned up" or come to nothing, but it also can act like a conjunction to Uranus, with a surprise outcome.

The term **void of course** means a planet makes no aspect before it leaves the sign it is in. It is particularly applicable to the Moon in a horary question since the Moon rules all the forward action in events. A VOC Moon means that nothing happens—the time you spend talking to the lawyer about your problem is a waste of time and nothing of value will result, for instance. Either there will be no resolution of any problem from the talk, or there will have to be another time and/or lawyer to talk to before the resolution materializes. In short, it's a dead issue or it goes nowhere or no action results from the event. Sometimes it just means there is "nothing" to worry about.

During a difficult period in his life a young man often asked me horary questions about things that worried him and 9 times out of 10 he'd do it on a void of course Moon. It got to be a standing joke that the universe was trying to tell him to cut it out and relax.

Sometimes the rules on horary are misunderstood. Any chart has a meaning—but what are called "strictures" (rules about judgment) always are crucial in the answer. Charts with 0-3 degrees rising can mean it is too early for an answer. Charts with 27-30 degrees rising can mean it is too late for the answer to be meaningful or useful. This is true except in the cases where the rising degree exactly (say within 20 minutes of arc) aspects a natal position. If the person asking the question has a planet conjunct the rising degree, the chart is definitely valid and should be read because it is particularly pertinent to the case.

I had a client once who asked when she would get her divorce and the rising degree was within 10 minutes of her natal 5th house Neptune, at about 1 degree. I told her that it was too early to ask when the divorce would be final because she and her husband had not worked out the custody problem (their son) and only after that was settled could she get the answer she wanted. She admitted I was correct because her husband refused to go "no fault" on the divorce until they settled that dispute. In some states a "no fault" divorce is much cheaper than the other kind, and many couples take that route.

If you have your natal Sun, for instance, at 0 or 27 degrees of a sign, those degrees rising actually may say the answer can be very, very important to you. Such charts are termed "radical," or "fit to be read." Cusp people are particularly apt to get exactly such degrees rising because they echo the natal pattern.

Sometimes people ask questions that are really already settled and they get an Ascendant between 27-30 degrees. That often means the answer doesn't matter because it's already decided, or it's too late to change, etc. Sometimes it is already decided, unbeknownst to the person asking the question.

The person asking the question is always ruled by the first house. A stranger, unknown to the querent (person who asks the question), is always the 7th. The chart is then mentally turned in a sense, so that the 7th house becomes the 1st house of the quesited (person the question is asked about). If the quesited is not a person but a matter—financial, or travel or the like, the technique is the same, only the house is different. It is an invaluable technique.

It is an irreplaceable natal technique as well when you sit down with a client who wants to know about her second brother's marriage and her third child's school work. People ask astrologers about many other people in their lives when they have readings. It's called the derived house system and I have information on that elsewhere in this book.

Some people try to interpret a horary chart like a natal, and it isn't. You have to be very, very specific with the question and answer business. In horary, the Moon is allowed all the aspects it can make going forward in the sign until it leaves the sign. Nothing counts in the next sign. Nothing counts that the Moon has finished aspecting. This is usually a shock to the student who is new to horary. Orbs are also tight and answers are specific.

For example, in a chart I did for someone asking if she would marry, Venus, natural ruler of marriage, left the sign it was in (Aries on the 7th) before the Moon could aspect it. However, the Moon's LAST aspect was a sextile to Mars, which ruled the 7th, saying yes, you will marry if you choose to. You might, however, change your mind when it comes right down to it (because Venus had already "left."). The option will be yours. She chose not to wed, which was the more likely answer anyway.

The potential partner was described by Mars, which was conjunct Saturn in that chart, meaning a possibly older man, and square Uranus. The Uranus aspect suggested he might be an engineer, or someone involved in high tech or a man of somewhat erratic emotions and of disorganized manner and life style, or all of the above.

He could be someone known before if the significator (Mars) is conjunct Saturn. The Mars/Uranus square also said that sudden attraction was possible. A somewhat darker description could also be made if there had been any harsher indications in the chart, but there weren't. Both the significators were in signs of debility (Mars in Taurus, Venus in Aries) but could get out of their difficulty because of the mutual reception. That said that neither partner was ready for marriage yet but probably would be later.

Horary rules are thus very specific and describe clearly all the elements in the question. The answer is valid as long as all conditions given in the original question remain the same. In actual practice, many astrologers think the answer is good for roughly 6 months to a year, though some questions have a long range element to them and the answer is given a long time in advance.

None of these "rules" work in natal charts. We are talking apples and oranges here. This is why it's important to be reasonably skillful with natal charts before taking on the new skill implied in horary. Natal work also will give you a better feel for how the planets function before you get into horary. In any case, get a good horary text and follow directions. Ivy Jacobson's book on horary astrology is a classic.

The Moon is your most important action indicator. It is the timing device most necessary in any horary chart. Each degree of the Moon is significant because it describes a development in the question. This is particularly useful when the question has a time element.

Speed is determined by the triplicity. Cardinal Moons do things as quickly as possible. Mutable Moons do things when they get around to it, and fixed Moons are slow but sure. Angular houses are the fastest, succedent next fastest and cadent, slowest. In an angular house a cardinal Moon can sometimes operate within a few minutes or hours. A cardinal Moon in a succedent house can be days and cadent can be weeks. For a mutable Moon angular the fastest speed is more like weeks, with months for a succedent house and years for a cadent one. The fixed angular houses are months, with succedent as years. Fixed and cadent is probably never. However, these meanings can change, and if the Moon is angular the answer may happen quickly regardless of triplicity.

A horary asked during a void of course Moon phase can often reassure the fearful.

For instance, a man worried about his heart asked me if he would have to have surgery. The ruler of the first was in the 8th house of surgery, reflecting his fear. The horary chart answer, however, was a void of course Moon. The answer was NO—there was nothing to worry about. And there wasn't. I did a horary chart recently in which a woman was waiting for the buyout of her company. It was in intense negotiations and expected to be completed within the week. She wanted to know how soon they would pay her the share she was entitled to receive. She wanted to use the money to quit her job and have a baby. When I saw the void of course Moon I told her the negotiations would fail. (She was not involved at all in them, by the way—they were way above her). I told her the buyout would not happen as it was structured. She could hardly believe me, because it looked so sure. But it fell apart four days later and the company was never sold to the expected buyers. As of this writing, it still has not been sold, to my knowledge.

Ivy Jacobson talks about peregrine planets in horary as symbolizing people who are aimless, in the wrong place at the wrong time and just sort of useless. Certainly not exerting any effort to help themselves or alter any situation they find themselves in. It's sort of like one's no-account cousin thumbing his way around the country. This definition becomes important when you are talking significators. Suppose you want to know if your brother-in-law will repay some money and the significator of the 9th house of in-laws is peregrine. Not exactly an indicator of reliability, right?

What's a peregrine planet? One which is not in any sign it rules or in a sign of any dignity, and not in a house that would give it any accidental dignity. (That's an angular house.)

Horary charts work because they accurately reflect present conditions. They tell us the future of those conditions as they currently are. That's why we may need a new horary if those conditions change. Here is a sample question a friend online asked me:

Question: *Will my Army Drug and Alcohol Counselor Certification be renewed? I have no idea how to supply a time and date for the question.*

Answer: *I took the time off the top of your posting. It gives 23 Sag rising with Neptune in Aquarius barely in the first house, retrograde, symbolizing your counseling work.*

The third house is the house of paperwork, certificates and the like and it contains a retrograde Jupiter in Pisces, showing that you are a good counselor, but the paperwork is being held back. The Moon at 22 Scorpio makes only two aspects before it leaves the sign: a trine to that retrograde Jupiter (which promises what it doesn't deliver) and a square to Mercury, also retrograde, which shows by the time you get it you won't want it.

My reading of the chart is that it would take nearly 5 years to get it, but you will have moved on by then and won't care. So much retrogradation in this chart (5 planets) including both Mercury, natural ruler of paperwork and certification, and the ruler Jupiter are indications of disappointment, but the clincher is Saturn in the 4th, showing a long time before any resolution would come and then it would be a negative answer.

In short, I think the answer to your question is no. Look for another line of work. The chart suggests to me you may return to some previous interest, so perhaps that is something to think about.

Chapter 37

What to Do, What to Do?
Finding a Career

As society becomes increasingly complex, judging a career direction for a young person becomes ever more difficult. And don't look at the really old books too much for help. They'll tell you Saturn types are undertakers and Mercury is a thief. Jupiter is dismissed as a shepherd or tinsmith. Some of the comments may apply, but there are careers you've never heard of in those old lists.

Mercury strong can indicate a terrific secretary (jobs that are already becoming obsolete) or a computer genius.

When I first began studying astrology there was no such thing as a computer outside of experimental laboratories some place. It would have been hard to guess that one of the most prolific Mercury jobs of the future would be in the computer industry or electronics. Mercury deals with sales, repairs and information, all part of the revolution of the 20th century. I could hardly have predicted careers in designing programs or electronic games when I first saw a chart with a strong Mercury. I might have thought of sales, though.

This is something all astrologers should keep in mind when looking at the charts of infants or young children. The world will be a different place for them when they enter it as adults so it pays to consider a wide range of options when examining planetary influences. The cross currents of several planets will sometimes confuse one, too.

Neptune's best known direction is often the entertainment world, where it can give acting skill and musical careers. But just being alone on the MC does not give musical careers. What it does seem to give is a Neptunian element to a career. That can also be a medical direction or one where the ties to industrial chemicals or the oceans are involved. Sometimes it just means a "stage name" or pseudonym.

Uranus does the same thing when it steers one to electricity and electronics. Venus is needed for all the arts to manifest and its ties to Neptune are quite common. But Venus can also be banking and other financial realms. Uranus can lead to politics, astrology or its modern equivalent, astronomy.

Venus alone—or even with Jupiter—is great for business in general. Throw in some Saturn and you get real managerial skill and the ability to reach one's goals with social grace. A study of successful people often shows the benefics strong in areas where social skills become important. Jupiter is always marked in the charts of outstanding people, perhaps because it opens so many doors to opportunity and ambitious people are quick to take advantage of such things along the way.

I have charts of two nurses with just Neptune on the MC. I have a postal clerk and a secretary for some Navy offices, both with Uranus on the MC. I have a doctor with a Mars/Neptune conjunction on the MC.

I must mention that former US President Bill Clinton has a Mars, Venus, Neptune conjunction rising. The Venus/Neptune combination is the music connection as well as personal charm. The Mars/Neptune can be movement. He probably is a good dancer, but I can't recall seeing a news clip of him doing it. However, we used to see a lot of clips of him running to get some fast food. (Mars is also appetite and Neptune is secrecy, and I know, I know, don't go there...) Or at least, we used to see it before he hurt his knee. In later life he had heart surgery to open up the cholesterol-clogged areas, probably from all those French fries.

His musical interest was well known. His sitting in to play a horn with a band during one of his election campaigns was a headline event.

The sign Pisces is said to provide stimulus for all the creative arts, particularly the theater but it alone doesn't gives musical ability. You have to look at Venus as well. It is Taurus that rules the ear and the throat, which produce song and tone. Venus is the planet of harmony. Often the sign Taurus is strongly part of the pattern for great singers. The famed tenor Enrico Caruso would be a good example. Modern pop singer Cher would be another, with platinum records in 5 decades.

An angular Venus is also an excellent indicator of business skills, marketing and sales ability. It can be jewelry design, painting, art, and hairdressing as well as fashion and design. Mercury and planets in Virgo can lead one to tailoring as well as library work.

Neptune aspects often bring out the artistic, but not necessarily music. I think of the chart of one man with it angular who ran an art school. Another Venus/Neptune client creates jewelry. A third angular Venus is a hairdresser. One former dancer/pianist I know has an angular Venus as well as a strong Mars. Another angular Venus person is an interior decorator.

Many with medical careers have sixth and eighth house emphasis in their charts. Sometimes the ruler of the tenth house of career will be there or the ruler of the sixth or eighth will be in the tenth.

Mars strong, and angular can indicate surgery. One young man seemed to have a Mars influence everywhere I looked in the chart. He was "passing through town" on his way to somewhere else and had been referred to me by an older client. He later told me he had just finished his medical internship and was en route to a surgical residency in the East.

The same rule applies to Mercury and the third or sixth houses. Any area that is heavily indicated with three or more ties usually sends one into the careers suggested by those areas. It is the secretarial skills, the personal aide and rules valets. I mention that only because this is another one of those careers that has practically disappeared from the world.

Many old books suggest that Mercury types were the "horse traders" of their day. In today's world they may sell cars, or drive them. They can also drive trucks, trains, buses and taxis. And, in a bow to Mercury's other love, the communication world, they may have jobs with telephone companies, radio stations and in public relations or advertising. It's also the mark of the repair man or the "jack of all trades," the handyman. And of course, the computer world.

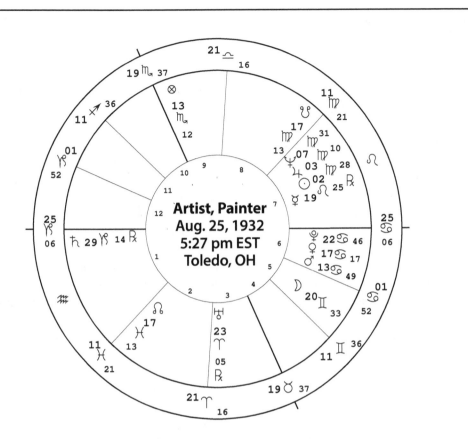

This is the chart of a woman who became a part-time professional painter and free-lance writer after raising her family of 7 children. Her humor articles sold well to a wide variety of venues and her paintings have been seen at exhibits and sold on eBay as well. Both Venus and Mercury form aspects to the Midheaven. She said she would never decide whether to stick to her painting or her writing, and so did both—a good comment by a Gemini Moon person. Chart is AA from birth certificate.

Charts of dancers and gymnasts usually show Mars/Pluto aspects for flexibility. Mars/Saturn in good aspect gives coordination for the body and either combination helps with dance if Venus is strong. Bad aspects give lack of coordination. Mars is helpful in occupations that bring injury since it helps one dismiss minor pain or ignore the possibility, such as in professional sports. It gives the courage for dangerous sports, as well, and sometimes goes too far in that direction.

Whenever a job has some element of danger (and there are many in the physical world), look to Mars. It may even show up in the charts of those who go up in tall ladders to fix telephone wires, particularly if Mercury aspects.

The feet are Pisces, of course and ballet seems to be particularly Piscean. Many ballet dancers are small people with foot problems who must be extremely careful to avoid injury when wearing toe-dancing shoes. With Mars, it is the head and face which need protection.

For musical instrumentation, examine Mercury also. All the wind instruments require fingering ability and air—that's Mercury. Guitars and pianos are particularly influenced by

Mercury. Harps and stringed instruments are also Neptunian, in combination with Venus.

I have the chart of a man who plays a stringed instrument, who went to college to get a degree in music but didn't fulfill any musical career, though he later had a government job. He has Uranus in 10—a dead giveaway to government work, and his Neptune is retrograde and squares it. He easily got that civil service job, but it wasn't music. It was only in later life that he found an actual job playing music.

You have to link Venus with Neptune and the 10th as well as Mercury for voice and instrument skills and usually Uranus and Mars/Pluto if it is dance.

Mercury in combination with Saturn can also lead to a job with numbers. Think of accountants and mathematicians. People with strong Mercury positions may do all kinds of clerical work as well as finding employment with companies that manufacture goods to serve such needs. One woman with an angular Mercury worked for a company that made golf balls and tees, small items that are easily replaced and which have a Mercury element to them.

Libra Venus is much less musical than a Taurus Venus. Libra is more the appreciator than the producer, in my experience. I have the charts of a couple rock types with angular Neptunes, Sun in Aquarius or Taurus, but Venus fairly strong. I'm sure there are many singers with Libra Venuses but most of those I know with that position tend to be fans rather than singers.

Libra Venuses may show up in the legal fields or in public relations and diplomatic areas. They make good labor negotiators or counselors in social work where their ability to stay detached helps them avoid emotional entanglements.

Venus can also hint that the career of choice may be in construction, architecture and interior design. Many florists and window dressers (those who create displays of clothing and ads to whet the appetite) have Venus prominent, as do beauticians and hair dressers.

I never expect to see Leo Suns for performers, but they do show up occasionally. They love the idea of it, however. Most Leos want to play something and will take lessons at some time in life, but it's not a particularly musical sign. Pisces, however, can be so creative, it produces artistic wonders. Leo often ends up as the impresario behind the great concerts and businesses that manage artists. A strong Sun is good for any type of management.

The late Pisces chairman of the board at the newspaper where I worked until I retired adored music and was a heavy patron of the Oberlin Conservatory. When he died he left the county park system his fantastic gardens, which were acres of flowers and beauty which had been a lifelong labor of love. His career was more on the money side of Venus than its musical side, but the artistic became an avocation.

Any strong angular Moon can be attracted to the domestic skills and you will find chefs, short order cooks and hotel managers with such positions. The Moon is also very helpful for furniture sales and acting ability. It can point to child care and enhance a teaching drive which comes from Jupiter. If there is a link to Mars and Taurus it can sometimes be construction of houses or carpentry.

Jupiter in 10 is often the mark of the publisher, editor as well as teacher. I am a retired journalist and I have it. I taught astrology for a number of years. I was also an editor. Many astrologers have the aspect. I also knew a lot of copy editors and most had angular Jupiters—many in air signs.

Strong Jupiter positions lead to training jobs and if they are not in schools these people may find an outlet through another job which has an instructional or teaching element. A woman with an angular Jupiter was a trainer for a retail company and traveled a great deal to locations where employees needed upgrading or tutoring. And of course, Jupiter deals with travel, travel agencies and exporting of goods.

I know an accountant who travels for a large accounting firm and an engineer who also does it. Both have jobs as advisors and consultants. Consulting is a seventh house occupation, so a heavily tenanted seventh house can turn one in that direction or include it as part of the job skills.

Venus can incline one toward finance, or even the financial end of some other field such as music, or concert management. It's helpful for working with volunteers, whether for charities or civil projects.

Career choices are always shown in more than one way in a chart. This is true of any major direction in life. The more ways they appear, the stronger the likelihood becomes.

Mars careers can take one into professional sports or the military, though our society is full of other ways it can be fulfilled. Often it merely lends the "cutthroat" image or ability to another type of work. Any career which uses cutting words or cutting tools of any sort will come under Mars and a great many industrial jobs require cutting or shaping of materials. Careers that deal with metal or recycling are also likely.

Mars will show up in the charts of mechanics, carpenters and plumbers. Uranus can be an electrician. Saturn is a farmer (and the Cancer/Capricorn polarity is strong in such people) and the Moon inclines to dairy farms and the production of food. Mercury can choose clothing manufacture or repair jobs of any sort.

It is the combination of planets that often shape the particular direction career interest will flow.

And of course, the times in which the individual lives, count greatly. In the world of tomorrow, many of today's careers will be out of the norm, just as we no longer focus on the careers of yesteryear. The planetary influence will still be helpful guides, however.

It just won't make us buggy whip manufacturers.

Chapter 38

A Little Numerology
Planetary Numbers

Why are planetary numbers useful?

Numbers underlie the entire universe in a way, and certainly are part of astrology. The numbers and the planets and the aspects are all linked.

Our very concept of aspects is based on a numerical division of the 360 degree circle. This is also the basis of the harmonic system of analysis. So, for a moment, imagine an empty chart and put the Sun on the ascendant.

The Sun is the number 1—only, sole, entire and complete, all by itself. Any planet that conjoins it is sort of taken over by its power. So, the 1 symbolizes the conjunction.

Now, put the Moon in the 7th exactly opposite the Sun. We now have 2 planets in the circle, divided by 180 degrees. This is the classic "you and me" set-up of relationships and the dynamic between them, both partnership and the tug of war for importance. We have yin and yang, positive and negative, male and female. The number 2 therefore symbolizes the opposition aspect and is the number of partnership and conflict.

Next we divide the circle by 3 and we have planets in either House 5 or 9, trine at 120-degree relationship to the Sun on the ascendant. We have bounty, we have ease, we have lack of problems with the 3. Things work out, there is talent to use, and advantages in what we choose. The trine is 3 and Jupiter, the Greater Benefic.

Put Saturn on the 10th and instantly the Sun receives a square. There is a problem because the square is not an easy relationship. It is conflict, and stress and requires resolution. This is the division of the circle by quarters or 4 into 90 degree chunks and symbolizes the square. Saturn, the Greater Malefic, is thus the 4.

Divide the circle by 5 and you get—tra la—the 72 degree quintile, used as the all-purpose 5- pointed star of humanity. Ever see any esoteric diagram with a man, legs stretched to sides, arms out at the points of the star? This is Mercury, the communicator, the "speaker" as the rest of creation is not. It symbolizes self-awareness or consciousness. The 5 is Mercury.

Again a division by 6 and we have the sextile, half of the trine. As the 3 or trine is Jupiter, the greater benefic, so the 6 is Venus, the lesser benefic, but this time the aspect acts to link houses in terms of potential (the Jupiterean 3 is talent fully realized). People with many sextiles have many interests. They are seeking where to develop their potential.

Neptune is 7, the number of priest and prophet and the septile of 51 5/8 degrees. It describes things that have the quality of inevitability, such as pregnancy, which are underway and difficult to stop. It's a very useful aspect to look for when trying to ascertain if a woman is pregnant. Computers find them readily for us since they are somewhat harder to see for most of us.

Divide by 8 and we get the semi-square, half the square, symbol of Mars, the lesser malefic. This, too, is a symbol of trouble and shows irritation and annoyance at the very least. This is the 45-degree aspect which is equally insistent on resolution.

Uranus is 9, the 40 degree aspect we seldom use. It is the number of surprise and the inner will of the spirit and is involved in scientific and technological work.

Pluto is given to the so-called "master numbers," 11 and 22. It is the number of completion and remaking.

Here's how I use these things. the best way to demonstrate is an illustration. Some years ago I sold a nine-year-old station wagon. It was gold colored. So, I chose a time to place the ad which was a Sun hour. I wrote a Sun-type ad using solar cues including the number one (For sale, Golden Oldie, one owner. New Michelins, air and all power accessories, etc.).

I wanted to appeal to a buyer who wanted top of the line but who couldn't afford it. Let's face it, a 9-year-old car is a 9-year-old car. But this one had been well-maintained and was in great shape, so I used the solar, number one attribution as much as possible. I made sure the ad would come out when the Sun was getting good aspects and was in a fire sign. The first buyer bought it. I got top dollar for a 9-year-old car. My numerology helped.

For many years I had what I considered the perfect address, all the numbers added up to 1. Then the county put in the 911 system, renumbered my street and I lost my no. 1. Now I have a Venus no. 6 address. Still good, just not No. 1. Since I'm retired anyway, it's probably a better number for me right now and doesn't make me work so hard. I decided not to fight the universe. Had it added up to 4, I probably would have moved by now or petitioned for a new number.

Numbers give you clues. Numbers give you another tool to use in achieving your aims. Numbers tell you where things are and where they are going.

I once had a checking account that I screwed up on a regular basis. Finally I added up the numbers of the account and they came out 4. I closed the account and opened one at another bank. Haven't had any trouble since. Sure, I could have done a chart for the time I opened the first account. I didn't. However, its number ID was quite enough to give me some help. There are a lot of things in life that we cannot get the chart for but that have a number attached.

You can request a different license plate for your car if it adds up to 8, the Mars number. That's dents, dings, accidents and fires. Of course, maybe you like to live dangerously and you want a "hot" car. But at least you know.

I like tools that are simple and reliable. You can't carry a computer around with you in life cranking out charts for every conceivable action or event. It's just not practical. We pick and choose what to study. So, a little numerology can be a handy thing. Beats some of the alternatives.

Chapter 39

Electional Astrology

An electional chart is a planned birth chart for an event in the future. Unlike an ordinary birth chart, which you are stuck with and didn't plan, an election can be chosen to give you the best opportunity for success. An example might be: A time to wed, a time to start a business, a time to ask for a raise. You want to set up a chart in advance for something that hasn't happened yet. That is an electional chart.

Election charts have specific rules. The one thing a lot of students don't understand is that they don't follow the same rules as a birth chart. You have to learn some new things to do them well. It should also be for something important enough to spend the time doing it.

The Moon assumes enormous importance in electionals because it deals with all the action ahead. If you are setting up a chart for something that lasts years, obviously you want all forward aspects of the Moon and planets to count because the action goes on for a long time. (Marriage, or setting up a business, for instance.) The Moon's separating aspects always refer to the past.

But if you are focused on a single event such as a surgery, and you can't get a long string of good aspects, settle for having the Moon make just one good one and no bad ones during as much of the 24 hour period in question as possible. Again, use only applying aspects.

If you want a letter to have some important effect, try to get the Moon aspecting what you want when you send it. **Example:** Letter is seeking a refund for bad product. Try a good Moon-Venus aspect. Venus will make people want to please you with money. **Example:** Letter is demanding repayment of an overdue bill, or even a bounced check. Get a Moon-Mars aspect. Mars is threatening, even if the letter doesn't sound threatening, and will (hopefully) galvanize the recipient into action. **Example:** You want an interview with an important man. Use Moon-Sun aspect— trine, or sextile.

The most likely election chart any astrologer is apt to do is for marriage. Marriage has some special rules. First, it is necessary to identify whether this is a first marriage or a second or third one. Many people today live together without benefit of a religious or civil ceremony which would give their union permanency.

Nevertheless, if the relationship involves the "Three B's" it qualifies as a marriage from an astrological point of view. The Three B's are simple: Bed, Board and the Bills.

When two people have a sexual relationship (Bed), live together and share the meals and the household tasks (Board) and have some sort of joint responsibility for the expenses of the establishment (the Bills), they're wed. People have been moving in together for centuries and marrying with just such a commitment. It's sometimes called a Common Law marriage in many jurisdictions, depending on the number of years it has existed and whether the couple gives themselves out in a public way as "married."

When an astrologer looks at a 7th house, the key thing to remember is that it rules all the marriages, in general, which one may have in life, and the first one in particular. The 9th house rules the second one, and the 11th the third and so forth around the wheel. Establishing the marital "history" of the individual can often help in selecting the proper house ruler for the election. It will definitely help the astrologer avoid dumb mistakes.

In a wedding chart the first house is the man, the 7th house is the woman. The 10th is their relationship, the 4th how it ends. The 3rd are HER in-laws, the 9th are HIS in-laws. The 5th are their children, unless either or both come already equipped with kids—in which case, the 5th are HIS, the 11th are HERS. The 5th is always the children they have together as well. The 11th is also their friends and social life. The 2nd is his income, the 8th is her income. The 6th is his health. The 12th is her health. You always want the rulers of the 1st and 7th –or planets in the 1st and 7th —to be in good aspect to each other. That's an obvious first step.

Now if you want to use the 10th as "how the public sees them," it also works that way and the 4th can also be used as the home or property they buy or build. Additionally, the 4/10 axis rules both sets of parents.

The first principle of any successful election is to know which planet rules the event. Too many people try to do an election for marriage with Saturn in mind. It's Venus that rules marriage. Saturn, however, is great for gardening if you are planting trees or for laying the foundation for a house. In a marriage chart it deals with a long commitment and the shared responsibility for raising children and should be strong in the charts of young couples. It also provides the glue needed for people to stay together.

Oddly enough, older people, particularly senior citizens or those in late second marriages who aren't planning any child rearing, usually find Saturn does not play a great role in their chart. Saturn rules permanency, though, and it's good to add a bit of its cement into the election for the young. If it's an older couple and Saturn isn't involved, don't worry about it.

Mercury rules sales of all kinds, anything involved in communication and any of the tools that link people: cars, streets, sidewalks, phones, newspapers, pagers, etc. A good Mercury aspect keeps them talking to each other. It's helpful if the marriage chart has a good Mercury link. Many marriages fail of their potential because people aren't communicating.

Mars rules sexual activity. If you want to choose a good time to launch a sexual relationship, pay attention to Mars. It also deals with sports and surgery and the use of sharp tools, and that's worth remembering, but sex is no. 1. Marriages aren't always made in the bedroom but they can be broken there. Always avoid retrograde Mars if the couple has not yet had any sexual relations.

It's important to fortify the planet that naturally rules the event. "Fortify" means to put it angular, in good aspect to rulers of the key houses and if possible in a sign it rules or one in which it is powerful and not retrograde. For instance—no marriage with Venus in Taurus in 10 is going to lack love. That, of course, is the top consideration in marriage. If the rest of the chart is too harsh the marriage may be fraught with all kinds of other problems, however, but the love won't falter. Lord knows we all need help because no marriage sails along completely untroubled.

The next most important rule is to choose the phase of the Moon most suited to the event. Whenever you want something to grow or prosper use the increasing or waxing phase of the Moon. When you want something to lessen or stay the same use the waning phase of the Moon.

Marriages that begin when the Moon is decreasing in light are about relationships that are as good as they're going to get. Suppose a couple has been living together a long time—their relationship is already set, in a way. The "marriage" is formalization and a waning Moon is a possible option for them. But most couples should get a waxing phase.

The Natal Chart's Indications

What is the indication in the natal chart to show that the time is right for marriage?

In either a man's chart or a woman's chart, Venus shows the desire for union. When progressions develop showing heavy Venus involvement for the year, take a close look because marriage may be in the offing. This presupposes that the individuals are of marriageable age.

In earlier eras the children of those in power were often married quite young to insure the stability of the realm or the kingdom, or to secure land or property. That doesn't mean they lived together or that the marriage was consummated until the proper ages, but simply that a binding contract was made. And, since marriage is a contract, such things showed up in their charts much earlier, I'm sure. The actual union came later. This is not usually the case today.

There will often be progressions that show both Mars and Venus active. Mars provides sex. But if there is no Venus activity, there's no contract. If there's no Mars activity, there's no sex. You need both. That's why no marriage is really a marriage until there is some sex. If people marry without those things, the wedding is about something else other than true love. One of the major qualifications for nullifying the marriage is lack of consummation—in other words, no sex.

In judging the natal for a time for marriage, look to the 7th house and its ruler, or a planet in the house and and/or those Venus aspects. The nodes will also be active (because the nodes are the knots and ties of human relationships) and often the MC/IC axis (new status in the community as a married person) or the Ascendant/Descendant axis (taking on a partner). The Moon indicates a new home. It usually shows in several ways in a natal chart. The fascinating thing to me is the number of dates unconsciously picked by people who know nothing about astrology. I've mentioned this already.

Those whose natal packages promise contentment end up with great wedding days and people whose natal charts show unhappiness in the marriage pick awful days. The universe is much subtler that we think. It also has a sense of humor, I suspect. I have found that no date will work until one "resonates" to the natal charts of both people. To get a good election, you have to tie it to their birth charts.

My youngest daughter wanted a night wedding and I found a dandy time for her on an evening with the waxing Moon in good aspect to a Venus/Jupiter conjunction. The ceremony was beautiful. As the two said their final vows and turned to face the congregation the setting Sun poured in through the church's stained glass window and shone right on them, surrounding them with a gorgeous natural spotlight just as if it had been planned. (It wasn't.) Jupiter and Venus were obviously on duty. The whole family showed up, it was a great party at the reception (I drank waaayyy too much champagne) and my daughter wore out her wedding dress. (Actually, it was the one I had worn when her father and I married.) She and her new hubby danced so much half the seams needed re-doing but what the heck, nobody else needed the dress any time soon anyway. They still seem pretty happy with each other.

It would be nice if an astrologer could always build a chart with a great aspect like that one. It's a very good boost that continues during the life of the marriage, though it won't eliminate all their difficulties in life.

All marriages have problems in some area—Keep the 10th (and the 5th) free of stress at all costs. The 10th is the relationship between the two. The 5th is their children. If those are good, they can work together to deal with whatever else happens. The 10th and 4th are their parents and you want them happy about the wedding or at least not meddling to the couple's detriment. Those are very clear reasons to avoid malefics in the 10th. A wedding chart is about the relationship between two people. It is not a birth chart for a person but for the new relationship and is read differently.

Never let Mars or Saturn be there because that gives continual fighting or coldness and control issues in the marriage. Uranus as the describer of a relationship indicates that both parties want to be free to do their own thing. This usually ends up in a relationship tug-of-war which ends the marriage. Only a very rare couple could use this to hammer out some new type of relationship and even then, they might not live together because it is such a disruptive planet. I once read for a couple who spent 30 years in side-by-side houses. Married, but—never actually lived together. Uranus was angular in their wedding chart.

I don't find Saturn in House 4 entirely bad—it just means that the marriage will not end until death. Even if a divorce comes in between, Saturn will still deal with the true ending of the relationship.

Sometimes the notion of "rules" can be very annoying. It really isn't a question of "rules" as much as knowledge of how the planets operate to affect the situation. This is really why we say not to put the malefics angular.

These things don't seem to have much to do with cultural differences either. A man and a woman who get along and have good feelings for each other can weather a lot of stress from other things in their lives. In fact, they turn to each other for strength and comfort. A marriage chart that reinforces this is all to the good, I think.

As I've said before, there is no such thing as a perfect wedding chart. If you can't find a day with good aspects between the rulers of 1 and 7, get a day when they are not getting bad aspects and settle for the Moon making a good aspect to the Sun. That is the best single aspect you can get, and has general rulership over both people anyway. But always get Venus strong and unafflicted.

Start your search for a date by marking the proper phases of the Moon in the ephemeris for the period you want to use. Then mark out times when the Moon forms squares or conjunctions to the malefics. Then hunt for days when the "pairs" are harmonious. What are the pairs? The two planets that rule opposite signs and that you would like to use for rulers of the first and the 7th. Those could be Mars and Venus (ruling Aries/Libra or Taurus/Scorpio). It is especially beneficial if the couple naturally have such a partnership axis already working in their charts.. He has Cancer rising and she has Capricorn, for instance. In that case, a good date for them would be when the Moon and Saturn are in good aspect to each other or a time when one of those two signs is rising and the other thus occupies the 7th.

Older authors often advocate a fixed Ascendant, probably for stability. However, this is not an absolute "must" in my opinion unless the couple already has that going. Practicality does play into this as well.....a fixed Ascendant at 3 am will not bring a large crowd to the wedding. Many religions will not allow a wedding during Lent or on a Sunday. Some people refuse to consider any but a weekend wedding. Others like a noon ceremony.

If you find a day when Jupiter and Mercury are in good signs and in good aspect to each other, that suggests using a possible mutable sign rising. A Leo/Aquarius package means a Sun/Saturn link would be appropriate.

The first house, Mars and the Sun are always the male indicators. The 7th house, Venus and the Moon are the female indicators. (In a same sex relationship the couple probably know quite well who is the dominant or bossiest of the two. In that case I'd give the dominant person the first house role. On the other hand, if they naturally reverse and the stronger house is the 7th although that person is not usually dominant, it can have the effect of balancing the relationship.) These house indicators are not reversible. Even an unusually dominant, aggressive female and a passive, subordinate male are still described as the Ascendant for the man and the 7th or Descendant for the woman. Even then I think such people are clearly indicated by the rulers of the 1/7 lineup.

Sometimes couples will ask you why they are having trouble in their marriage. You get their date and look back at the chart, and the answers are plain to see. Saturn culminating (in the 10th) says the relationship is full of domination or dictatorial attitudes and power struggles leading to coldness and distance. Uranus rising says the man is emotionally erratic and the Moon in Pisces square Neptune and Jupiter says the woman is unrealistic and not seeing anything clearly. Mars in 10 is too much arguing. If you're selecting a date for the marriage, obviously you would want to avoid such aspects.

Marriages are not made in the bedroom but they can be spoiled there. You want to get a good Mars aspect for sex as well. It's the one private time some couples treasure most and can provide comfort and glue when life is not going well.

I've said you also always want to fortify the 7th and Venus and the Moon. Why? Venus rules harmony, satisfaction and love. Sex is ruled by Mars, primarily a male indicator. As the old joke goes, a woman needs a reason to have sex, but a man just needs a place. If Venus is powerful, the woman will more likely be happy and her satisfaction is important. And as they say, if Momma ain't happy, ain't nobody happy.

If Venus is good, and the first house ruler is in the 7th house of the woman, that means it's up to her to decide how happy the relationship will be. If the 7th house ruler is in the 1st, the man and his attitudes determine how happy she will be.

You always want the Moon in good shape. Since the Moon rules all the future development of an event like a wedding, you don't want to handicap yourself. The Moon is also the general ruler of children and nothing is as stressful for a marriage (aside from issues of sex and money) as children.

So, let's construct a good marriage chart. You want to link the chart to the natal charts of the two people—particularly their 1st and 7th house rulers. We want those rulers in the election chart in harmony. We want Venus angular, preferably in 10, in one of her signs. Keep the malefics out of the angles unless one rules house 1 or 7. Even then I try to avoid angularity.

Now, we have the rulers of 1 and 7 in good shape, we are using the waxing phase of the Moon and we have Venus potent. Maybe we can't get Venus in 10 but we can get it in good relationship to the rulers of 1 and 7 and perhaps to the 10th house ruler or a planet there. That works. During a daytime event, the Sun is above the horizon. If possible, keep the Moon below it. During an evening event, put the Moon above the horizon and the Sun below. Those are natural places and enhance things.

Now the key things for the Moon to do are to apply to benefics (Jupiter and Venus) and/or the rulers of 1 and 7. If you can't get the Moon in aspect to the rulers of 1 and 7 get the Moon in aspect to a planet in the first or 7th. Both preferably. If all else fails get the Moon in trine or sextile to the Sun. As I said, that aspect alone improves any election.

The ruler of the fifth or planets in the fifth tell about the children that will be born to the couple. You want that ruler, or a planet in that house to be either a benefic or in good aspect to the benefics or the Moon aspecting it. This is much less important if the people are in their 60s or beyond. Adult children do their own thing anyway so if there is stress, it's not as immediate in its effect on the marriage.

Don't put any afflicted planet in 5. Now obviously you have to put them SOME-WHERE. It's better to use 3, 6, 9 and 12. Everybody has problems, but a problem with health, in-laws, brothers and sisters or cars or the like is far better than a handicapped child, stress from a mother-in-law or job losses.

If you avoid putting the malefics in succedent houses you protect income, investments, social life and the children. If you avoid stresses in 1-10-7 and 4 you protect the couple, their relationship and their home and longevity.

What role do the outer planets play? A good aspect to Saturn is stabilizing. A bad one implies problems from the area the planet rules. A good aspect to Uranus keeps the relationship interesting. A bad aspect can mean one partner continually strives for independence and is likely to see the relationship as being less important than his/her own desires. Neptune—well, don't put Neptune in a powerful position unless you want an alcoholic or a drug addict, or major health problems or handicaps. However, if you marry a research doctor, that's a little different. But I still wouldn't use it. Research doctors can be losers, too.

Pluto can bring a lot of personal change. In the first house, the man will drastically change his appearance and behavior over the years. In the 7th, it would be the woman. One case I had was a young man who had a string of speeding tickets and bad debts. The wedding chart was a good one, though Pluto was rising. It is not technically a malefic but there was little option to change it. Anyway, he married and grew up. He paid his bills, changed his appearance a lot, owns his own business and became a respected member of the community.

If rulers of 10 and 4 are in bad shape in a marriage there can be problems with property and parental involvement. One of the most afflicted marriage charts I ever saw horrified me. I knew it wouldn't last. There was not one good aspect in it and the marriage suffered from every imaginable problem. It was defunct within a year. There was excessive drinking, drug use, physical abuse, parental meddling, landlord disputes, money stress, legal problems and more, it just went on and on.

When it comes to rulerships, I use the old rulers first. Period. The outers add to but do not always determine the quality of the marriage. The nodes are important. They are the relationships of life.

In a general, the eastern side of the chart is the male side and the western side is female. If more planets are on one side than the other it puts the advantage, or the power, on that side.

Years ago, all Catholic weddings were a.m. weddings and that usually meant most of the planets were in the east. Afternoon weddings put the emphasis in the west. Noon weddings and midnight (if you want) give a more balanced time. Everything in the east makes the woman feel more helpless to affect anything. In the west, the man feels powerless. It's not good to have unbalanced relationships.

There are a number of other possibilities in marriage elections. You can tie the Moon to a favorable fixed star if nothing else works. I put the Moon on Spica for one marriage date since they insisted on being married on that date. It was the only good thing I could find but it seems to have worked for them since Spica is the star of sweetness. They're still married, anyway.

Some time periods are rotten to work with. A marriage begun with an eclipse in the offing is going to have significators that will run smack dab into it by progression. For example a wedding two days before an eclipse is not a lot of time. It works out to about two years as progressions go which means the couple is going to meet a crisis point then.

A classic case of an eclipse too close to the wedding happened to Prince Charles of England and his first wife Diana. The strains tore their marriage apart. Oddly enough though, Prince Charles married his second wife near an eclipse as well. Such dates tell me no astrologer helped them to be picked.

You never want the ruler of the event retrograde. It's rough for people who marry with Venus retrograde. Just ask them. Nothing ever satisfies either party. Venus deals with satisfaction in life. A good Venus is happy with whatever it gets. Retrograde, nothing does it. However, it wouldn't be bad if it was a re-marriage of the same couple (and there are some, you know), because a retrograde works fine then.

Speaking of retrogrades, I should re-emphasize my advice not to start a physical relationship with Mars retrograde. If a couple asked me for a wedding date during a Mars ℞ period I would tactfully tell them the period was not good for starting a sexual relationship. It should have been started before. In the case of one couple, who heard my explanation, they said it would not be a consideration for their marriage. We were all happy.

All too often Saturdays are picked for a wedding date because it's when people aren't working. Sunday is usually omitted because of religious angles. One couple I counseled first chose a Saturday but later changed their minds and got married on Tuesday. Luckily their natal charts were harmonious to start with and the date they selected worked.

Saturday is SATURN'S day. It can stabilize some marriages to the good, of course. An Aquarian or Capricorn can benefit from it. Many young people assume a heavy burden in home construction or renovation and child rearing, and elderly couples are already under Saturn's sway. Many of us like Saturn and Saturn qualities. We like the stability and the reliability and the truthfulness. We like good things that endure and people who don't run out on us when the going gets tough. We like their loyalty.

Life is never easy. Saturn tests us and rewards us when we do well. Good Saturn people are who they say they are. They have common sense and a practical outlook on how to get things done. There are a lot of good qualities under Saturn. Saturn is the good father in the zodiac and Saturn people are the grown-ups of the world, willing to take on the responsibility and keep trying until they get things right.

Of course there are undesirable Saturn types. But there are undesirable Mars types, or Mercury types or anything else. Saturn is far from being all bad. But I still like Friday for weddings, since it's a Venus day.

Avoid retrograde planets that are involved with the rulers of one and seven. All retrograde planets affect events started during that phase. If they go direct later, the affairs change direction, too. We can wait for a good day to buy a car, or pick out a decent washing machine. Why can't we wait for a good time to marry?

There will be times when Jupiter (the Greater Benefic) is not well situated. But Jupiter does not rule marriage. Venus does. If Venus is in good shape, the marriage will be fine, but the job opportunities or travel possibilities or something else under Jupiter's sway may be limited in the couple's lives. We all have limitations somewhere.

There may be times Pluto operates beneficially, but as a rule, its function is to clean things out of the life, and allow new things to come in. This pretty much boils down to a lot of trauma and marriage already has enough trauma without making it worse, I think. In wedding charts where Pluto is angular, something major changes the relationship. It can relate to the individuals themselves in Houses 1 or 7—meaning mental stress and serious problems, for instance. I think most folks are better off keeping Pluto in the background where it can help you clean out the closets and stay away from the touchier stuff.

Since all retrograde planets promise more than they deliver, I think couples would rather not have pie-in-the-sky as part of the marriage plan. Most would prefer to have good things not yanked away at the last moment.

The older I get the more convinced I am that couples choose times suited to their relationships or their needs in their relationships. And they often do it quite well without our help. But, just as many people never buy a car under retrograde Mercury, many will. Those are the ones who plaintively ask the astrologer, "Why, Me?" when the thing falls apart. These are the ones we counsel. And if a couple asks an astrologer for help, they should be able to get help that works. Some people will marry under the waning phase of the Moon and have happy marriages. But the waning phase tells me that the relationship was "set" at the time of the marriage and didn't "grow" beyond that later. It was already as good as it was going to get. If we are talking the love affair of the century, that's dandy, but most relationships aren't. A lot of couples expect to see development and growth and when it doesn't happen, they stand around and ask, "Is this all there is?" Then they meet somebody else who pushes the right buttons and it's one more marriage down the drain.

Maybe that is part of their karma. Maybe they need the practice of marrying more than once. OK by me. But if somebody asks me for help, I won't give them a date that will offer zero possibilities for success. If they choose it on their own, that's their business.

Going back to the natal for a moment, we can look at the marriage possibilities in the charts. In a woman's natal chart, marriage is sure to happen in her life if the Sun is aspected by Mars in any way, parallel, minor aspect or whatever. In a man's chart, marriage is sure if the Moon is aspected by Venus in any way. Same rule. Don't overlook the possibilities in the parallel. Declinations provide a "sure thing" even if there is no aspect in longitude.

Of course, if you are dealing with gay people, these can be partnerships also, just not with the opposite sex.

The natal quadrants can help with timing. Houses 1/2/3 and the 7/8/9 suggest early marriage if the ruler of the 7th or the chart emphasis is in those areas. Houses 4/5/6 and

12/11/10 indicate later marriage. House 7 also rules roommates without sexual relationships, but that's not "marriage." When people tell me they never married and it's all over their chart that they did, I am pretty sure it's one of those "living together" deals. I always ask now—saves me from a lot of dumb mistakes. The clue to decision is those 3 Bs (bed, board and the bills). The other house to keep free of stress if at all possible, as I have said, is 5—that's the children. Families where mom and dad love each other and their kids are wonderful. They can be poor or full of health or other problems, but if there is love and the relationships are good ones, they are blessed. Any legitimizing ceremony, civil or religious, is house 9.

If you can tell the couple exactly what time to say "I do," do so. If you can't, you try to closely estimate the approximate time it was or will be done.

In the case of my own wedding, it was done at a nuptial Mass, the custom in those days. When I tried to figure the time many years later, I knew the time the Mass started and about how long it took to get to the vows part, so that was the time I used. I think I was pretty well on target because the chart told me the story of the relationship.

You do the best you can to get the exact time, but if it is being set in advance, sometimes you will only get within a few minutes or so. When I set up an election, I try not to get it so tight that there is no leeway. Better give the couple a time a few minutes early (to allow for normal messing around) than too late, I think.

Buying and selling

In any chart, the first house is the initiator of the action. The 7th house is the recipient of the action So, if you put your house on the market, you are the first house and the buyer is the 7th. However, suppose you're sitting there having coffee one day and somebody bangs on your door and offers to buy your house on the spot for a million bucks. In that case, that strange person who initiated the deal is the first house and you are the seventh house.

For a sale—say of a car, or a collection of toy trains— or anything where you want to get public attention use the full Moon phase, preferably close to the full Moon but not after it. It's amazing to me that any astrologer would ever attempt to have a conference or a public event during a waning phase, let alone the dark of the Moon. That guarantees you won't see very many people there. Mostly we want things we start to go well. They won't if we don't use the right planet and the right phase of the Moon.

Angular houses have power. Always put the planet ruling the event angular if at all possible. However, there are times to alter that rule. Surgery, for instance. Mars rules surgery, but if you have to have it at a time when Mars is in bad shape (square Uranus, Saturn or Pluto or retrograde), use the ruler of the surgeon instead. In any surgery the surgeon is the person in charge—10th house.

When I had surgery some years ago I didn't have a choice of day or time. But, I was greatly comforted to realize I had a 10th house Mercury powerful, unafflicted and in good shape even though Mars was not. The Moon that day didn't make any bad aspects at all. Its only aspect was a trine to Mercury in the 10th.

Thus, if you can't get good aspects, try for a time when there are no aspects for something that is over quickly, such as surgery. That wouldn't have been suitable as a choice for other things, but for that day it was as good as I could get. And surgery is often done on an emergency basis or the doctor's personal schedule and the day you want may be completely unobtainable. There isn't much you can do if that's so. That's life.

To recap, Rule No. 1 in electional work is: use the correct phase of the Moon.

Rule No. 2, get the Moon fortified (strengthened) by sign, speed, aspects, etc., for success. Some phases of the Moon are more successful for some events than others. The Moon varies in its speed and faster is better, as a general rule. Of course there are exceptions, particularly when you don't want hasty action.

Rule No. 3, Fortify the planet that naturally rules the event (Mercury for sales or Jupiter for travel or going to college). That means put it angular and/or in good aspect to the Sun or a benefic. The other option if you have no choice is to put it in the house it naturally rules, such as Mercury in 6, or Jupiter in 9.

Rule No. 4, Keep the malefics Mars and Saturn out of the angular houses unless one rules the ascendant or the topic in question. Buying a house, for instance, comes under Saturn, natural ruler of real estate. Capricorn is the appropriate sign for this. But you don't want Saturn in 4 because it implies an old, run-down property. If that's actually what you want, you might consider Saturn in 5, the price of the property. Saturn gives you its value and Jupiter what you pay for it, as a rule, but the 5th house is always the final price.

Rule No. 5: Examine carefully the natal chart of the individual (or organization) that is beginning the project. If this chart is in trouble, NO, repeat NO, election chart can override it and be successful.

I know of a woman who twice started businesses with wonderful election charts. Both failed because her natal chart was a disaster at those times. The election chart rests on the shoulders of the natal, so to speak. It does not have a separate existence. When I am looking for an election for anything I do some serious thinking about what Moon phase I want first. That gives me a target time each month and I limit my search to those periods.

When you want to "diminish" something or "lose" something or "get rid of" something, use the waning phase. When you want to expand something, add something, improve something, use the waxing phase. If you want to sell something and get rid of it at any price or just give it away, use the waning phase. If you want to get the best price, use the waxing phase. If you want to buy something cheap, use the waning phase. If you want to buy a luxury item and don't care how much it costs as long as you get good quality, you can use either phase.

Price rises toward the full Moon and then diminishes. I'd never buy a car on a waxing Moon. Cars never improve from the day when they are "new." They just get older. Therefore, use the waning phase and get a good price.

Well, as soon as I wrote that I thought about antique cars, but those are apt to be pretty rare and you won't know what will be a collectible car when you purchase something manufactured in the thousands. Unless you are buying a special edition or a custom built car I wouldn't worry about it. Use the waning phase.

If you want to get attention for something (say a speaker for your group) or attract attendance (perhaps for a garage sale), use the week before Full Moon—better yet, a day or two before. Or end the event (if it goes on a few days) on the day of Full Moon. In other words, you are expanding interest, attracting attention and improving the gate, so to speak.

If you want surgery to rid yourself of cancer, use waning Moon. If you want surgery for a face lift (the "improving" rule) use the waxing phase.

Retrograde planets often "promise" but don't deliver. With retrograde Mercury, keep every little relevant piece of paper, as you will probably return to the matter.

Venus rules money. Venus is the cash paper, the asset. Jupiter has financial influence only in the sense of philanthropy. It actually has more social function and is the planet that opens doors of opportunity. Thus Venus is what you earn, or have or spend personally and the gifts you give. With Jupiter you get into corporate giving, and family trusts and that sort of thing. You never want the benefics retrograde.

The phases of the Moon are critical. The day of New Moon is not good until the Moon has separated from the Sun by at least 12 hours. 12 degrees is better. Same thing with Full Moon. Don't have surgery then—too much bleeding—don't plant anything under Full Moon and don't start a major development under it. The Full Moon is always followed by a decline.

If there is a major aspect like a Jupiter/Saturn conjunction happening that day, pick another day. Ditto something like a Saturn/Pluto conjunction or opposition. These big aspects are like time bombs sitting in the chart and will go off eventually to affect the affairs of the house they are in. In every year there are a few times like this to avoid like the plague. Once every other year it might be a Venus ℞ period for marriage, money making schemes, jewelry buying or home decorating.

Despite all its bad press Mercury Retrograde is an excellent time for certain things—re-initiating a contact is a classic. Anything you didn't accomplish before and have to redo is definitely a positive for Mercury ℞ phase. That's true for any retrograde planet, which allows us a chance to go back and redo something. Sometimes things you started under previous Mercury ℞ phases can finally come to a conclusion under this one.

I had a knitting project for a linen tote bag I unwisely started under Mercury ℞ (even smart astrologers are stupid sometimes) and didn't finish. I thought it was a small project which I could finish before Mercury went direct. Nope. Every time Mercury went retrograde I'd pick it up again, mess with it a while and put it aside again.

Finally after about three Mercury ℞. periods I gave up. I just unraveled it, wound the yarn into balls and put 'em away. Lord knows if they'll ever get used but that project was never going to see the light of day. Still hasn't, for that matter. However, periodically –usually during a Mercury R –I think about it and then decide to forget it again.

The rule is that anything you "go back to do" or "re-do" under Mercury ℞ is favored. Just remember, if you start a project under Mercury ℞—especially one like a knitting one that involves string or yarn (Mercury) and fingers (Mercury) be sure to finish it before Mercury changes direction. There are other specific times to use Mercury ℞.

Example—a local jewelry store sold out its stock, ostensibly to honor the retirement of the owner. He was ill and the retirement was not voluntary. Wife had decided to reopen it and give the place a whole new look and feel. She planned to remodel the inside, set up new areas of interest to display the goods, select a younger, trendier inventory, etc. She even considered renaming it. Calling it a "Grand Opening" under Mercury ℞ was inappropriate here because the same people still owned the same basic business. It was just a major overhaul. The term should have been "Grand Reopening."

A Grand Opening under Mercury ℞ might be an opening that was scheduled and then delayed for some reason. It might be there was a bad storm, perhaps, or fire in the neighborhood which left soot on the windows. Mercury ℞ is a chance to go back and redo things. So the second scheduled Grand Opening could be entirely different, such as the time, festivities, etc. That is not a re-opening.

The key thing here is that a reopening is not a "new" venture or a new event, but rather one that is somehow a reissuing of the old one. This happens more often than you think with redecorated businesses, etc. A Grand Reopening gives them a chance to plug their merchandise, offer prizes and special deals and attract traffic.

How about a car dealership offering a whole new line? They just became the Toyota dealer and ditched Chevrolet, for instance. Again, it's a valid use of Mercury ℞. The business did not change, just a product they were offering.

Nothing is always bad, even Mercury ℞. However, the jewelry store didn't make it. It closed despite its long family history in town. The owner's chart was obviously not in good shape and natal charts of owners are primary, no matter what.

Eclipses are risky. Never launch a major event (unless maybe a divorce) just before an eclipse. In fact, the time between two eclipses is a no-no for almost everything. I'm not talking about ordinary affairs, but the biggies that start important things. Let's face it, if you go out to buy underwear it's not earth shattering. Buy it any time. But don't start a business then.

Time works both backward and forward. It's the reason that converse directions work and why eclipses get triggered before they happen. If you already have a good date for something to happen with good aspects, etc., then all the preparations leading up to it go smoothly. It's as if the proper election date produces a "clean pathway" for you to follow to get there. But, if you have a lousy date ahead for an event, it muddies up the road to it and the pathway is full of thorns and old tin cans. The path afterward is equally unpleasant. This can be dangerous if it's an election for a wedding, for instance. Not only is the path TO the wedding date rocky, the path FROM the wedding will bring a rocky marriage in some way.

If you have planned for something on a specific day and you keep running into major snags, it's a tip-off from the universe. Quick—go pick another date.

Now, if you have a clean election, such as choosing a good time to put a house on the market and a minor snag develops, it's sometimes like a misplaced sign on the road saying, "turn here." By ignoring it, you stay on the main path which is clear and smooth. That's what one landlord's "tenant problem" was. By choosing to go with the original path only, and ignoring the tenant's desire to sell at a later time, the seller sidestepped the problem. The tenant probably wasn't happy, but the tenant wasn't happy about losing her home anyway. You can't please everyone.

Most of the things in life have mixed indications, but I always know if I have a good election for something because suddenly the problems disappear. Time has worked both backward and forward for me. Think of a party you plan. Some parties are a ball, and things just "fall together" easily and "everything works." Obviously the choice of the date has unrolled a path to it that you will find smooth. The day of the event is good weather, everyone comes and the food is better than you expect, etc.

Other times all hell breaks loose—the caterer cancels, the toilets jam up, your favorite people are in Florida, etc. The party itself is not as good as you had hoped. Your neighbor gets tipsy and makes an ass of himself, somebody gets dinged in the parking lot, etc. etc. But when the party-giver's natal chart is in good shape, a good date is selected.

Not everyone will have a great party and not everyone plans a party when their chart shows good aspects for entertaining. They need a bit of help selecting the best path. Much of the time it won't be possible, for one reason or another, to get the "optimum" time. So, you settle for a pretty good election that has a mostly clear path with only a few tin cans on it. There's no such thing as perfection, after all.

But once you choose the date, it's amazing how quickly you'll find out whether you chose rightly. It's like throwing a rock in the pool—it affects the water everywhere.

There is not a great deal of published material available on elections. Ivy Jacobson has some at the back of her book *Simplified Horary Astrology*. There are dribs and drabs of it in some older authors, but the best book I have studied is Vivian Robson's *Electional Astrology*.

If you get into some of the classical authors you will find additional material. If you can't remember all the rules, follow these three:

1—Fortify the natural ruler of the event (marriage, sales, whatever).
2—Use the proper Moon phase
3—Keep the malefics out of the angles. You can't control everything.

The modern computer programs that enable you to "rectify" are marvelous to use and quite helpful for elections. I can remember spending days—literally—casting charts for elections in the years before computers. Now, you can just punch buttons to re-jigger the chart and get it the way you want it. And most important in an election, use the KISS method—keep it simple, sweetie.

Getting Engaged

Any time when Mercury, Venus or Mars aren't retrograde and the Moon is not void of course. Other than that, leave it up to the groom.

Divorce

I don't consider divorce the acquiring of freedom as much as a recognition of failure. I am not being critical, merely practical. In filing for divorce, use the waning phase of the Moon with the Moon aspecting either Uranus or Neptune.

If you want property matters to be settled comfortably, try to get a good Venus aspect. The tenth house rules the judge, so it's always best to keep the malefics out of that house.

If Jupiter is in the fourth it means the ending will be a blessing in some way. There are many endings that are peaceful and that leave one or both partners better off. The rule on keeping malefics out of the angles is still valuable.

Conception

I have only worked with this a little, but I think one of the problems some astrologers run into on choosing an election for this is they use only part of the requirements needed.

First of all the woman's natal Sun/Moon angle is the key. It must be replicated during the proper time of the month for fertility. But you can also use the solstice points of the Moon to the Sun and that provides a secondary time each month.

It also seems that Mars is required to "activate" the cellular response and when it transits the angles of the woman's chart it is the most likely to produce conception.

Selling a House

One Monday night my sister e-mailed me that her son wanted to sell his condo but would wait for me to select the dates to put it on the market.

After I looked at the ephemeris, I told her to do it immediately. Tuesday if possible, Wednesday at the latest.

So, my nephew went into high speed action and got it listed while the Moon was waxing in Cancer before the full Moon in Leo later in the week. He held an open house Sunday, 6 days after asking me for help.

That evening I got a note from her that her son had an offer in hand and another one coming in later that night and he was thrilled to death. Pretty good for a week's work, right? He got his price, too. The key was the starting time. If you want to do something fast, always use a waxing cardinal Moon. Cancer is excellent for listing a home. For a quick sale use an afflicted cardinal Moon. Pick a day that plugs favorably into your natal chart. In my nephew's case, it worked like a charm.

Now obviously it helped that the real estate market was good at the time. During the real estate collapse of 2008 and beyond it might not have worked. You can't swim up Niagara Falls and the terrible collapse in real estate was akin to Niagara. Many people asked for my help during that period and I tried, but property just wasn't moving. Any property.

If you want top dollar sell before the full Moon. If you want to buy something cheap, get it late in the lunar cycle, of course. The rule, remember, is that the price rises to the full Moon and then starts to fall. Above all, avoid the void of course Moon to launch your sales effort. Nothing will happen. These rules are good for all buying and selling.

A sale chart has a few special rules. It's a transaction between two parties, the seller, who is House 1, and the buyer, who is House 7. The 4th is the property and the tenth is the price negotiated in the deal. The 5th house is what the 4th house is worth, of course. The 8th house is the buyer's money. 2nd house is seller's finances. Third house is advertising, 9th is title work, etc. Since the 4th house describes the property, there might be a link to the 2nd or 11th or even the 8th, which helps analyze it.

If the sales effort is not working, the only thing to do is take it off the market altogether and wait for a better time and then start the process all over again.

The lunar rules are pretty simple:. A cardinal Moon gets things accomplished as quickly as possible. Mutable or common signs, things happen when people get around to it. Fixed signs take forever and are constantly being delayed for one reason or another.

Whenever you have a project you want to start, always do it with a cardinal Moon if you are impatient or in a hurry for some reason. Cardinal Sun people tend to be impatient, of course. Fixed and mutable Sun sign people are different. Use mutable signs if you just want to go at your own pace and enjoy the process, or if it has a "people" element, such as where you need to do some negotiating or dickering of some sort. Fixed signs are best if you want something to last or have some permanence about it, you don't care how long it takes but it has to be right, etc. The fixed Moons take the longest but are the surest. If the fixed Moon is in a cadent house you may never get the deal finished until long after you've given up on it.

In the cadent houses a mutable Moon sometimes springs a surprise ending, so the deal doesn't end up as you think it will. If the Moon and Neptune are conjunct, trade on it. Play up a water/beach scenario, a pond with fish, or a stream, etc. Otherwise it can merely bring confusion to the deal.

One of the reasons people have trouble with elections is that they want to use the wrong kind of rules and end up confusing themselves so much they have a difficult chart. Here's a classic example: Somebody with Scorpio rising and a Moon/ Neptune aspect in her natal chart and Pisces on the fourth cusp used a Scorpio new Moon for the sales chart and put Neptune in the 4th and the Moon in the 9th (thinking, perhaps, to attract a foreign buyer). Yikes. What she gave herself was awful. It guaranteed slow action or none and a property with water problems or in serious need of repairs. Who wants to buy that kind of a mess?

You have to be very clear in your own mind about the sales chart. If you put your property on the market at a rotten time, take it off the market as soon as you can. Put it into limbo for a while—months, perhaps. Then, pick a new and better time to hire an agent and advertise it. If possible, make some face-lifting changes to the property while it's off the market so you insure that the new time is truly a new deal.

Finally, you can't fight city hall. If you are trying to sell a high priced piece of property in a disastrous market, you can have a wonderful chart (though that's highly unlikely) and still have trouble selling it. It's like trying to peddle ice cream on the Titanic while it's going down. About all you can do is seek shelter and wait for things to change.

The date you want to use is when you start the process of selling—list with broker, or advertise, etc. The first showing is, as a rule, not the first step. You want to be very clear on exactly what is the first step to selling. Soooo—list with the broker or do your first advertising after the Moon has passed any stress aspects like a conjunction to Saturn. Make sure the Moon is about 12 hours past the new Moon if you can to open the doors for best action.

When Saturn is active, that's when you may buy or sell property. Saturn is real estate in general. If you have Aries on your fourth (which rules property) and you are considering an open house to sell property with the Moon in Aries I'd say it's a good choice. The Moon illuminates or lights up the area where it is.

If you want to key the whole beginning to your own chart that's an extra plus. When I told my nephew to get himself in high gear to launch the process of selling his condo I didn't even bother trying to coordinate with his personal chart. I knew it well enough to know that if he was ready to sell there would be some tie operating, so I didn't worry about it. Apply the KISS method (Keep It Simple, Silly). When I hear people complain about property that has been on the market for months without a nibble I have to bite my tongue not to say something. It's so much easier to do it with a little help from astrology. Isn't that why we learned all this stuff?

Buying a house or property

You want to get a chart with the ruler of 4 in good shape or with planets there well aspected. That gives you a good property to buy. Do a chart for the moment you first see the property or first read the ad for it. That will give you lots of information.

If the property has not been advertised, make an offer when ruler 1 is stronger than ruler of 7 since that gives you a better shot at getting your price. You are the initiator of the action. If you were attracted by an ad and made an offer after seeing it, you are house 7, and want to make that house stronger than the 1st house.

The chart of the first viewing of the property is key. That's an event chart, not an election. Use the chart for the time you first see it as the key chart which will tell you a lot about it. Refer to Ivy Jacobsen on property purchase—she's got great material in her horary book.

You can't control the condition and value of the property—only your response to it. Thus, you do not want a Neptune/Saturn conjunction in 4 (old, rundown, possible water problems) or Mars there (probably had a major fire leaving it badly damaged). Uranus in 4 can sometimes point to electrical problems or subsequent urban renewal which will alter the property or its environs.

Good aspects make for good property. A good Saturn aspect might mean the property is simply a bargain. Poorly aspected Jupiter shows the seller wants too much for it. Study the 4th house carefully, it has lots of information for you.

You can use an election chart to buy a dog. But, there will be lots of dogs to choose from at the time you go to the store. It doesn't work that way with land. The land is what it is.

Charts of Buildings and Home Renovation

If the only date one has is the "official" opening of a business, that can be used as a birth chart for the building.. If you have the date the residents (or the first residents) move in, especially in the case of apartment buildings, that's preferable.

But best of all is the date the building's work began. That's always the date of choice.

It's not easy to find out when the work was commissioned on the building or when architects were hired. I don't know any building where that was available.

A lot of times (such as ones damaged or destroyed in the World Trade Center catastrophe) the date of completion or the date of "opening" is what is available on the buildings. But if you actually have the date the first shovelful of dirt was dug, that is the best. As an example, to do an election for a public building (choosing the time to start the work), you are choosing when that first digging commences, not when the building is opened to the public.

If you don't have that, you can use the date when the building is opened to see whether you want to buy it. And if the planning is already under way, you can choose a date for the first shovel full as an election if you are asked to do so.

I would hide in a rat-infested hole for a month before I would start work with a contractor under retrograde Mercury, though. Some of those guys are bad enough just getting them motivated to finish the job but adding a retrograde Mercury is a nightmare.

Start any building or renovation project well before it goes retrograde or wait until it's over, is my advice. It's not like emergency surgery—you don't have to have it then. I once spent half a summer on a bathroom renovation, so I speak from experience. And I did NOT have Mercury retrograde.

Moving to a New House

If you are returning to a place you have lived before, travel under Mercury R should be OK—anything that is a repeat or a return or a going-back-to-do-over is part of what the retrograde phase is all about.

If I travel to a familiar place near a retrograde phase I leave on a direct Mercury and come back home on the retrograde phase. This is not a good plan if this is a brand new location. You don't want any retrograde influence then.

If the papers you have to sign for the property are in any way a duplication of something begun earlier, or are a correction of something done earlier or the like, the retrograde phase is the time for it. Or if they are phase 2 or something already begun, that's fine. What you should not do is launch something brand new under Mercury R.

Renting Out a House

The Moon phase to use depends on what you kind of tenant you want. For a quick, short term renter (a vacationer in a summer cottage, perhaps) you might use a waxing cardinal Moon but for a long term tenant who would be stable you are better off using a fixed waning Moon. A little fixity is in order then, though too much could handicap you if the tenant does not turn out well and you'd like him to leave.

Look at your own natal 6th since that is the house of tenants. If you have a benefic there, try to target that for your choice of time. Try for a day when the Moon is in good aspect to your 6th house ruler or a planet in the house or in good aspect to a benefic.

People who have serious problems in their natal 6th house will not be happy land-lords. People with benefics there in their natal pattern could find it a good source of income. Check your natal pattern carefully before deciding whether to rent out property.

Renting a House to Live In

For happiness a good Venus aspect is primo. Of course you want some other good aspects too if it's a rental, but no stress with Mars.

The 10th house is the owner or landlord, and since you are responding to an ad (if you are) you are the 7th house (a stranger). Make sure the 7th and 10th rulers or planets are harmonious.

The property is always the 4th. Jupiter aspecting the ruler of the 5th (cost of the rental) could be a high price, so check to see if the rent is reasonable and there is a good Venus aspect for satisfaction.

Applying for a Job

In a man's chart, the Sun is always the significator of the work he does, and in a general way, is the significator of the "boss" or authority who has a job to confer. In a woman's chart, the Sun can also refer to her work if it is a "career" which requires training vs a job, which may not require much education or learning.

Ergo, you want to get the Moon (ruling the action of the day) making a good aspect to the Sun of the day. Using a Sun hour is also good if you have access to a planetary hour list when you are making an appointment for the interview. If you can find a benefic conjunct or in good aspect on that day to your natal Sun as well, it is a great help.

No aspect to your Sun? Try to get Jupiter or Venus making a good aspect to your MC or ruler of the MC or planet in your 10th.

The 10th house is the job, the first house is you. You are signified by the planet ruling the first, a planet in the first and/or the Moon. The 10th is signified by the ruler of the house and/or a planet in the house. It is helpful to echo part of the natal pattern if you can.

The Moon phase is vital. If you want a job that will improve and get better—i.e. grow—you want a waxing phase of the Moon. If you expect the job to give you a better position than you have, wait until Jupiter is direct, since it rules opportunities to advance.

A good aspect between 1 and 10 can be between the rulers of the signs on 1 and 10, or planets in 1 and 10 or the Moon in aspect to the 10th house ruler or planet. The Moon can always stand in for you as house 1.

The job is described by the 10th. If you want to be the boss, put the Sun or Saturn in the 10th. If you are looking for a clerical job, use Mercury. If it's handling money or luxury items or jewelry, use Venus. Saturn and Jupiter deal with more responsibility than the inner planets. What kind of job you want is described that way.

Unless you are after a high tech job, I'd leave Uranus out of that house. Neptune is kind of undependable, too, unless it's acting, dancing or the arts. Also avoid Mars unless you're after a Mars type job (butcher, soldier, surgeon etc.)

The company and the person with authority to hire you are also the 10th. That's why it is especially important to get 1 and 10 in good relationship to each other. If you talk to the personnel department, that's 7. Your resume is house 3. Co-workers are 6. Your past jobs are 12.

Be sure to get the Moon in good shape, not applying to a retrograde planet and neither 1 nor 10 signified by a retrograde planet. You or they will change your minds if so.

If you just want a job that replicates the one you have, you don't need to worry about the phase of the Moon as much, nor the outers being retrograde, unless you have them angular. It's best to keep Mars and Saturn out of the angularity unless one rules 1 or 10, too. Even then, it's best not to have them angular.

If you can get a good Saturn aspect to the ruler of 10 or planet in 10, it could enhance the permanency.

When you are considering "going back" to a firm you worked with before, a retrograde Mercury is fine.

Unless you have Venus ruling your natal or the career houses 6 or 10, a retrograde Venus is not likely to be particularly damaging, but it could lessen the money being offered, especially if it has anything to do with the second house.

I'd use the time you actually apply for the job for the chart. That way any interviews refer back to the application chart.

Improving your Business

If you already have a business operating the chart when you first began doing business is the key one to use for information. You already should have the information—perhaps when you saw your first customer, or took your first order or actually opened the door the first day. The next charts you want to calculate should key to that one. Taking a new name? Tie into the MC of the original chart and get good aspects to it, or the ruler of it and/or planet in it.

Do the same thing with the 8th house for relations with the IRS—you want no malefics there and the ruler in good aspect to the owner/10th and if possible to the 2nd/income.

If you want to change your merchandise line, use a good lunar aspect to the 2nd house ruler, which is the goods you sell.

Take some time to hunt down your original chart. If it shows changes now such as you want to do now, like expansion (Jupiter aspects, perhaps), you know you have the right one. That's the business chart.

If you are starting a business, you want different aspects. If it's a partnership, you want some of the same things as in any other relationship, including a good aspect to Saturn for stability. Skip the Mars, of course. That's too much like trouble for a business relationship.

You want the ruler of 10 (the business) in good aspect to ruler of 2 (money). You want the ruler of 7 (competition) weak. Stresses in 6 are the workers, and stresses in 12 are their union. Public relations and advertising come under 3. Export is 9th house and financing (all businesses borrow for expansion—or most of them) comes under 8. Taxes do also. 5th house is not as important unless you are a toy maker or movie production company, then you definitely want the creative juices enhanced. The 11th house is your board of directors.

Buying a Car

When I do a chart for the purchase of a vehicle, I use the first person for the buyer, since the buyer in this case initiates the action (the auto dealers are always "ready" in a sense to sell, so therefore respond when customers want to buy). Dealers are thus the 7th house.

If you have your birth chart, haul it out and look at the ruler of your 3rd house of vehicles and any planets in it. Are they currently under any horrible stress? If so, wait until you can find a day when the afflictions are separating by at least a degree. If they are applying, you are walking into trouble. The best electional chart in the world won't fix that.

Next, get an ephemeris for the time when you want to order the car if you are not actively choosing one already in the dealer's inventory. This year? Next year? Why do you want to do this? Because you are going to set up an electional chart for the time you order your car.

Let's face it, every car rolling off every assembly line in the world is not necessarily as good as the one before or the one after. The people on the line have bad days. The machinery gets out of whack, or the tolerance gauge shifts during coffee breaks and nobody notices until an hour later and rather than stop the line (admitting they took too long on their break) they pass the bad pieces right on through. Some of the cars get those bad pieces. Some are what we call "lemons." But when everything is working right, the company makes a cream puff. You want to set up your order so that when the car is made for you, it's one of those cream puffs.

The car is the third house, its ruler and any planet in it— but like all "moveable" items (as opposed to immovable items like real estate) also is influenced by the second. The price the seller wants is 8th house; the buyer's cash is 2nd house. Of course, if the buyer wants a loan, it doubly emphasizes 8th house.

You should choose a time of the month when Mercury—ruler of all transportation— is in good shape. You should never use a day when Mercury is debilitated, squared by anything, conjunct a malefic or retrograde (or near to going retrograde.) or too close to the Sun unless it is Cazimi—in the heart of the Sun (conjunct by 10 minutes or less).

You want to get the Moon in good aspect to Mercury. You want the Moon strong by sign (not in Capricorn or Scorpio), fast in motion (check the speed) and not afflicted in any other way. If possible, get either Mercury or Moon also aspecting your natal third house ruler or any planet or planets in it. That is double insurance. Make sure the aspect is applying if possible, but if not, at least not making any bad aspect. Mercury is the general ruler of cars so good Mercury aspects are always important. Any aspect to Mercury will dominate the deal.

I once bought a car with a Mercury-Neptune conjunction in 9 and first the bank lost the papers for the loan and then issued two loans before finally straightening it out. The rest of the chart was so favorable it overcame any Neptune problems. I loved that car—kept it for years and passed it on to one of my kids who ran the legs off it. It was, of course, foreign made.

Set up the chart for the time of day that will hopefully put either Mercury or the Moon in or ruling the 3rd and the ruler of the first house (that's you) in good aspect to the ruler of the 2nd or at least not in bad aspect to it or any planets in the 2nd. The second is what you will spend on your cream puff. If you can't get either Mercury or the Moon in or ruling the third at the absolute LEAST make sure that the ruler of the third is not afflicted by malefics.

The car's price and value is a combination of Jupiter and Saturn. Jupiter increases price and size. This can be favorable with good aspects, and overblown or over inflated (good Jupiter words) for bad aspects to Jupiter. Saturn's good aspects improve durability and value. Saturn's bad aspects imply the thing needs a lot of repair or is in bad shape or a bad model or a lemon and won't be worth anything for resale.

Use Saturn as ruler for Aquarius and Jupiter for Pisces

Venus makes for a pretty car, often pastel or light-colored. Bad aspects from Venus can mean a rotten paint job or interior fabric that is sleazy or unattractive, or a style that nobody likes when you go to resell it.

Mars makes it hot, or fast, or exciting. Never buy a car under retrograde Mars—it points to engine fires or things breaking at crucial times (control rods, brake linings, etc.). Neptune poorly aspecting can be trouble with fluids (gas tanks, power steering fluids, etc.) or in nice combination with Venus can be a dream car, beautiful styling, classic design.

Uranus well aspected shows innovative ideas or electronics. Bad aspects from Uranus? Don't touch it. It will have sudden and devastating problems, particularly in the electronics. That means power systems, steering, brakes, etc. It will be unreliable, and tires or anything operating with air or hydraulics is bad news.

Some years ago French-made Peugeot cars would literally rise up when started and sink down when stopped. Obviously a hydraulic design. It was weird looking, I always thought. Definitely a Uranian vehicle. But many of them were well made and loved by their owners.

An unfavorable Pluto can show the car was stolen (if it is used). A rotten Neptune can show car was in a flood or accident. Ditto Uranus.

Look at your own third and you will see the kinds of cars you buy. Every car I have ever bought for myself has been dark blue. They all have seats that fold so you can haul things and they all carry a lot and are thrifty on gas. I have Saturn in 3, and keep a car forever. I don't care for black, so I never buy black cars, but many people with Saturn in 3 would buy a black one. Interior comfort is usually Venus—how cushy the seats are, how well appointed it is in terms of comfort.

The Moon is critical. The phase the Moon is in will tell you about price. If you buy during a rising Moon (between new and full) you will pay more. If you buy during a waning Moon you will get a better deal. Never buy under the full Moon: you will pay top dollar. Wait a few days and dicker.

Don't sign the papers if the time shows the Moon common (or mutable) and cadent— this is the one that lands you in the soup. You won't know where you will end up with it. Try to make the deal when the Moon is making either a good aspect to the third house and its ruler, or to Mercury or to the Sun. There is nothing better than a nice lunar trine to the Sun so use that if you can't get anything else. If the papers you have to sign are in any way a duplication of something begun earlier, or are a correction of something done earlier or the like, the retrograde phase is the time for it. **Plan this out before you go to the dealer.** It's the best way. Then you won't be left saying, "Oops, wait a minute here. I have to check my ephemeris."

Never buy between two eclipses or just before one. If you buy under a retrograde Mercury you will be sorry, believe me. Or, you won't keep the car long.

I once told a class this and one of my students went home and told her dad not to buy the car he was planning to the next day. He was very snotty about her comments (he was a Leo and was not amused), bought the car anyway, drove it two miles to the mall and the engine actually fell out at a stop sign. This is a true story.

My student didn't have the nerve to even look at him for days. We all laughed hysterically in class the following week when she told us. He resold the car back to the dealer almost immediately after he got the engine put back into it.

If you are going to buy a foreign (Jupiter) car, it sure helps to have a nice Jupiter transit to the 3rd. Now Honda makes cars in the U.S. but it didn't in 1982 when I bought one and it was strictly a foreign purchase then.

Just don't put the Moon in a mutable (also called common) sign and cadent house. I like to think of the common-and-cadent Moon as a Uranus blind date: you don't know what you will get, where you will go or where you will end up. If you like surprises, be my guest, but I'd rather have a tad more certainty when I'm spending that much money, thank you very much.

Try not to buy on a day when a major aspect of any sort is happening, such as a Saturn/Pluto square. Don't buy if the aspect is still forming. You can buy when they're separating and when Mercury is in good shape by sign and aspect. Get the Moon applying to Mercury or the ruler of your 3rd and you'll be fine. Since Mercury pretty much rules cars, you want Mercury in a good sign or in mutual reception with a planet in a Mercury-ruled sign. Either Gemini or Virgo is good.

When retrograde Mercury goes stationary direct, many people get the urge to rush and buy a car then. Don't do it until you check the rest of what's happening in the sky. While Mercury is the most important planet here, it isn't the only one with influence. Still, it is at its best and most powerful the day after it goes direct so if you get good aspects that day, buy then.

Feel free to use the waning phase for buying a car since you want a good deal anyway. Waxing phase is used when you want something to grow or improve over time. Cars are as good as they're going to get when they're new. And a used car never gets less used. So, the waning phase is fine.

Selling a Car

In the sale of a car put the ruler of 7 in the 1st house and it brings the buyer to you. You don't want to put the ruler of 1 in 7 because then you are at the mercy of the buyer and end up accepting whatever he offers, but the ruler of 7 in 1 brings the buyer to you quickly and he pays your price. I used this tactic quite successfully several years ago. I had bought a gold colored station wagon that was now 9 years old. To advertise it, I chose a Sun hour on the day just before the full Moon. The ruler of 7 was in 1 and the Moon was aspecting Venus (money). I offered the car as a "golden oldie," well maintained—which it was—and emphasized its luxury features, such as a new set of Michelins and power equipment in the ad. The first buyer bought it for what I asked.

The rules are the same for buying and selling anything. The fact that a house is the biggest thing we usually ever sell prompted me to suggest the use of the Cancer Moon quite often since Cancer rules "home" and domicile. This is kind of like doubling up on the likelihood of a good deal. This may be why spring is a good time to sell a house, you know. Cancer Moons are waxing then.

However, any cardinal Moon is good for a fast sale, though a Gemini (waxing) Moon is obviously good, too, for a used car. Gemini is not usually as quick, but a lot of folks just like to go look at cars and kick the tires and if you don't mind that, go for it.

Personally, I'm an impatient cardinal type and just want the whole process DONE. So, you could use a Libra Moon, for instance, which attracts a nice person to buy your "baby" and is another air sign. When I want speed I just look in the ephemeris for the next cardinal Moon that's waxing and avoids a major conjunction (like to a malefic) and do it. It simplifies things enormously.

Choosing a Doctor

I usually do two things—one is find out the doctor's Sun sign. If it falls in your 6th he'll usually take good care of you. The same is true if his Sun is near your part of fortune, or conjunct your Ascendant. The other thing to to examine is your 7th. Since doctors are consultants, not really 6th house service people, I check transits for the first appointment and whether or not the 7th is favored, especially by Sun or Moon. If the Moon is strong, it's helpful for a woman doctor.

If you want a good surgeon, check his or her natal. Surgeons are all very Mars types, so if your own natal or progressed Mars is in good shape by sign or position, you'll get good surgeons. If you have afflictions to natal Mars, I would proceed carefully and get physician birthdates if possible. One of the most arrogant surgeons in my area (now dead) was also the best and did a dandy job on my gall bladder years ago. His Sun was on my Ascendant. The man who did my hip replacement had his Sun conjunct my Part of Fortune.

Anyway, those are techniques I use. Not perfect, but it isn't always easy to get birth data from surgeons. Ask their office nurse for the birth date, at least. She probably knows.

Making a Medical Appointment

The third house rules appointments and tests (or examinations) of all kinds. Get a good lunar aspect to Mercury for the appointment day. You want somebody who will see what needs to be done and communicate well with you about your needs.

The outcome of a test is the 6th, obviously (4th from the 3rd), and deals with whatever treatment will be needed.

Surgery

In the chart of surgery the first is the patient, 10th is the surgeon, 8th is the cutting work itself and 4th is the outcome. If you have a good 10th and 4th in your natal chart you're in business. The 6th is the nursing, the treatment, care and rehab afterwards. 12th is the hospital where you stay. The 7th is any additional consultants, 11th is the doctor's fee, 5th is how you do once you get home, 2nd is how you pay for it.

You want a good lunar aspect to the part of the body involved and a good Mars. The eyes are generally under Mars as is all surgery. Specifically, however, the right eye in a man is ruled by the Sun and his left eye by the Moon. In a woman, the rule is reversed. The right eye is the Moon and the left is ruled by the Sun. If all else fails get a day when the Moon makes no aspects to anything if it doesn't aspect something well.

Rule No. 1 in all elections: Fortify the planet that rules the event.

Rule No. 2: Get the Moon in good phase for what you are doing and in good aspect to No. 1 if possible.
Rule No. 3: Do rule 1 and 2 again.

The rest usually falls into place. Never schedule surgery on a part of the body when the Moon is in the sign ruling that part of the body. For example for eye surgery, don't use the Moon in Aries. Libra is dandy, however.

Mars rules surgery and you want to avoid retrograde Mars if possible. Unless you have a first and 8th houses ruled by Venus, retrograde Venus is immaterial. Ditto Mercury.

Try to schedule surgery when the Moon makes a nice aspect to either your Ascendant or its ruler or 8th house ruler.

The oldest rule I know on elections I can't quote exactly but it goes something like,

"Pierce not the part of the body ruled by the sign the Moon occupies." The stricture goes back a couple thousand years, so it's one to pay attention to if you can.

Some years ago when my son was small he had an infected toe nail. The doctor removed it during the Pisces Moon and it was nearly two years of treatment before it finally healed up. I often thought that I should not have allowed it to be done under that Moon but it was too infected to wait two more days until the Moon changed signs. Sometimes you are just stuck and medical treatment has to be done right now. It would be nice if we could change the way the Universe operates but we can't and sometimes we just end up on the wrong side. That's life.

The transiting Moon conjunct one's natal Moon is not particularly recommended—too much changeability, and you want a stable outcome. You also don't want transiting Moon conjunct the Sun. Wait 12 hours after a new Moon so it isn't under the Sunbeams or combust. I wouldn't use a void of course Moon for anything and usually I find that things gets canceled under it anyway. If it doesn't, sometimes the surgery doesn't work.

Surgery on Varicose Veins

Aquarius rules the lower leg and ankle, Capricorn the knees and Sagittarius the thighs. You don't want the Moon in any of those signs for work on that part of the body. Veins are Venus-ruled, so a day when the Moon is in good aspect to Venus would be best. Use the waning phase of the Moon and avoid a lunar aspect to Mars.

Dealing with Ovarian Cysts

One of the real benefits of using the Moon in Leo for a procedure to get rid of them is its function as a non-fertile sign. Things tend to die when attacked under Leo. This is why Leo and Aquarius are such excellent signs for weeding one's garden. It's also good for going after other kinds of growths.

When you are trying to get rid of cysts or things that shouldn't be there, a Leo Moon, therefore is a pretty good choice. I would not recommend a Libra Moon because the sign rules the ovaries.

Eye Surgery

The eyes and all areas of the face and head are a first house matter, a 6th house health problem and 8th house surgery.

The other houses are less important in this election. Try to schedule surgery when the Moon makes a nice aspect to either your ascendant or its ruler or 8th house ruler. In eye surgery never use the Moon in Aries. Libra is dandy, however.

Try to schedule surgery when the Moon makes a nice aspect to either your ascendant or its ruler or the 8th house ruler. Don't use the full Moon. Since cataracts are removing something permanently, you can use the waning phase of the Moon so it gives more flexibility in scheduling. The best aspect for cataract surgery is to get the Sun and Moon in good aspect with each other and no bad aspects to either on that day. A Sun-Moon trine is great. The Sun rules the right eye in men and the left in women and the Moon rules the left eye in men and the right in women.

Dieting

First look at the natal chart. The advice differs depending on which Sun sign type you are — cardinal, fixed or mutable. I once knew a woman who lost 30 pounds one year by eliminating one piece of bread and two pats of butter daily. She was a Virgo. Only a Virgo would think of doing it that way and then stick to the plan.

Then look at the 6th house of whoever wants to do the dieting. It will give you some ideas about the best Moon position for that person. Ordinarily a Taurus Moon is not a good idea since Taurus is such a hedonist, but if the person has a Taurus 6th, the interest in "looking good" may help. Leos either diet forever or almost never do so if a Leo asks, they're serious.

Always start a diet in the waning phase of the Moon. If possible, use a fixed sign so the individual will have some help sticking to the diet. Cardinal types want fast results and may think they want a cardinal Moon but that doesn't have a lot of staying-on-the-diet power. Avoid any time when transiting Mars (appetite) is near the Sun, Moon or angles of the natal chart. Do not place the Moon in aspect to Mars on the day the diet begins. If the individual is a mutable type, small changes (like the Virgo's I mentioned above) may work.

Fire sign people are best at dealing with exercise programs to go along with the diet. Earth signs may groan about it but will see the necessity for some activity. Water signs (except Scorpio) just want to forget the whole thing until it goes away but you can usually coax them into a pool or doing some seashell collecting in walks on a beach. It has to seem like it isn't really exercise. Maybe mall walks? You have to get creative with water people. Air signs are the ones who love those mall walking things and water-walk classes and aerobics classes. They like anything social to get their exercise.

Strangely enough, Sagittarians will usually stick to an exercise plan (especially if it involves biking, or hiking, or something they like) better than they will a diet. On the other hand, it works for them. Avoid those "heavy protein" diets for Libras—too hard on the kidneys. Leos mostly like diets with plenty of meat. Virgos need lots of cooked produce. Aries just wants to eat anything handy when hungry so they need to do a lot of preparation like keeping raw veggies in the fridge for impulse time. Mostly they don't diet anyway. Ditto Aquarians.

Keep cold stuff handy for Capricorn, tepid stuff for Cancer and don't let Scorpio convince you that one meal a day is healthy. Except for them. Pisces better check with its doctor and Capricorn has to be watched—they're the ones who believe that garbage that no one can be too thin or too rich.

A lot of this applies to rising signs, you may notice. But diet and exercise are health matters and come under House 6, which is why you need to look at that. Anyone may actually have a Sun sign, rising sign and 6th house that conflict. Use 6th house as much as possible. It will show you how to plan the weight loss program and what the snags are.

Saturn and Jupiter transits through 1st house are so typical they are textbook. Saturn is the best time of all to lose and Jupiter is the best time to start an exercise program.

Transiting Mars coming to Neptune is no help. Mars coming to the Sun, Moon or angles can be problems, however, when you want to start a diet. It's never wise to underestimate the strength of Mars and its rulership over our appetites in life.

Weight problems are endemic for those of us with calm dispositions, lots of water planets and sit-down jobs and hobbies. The only thing that helps is finding some sort of exercise program that is what you really like doing. Think about what that is. If you like dancing, go for it, even if it's only you and the ear phone. But if you can't dance, walk.

Under all circumstances a good walk every day does wonders for both your appetite (which it will help regulate) and your waistline.

To Quit Smoking

The Moon gives you tips on how to do just about anything. You use the increasing Moon when you want to increase something. You use the waning Moon when you want to lose something. I quit smoking many times, but it finally "took" when I used a time period after a Full Moon on my 3rd house Saturn. I picked a quarter Moon day when the Moon was in Taurus square the Saturn for loss. I lost the weed at last. Habits and habitat all come under the Moon. That's why it's vital to use the Moon to change a habit.

Smoking and tobacco —all physical appetites in general—belong to Mars. Be careful not to use a lunar aspect to Mars if you want to quit smoking or go on a diet or it will just intensify the cravings. If Mars is aspecting your ascendant it's the same thing. Try to find a time when Mars is ignoring you.

Travelling

If you're driving, the time you pull out of the garage is the beginning of the trip. Under almost all circumstances I use this time, though there can be modifications. Some people use them. They are:

If one is flying, the time the plane takes off; going by ship, the time of the sailing; by bus, the time of departure. etc. However, most of us drive to the airport or the dock, and leave the car in a long term parking lot there to be picked up on the way back, so that's why I use leaving the house as the time the trip starts. Even if you take a bus or taxi or your sister drives you to the airport or whoever, your trip really starts when you leave your house.

If you are returning to where you originally came from or to a place you have been before, travel under Mercury R should be OK—anything that is a repeat or a return or a going-back-to-do-over is part of what the retrograde phase is all about.

If I have to travel near a retrograde phase I try to leave while Mercury is still direct and come back home on the retrograde.

Financial Matters

Getting a loan or a mortgage or investing assets are an 8th house task. Putting Saturn there is sure not a good idea. It makes repayment of loans seem forever and can deny you good rates on a mortgage or investment. You want your money to grow, not to shrink.

Many people want to invest or put their money in the kind of accounts or projects that have lower tax implications than others. IRAs come to mind. That's a valid rationale. "Shielding" is often a euphemism for hiding money to avoid tax altogether and that rationale is not. There is never a "good" time to do something illegal.

Follow the two big rules in electional work: Fortify the Moon and strengthen the area or planet ruling the matter at hand. If the Moon is increasing in light, in Taurus (exalted), that is "fortified." The Sun in Aries or Leo is fortified. Make use of dignities and debilities whenever possible. They improve your election.

Look at the planet in the best shape at the time and make that the ruler of the 8th

Fitness Center

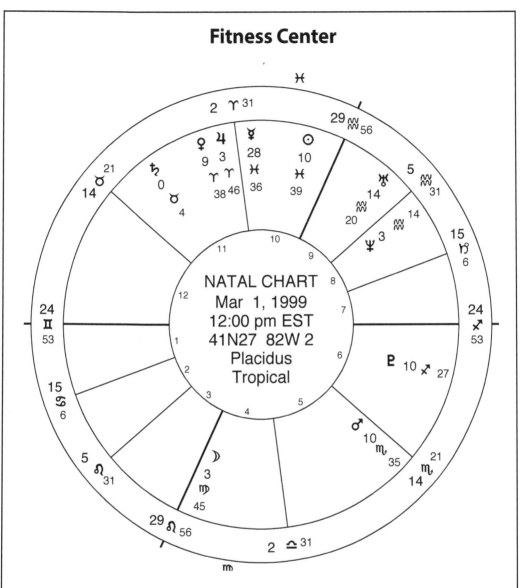

NATAL CHART
Mar 1, 1999
12:00 pm EST
41N27 82W 2
Placidus
Tropical

This AA chart (time taken from company records) provides proof that even a debilitated planet such as Mercury in Pisces as chart ruler works well when it suits the description of its function. Many businesses choose poor election times to open, but this one was a superb choice. This athletic center is sponsored by a hospital and is used for rehabilitation work as well as public health needs. It has all the bells and whistles one could wish. The Moon coming to full brings a wide public to the doors and there are seldom times during the day when the parking lot is not packed. The Jupiter/Venus conjunction and Moon trine Saturn ruling the money houses show strong income potential. Sun in House 10 insures that it will prosper, as well.

if you can. A good aspect from the Moon is important, of course. Always keep the action clearly in mind. Seeking a mortgage or loan is best done under a waning Moon. Investing is best done under a waxing Moon. It's the fundamental rule of things growing when waxing and shrinking when waning.

One person's assets are House 2. This is your own paycheck or what you have in your purse or the cookie jar or your own bank account. When it is corporate or business or partnership assets where you are dealing with the money of others as well as your own, it's House 8. All investing is House 8. Even a savings account, which contains your own money, comes under House 8 when you get interest on it, because that interest comes from "other people's money."

I think half the job of doing astrology is being clear on which house rules the activity at hand. All interest on money that is loaned or borrowed comes from other people. You didn't earn the money—your money earned the money. That's always the eighth house. When you earn your money with your own efforts, that's the second house. Once you —in effect—lend someone your money in a savings account, you are putting it to work.

You can keep the interest because you own the money. When you pay interest on a loan you are repaying "other people." Same when you earn interest from them. That's why the 8th house will indicate things like money from law suits (which other people pay you) and bankruptcy as well as mutual funds and bonds. For instance, if you sell a house, but hold the mortgage for the buyer, then the borrower pays you back. That's 8th house. Insurance is 8th house. Inheritance is 8th house.

With all the financial things we need to keep up on these days, a lot of people could use a better understanding of the 8th house. It's the price we pay for having charge cards, debit cards, ATM machines and travelers' checks. All those fees are 8th house.

Paying Your Income Tax

Is there a "good" time to go to the accountant? I always do it during the dark of the Moon (or as close as I can comfortably do on my schedule)—not the void of course. But the void of course period is OK too. Once you're in the last quarter of the Moon phase I think it's a go. One accountant friend likes to mail the returns during void of course. Why? Well, obviously we don't want to have to do the work over again in case somebody at IRS finds an error in the return.

Obtaining a Loan

A waning lunar phase means the loan won't "increase" and the debt will get less and less with time. That implies steady repayment. Loans are an 8th house matter and Mars is the natural 8th ruler. In your chart, whatever planet rules the 8th is your key. If you can get the Moon waning and applying to a nice aspect to Mars or your own 8th house ruler, it is a good thing.

Try to get Mars in good shape (not square Saturn of denial) or Uranus (something unexpected comes up.). Trine Venus would be excellent, since Venus is the general ruler of income or the money needed to pay for the loan, or trine your own second house ruler.

If you want a loan for a long time (home mortgage, open credit line for a business or the like) a fixed Moon is good. If you want it on your signature, Leo is good. If you want it to be repaid quickly, I like the Moon in a cardinal sign. If you use a cardinal Moon, be sure there is no penalty for fast repayment.

Writing a Book or An Article

If you can start and finish a writing project during a retrograde Mercury period, it works fine, in my experience.

If you don't finish then, you'll either wait until the next Mercury R period or not finish it at all or there will be so many changes that you'll end up starting over anyway. We're not talking routine things here, but special projects, you realize. If you were born with Mercury retrograde the period is particularly good for you and most of the Mercury ℞ rules don't apply to you. Thus, you can see that writing an article during the period is feasible. A book is probably not.

Setting Up a Blog

You want the Moon in House 10. The "owner" of the blog—you—would be signified by the Moon and its aspects. The blog itself is the first house.

If you want it to grow, use a waxing phase of the Moon in good aspect to Mercury. A good aspect to Saturn gives it stability and longevity. Since it is a blog you might want to beef up Mercury's importance in the chart. Maybe use Gemini or Virgo as rising sign with Mercury in good aspect to the ruler of the 3rd. Put the benefics direct and in some sort of good aspect to Mercury or the Moon.

Setting Up an Astrology Organization

First decide what you want your organization to be: A comfortable group for professionals to swap ideas and research and network? A mainstream outfit that works to upgrade professionalism or astrology's image and relates to the press whenever astrology comes up? A group to fight ignorance and foster education? A money making publisher of new works? What? If such a purpose is already part of your charter, you have your answer.

We have all of these purposes in American astrology. Depending on what you want, the planets you might want prominent are: publishing/money making: Jupiter and Venus: networking and research, Mercury and Saturn (just the facts, ma'am); mainstream and education, Jupiter and Saturn and the Moon. You'll notice I didn't mention Uranus. I think Uranus too strong undercuts any group because it fosters so much individualism that "the group" doesn't benefit much and the average astrologer already is about as individualistic as it comes.

For a chart, I'd consider a waxing phase of the Moon in a good sign if you want growth. If you want it to get attention and have people eager to join, use the day of the full Moon but before the Moon is actually full. You can use the day before as well.

For a venture that grows, always use the waxing phase of the Moon, and when you want to pull people in, the closer you get to the Full Moon the better. Have the social planets Jupiter and Saturn emphasized, in addition to Mercury. If public relations/money making is important, get Venus angular.

At all costs keep the malefics out of the angles, even if you have to sacrifice angularity for a benefic. Angular malefics bring down an organization faster than anything, I think.

The first house is the members, the 10th house is whomever they elect to run the show, the 7th house is people who disagree and/or start competing groups and the 4th house is the outcome of the effort.

Try to avoid having the first house ruled by a planet that is debilitated. Don't use Leo with the Sun in Libra, for instance. Don't use a debilitated planet to rule any angle if you can avoid it.

If you can't get the Moon applying to the planets you want, find a time when it doesn't make any bad aspects. A lunar application to a retrograde planet doesn't pay. Retrogrades promise more than they deliver.

Baptismal Date

The first question to answer is why do you want to pick a special date for this religious event? Are you hoping to have a big family party afterward? Do you see this as somehow spiritually critical to the child? To the parents? Does your view of the rite make it important in determining the child's approach to religion?

In other words, what do you want this date to accomplish? Before you can pick a date for something that is usually a routine ceremony, you have to decide why it needs a special date. I am not being facetious. I think this is an important element of the electional process. Once you know the answer to that question you can choose the election.

Opening a Coffee Shop

Coffee is black and acrid. Almost a clear description of Saturn, except for its ability to stir the body. As a stimulant, though, Mars is involved. Cream—the Cancer ingredient—tames it and sugar, the Venus component, sweetens it.

Coffee houses—obviously Moon places where liquid is served—or Venus, where pleasure and sweet pastries are available.

I say we use cardinal sign power in an election to open a coffee shop. Coffee is a quick starter (definitely cardinal) in the morning (Sunrise—Aries—stimulation) and we even call it an eye-opener. Eyes come under Aries.

When we get weary we drink some more. It's considered a good ending to a meal (Libra—fourth house from food-serving Cancer) and we even try to boil it down to make it intense and strong (espresso) which is very powerful (Capricorn) and then we add sugar and milk to make it palatable.

Yes, I think definitely cardinal angles. Saturn/Mars for the beverage.

The usual election rules would apply.

Chapter 40

Decumbitures
An Old Way to Look at Illness

Decumbiture charts are practically unknown in modern astrology and yet, like many old techniques, will give us a considerable amount of information in cases of illness or injury.

A decumbiture is cast for the moment one is said to "take to one's bed," and admit one is ill or needs to rest in order to heal an injury or recover from illness. If the exact time of the injury is known, that can be the time of the decumbiture chart.

If you come home from work, because you are sick and crawl into bed, that's the time you use. If you've been working for days and finally admit that you are ill and make an appointment to see the doctor, you can use the time you call for the appointment or the time you actually see the doctor if you forgot when you called. You don't use the time of the appointment but the actual moment the doctor walks in and asks you what the problem is.

This is very similar to a horary chart in that the exact moment has to have certain rules applied. Many older writers and doctors in earlier ages when birth times were less apt to be exact made heavy use of the decumbitures as a guide to treatment of their patients and there are a few rules to follow.

As in horary, the Moon's triplicity is vital information. Cardinal Moons heal quickly, take their medicine and are back on their feet before expected. Mutable Moons take their time, may have setbacks in the healing process or the condition can become chronic. Fixed Moons are deeply serious situations which involve a long time of recovery. If there is any tie to natal Saturn or the decumbiture chart has a rising Saturn which the Moon aspects, it can leave damage one suffers the rest of one's life. Such an example might be the loss of a limb. Depending on the severity of the aspects, such a Moon can also point to the end of life.

The long recuperation element of the fixed signs alone is enough to gives one a desire to stay on one's feet until the Moon changes sign.

In medieval times the decumbiture was a crucial piece of information for the astrologer and physician in an era when medicine had few remedies more useful than herbal ones and relied on diagnostic tools far less effective than modern ones. Both William Lilly and Nicholas Culpepper wrote of them. Lilly was the author of *Christian Astrology* in 1647 and Culpepper wrote *Astrological Judgment of Diseases* in 1651. The Culpepper text is considered the authority on the technique.

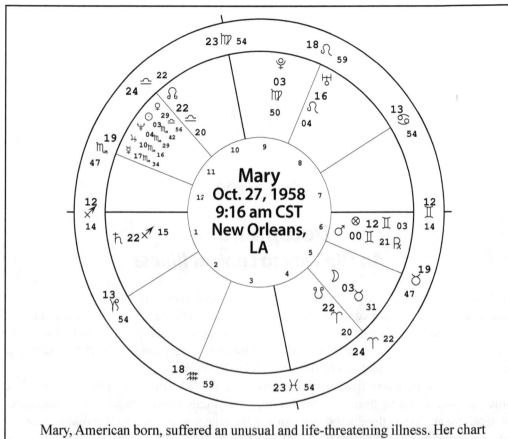

Mary, American born, suffered an unusual and life-threatening illness. Her chart is AA from her birth certificate. She was living in Vienna, Austria, at the time.

Here is the explanation for a decumbiture I did in 1998 when an online friend in Austria fell deathly ill and was taken to the hospital by ambulance. I wrote it for members of our online astrological group as she was undergoing treatment in a hospital, Her name has been changed to keep her privacy.

Our friend Mary has provided us with a fine example for analysis and her friend wrote with the time of the ambulance arrival at the home, Jan. 5, 4:30 p.m. CET, Vienna. Her birth data is Oct. 27, 1958, New Orleans, LA, 9:16 a.m. CST. I would recommend watching these two charts as I go through my technique, if you are interested. It will make it a lot easier to see. The first chart is Mary's natal and the second chart is for the time that the ambulance arrived.

A decumbiture is the chart cast for the time an illness begins, and the ancient rule was the time the individual "took to their bed." In other words, it was the time when the individual ceased to be able to function.

Four steps in the Process of Working with a Decumbiture Chart

First, compare the decumbiture with the natal, or radical chart. For this example, I cast two charts, one for the ambulance arrival (a known time) and the other about 20 minutes earlier, a "guess" time which her friend who was there said was "about" when she collapsed. It did

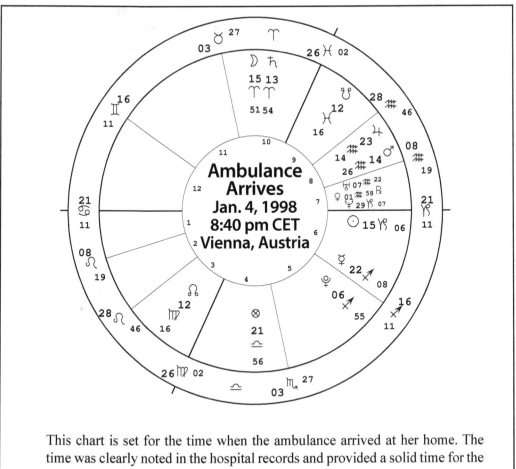

This chart is set for the time when the ambulance arrived at her home. The time was clearly noted in the hospital records and provided a solid time for the decumbiture chart to be cast.

not surprise me to find that the first I did, the one when the ambulance came, was the time most closely linked to her birth chart. The known time always seems to have the edge in these things. Don't ask me why.

The MC of the decumbiture is conjunct her natal 4th House cusp by minutes. Mercury in decumbiture House 6 is exactly conjunct her natal rising Saturn by 7 minutes of arc. This is a VERY tight package.

The ruler of her natal 6th, Venus, at 29 Libra in her natal chart is exactly square the Neptune of the decumbiture chart, 29 Capricorn, again closely tied by minutes. The decumbiture chart has a retrograde Venus at 1 Aquarius, in tight trine to her natal Mars in House 6 at 0 Gemini. The Moon of the decumbiture chart, which rules the ascendant and the course of the illness, is exactly semisquare that natal Mars in 6. These are all extremely close, specifically linked to the natal rising planet, angles and 6th house. You don't get a much tighter decumbiture, in my opinion.

An aside here: I am not using any directions or progressions to the natal chart. A decumbiture stands on its own, even as a horary does and has its own "niche" in astrology. However, to decide if the decumbiture is "radical," or fit to be read, the ties to the natal are of great value, if the natal chart is available, and this is a centuries-old rule.

2nd step is looking at the decumbiture alone for the seriousness of the illness and the significator. Cancer rises here, so the Moon is both significator and timer, describing the patient, the illness, her chances of recovery and how fast she will get well.

The Moon is conjunct Saturn (a nasty problem), square Sun, and opposed the part of Fortune, all strong and angular. This is a very serious situation, will require major medical care from a good physician and appears life-threatening. The ascendant is exactly square Fortuna, opposed Sun, square Saturn and widely inconjunct Mars in 8 and Mercury in 6. On the plus side, the Moon is also sextile Mars and Jupiter and Uranus (within an 8 degree orb) and trine Mercury in 6. (By 9 degrees).

The planets are all western in this chart, except for the Moon/Saturn in 10, meaning her cooperation with physicians will be key to recovery because she can do little to help herself.

The significator Moon in Aries says this is a "head" problem—brain—and can affect the eyes (or be affected by things seen) and because of the sextile to Mars, has a bleeding-injury-or-inflamed element to it. As I understand the explanation we have received from her friend it could be described as a swelling, or inflammation of the brain.

The aspect to Uranus says it is an unusual problem (in Aquarius, sign of the circulatory and nervous systems, probably affecting both).

Note—I am NOT medically trained and am using astrologer's terms and rules, not medical knowledge.

The doctor in the case is Saturn in 10—a dignified position and powerfully in control here. He may have been consulted initially by a second man, the Jupiter (co-ruler 10) in Aquarius doctor, who later stepped out of the way. He has taken over. Neptune, co-ruler of 10, is in 7, the consultant's position, and suggests a (third doctor) neurological specialist in the twilight of his career—old and very experienced—who has been very important in helping with her case. The Jupiter in Aquarius person may even have been a doctor in the ambulance, or one who handled the trauma unit or emergency room. (The 8th house is trauma as well as surgery.)

Her nursing care will be also indicated partly by that Jupiter, which rules 6, as well as the Mercury there (trine Jupiter) and the Sun. Even an afflicted Sun in 6 helps with nursing care. Mercury is debilitated in Sagittarius but the sextile to Jupiter helps. My impression is that she will have a lot of nurses or caregivers, some quite young, as well as men (the Sun)—or at least one man. (This may perhaps refer to her friend later during her recovery.) Caregivers or nurses are not physicians.

Both Mercury in 6 and Jupiter, ruler of 6, are inconjunct the rising degree. Inconjuncts show things "take time." This is in contrast to the speedy Moon, hinting that while the illness will "take time" to heal, it will be "fast" for the kind of illness it is.

OK, we have established the situation. Now where will things go?

Third step is to use the Moon as timer. The Moon is separating—an excellent sign—from conjunction to Saturn and (barely from) square to the Sun. If it were applying, it would mean the worst was yet to come. The separation says the situation is bad but at least all the bad news is already on the table.

It separates from Saturn by about 2 degrees, showing the first signs of what was wrong may have occurred two days before her collapse, but a definite hint of big trouble showed two hours before...some symptom like vision difficulty, or pain or etc.

As the Moon moves forward in the sign, it opposes Fortuna in 4 degrees, trines Mercury by 7, sextiles Jupiter by 8, and lastly squares Neptune, by 14. The cardinal, angular position says these are "days" as well as developments in the case.

Aspect to Fortuna shows prognosis, or outlook, being established; Mercury shows tests, Jupiter shows treatment, Neptune shows medicine. Neptune also rules hospitalization and sleep treatment, which was the chosen method of helping her. She was in a medically induced sleep—or coma, as they sometimes call it—for several days to give her brain the time to heal.

The Moon is in Aries, the speediest sign of all. Given the seriousness of her condition, she will make a much faster than expected recovery. The ascendant in Cancer says food and emotions will be significant in that recovery.

The fourth step is recovery. It is ruled by the fourth house, or outcome of the event. Fortuna is there, trine Jupiter and sextile house ruler Mercury in 6.

Jupiter is inconjunct the fourth house cusp, however—another hint that this will "take time" and she will have to make major adjustments in her life. She will recover, however, and that is no small feat with this kind of problem. Her friend has not said so but I suspect this was not thought to be a given in the beginning.

The Moon's last aspect to Neptune says the last treatment or prescription will be about two weeks after the onset of the illness. This can also mark the end of hospitalization, but the last aspect being Neptune can also show a need for ongoing treatment and medication.

In conclusion: She should be home on the 19th. She will make a full recovery, against all odds.

I wasn't kidding about good food. The patient will need it and will need to be very careful about medication and drink only bottled water for a while.

She did return home on the 19th and to my knowledge to date, there has been no recurrence of the problem.

Some feedback from her friend who wrote to tell us of her illness at the time:
It was diagnosed yesterday that she has "para-infectuous encephalitis" from a virus like from a children's sickness or Herpes-Simplex. M.... says no she doesn't think so because she has had the problems so long but the doctors say brain swelling is there and so it must be treated. They are giving her medications and injections to make the swelling of the brain tissues go down and to stop from having more seizures and many antibiotika (sic) to fight the infek(sic)t. As before she has no pain and does not feel so sick and so she is getting sedative drugs to make her restful. She must not read or watch tv, not listen to music, all must be quiet as possible and she is bored. This is a dangerous sickness only they don't think she has the most serious form and after a week the worst is over. I hope it is so. Then after one can see if there will be continuous damage in some parts of the brain. She says it will not be more crazy than already is."

After Mary came home from the hospital where she had had extensive sleep therapy and read my comments on the decumbiture chart she sent me a number of remarks. Here are some of them:
Dear Pat!

WOW!!

This is quite an analysis and so damn accurate! I just wish i could think of a better learning method than always having to experience at first hand.

And thank you for taking the time to explain - I think this did much to also ease (her friend's) worries.

I'd been watching those coming transits and had figured something might happen but I was more prepared for a recurrence of an inflamed jawbone - a problem I have had in the past once and that was what I had thought was wrong with me. I did not expect this more drastic manifestation, although in retrospect I think I should have seen it coming.

(My comment that it was a life-threatening illness prompted her to say:) *Unfortunately and although it didn't feel that way to me, it apparently was so.*

(I mentioned she could do little to help herself:) *Err...yes,. sorry to say. I was busy being extremely irritated - and from what I see you guys were pretty feisty at about the same time - and couldn't or wouldn't calm down. So I had to be convinced to be put under completely for a while.*

(I said the aspect to Uranus made it an unusual problem.) *Again yes. What I had/have is not common at all and I would seriously like to know how I managed to pick up something like that. Not a question anyone can answer, though.*

(When I said the doctor was probably old she replied:) *Not really old - just very, very capable and able to convince me. A real authority I guess. (Saturn). I wasn't going under without having someone make it very clear why that would be so necessary. The worst, inflammatory part is over. It's not sure yet if anything was damaged permanently but I don't think so, at least, judging from how I feel now. Altogether I'm brainwise in much clearer and freer shape than I was for a long time before. But...I am in for at least a month of no work and a long time of regular and intensive neurological checkups.*

(I mentioned she might have had symptoms about two hours before the ambulance came.) *All I felt was being even fuzzier than I had been in the days before. There never was any pain (thank God).*

(When I said she should be home on the 19th, she wrote:) *Laughing...and yes, here I am! On the premise that they don't need to jab objects into me anymore, I much prefer my yelling cat to even the friendliest and kindest of nurses and they were! They really were all good and caring people who took a lot of trouble with me but still...I'm glad to be home, glad to be back and know there is a good deal I will have to change and adjust.*

Food doesn't interest me much right now but before you say anything...I am eating and eating well. You are a Cancer Sun aren't you? :) Thank goodness water in Austria is the best there is. Vienna's water is essentially clear spring water that comes straight down from the mountains. Its quality is often much superior to bottled water.

Pat, I thank you again for your analysis. Not only am I impressed but also feel much more hopeful that what happened will have a lot of positive effects in the long run.

The decumbiture chart eased my worries considerably but I am so pleased you took time for feedback on it for others to see who have never worked with a decumbiture.

Love, Mary.—who is off to bed again

Note—a jaw problem is ALSO an Aries difficulty, as was this brain inflammation. Her natal 6th house Mars is a clear indication of Mars problems during her life.

Chapter 41

Zeroing in on Time
Rectification

Rectification is not something I enjoy. You'd think I would, as many crossword puzzles as I do, but I find the whole process painful. However, I have been asked (yes, really) for tips on how to do it. Therefore, I offer some thoughts you may find useful when faced with a completely unknown birth time. There is a big difference between a 24 hour unknown time and one that's "off" by a few minutes. The first is a wild stab at the unknown and the second is mere tinkering. Usually, questioning may give you some idea of night or day, but that can be wrong, so don't think the answer is written in stone.

First of all, figure out the rising sign. If you get that wrong, you might as well hang it up on anything fancier in the way of rectification.

The first house deals with the body and its ailments and those are a dead give away to a rising sign that is different from the Sun sign. If it's the same as the Sun sign the influence of that particular sign will be quite strong but it makes it hard to be sure some times. You can also think of the natural 6th house ruler to a given Sun sign as helpful, too.

Not all the indications I give you will be present in any rising sign, but some of them may prove a tip you can follow to see if it works.

Bad knees, taking after "dad's side" of the family and being small or lean and dark are tipoffs to Capricorn. Bone problems and skin troubles can plague **Capricorn rising**. Sometimes there are beautiful teeth and very strong bones if Saturn is in good shape in the natal pattern.

A soft, rounded body, trouble with digestion and food and looking like "mom's side" of the family suggest **Cancer rising**. Also, a body with the weight in the stomach and with thin legs, the "apple" shape. Moody.

Teeth problems, back trouble, slipped discs, broken bones, heart difficulties point to **Leo rising**. Strong shouldered, upright carriage. Lean in the hips. Hair sometimes long and combed straight back in a "mane" look. May wear striking jewelry, particularly gold. May seek to run the show, no matter what's going on.

Deep set eyes, a looming brow, hemorrhoids and generous hips belong to **Scorpio rising**. Also, constipation difficulties when away from home. In later life the men get prostate trouble and the women may have female ailments of various sorts, depending on how many children they've had. Hair tends to be extremely curly or very straight and may be very dark or very fair, but seldom "average." May tend to eat irregularly or only one meal a day. Thin lips and sometimes piercing eyes.

Bow-shaped mouth, thick neck, a tendency not to move the head much but rather the eyes only, and strep infections can be **Taurus Rising**. Men are often pretty in youth (and spoiled by their mothers) and women can be stunning. Sometimes good or even great singers. Kidney stones and inner ear difficulties. Thyroid problems can show up.

Very youthful appearance, even in old age, with a tendency to talk a lot is usually **Gemini Rising.** They like to multi-task and seldom want to sit very long and do nothing. They fidget when they sit. They run into lung problems unceasingly if Mercury is afflicted and can have arms and finger troubles. They may tend to avoid talking about problem areas.

Sagittarius Rising can be the tallest member of the family, stoop shouldered or well-padded in middle age, but athletic appearance in youth. Often long-legged and likes horses or bicycles. High forehead, open face and smiles or laughs a lot. Animals in the family show up when they come around. Hip problems, gout and liver difficulties.

Virgo rising may run into Crone's disease or other bowel ailments, usually has allergies and/or hay fevers and is sometimes mistaken for Gemini. Both look youthful and the men keep their hair in middle age and beyond. Virgo may have curly hair and small feet. When you ask them, "How are you?" they may give you a medical summary.

Pisces rising can have an array of ailments, usually ones nobody else in the family has. Chronic ailments like asthma or food troubles. It can run to eczema as a baby, or club feet or just foot problems in general, such as bunions or ingrown toenails. Soft bodied. This is a sign that is particularly vulnerable to whatever is "going around."

Aries rising men have skimpy beards and **Aries rising** women don't seem to choose a good hair dye unless they have a really tactful beautician. They have sinus problems, jaw ailments, ear aches, dental infections and quite often scars on the head or face. They tend to lean forward with the head when walking or talking. They are often annoyed by the necessity to eat and seldom cook unless the Moon is angular.

Libra rising almost always appears to have a symmetrical body even if the arms are too short or the legs too long. They also have the pretty mouth Taurus gets, but with a more refined appearance. Their ailments run to kidney stones, or infections. Women may have ovarian difficulties and men problems with impotence. Early baldness.

Aquarius rising has a classic profile and usually very high set calves on the lower leg. The ankle goes on forever. Circulation difficulties in middle life and a tendency to varicose veins or nerve problems. They tend to have quite regular habits—meals at the proper time and amount, regular sleep and regular exercise. Can be stunningly beautiful if Venus is involved..

Those are just a few things to watch for. You may know many more if you are perceptive and study people. When one is doing rectification and looking at the client who wants a forecast, you have to know what you are seeing in order to pin the chart down.

Broken bones and surgeries in children are among the best anchors for a rising degree. Use a simple one-degree measure to establish this if you have some events to work with. You can also use deaths of grandparents, who are ruled by house 1 and 7. (Parents of one's parents, you know.) Next best thing to use is marriage, since that involves both house 1 and 7. The age at which it occurs by one degree will bring the 7th house cusp to Venus or a planet in the 7th or the ruler of the 7th will aspect Venus or vice versa.

The angles are the next thing to decide on once you pick a possible rising sign. A good knowledge of the family is a big help. The father's occupation and nature and the mother's role in the home should be described by the two signs on the MC and IC. The two parents may switch from 4 to 10 also. The kind of home an individual likes, the family heritage, standing in the community and the like should "fit" the signs.

Using the simple one degree measure, check for those childhood surgeries and broken bones to form squares, oppositions or conjunctions by the possible Ascendant to Mars and/or Saturn. That will give you a likely degree rising and a possible degree for the MC.

The individual's own career should be described by the MC. A dual career is a Mercury thing so look to Virgo or Gemini. Honors and recognition will come from Jupiter, and management sometimes from the Sun. Uranus may point to a government job or even astrology. Sometimes both. I never bother with events in the life that strictly belong to the succedent and cadent houses. You need to get the correct angles first or you're really whistling in the dark.

If you've gotten this far and you have possible angles, start moving planets by the one-degree method around to aspect them for major events in the life (job changes, purchase of a home, moving, etc.). If you can justify the time that well, run up a secondary progression for an important year and see if it matches the events. If not, keep trying.

If you find this interesting—and some people do—go get a good book on rectification and dig in for more details and do the mathematical refining. Don't be too disappointed if a major event fails to show up. It takes time to do this and it's not as easy as it sounds.

This is as far as I want to take you. As I said, it's not something I like to do. The practice, however, will teach you a lot about how much you really know and will introduce some new elements into your thinking.

Take a chart—any chart—that you are absolutely sure is dead accurate and do the measuring to see how it works in practice. Don't use an infant since their life is still ahead of them. Take an adult's chart so you can check your accuracy. If it doesn't measure properly to the big events in the person's life, and you've exhausted the book you bought, start over and find a good teacher to help you.

If all else fails, use a simple solar chart. Events in the life should be followed for some years to be sure of a rectification. When things occur on schedule you can be pretty sure you got it right.

One of the best rectification events I know of is that childhood accident which results in broken bones. First of all, such an event usually involves both Mars and Saturn natally and both are reliable transits as well. I rectified my father's chart some years ago using the fact that he had broken both collarbones as a child in falls. He was born at home on a farm, one of a family of 11 children (9 lived) and all he knew of his birth time was that it was "slightly before dawn."

The first time he was jumping on his father (Saturn, obviously) in bed and slipped off the bed and the second time he fell in the barn. He had a natal Mars Saturn conjunction, which I put in the third because of the tie to the arms and shoulders and it squared the Scorpio Ascendant by solar arc exactly during the years of the accidents. His chart worked practically to the minute for the rest of his life.

I had a client who had broken a leg at 12. Another had a broken arm falling out of a tree at 8. A third had broken teeth in a fall at 9. All of these are excellent to use. It helped me nail their birth times very quickly. One of them was not a complete unknown to start with but the pattern was there.

Also excellent are surgeries as a child. Tonsillectomy, for instance, was quite popular years ago, though they don't seem to do them so much anymore. This is probably because antibiotics cure a lot of the infections that used to be so common.

Events after age 30 are much tougher to use initially, I think. Once you have an accurate time they show quite well.

All rectification is tough except for the mathematically inclined. I think you need feedback from a client on how the selected time works unless you know them very, very well (as I did my father). I don't trust rectification unless any major event the person can come up with can be verified by the chart and even then I wait a couple of years to allow for plenty of transits to set things off before I'm sure.

I have no compunction at all in throwing out my work if it doesn't measure up. Close, but no cigar, as Groucho Marx used to say.

There are lots of people who are better at rectification than I am. Math is not my preferred mode of action. I do it under protest and whine all the way. But occasionally it's vital and there just is nothing else to do.

But as far as the so-called pre-natal epoch is concerned, my advice is to skip it. I never figured out any particular value in it and if there is one, nobody has proved it to me.

Of course I'm a lazy astrologer and if there is a complicated technique on one side of the table and a simpler one on the other, I'll pick simpler without any hesitation at all. Besides, simpler is just as valid most of the time and a heckuva lot less work.

If it doesn't work, and you can't get out of the rectification, grit your teeth and do it or find a new way to weasel out altogether. If you know a lot of astrologers there will surely be one among them who likes to do rectification and you can refer the client to that person. I highly recommend weaseling out.

Author's note: I wrote this chapter in late 2002 and published it online in early 2003, before the U.S. war with Iraq had started. Many other things have changed since then, but some may find what follows interesting, as an example of what the astrologer can "see" at some points.

Chapter 42

Follow the Money

There's a story to tell about the proposed U.S. war against Saddam Hussein that goes back many years. But astrologically, let's start with 2000. That was the year of the latest Great Conjunction of the planets Jupiter and Saturn at 23° of Taurus where it landed dead on the U.S. Part of Fortune in the 8th house of investments and other people's money. It squared the U.S. Moon at 24° Aquarius in the 5th house, which rules the national Sun sign, Cancer. The U.S. strike was a bull's-eye by any standard. A Great Conjunction occurs every 20 years or so and marks a new generation of events in the world.

Obviously, I am speaking of a U.S. chart with 13° Libra rising and 15° Cancer on the MC. This is not an argument for or against this or any other U.S. chart, merely an explanation of the one I use and have found reasonably accurate in predictive work.

At the time it was obvious to me that we were entering a far more economically conservative time (Taurus is the pre-eminent sign of conservative views) and one that would seriously affect the stock markets, the economic climate, the banking system and the currencies of the world. It would have particular impact in the U.S., given the points it hit in the chart.

I had begun warning people about the coming economic downturn as early as late '99, particularly since the Millennium eclipse in August of that year involved a massive grand cross in fixed signs which always targets money and the status quo.

This was not popular of me, because all of the U.S. markets were blowing full steam ahead, but a few prescient economists also warned that it was a bubble on borrowed time. I urged friends and family members to get out of the market. Not all of them paid much attention. I sold my own stock in the spring of 2000, before the markets began to fall later that year. They have continued to drop ever since.

Many astrologers have considered that market downturn the major effect of the Great Conjunction. But much more was involved. Many banks and financial institutions merged, went under or restructured in the following months and years.

In Japan, where economic recovery had stalled for more than a decade—they missed the whole prosperous '90s as a result— due to the nation's reluctance to allow its unsuccessful banks to go under, times got tougher. The healthy banks were constrained by the need to prop up the dying ones. The situation worsened year by year as the government refused to take the hard steps to allow bankruptcies or to fix the system. Institutions and businesses in Japan scratch each other's backs and prop up each other's stocks as a matter of common policy. They don't let each other fail. After a while nobody was doing well.

By comparison, the huge U.S. savings and loan scandal which had come in the 1980s was long over because the U.S. government moved in and took over, allowed failed institutions to go under, sold the viable ones and restructured the system. It cost a fortune but it saved the U.S. from paying a much higher price later. It also protected the U.S. banking system.

Last year some Japanese banks were finally allowed to fail. It was too little and too late, of course. The Nikkei standard of stock performance is a shadow of its former self. The Japanese market has lost far more than that of the U.S since the conjunction, although many investors caught in the U.S. "tech wreck" might not think so.

However, in Japan, the world's second largest economy, a great many loans—business and otherwise—were underpinned by the enormous real estate values of some years back. The banks didn't revalue those loans although the real estate had lost its luster. Nor were stocks routinely marked to market—a process whereby stocks held as collateral are given their current values rather than the value they had when the loans were first obtained. If the collateral were ever called in, it would be worthless or greatly diminished in value, of course, by lower current prices. The stocks, far from being worth their original price, would then be worth only what they could actually be sold for on the open market.

Thus, while Japan is still rich and the Japanese banking system is still viable, there has been an enormous, unhealed wound in its side for many years. Its troubles have become common knowledge since the conjunction and the value of the yen shrank against the dollar. There is no doubt the U.S. has also been hit hard by the conjunction. For one thing, U.S. currency itself has changed its appearance. Some say the overhaul was overdue and perhaps they are right.

The 8th house rulership over insurance, tax matters and money saved for things like retirement has also been nailed to the wall. Many huge corporations have gone under, their books awry with lies and deception and theft, often from their own employee retirement accounts. Workers who saved and invested in their company's stocks have been devastated.

The Enron scandal was the biggest, but hardly the only one. Many companies "borrowed" from retirement accounts to fund stock market speculation and replaced the borrowed money with company stock. When the company stock went down, so did the retirees' savings. Even Social Security seemed threatened, although immediate steps were taken to reassure the public that it was safe even if all else failed.

But in another huge economic development since the conjunction, the Euro has become a major currency in the world. For a very long time the U.S. dollar has been the world's key money, its so-called "reserve" currency. All oil trading has taken place in dollars. Countries who sell oil want dollars for it. If you want to buy oil, you convert your money to dollars and then make the purchase. This has been great for the dollar. It has forced other nations to keep a continual "reserve" of dollars in their banks.

Since banks never have unused money sitting around, that money has been invested in the U.S., mostly in bonds. Japan alone probably owns 15% of the U.S. Treasury market.

And oil trading is ubiquitous. The whole world runs on oil. So the whole world has dollars in "storage."About two/thirds of all official exchange money held in reserve is dollars. More than four-fifths of all foreign exchange transactions and half of all world exports are in dollars. In addition, all International Monetary Fund loans are made in dollars. That gives the U.S. a finger in everybody's pie.

Now to digress a moment, the U.S. owes the world a lot of money. Why? Americans like to buy the world's goods. We pay for them with dollars. Thus, a lot of U.S. money goes out of the door all the time and since foreigners don't buy nearly as much of our goods, not as much foreign money comes into the U.S. to keep things even. It's called the balance of payments, and it's very lopsided in favor of the foreigners at the moment.

It wasn't always so. For many years the U.S. produced the most desirable goods and services and the whole world beat a path to the door to buy. Now the U.S. does the buying. That's no problem for us-if we need more money, we just print it. And because of the oil buying business, people ALWAYS need our money. The more dollars at work outside the U.S., or invested by foreign owners in American assets, the more the rest of the world gives the U.S. its goods and services in exchange. The dollars cost the U.S. next to nothing to print, so this means that the U.S. is importing all those foreign goods and services practically for free. How bad could it be?

But what if they don't need our money anymore? What would happen if the dollar weren't the world's reserve currency any more? What if oil producers decide to accept payment in Euros?

That would be a very large problem for the U.S. Other countries would scramble to trade their dollars for Euros. Their money, currently invested in dollars (as in our Treasury market) would be pulled out of those dollars and re-invested in European banks in Euros.

That 15 % Japanese investment in the U.S. treasury market? Gone.

All that wonderful foreign investment in U.S. companies? Gone.

All those cheap goods and services? Gone.

All that U.S. debt? Bigger and bigger.

And what if the U.S. had to swap its dollars for Euros at a time when the dollar is falling in value and the economy is already in trouble with U.S. companies coming unglued right and left? Printing more money wouldn't help us then. Not only would the stock market fall, so would the whole U.S. primacy in the world's financial affairs. From being top dog we would drop to the bottom, owing everybody a ton of money and they wouldn't want our dollars for it. They'd want Euros.

And oil? Forget oil. It would be bicycles and walking in the U.S. again as oil's price in dollars goes through the roof. We'd simply be too broke to buy very much of it. The big oil embargo of the '70s? Mickey Mouse stuff by comparison. At this point, oil is the only game in town. Despite options such as hydrogen and methane, the world still runs on oil and the U.S. is the biggest consumer. The amount of oil found on U.S. soil is pitifully small by comparison to the demand of U.S. industry and consumer.

Big bankers and big oil men understand how this works. The U.S. government currently has a number of people with backgrounds in oil, starting with President George W. Bush, and they know loss of dollar power would be a terrible blow to the American economy. So imagine the shock it caused in certain circles when Saddam Hussein stepped up to the plate in November of 2000 as the first oil producer to say yes, I will take Euros for my oil. They thought he was just desperate. It seemed insane. The Euro was also at its lowest value compared to the dollar. Unfortunately, he was also looking ahead. The Euro has since risen nearly 20% and generated a lot of profit. Before long other countries began considering the move from dollar to Euro. Iran has said it is thinking about it. North Korea began accepting the Euro in November last year. All three have been dubbed the "axis of evil."

Another willing to take Euros is Venezuela. And it has been in the throes of a terrible national upheaval with halted oil production ever since President Chavez said so. Certainly it's another odd coincidence in the oil and money struggle. The U.S. would be happy to see Chavez go and has not been particularly subtle about its opinion, either.

And of course now, war is imminent against Saddam Hussein, who started the whole thing. France and Germany are against the war. They have no problem with the Euro being accepted for his oil. They use the Euro. They ARE the Euro. Or a large chunk of it, anyway.

The big supporter of the U.S. is Great Britain, which did not convert to the Euro. The British still use the pound and they aren't particularly eager to see the Euro become any bigger.

Meanwhile, another element in the restructuring of the world's financial affairs is taking shape quietly in the background but it has enormous implications and it involves gold. When Richard Nixon was President he gave the order which took the U.S. off the gold standard. Before that time, every dollar printed, once considered "as good as gold," was backed by an equivalent amount of gold stored in Fort Knox, Kentucky. Now the stockpile of gold has become somewhat immaterial.

Today the U.S. dollar is only backed by the U.S. government promises. It "floats" among world currencies, as they say. But the Russians, who suffered greatly when the Soviet Union collapsed along with the value of the ruble, are considering a gold standard.

Iraq has said that accepting gold for oil would be a blow against the dollar's premier position in the world. And if the surging Euro would cause a huge commotion in world financial affairs as OPEC nations begin accepting it for oil, imagine what would happen if Russia had a currency based on solid gold.

More amazing still is the fact that this currency war is being played out in front of the whole world's eyes and hardly anybody sees it—truly a Jupiter/Neptune opposition keeping people deluded.

And so the Great Conjunction and its effects continue with the world looking for value and reliable money. Will it be the dollar in the years ahead or will Saddam Hussein be crushed for his temerity in giving the Euro a foothold in the economic future of the world?

The U.S. has a huge stake in this and if it can't do anything else to stem the tide of the Euro it will use its second largest weapon against Saddam Hussein: military might.

The nations of the Euro are bound to get the message.

Chapter 43

Mundane Charts

The word "mundane" in charts refer to the charts of individual nations and worldwide groups and events that affect human affairs. They are a separate branch of astrology and require far more than a quick thumbnail sketch.

For those interested, Nick Campion has a fine pair of books out. One is *The Book of World Horoscopes* and the other is a book on interpretation of the mundane. I strongly refer those interested to his works.

The course of wars and social movements require somewhat different approaches to the houses, just as business charts require a modification of analysis to do well. The natal patterns of both are in the same areas as those of individuals but have broader scope. In the second house, money earnings and savings is reflected in the banks and tax receipts of the national chart, for instance.

Other authorities on mundane work are from the ancient world and can be read and studied in translation from the Greek, Latin or Arabic of the astrologers of those times.

Why do they work? A mundane chart works precisely because people en masse tend to take the path of least resistance. That is not to say they can't change their mind in the future or take steps to change events. But that will also be reflected in a major shift in the chart, just as it would be in an individual's chart.

If we want to be accurate in prediction we need to use things as they are, not as we wish they were. It would be wonderful if every national action was all voted on so that every governmental decision truly reflected national thinking. In fact it doesn't work that way, here or any place else. It tends to reflect the dominant thinking or force—whether that is by a head of state or the legislative body or the majority of the populace.

Today this forecast is more than 10 years old and much has changed. Currency wars are going on now, though less obviously than the average reader may realize. Saddam Hussein is gone and President George Bush's rush to judgment and then to war in Iraq has been exposed by those who tried to warn him that the "evidence" on which he relied was not accurate or reliable. Osama bin Laden has died at the hands of U.S. soldiers and El Queda has lost its base in Afganistan.

The enormous cost of this war has the U.S. finances reeling. It is considered politically correct to ignore war spending and blame the economic mess on entitlements and the like but the truth is that military spending has been incredibly high and continues to be during a time of peace. It is the largest single element in the U.S. budget.

Where will it all end? Even as I write this I know of the vast discoveries of underground oil and gas in the U.S. which may spark a new financial boom and a renaissance in American prosperity. The U.S. chart with its powerful and benefic Jupiter/Venus conjunction to the Sun is coming through again. One can only hope that this time the budget will be balanced and debts will be paid before legislators send the deficit soaring again.

Following is a series of rules that I created as a baseline for people who want to do serious astrology. It turned out to be a good start for those who wanted to go beyond serious astrology and into the professional areas. My first rule has been picked up and quoted by many more people than I realized when I first compiled it.

Chapter 44

Ten Rules for Astrologers

One of the problems every student in astrology runs into is why I have always taught one rule first. Every class and every student needs to know it. It is astrology's fundamental basic, rock-bottom principle. Ready? Here it is—the biggie—write it on your forehead in big gold letters:

EVERYTHING MODIFIES EVERYTHING ELSE.

In order to learn astrology you have to learn how planets and signs function as if they were there all by their lonesome. When you learn a little more, you realize that they almost never are all by themselves, but linked in such a way that they affect each other. Thus:

1. Everything modifies everything else.

2. Nothing is as good or as bad as you think it will be.

3. Forecast conservatively—it's better than looking like a complete fool when you're half wrong.

4. Study love, money and health issues. If you become a professional, 99 percent of your clients will want information on them. If you stay an amateur, it's probably what you want to know. The rest is frosting.

5. Don't take your transits too much to heart. The word transit means "passing on by.' The stations are the more reliable indicators.

6. Continue to study. Pay attention to the old timers. They're the ones who taught the astrologers that you think are so wonderful.

7. Take astrology seriously. Don't give away what you know too cheaply. It cost you plenty to learn it. Charge a fair price if you charge.

8. Keep your mouth shut. Don't talk about what your clients tell you and what is confidential information. Before long, nobody will tell you anything and you will stop learning.

9. Listen. Half the time your clients just need somebody to talk to. Most of them will solve their own problems if they get a little moral support from you. They probably don't need a forecast as much as the hand holding.

10. Share what you know with others trying to learn. It keeps astrology vital into the future. It is your gift to the world.

These aren't the only rules, just a few of the big ones.

Chapter 44

Tidbits and Aphorisms
Some Common Sense Answers

Until a child takes an independent breath it has no individual life—it is merely living as part of the mother's life. You can't do a chart on an individual until he or she is born. You can do a horary, asking about the birth of the fetus, or an election chart, if a Caesarian birth is planned, but you can't do a valid birth chart before that first breath occurs.

Don't check your chart constantly. It is not meant to replace your legs or your common sense but to help you over the rough spots and provide a road map for travel.

Learning what rules what is one of the most important things you can do to be a good astrologer. It's useless to do a horary chart for a lost object if you use the wrong house. Only one works for most items—the 2nd house of possessions. Of course, there is also the 3rd house which rules cars, the 4th, which rules houses and the 6th of pets. If you are a farmer with horses or cattle you might need to use the 12th, but any possessions which can be picked up belong in the 2nd house. You can, however, use the derived house system, explained elsewhere, for the possessions of others.

There is no such thing as a sexual relationship between mere friends. Once two people take their clothes off the friendship has changed from an 11th house matter to the 5th house one of relationships with lovers. If the two get around to marrying things change again, and go from the 5th house to the 7th house of partnerships. It never returns to the 11th house. If they end the sexual affair or any subsequent marriage their relationship becomes a 12th house matter of the past. Sex does change things. No matter how people "feel" about each other, you can't answer questions until you clarify their actual relationship.

A person who can hire or fire you is never a 6th house person, such as a co-worker or subordinate. The role is a 10th house one, no matter what term they use at a particular company or how congenial the relationship may be. A boss is a boss is a boss.

Law in the abstract may be a 9th house study but lawyers are 7th house people who are professional consultants. Judges are 10th house authorities who decide the outcomes of legal matters. The 8th house deals with financial settlements in the case of lawsuits and insurance claims.

Pets never become "children," no matter how doting the owner is or what the owner thinks or if he or she calls the pet "baby." Pets are 6th house creatures that make our lives more comfortable or pleasurable. The only way they become any part of the 5th house is if the owner breeds pets as a hobby or shows them in the ring. The pet itself stays as a 6th house creature but the breeding and showing hobby can be a 5th house interest. If money is exchanged for them or earned by them it becomes a part of House 6, 7 or 11, depending on how intensely involved the individual is. House 6 produces side income from a hobby, in jobs anyone can do, House 7 reflects money from the sale of the animal and House 11 is money from one's livelihood or from a career that requires training.

Children of the body are 5th house. Adopted children may be 11th house until the adoption becomes legal, when they are henceforth 5th house persons. All children of other parents belong to the 11th house. It is the house of step-children.

When in doubt about what planet rules anything, think it through, using the basic nature of the planet. Jupiter is anything that gets larger or increases. Saturn is anything that shrinks or condenses. Venus is sweetness, Mars is sour, hot or angry. Mercury is whatever has elements of any two contrasting things, such as androgyny or salt and pepper. Neptune hides, Uranus reveals and Pluto just likes the mystery of it all. The Sun is warmth and light, the Moon is nurture and nature. Those are fundamental qualities that never fail to steer you right.

Astrology is a forecasting tool. Anybody who tells you differently doesn't know anything about astrology and probably can't forecast either.

There are a great many specialties in astrology. Make use of the referral system if someone wants information you don't have. This is particularly important with health and money matters.

If you don't know something, it's OK to say so. Nobody knows it all.

There is no such thing as a "quantum leap" in astrology to help you instantly understand a chart. It's a slow, hard slog and if you get to a point where every chart you pick up means something and tells you a story, then you are there. You can only get better after that, but you don't get to leapfrog over the work and reach astrology "heaven" immediately.

Don't make public predictions unless you are dead sure of the birth data. You always end up with egg on your face when the forecast goes wrong and you find out the real time and it wasn't the one you used. It's a law of the universe.

All things being equal, never expect people born under the mutable signs to stand up for you when you get in trouble. Pisces and Sagittarius people vote with their feet and the Gemini and Virgo types stand back to see if you need to talk things through. If you need somebody to guard your back, get a fixed sign person. There is nothing as comforting as a Scorpio, Leo, Taurus or Aquarius in the crunch. Meanwhile, find a Libra to start defusing trouble, a Capricorn to provide the serious social or legal clout, the Cancer to find a few bucks you need and the Aries to guard the door.

Enemies have two houses, the 7th of "open" antagonists and the 12th of "hidden" or unknown ones. House 7 enemies are known to one, or step forward boldly to confront us. House 12 produces the sneak attack, the burglar in the house or the person who operates under cover.

All tools of any sort are Mars ruled. Guns, from derringers to cannons on ships and planes are Mars instruments. So are frying pans that get hot and furnaces in the basement that warm the house in winter. Isn't it amusing that one of the slang words for armaments is "heat"?

Anything that cools or chills us or the house comes under Saturn. That includes air conditioning in house or car, fans and ventilation systems. Above all it is ice. Ice can be cubes in drinks or actual large hunks of ice which were once used in the "ice boxes" of long ago to provide refrigeration for food.

Chapter 46

Terms That Mean the Same

The **birth** chart or **natal** chart is the same thing as the **radix** chart. The study of natal charts is sometimes called **genethliacal** astrology. A chart is **radical** if it pertains to the natal chart. Occasionally in horary work a question is called "radical" because some of the planetary positions or angles match those in the natal chart of the person who asks a question. In a chart comparing aspects by progressed planets to natal the natal ones the natal positions are referred to as "radical."

The **Moon's nodes** are sometimes called the **Dragon's Head** (the **North** Node) and the **Dragon's Tail** (the **South** Node). Sometimes the nodes are called **Draco**, the Latin word for dragon, or simply **The Dragon**. *Caput* is the Latin word for head and *cauda* is the Latin word for tail. So, you will occasionally see *Caput Dragonis* (head of the dragon) or *Cauda Dragonis* (tail of the dragon) used in older books.

Sun and **Moon** can be called **planets** (even though they aren't planets) or **stars** (even though the Moon isn't a star) or the **Lights**. They can also be referred to by their Latin names, *Sol* and *Luna*

Moon also may be referred to in some older books as **Diana** (who was the goddess of the Moon in the Greek mythology). Moon is feminine in the west, but in some parts of the world is considered masculine. It is a satellite of the earth and not a planet at all. It does not have any energy of its own.

Sun is sometimes called **Apollo** after the ancient Greek name of the god said to drive the chariot of the Sun and is masculine in the west but feminine in some eastern traditions. The Sun is actually a star and gives off its own energy.

Mutable signs Virgo, Sagittarius, Pisces and Gemini are also referred to as common signs.

Cardinal signs Aries, Cancer, Libra or Capricorn can occasionally be called **changeable** or **moveable** signs.

The **Part of Fortune** may also be termed *Pars Fortuna*. Or even simply *Fortuna,* **Fortune** or *Pars*.

The **150 degree** aspect between two planets is an **inconjunct** or a **quincunx.**

The **square** and the **quadrature** are the same thing, a 90-degree aspect.
The **sesqui-square** and **sesqui-quadrature** are the same thing—the 135-degree aspect.

Partile means an aspect is **perfect** or **exact** to the degree.

The Antiscion or (plural **Antiscia**) is the same thing as the **reflex point** or **solstice point**.

To find the solstice point of anything, imagine the zodiac as a rubber band stretched between 0 Cancer and 0 Capricorn. Points opposite each other are solstice points. An example is 2 Cancer which is opposite 28 Gemini. 14 Cancer is opposite 16 Gemini. 2 Gemini is opposite 28 Cancer.

A point 45 degrees from Cancer on one side is 15 Leo. Opposite Leo 45 degrees from 0 Cancer on the other side will be 15 Taurus. All the fixed signs have their solstice points in other fixed signs and this has sometimes been thought to account for the power which planets in the middle of the fixed signs have. Cardinal signs have their solstice points in the mutable signs and vice versa.

Chapter 47

Dealing with Problems

Raising a child with a Pisces Moon is a fearful responsibility. They are so sensitive and loving and will try so hard to please that any lack of positive response is devastating to them.

A child with a Pisces Moon who accidentally got a cross word in childhood can spend an hour weeping. I kid you not. A frown from mother is a big deal. It meant the child had failed somehow. A child with a Pisces Moon can be an absolutely wonderful, happy child who will do anything asked of him or her and can learn so fast it is scary. They are very easy to raise. But handle with care.

It makes me sick when I think of Pisces Moon children without a good upbringing or good parenting who grow up with that walloping sensitivity. They can absorb the negative and the sad and the frightening just as fast.

When someone with a Pisces Moon tells me he or she doesn't "feel" any of the lighter, happier, joyous emotions easily, I grieve. It means —to me, at least— that somewhere along the line he or she learned not to have them. It means the lonely, sad emotions were learned instead. Pisces Moon people just pick up on everything.

All watery Moons can be highly sensitive. Cancer and Scorpio are a bit sturdier than Pisces, however. Scorpio has the benefit of a Mars boost to toughness and will fight back, not always wisely but too well. Cancer timidity and fears can be outgrown or defended with that hard shell. But the child with the Pisces Moon seems to come into life with "marshmallow" written on the forehead.

Over the years I think the one unalterable fact I have learned in astrology is that all the problems people have stem from not getting enough love and not learning how to love others. Out of that comes more grief and pain than anything else I know.

Why don't people give their children all the love their arms can hold? I don't know. I wish I could change the world, but all I can change is me. Frankly, me is a big enough challenge and I am nowhere near succeeding with that one.

When the chips are down...

For the best all-around help in a crisis situation, give me a Gemini or Virgo Sun native with a good strong Mars any day of the week. Those Mercury-ruled folks are always thinking, even in the crunch. Or, especially in the crunch. It is no coincidence that many

Virgo Sun natives end up in the medical field where a crisis-an-hour can happen. Mars in either of the two signs is a good indicator of being able to deal with emergencies in a hurry.

Mars in Gemini thrives on pressure and can deal with a sudden, overwhelming need for speed to get out of trouble (you see this one in the charts of a lot of race drivers, air traffic controllers and media types with deadlines for that reason). Mars in Virgo folks rarely lose their head when the going is tough and often apply logic to get out of trouble when other people are still too stunned to think.

Mars works so well because it sees any type of crisis as "threat, attack, danger" and responds instantly. Folks with angular Mars positions or rulership (Scorpio or Aries rising or as Sun signs) are really, really handy to have around at such times. However, speed belongs to Mercury.

People with a lot of water (except Scorpio) or earth and no real Mars power usually go into shock during a crisis and are absolutely useless. Sometimes they collapse and become secondary crises.

I remember talking to a professional Gemini photographer one day about some of his more interesting experiences. He told me how he dealt with one idiot at a rock concert in the '60s where his assignment was to take a picture for his newspaper. A large, intimidating man went bonkers (apparently on booze or drugs. That did happen sometimes at rock concerts), tried to grab his camera and punch him.

The Gemini only had one hand free and he certainly wasn't going to let go of his camera with the other, so he stuck his forefinger up the man's nose, practically lifting him off his feet and then moved away as soon as the other man let go of him. The aggressor collapsed like a wet balloon. A finger forced up your nose is extremely painful.

Gemini rules the hands, but not too many people would think of a finger defense like that one. Leave it to a Gemini.

Something Broken? Look for Virgo

There is nothing in life I so value as someone who can fix things since I don't have that talent. When my oldest Virgo Sun daughter left home after college, I thought, there go my repairs for the next zillion years.

Luckily, I had a second daughter with the Moon in Virgo who developed into a whiz at fixing almost anything. She kept me on the straight and narrow for a long time, repairing towel racks, leaky faucets and light fixtures. Whenever the two come back for visits they all but mow me down improving my life. Before long I will be so improved I will have to die of excessive perfection.

Sleeping Problems

Look to the 8th house for information on sleep and sleep-related disorders. Many teens in puberty or shortly after seem to crave sleep and I think it is connected to the hormones and endocrine system. Too much sleep is just as bad as not enough and both need attention.

While I have no medical training, I notice stress to the rulers of 8 or planets there often show up in sleep disorders. You should also look at Mars and Pluto, the Aries/Scorpio rulers. When you can't get out of bed, there is something wrong with the energy system and that is controlled to a large extent by the endocrine glands, which are—in turn—under Venus/Neptune. And Neptune appears to be in charge of the dreaming process.

Neptune is also involved when drugs, allergies and sensitivities of all sorts are causing problems. Toxins can come from the very air for people with hypersensitivities. All cases of abnormal sleep habits should go to a physician for analysis.

I remember reading about a case of a woman who suffered extreme fatigue who turned out to be allergic to just about everything in her environment and doctors required her to find a place where she was practically living in a bubble to begin healing. Sleep was her body's way of trying to heal itself. It was the body's cry for help, obviously.

A good internist should be consulted. Any allergy history might also be re-examined.

Psychic Talent

Water signs are naturally empathetic but the best psychic I ever met was a Leo. Fire Sun people are more intuitive than you think.

I collected several charts of psychics at one period and Sun signs varied completely. .The clearest "signature" was the house of the Moon. A 4th, 8th or 12th house Moon, in any sign, forming any aspect to Neptune or Pluto was psychic. Period.

Not all were professionals. One Virgo was spot on but you'd never get her to admit she could do it. A Libra with a zillion air planets was dynamite with Tarot and the Leo I mentioned (a professional) was remarkable. A Gemini palmist blew me away.

But when I could get the charts and especially if I got birth times, I always found the Moon business clearly operating.. Occasionally an angular Moon did not inhabit a water house but the power of angularity seemed to fill in the difference.

Many psychics have the water houses (4, 8, 12) occupied—some have all three with planets there. Planets in the water signs work well, too. Pisces is known for its hypersensitivity and Scorpio reacts to unseen danger instinctively. Cancer has a string attached to all its children and many are aware immediately if anything interrupts their child's well being.

Migraine Headaches

Migraines are the super headaches of the world and those afflicted with them can become highly sensitive to light, unable to eat and quite ill. The pain is severe. Some have to lie down or sleep until the headaches end because they are unable to function at all. There can be visual or auditory hallucinations or even vomiting.

Any planet or rising sign in Aries is vulnerable. The same is true of anyone with any planet in the first house. One Aries rising woman has to go to the hospital emergency room when she gets hers because nothing short of an opiate will help her. Luckily they don't come very often. A man with a rising Venus has suffered from them for years. He just goes to bed.

I have had a number of clients with migraine problems and there are obvious dietary links (afflicted Moons or the Moon square the ascendant, etc.) and stress on the rising degree or rising planet. Some problems seem tied to outright allergies when there are a preponderance of planets in the 6th.

One client with an Aries Sun was helped about 60 percent by some of the suggestions I made about diet but of course needed more help from a medical source and found a headache clinic that was a godsend to her. The charts I am most familiar with have Uranus or Mars tied to the Moon. Sometimes Mercury is linked to the rising planet or degree.

Diet and the links to Mars are easy to see. Mars foods like coffee or chocolate are known migraine triggers. Men tend to experience digestive upsets rather than the hormonal ones which women get.

Smoking, for instance, is also a Mars thing (all that smoke and fire goes in the mouth, you know) and those with migraines who stop smoking can find some relief. The tie to Uranus and the Moon shows the hormonal imbalances which can affect women. Three migraine charts I can think of offhand belong to women who have no children. Some women stop having migraines when they move into menopause.

One woman with the problem found what she called a new "miracle drug" for migraine sufferers. It was a prescription her doctor gave her. Modern medicine is a wonderful thing. She gets every symptom you can think of and a few more besides. If she has no access to her prescription medication when a migraine comes, a strong dose of codeine is the only thing that helps her.

Some of those with migraines also are lactose intolerant. That's also signified by the Moon. Lactose intolerance is probably behind the relief experienced by omitting dairy products from the diet. Again, cheese, a milk product, is one of those foods known to trigger migraines. Lactose intolerance seems most likely in fire Moons and the Moon in Capricorn, as well. It can sometimes show in Scorpio Moons.

All of this lunar contact also suggests a strong, emotional trigger to the migraines and I am sure that is part of the problem. We are all creatures of both body and soul and the interaction of emotions on the body has long been known to exist. Several people have told me their migraines followed periods of intense emotional stress.

Danger at the Track

Some years ago I was very interested in Formula One racing. I attended several of the races at Watkins Glen, NY, in the '60s and '70s before they moved out of that venue and even won a newspaper photography award for a photo I took of a win during my journalism days. The flagman was leaping into the air waving the checkered flag as the winning car went by in a blur apparently right under his feet. It wasn't really that close, but the photo turned out great.

Since I am not an experienced photographer, and had only an old, borrowed camera without a flash, and was pushing between ranks of pros with fancy equipment and made the shot from down on my knees with my eyes closed because I got jabbed with an elbow at the last minute, it was clearly a miracle picture. Nonetheless, I got an Inland Daily Press award for it and my photography friends called it sheer dumb luck. They were right, of course, but I remain smug about it to this day.

Anyway, I wondered about racing accidents and began amassing a lot of birth data on then-active top drivers. I used some of the Indy car drivers but generally only those who were well known in both Europe and the U.S. All I had were dates, so I calculated simple solar charts using noon positions.

One year, in the '70s—I forget which—my husband had asked me if Jackie Stewart would win the race at Watkins Glen, NY. I told him that I thought it would be Stewart's last race there and that he would probably win or die trying. It was meant as a flip remark, but I was serious in telling him that I thought Stewart's career as a driver was about to end.

I couldn't go that year but my husband was there in New York when one of Stewart's teammates crashed and died during practice runs on the course. Stewart withdrew from the race and a few months later announced his retirement.

Stewart, a Gemini, became quite well known later on as a racing commentator on TV, but he never raced at Watkins Glen again after that year. Eventually racing grew more safety conscious and some things changed. Formula One races were no longer held at that course.

Anyway, I began studying the solar charts of all the drivers living or dead that I could acquire and spotted something that was very significant. All those who had serious, life-threatening accidents had malefics with the south node. Mars, Saturn and Uranus were the keys. They were usually conjunct that point. Mars and Uranus would bring the accidents and Saturn, the damage. I did not find Pluto or Neptune very often so I suspect that when they were involved, it was more incidental.

If one planet was involved, there was an accident and serious injury. Two was danger of death and all three were surely death. They could be square the nodes, but if so, that was accidents too, but not always death. Contacts to the North Node alone seem to be more forgiving, There were miraculous escapes, or fast healing, or the right doctor at hand when needed. Conjunctions to the south node were deadly.

After I was done with my study, I made a list of drivers with terrible patterns that I feared would die in accidents. There were five names on the list. All died later in racing accidents. Some drivers had only good contacts to the nodes and they retired happily and safely. Stewart had good natal contacts, but during the year in question Saturn was transiting his south node making an aspect to his Mars and I was greatly relieved when he quit. He became a leader in the movement for track safety, though, and today's drivers are the beneficiaries. Another interesting thing I saw when I did the driver charts was the prominence of Venus—and of course, all the charts I did were those of men who made a very good living indeed. Some were quite wealthy and collected art or were even artists themselves. Venus always shows.

I lost interest in sports car racing as the years went on, so I have no data on current drivers any more, but for those interested in the safety issue, I would say look to the nodal contacts.

Planets for Astrologers

I have found Jupiter prominent as often in the charts of professional (not amateur) astrologers as Uranus, because so many of us write, teach, publish, travel, and lecture.

I also have quizzed most of the pros I know about having a Moon/Uranus and Sun/Uranus aspect and most of them have both. They don't have to be just "good" aspects—any strong one will do. The Moon is necessary because you can't stand up in public and say, "I am an astrologer," unless you are willing to be seen as somewhat "different" and the Sun refers to the career of all of us in some way.

I think Jupiter is a big help in dealing with the culture as well, since it and Saturn are both planets of social consciousness. Let's face it—if you want to be a professional astrologer, you are likely to be regarded as a bit odd. It helps to have Jupiter on your side.

I have had students who fully intended to become professional but who somehow never did—they lacked either the Moon/Uranus contact or the Sun/Uranus. One student with no Moon/Uranus contact just couldn't bring herself to tell her friends that she was an astrologer. She could call it her hobby, but she said she just couldn't wear the "professional" label.

Mercury is usually strong. I suspect most people will never "get it" in this field or like it sufficiently well to do the work it takes to get good at it. One man told me once he thought someone had to have a 12-track mind to do astrology. The best astrologers usually have a very good intellect.

Other planets can also show strongly. Neptune is called the old soul and I think many interested in astrology intensely relate to the planet, and Pluto is the sleuth who digs for the real reasons people do what they do.

If astrologers got rich, they would also have strong Venus positions, but I don't know any rich astrologers. Some nice ones, but no rich ones. If they are, I suspect it's because they did something else to get rich.

The "Elite" Corps

When it comes to groups one of the most common aberrations is the notion that there is an elite group among mankind and that "we" belong to it or someone else does. This, of course, gives people in such groups the right—indeed, the obligation— therefore, to make decisions for others. They know they make the best decisions and they should do it just to save society from the ignorance of the rest of us. They operate under all kinds of guises—from the food police to the fashionistas.

It doesn't matter whether it's a religious group (almost every church is full of elite-ness), a political group, a social group or an esoteric "brotherhood" of some sort. It's always the same. "We" are the elite because "we" say so, or we are divinely ordained or we are the smartest, or "God told us so." etc. etc. Scientists are just as liable to this particular aberration as religious figures. The most educated among us, who should know better, often think that their very education makes them members of the (potentially ruling) elite and the one with the best degrees wins.

I strongly suspect this idea comes from an afflicted Sun. There is probably a square to Saturn and Jupiter may get a square from Pluto. The Sun rules power and our ability to affect our environment and impose our will on the world around us. It's "us" against "them" and unless we keep "them" under our control they will do bad things to "us." This can be mild or as extreme an opinion as that of Hitler's SS was. They were told –and believed— they were the elite.

This is the source of the urge to control others and manipulate the behavior of other people. It starts as fear. And of course, Saturn is the planet of both fear and control. Jupiter can be an over-inflated ego when it squares the Sun, thus justifying one's "elite-ness," but with any good aspects Jupiter may not do any real harm. A Pluto aspect seems to intensify it, providing confirmation for the opinion and tempting one down a primrose path.

The "elite" idea has been around for every generation. Isn't it interesting that there is truly no new idea under the Sun?

No Angels, Thanks

I have the same problem with "angelic sources" as I do with astrological readings based on "past lives" which nobody can confirm and psychic sources. They are all so much Moon-shine to me without some sort of concrete evidence. I really don't think we should let people (and I include Max Heindel, founder of the Rosicrucians) snooker us or the public.

Back in the 1950s when I was learning astrology, I read his notion that the planets Uranus, Neptune and Pluto were somehow "octaves" of the planets Mercury, Venus and Mars.

Now as a parent, you can't convince me that any child born is an "octave" of an earlier child. Every child is a unique individual, totally him or herself. There's no such thing as octaves except in music.

So I wrote to the Rosicrucians and asked where he got this notion and what research he used and could I study it, too. I got a rather snippy letter back saying that he was already dead and as far as they knew, there was no research available, but that he obviously had "his own sources of information." In other words, he made it up.

When I was teaching some students used to ask me in class, "What about past lives. Don't you get into that?" I would always explain my belief that studying the birth chart would explain events in this life quite clearly without the use of unsubstantiated esoteric ideas. Past lives might be true (or not) but information about them was irrelevant, unnecessary and mostly without actual evidence anyway.

Astrologers who spend half their time in readings discussing nebulous past lives only convince me that it's a) a snow job by b) somebody who doesn't know enough real astrology to read the birth chart otherwise.

If Max Heindel started his whole octave thing because the angels told him so or he had a psychic flash, he did a disservice to astrology, in my opinion. The octave notion is hog wash. I've heard it repeated for years by people who should know better. We have enough battles to fight without explaining the delivery of inside information via special visitations from on high. And that goes for past life discussions, too.

Inadequate research is one thing. No research is something else. I have several books on the meaning of the degrees of the zodiac but only one of them is based on any sort of research by the author. One is from psychic impressions and two don't say how they got their information. More angels?

Please don't misunderstand me. I personally might believe in angels and past lives and lots of other things. But there is a big difference between beliefs and practical knowledge that can be verified. Yes, I know we're talking interpretation of abstract patterns, but we have to have some sort of standard for the information we use and base our work on. I believe in reading charts from this lifetime and I believe there is no such thing as octaves of the planets.

And angels don't do it for me, either.

Lies We Tell

One kind of lying is lying to oneself. It's called rationalization, telling yourself that a situation is the way you want it to be no matter what it really is, or that you did something for a good and noble reason when either the reason was selfish or bad and you just don't want to admit it. For rationalization, look to Mercury square Neptune.

Another kind of lie is done out of fear, usually of getting in trouble if you tell the truth. Here you should look to Mercury square Saturn and with a tie to the Moon—any aspect, as long as it links the Moon to the Mercury/Saturn affliction. If one of them is in 12 or two are in the 3/9 axis, it may be practically a way of life.

A third kind of lie is the one which comes out of too casual an approach to the truth—sort of like the people who never let the facts get in the way of a good story. For them, it's a Mercury/Jupiter square. Sometimes they are just excessively hopeful that all will turn out well, so they exaggerate the truth with the Mercury/Jupiter square. This is one that Sagittarians can fall into rather readily.

Bias or prejudice, is usually fear and rigidity—Mercury in a fixed sign, such as Taurus, for instance, and squared to Saturn or Neptune.

Not everyone who has these aspects will lie. The same aspects that make for imagination and the charts of fiction writers may contain them. Mercury/Saturn squares are common in depression, for instance, as well as math and communication skills. Mercury/Neptune aspects add to musical ability. However, people who get depressed or lie to themselves don't want to accept the truth about something and people who live in pretend worlds don't want to live in the real one.

It's never a good idea to kid yourself or others. The same stresses that lead to lies can produce ill health as a result. Life is the fine art of taking our lemons and making lemonade—and that means the truth, no matter how sour in the beginning, can be a very good thing after all. Especially when the going gets tougher. The tendencies show up most clearly in the squares, but the conjunctions and oppositions and semi-squares will have them, too.

But I hope my caveat is clear. I am talking about tendencies. Old people have a tendency to fall asleep in their chair in the afternoon if nobody is around and it's been a hectic morning, but most probably wouldn't do it if someone were visiting.

As always, you have to look at the whole pattern, and if you are reading for someone who is telling you about a problem, you'd better know about it. It may warn you that you need to ask some probing questions to make sure you get the whole truth about the situation.

There are many Neptunian types who are not liars, and many Saturn/Mercury squares who tell the truth. But—and it is a big but—when you see these aspects you know there is a tendency. You need to consider the entire chart for clear judgment.

No single aspect is responsible for all the choices we make as human beings—whether it's lying or any other unpleasant option. We ourselves are responsible for our choices. People with Neptune rising and under stress often just suffer confusion between what they wish were true and what is.

There are many aspects that can counterbalance any harsh indicator, but unless we know what the indications are, we will never be able to reach the point of being able to make sense of any chart. Too many textbooks go all lofty and psychological when what you really need to know is will this person rip you off or can you trust what they say.

Places on Earth

When you travel, aside from the obvious look at tourist info, check the birth charts of the places that interest you and see where your Venus and Jupiter fall and where their Venuses and Jupiters fall. One or the other places may have strong contacts to your birth chart, or that of your travel partner, making it a good choice for you.

Venus brings pleasure and Jupiter brings protection. Those are good things to plan for. If you are looking for a possible residential change, look at Moon lines and Moon contacts.

Your Saturn conjunct a place's key planets could bring you problems or a desire for permanency there. Unless you're positive you want to stay, don't go to a Saturn location. You'll have a hard time leaving or you will experience things that are disappointing.

Another way to check your destination would be to study your Astro*Carto*Graphy map or a locational one if your computer program will do it and see where your natal lines fall.

Look again to the benefics and chart ruler for contacts. If you see a major problem—

like Pluto or a malefic on an angle—skip that place. Go elsewhere unless you like to live dangerously. But if you run into trouble there, remember I told you so.

A Question of Secrets

One of the problems with exoteric vs esoteric knowledge is the times we live in. A thousand years ago knowledge we consider "common" today was kept carefully hidden except to initiates of various disciplines. The movement of the planets was very esoteric or "hidden."

When I held my first seminar on astrology in 1974, one of the old time astrologers who came (bless his heart, he's long dead now) was horrified that I was giving out all that good information and telling students the truth and answering all questions freely.

His approach to astrology was to teach only enough to whet the student's appetite and to actually give wrong information on many occasions. If the student was smart enough to question it, he/she got the right answer. Otherwise, the student was too dumb for astrology. It was his way of keeping astrology hidden. He was doing his best to protect what he considered a noble study that you had to earn the right to share. He saw it as an esoteric discipline.

I was horrified by his approach because when I was young, my parents felt that if I were smart enough to ask the question I was smart enough to get the answer. I grew up taking it as the norm.

In many times and places, the actual motion of the planets, the cycles of eclipses (the Saros cycle is a prime example) and other "ordinary" information was considered too important to give out. And an ephemeris that just anyone could go and buy? Be real!

Some of this was ignorance, of course. Nobody wanted everybody else to realize how little they were sure of, but much of it was an actual attitude about the sacred science of the stars, as it was known.

Today we live in the information age and all information is freely available. We think that if you seek, you should find. We see information as the building blocks of the world. Part of this is our scientific approach—facts simply are, and what's such a big deal about that?

Part of this also is the waning of the days when religious or political groups could outlaw information that they found uncomfortable, or that threatened their domains in some way. The biggest thing destroying it (it all started with Gutenberg and the advent of the printing press, you know) is the arrival of the telephone and computer technology which has made possible the Internet.

Now, almost all of what we know is exoteric—open, available to all for the asking. I exclude here, for the moment, the kinds of information politicians and governments may seek to suppress for political reasons. It's fairly obvious that much "official" information is skewed by the time it gets to the public.

Is there still an esoteric?

Some people think that psychic perceptions and so-called "channeled" information is esoteric. It isn't. It is merely another type of exoteric astrology, freely available. You can buy the books. You can read the material. You can hire a psychic. You can write books about it.

What then, is esoteric astrology? One astrologer I know is convinced that a hidden mathematical configuration will explain to him why people win lotteries. Another man thinks a mathematical principle is behind the secret of planetary movement. Is this esoteric? It is today. Tomorrow it may be exoteric.

Any time research "reveals" a truth unknown up to that time, esoteric becomes transformed into exoteric.

I repeat the question—is there still any esoteric knowledge? My answer is yes, there is. It is all around us, in every chart we study. It is the magic of reality. It's the mystery at the heart of existence. It's the hidden hand of the Creator. The esoteric needs no defense. Those who might misuse it, can't see it anyway. You can lay it right out in front of them, and they go whippoorwill-ing off after some pipedream.

The secret is this: The esoteric is "Why Things Happen." The longer I am in astrology, the more I see the ultimate answers go glimmering off into the distance and we who want to know are still in the hunt. It looks like it will go on a long time.

Good and Bad Descriptions

A lot of what the old-timers wrote was not solely intended for personality analysis but some of it certainly was. We have to remember that horoscopes for ordinary people are really a modern conceit. In the old days, only rulers and potential rulers were considered important enough to have their own charts constructed.

One comment I stumbled into out of old literature, that Aquarians "hate" their families is very nearly so, in my experience. Most Aquarians decide exactly which members of their families they like and are sympathetic to and ignore the rest. To all intents and purposes, they give themselves the liberty to "divorce" the ones they consider idiots and fools.

They can also be remarkably callous and undiscerning about the needs of people in their families, to the point of causing pain—which they also don't see— and in the old days I suppose that seemed like hate. Aquarians often like working in metal and hard things—a lot of invention involves machinery, right? This sign is highly scientific. That struck people in other eras as a symptom of cold-bloodedness.

I have found Aquarians the most personally private of all the signs—far more so than much maligned Scorpio, which will be quite blunt about itself when it trusts you.

The old timers also called Aquarians impious, scoffers without faith. Certainly by the old standards that was probably true. Most of them whom I know will only trust a religion that is reasonably logical. That didn't exactly wash in medieval times when you were supposed to believe blindly or be socially excluded and considered heretical. There were even eras when that was dangerous.

Aquarians love to poke pins in egos, things and ideas they consider inflated. They are first class iconoclasts. It is definitely a barren sign and one of the best for pulling jokes and people's noses when the Moon is there.

I think there are many reasons for some of the descriptions given in these old texts, and it is necessary to sort them out. Not all are meant to apply to people. Some were instructions for weather interpretation, or crop lore or the like. I also think that we spend much too much time giving all the signs sweet little New Age credit for nothing but good. Most textbooks practically canonize Aquarians unfairly. There are a lot of bad eggs out there— and they are bad in the ways of their own signs. If you don't know what those are, you can really miss the boat. Hitler, for instance, was not just a dear little flower-smelling Taurus.

But that's another story.

The Magi

Brace yourselves for a bit of poetic feeling. I'm in the mood.

It seems to me that all astrologers around the world should pay special attention to the feast of the Epiphany—or the Three Kings, as it is called in some parts of the world..

The tale of the Magi who came to see the child whose birth they had predicted is not only the most famous story of an astrological forecast, but the only one I know of from ancient times. Some may know of others, but this one is familiar everywhere the New Testament is read. You don't have to be a Christian to appreciate it.

I for one plan to pay a lot more attention January 6 to the notion that my astrological forebears went on a long journey on camels across the desert thousands of years ago just to see how their forecast turned out. I'm not sure I would drive to Toledo in my well-heated car for that! (Toledo isn't far from me—couple hours by turnpike. Piece of cake.)

Anyway, this year I plan to light my own little candle to remember those guys who validated our profession so well.

Dang, don't you wish you'd been there? Smelly camels aside, think of the adventure of it. Tents in the desert. The sound of wolves, perhaps. The wind blowing. Dates in your pocket for a snack while the camel rocks away the miles. The chilly stars at night. A whole sky full of them that we barely see in our smog and light-filled modern world.

Servants brewing that hot glue they call coffee in the dawn—the sky streaky red and gold, and off across the dim horizon a child they think will change the world.

Wow. Such pictures I get.

Chapter 48

Destiny and Free Will

There is a modern tendency to see the birth pattern in strictly psychological terms and describe the life experiences in terms of the internal change the individual undergoes. The ancients saw astrology as the story of events and how one faced one's life, both the good and the bad challenges, decided the issue of 'fate.'

The truth, I think, lies in the middle.

There are many things in each life that cannot be changed. We are born to parents at a time and place we did not choose. We did not choose those parents. We arrived in a package of sex (later surgeries don't count), size, and coloration of skin, hair and eyes. Some of us spend a lot of time altering those parameters as we age. Each body has areas of strength and weakness we didn't opt for but are stuck with. We can't change what we were given, only try to modify it with diet, proper care, cosmetics, dye and the like.

The births of siblings, the timing of a father's job or a mother's emergency surgery are not within our control. Grandparents die no matter how we might want to change it. Companies we work for go out of business. Government programs we had no hand in choosing help us or hinder us. In short, a great many events on every native's time-line are inescapable. The astrologer can see accidents coming, times of illness, job change and the like.

But living is not so much what we face as how we react to a particular happening and the inner road we choose to grow and develop as human beings. Joining the human race at birth does not give us unlimited options of the road we will travel. If we are going to Chicago that's where the car is going and the birth chart can show how we travel, how fast and where the detours will be. But who we will be when we get to Chicago is always within our choice.

There is a very old saying that "the stars impel, but do not compel." That means we were born with a tendency toward certain patterns of behavior. If we drift through life, not bothering to analyze where we are headed, we may take the path of least resistance and see all events as destined and out of our control. But if we examine our selves we may find many things we can alter, improve, upgrade and modify.

We just can't do that to everything. Are we "pressured" by the planetary energies? Of course we are. Are we locked in to catastrophe? Maybe. We are the product of the time and place in which we are born. If that time period includes a world war, a depression, a tsunami which hits our village all we can do is cope and develop the inner strength to deal with such events.

We choose many things in life.
We just don't choose everything.

Chapter 49

The Road Most Traveled
The Esoteric Path?

There is no truly esoteric or "hidden" path to wisdom, in my humble opinion. This may be a shock to you. There is only **one** path and we are all on it. It has many names and fits them all. It is so wide and broad that we may think our particular part of it is unique or some other part is hidden or better. Or, perhaps, worse.

It isn't.

The path is the all-inclusive journey of everything that was created from its beginning back to its source. It is circular, so the route is pretty simple. It goes from A to A.

There are many among the wise who have differing opinions on the purpose of the journey. Most of them believe we are happily gathering experiences for the pleasure of the One from Whom we all come, and that we return joyously to our reunion with hands full of souvenirs and spiritual home movies.

Perhaps that is an over-simplification, but perhaps also we are making this understanding unnecessarily difficult. Maybe we're just doing this for the fun of it.

As do all journeys, this one goes through a wide array of scenery with many pit stops and side excursions along the way. We are at liberty to make any selections on how we travel, from a high-speed pursuit of the end to a slow and gradual ramble or even a quick start and stop, with many reverses to avenues of interest. We are free to stay anywhere a long time or a short time, but certainly as long as we choose to.

If we enjoy melodrama, dressing up in costumes and exchanging "secrets" with each other, that, too, is allowed. This confuses many who think there really is a secret.

Any part of the trip may be described or given a label by anyone. All such descriptions are bound to be right about something because the path includes everything anyway and sooner or later all the conditions are met and experienced. You can't possibly lose.

Few of us are on the same portion of the road at any given moment. Thus, each of us sometimes appears to be traveling a separate way. In fact, we are following the footsteps of many who have trampled the soil flat for our convenience. We will be followed by others in their turn so it behooves us to leave the place tidy as we pass by.

Many people think there are short cuts and try them. They are usually wrong and find only dead ends, but the experience itself is part of the journey.

Some look for inns along the way, pleasant places to stay and enjoy themselves for a while. They can do this all they want. Usually some unexpected event will prompt them to leave and resume their trek (if sheer boredom doesn't do it after a while), but meanwhile they may mistakenly think they have found the final answer and that those who continue to toil past laboriously are missing the point.

Some folks set themselves up as authorities and attempt to exact tolls on their portion of the road. The wise merely smile and step aside and keep on going. There are endless curb lanes for such purposes. The wise make use of them. The credulous may need the experience of dealing with toll takers.

There are a number of structured tracks along the way. We may follow any of them we choose or for as long as we believe they take us in the right direction. They are like buses going part of the way to where we wish to be. We may need a transfer to a new route after a while, of course.

Some of these tracks are labeled religion, or the esoteric (I know, I know, I just told you it wasn't real—but, some folks think it is.), science, art, or community service, business or the professions. Some might be physical achievements, such as sport or dance, or creative ones such as music or sculpture. Any track which fosters the growth required to help us continue along the road is a good thing. Some tracks merely have better reputations than others and those who travel them sometimes seem to be credited with more prestige as a result.

Should a strip tease artist who finds a key to truth be considered less accomplished than a hermit who finds the same key? No, but the monk probably gets better press releases. All parts of the road, however, are valid. All insights, lessons and growth are valid.

As the road begins to climb, it can dismay some travelers who may need to do some spiritual training exercises in order to cope with the new demands of the altitude. When it dips, and goes into dark valleys of the soul, some travelers may despair and try to turn back or follow what they believe to be other paths, blaming themselves for taking wrong turns or making errors.

But those farther on, then, we are say that following the rise and fall of the road is required of us. It's part of the journey to face such challenges. And what's more, when we have done this successfully and begun to think we are actually getting somewhere, we usually have to keep stopping because of the increasing number of distractions.

The distractions most often involve other people who need some form of help. They may need help understanding where they are going or a strong arm for part of the way or some of our spiritual "cash" in the form of encouragement or comforting to continue their own journey. Sometimes their needs, while serious, seem to have little to do with our own trip at all. We may spend so much of our time helping others that we may even despair of making further progress of our own. We find we may have to shelve our personal preferences in order to be useful to our fellow man.

But such distractions are also part of the path. Only by bringing others with us do we continue forward. There is no loss of progress when we stop to help a friend. "Service to others" is one of the main steps along the road after a certain point for all travelers. To ignore it is to miss the message.

At various points we need to reassess the baggage we are carrying. Some of us are carrying more than we need in our knapsacks. Not all of it is useful. As we go on, we learn to get by with less and less. Pretty soon we leave behind most of what we thought was so necessary once upon a time. We just get tired of carrying it and it really doesn't serve us any more. At some point we walk away from it all and like Gandhi, settle for a bowl and a spoon and sometimes we even forget those.

Some people think we aren't able to follow the road from start to finish in a single lifetime. They think we apparently need to refresh ourselves with new vehicles—bodies—periodically. In each lifetime it takes a while to get back "on track" but those who have the goal clearly in mind are quicker to do so than others, they say. They could be right. It certainly explains a lot about why some of us catch on quicker than others.

There are many pleasant lanes to investigate. There are also less pleasant ones, which seem to go a long way and often appear to be those I referred to as apparent "short cuts." They wear many labels—sex, violence, warfare, intellectual development, scientific achievement, psychic powers, magical mystery shows and the like.

Follow any that appeal to you. They may or may not be fruitful. You'll find out, anyway, after a while. Usually the sheer discomfort of a wrong choice puts us back on the right footing eventually.

The Hindu holy book the *Bhagavad Gita* says that whether one follows the route of meditation or intellectual development or devotion or right action to the goal, after a while it merges with the others anyway. One fiction writer even titled a book, *Everything That Rises Must Converge*. I've always thought that writer knew something. It seems that all areas of the road begin to appear the same beyond a certain point.

There are only very simple rules on the road no matter what anyone tells you. If they weren't simple, it wouldn't be fair, and it is always fair since we are all intended to make the journey successfully. This is not always understood by those who hold themselves up as the authorities and toll takers, but in the end, their opinion doesn't matter anyway. We are all expected to make the trip, so it has to have simple rules that everyone can grasp.

Here they are:

Love the creator or your version of the Ultimate Good or the Divine Light
(whatever you call Him, Her, or It) as much as you can and try to take care of
your neighbor on the path as well as you take care of yourself.

That's about it. Following the so-called Golden Rule to do unto others as you would have them do unto you is also a pretty good guide.

Complicated people think the path is complicated. But the farther you travel, the simpler it becomes. And simplicity is the mark of the experienced traveler.

**As for the esoteric "secret" that everyone is hunting for
and few really find, the secret is simply this...**

The truth of the Universe is Love, and light is everywhere. Ally yourself with it, and you have found the only true shortcut there is.

You can't ever get lost because you are already there. You can find guides along the way if you look for them. But they aren't really necessary. You contain within yourself the light that will lead you unerringly on, if you are honest about what it shows you.

No matter where you are, all you have to do is turn your face to that light and take a single step toward it.

All the rest will follow.

Bibliography

Note, some of these authors have many more books out than the one or two titles I have listed. All are worth exploring.

Adams, Evangeline, *Your Place Among The Stars*, 1933, Dodd, Meade Co., N. Y. N. Y.

Bills, Rex E., *The Rulership Book: A Directory of Astrological Correspondences*, Macoy Pub. & Masonic Supply Company, 1971

Blavatsky, Helen, *The Secret Doctrine*, 1888, The Theosophical Publishing Co. Ltd. London, England

Boehrer, Kt, *Declination, The Other Dimension*, 1984, Fortunata Press, El Paso, TX

Burgoyne, Thomas, *The Light of Egypt, Vol. 1 and 2* 1888 reprinted 1963, H. O. Wagner, Denver, CO.

Campion, Nicholas, *The Book of World Horoscopes*, 1996, Cinnabar Books, Wiltshire, England

Carter, C. E. O. , *Symbolic Directions*, 1947, Macoy Publishing, New York, N.Y. deVore, Nicholas, "Encyclopedia of Astrology," 1977, Littlefield, Adams & Co., Totowa, N. J.

Hammacher-Zondag, Karen, *The House Connection*, 1994, Samuel Weiser, New York, N. Y.

Jacobson, Ivy, *Horary Astrology*, 1935, Pasadena Lithographers, Pasadena, CA.

Jones, Marc Edmund, *Horary Astrology*, 1966 and *Sabian Symbols*, 1969, Sabian Publishing Co., Stanwood, Washington.

Koparkar, Mohan, *Moon Mansions*, 1974,

Lavoie, Alphee, *Lose This Book and Find It with Horary*, 1995 AFA, Tempe, Ariz., *Horary At Its Best*, 2002, AIR

Lewi, Grant, *Heaven Knows What*, 1935, Llewelyn, St. Paul, Minn., and *Astrology For the Millions*, 1969, Llewelyn, St. Paul, Minn.

Lineman, Rose, *Eclipses*, 1984, AFA, Tempe, AZ

Noonan, George, *Classical Scientific Astrology*, 1984, AFA, Tempe, AZ

Robson, Vivien, *Fixed Stars and Constellations*, 1923, Samuel Weiser, New York, N. Y. and *Electional Astrology*, 1972, Samuel Weiser, New York, N.Y.

Rudhyar, Dane, *The Lunation Cycle*, 1967, Llewelyn, St. Paul, Minn.

Watters, Barbara, *Horary Astrology And The Judgment of Events*, 1974, Valhalla.

Velikovsky, Immanuel, *Earth In Upheaval*, 1955, Doubleday, New York, N.Y.

Volguine, Alexandre, *The Technique of Solar Returns*, 1937, reprinted 1976 ASI Publishing, New York, N.Y.

About the Author

Pat Geisler began studying astrology in 1958, an era when astrology books were as foreign as gardening instruction on Mars, and read everything she could lay her hands on. It took her more than 6 months to teach herself to cast a chart with house cusp corrections using what few second-hand books she could find.

She began teaching, lecturing and consulting work in 1969 and put in nearly full time hours as the years went on, despite also working a full time job as a journalist.

In the newspaper field she earned awards at state and national levels for writing, editing and sports photography. She worked as reporter, copy editor, Metro editor and Sunday editor for her newspaper before retiring in 1996.

In astrology she taught non-credit astrology courses on two community college campuses, held seminars at two others and was active in private tutoring. She was among the first in the nation to teach courses on college campuses. She lectured everywhere she could find a podium, from state and national astrology groups to conferences abroad. She spoke at high schools, and to a wide array of civic and educational groups.

Her television and radio work was primarily in northern Ohio, where she was a regular on various programs. Her consulting practice was extensive and included many clients abroad.

She is a member of AFAN, NCGR and ISAR and served a term as a member of the national Steering Committee for AFAN. She also served on the UAC board for the Orlando conference in 2002. She was active in AFAN's mentoring program.

She is a widow with four accomplished children and five exceptional grandchildren. She lives near Grafton, Ohio.

Also from Starcrafts LLC
Imprints: *Starcrafts Publishing, ACS Publications*

All About Astrology, a series of booklets by various authors
The American Atlas, Expanded 5th Edition, Thomas G. Shanks

The American Ephemeris 1950-2050 [at Noon or at Midnight],
Trans-Century Edition, by Neil F. Michelsen and Rique Pottenger

The American Ephemeris for the 21st Century 2000-2050 [at Noon or at Midnight],
Revised & Expanded Third Edition, Neil F. Michelsen and Rique Pottenger

The American Heliocentric Ephemeris 2001-2050, Neil F. Michelsen
The American Sidereal Ephemeris 2001-2025, Neil F. Michelsen
Archetypes of Astrology, Ena Stanley
The Asteroid Ephemeris 1900-2050, Rique Pottenger with Neil F. Michelsen
Astrology for Career Success, Gayle Geffner
Astrology for the Light Side of the Brain, Kim Rogers-Gallagher)
Astrology for the Light Side of the Future, Kim Rogers-Gallagher)
Astrology: the Next Step, Maritha Pottenger
Astrology and Weight Control, Beverly Ann Flynn
The Book of Jupiter, Marilyn Waram
Dial Detective, Revised Second Edition, Maria Kay Simms
Easy Astrology Guide, Maritha Pottenger
Easy Tarot Guide, Marcia Masino
Future Signs, Maria Kay Simms
The International Atlas, Revised 6th Edition, Thomas G. Shanks & Rique Pottenger
The Michelsen Book of Tables, Neil F. Michelsen
Moon Tides, Soul Passages, Maria Kay Simms, with software CD by Rique Pottenger

The New American Ephemeris for the 20th Century, 1900-2000, at Midnight
Michelsen Memorial Edition, Rique Pottenger, based on Michelsen

The New American Ephemeris for the 20th Century, 1900-2000, at Noon
Michelsen Memorial Edition, Rique Pottenger, based on Michelsen

The New American Ephemeris for the 21st Century, 2000-2100 at Midnight
Michelsen Memorial Edition, Rique Pottenger, based on Michelsen

The New American Ephemeris for the 21st Century, 2007-2020:
Longitude, Declination, Latitude & Daily Aspectarian,
Rique Pottenger, based on Michelsen

The New American Midpoint Ephemeris 2007-2020,
Rique Pottenger, based on Michelsen

The Only Way to Learn Astrology, Volumes. 1-6 series
Marion D. March & Joan McEvers

Past Lives, Future Choices, Maritha Pottenger
Pathways to Success, Gayle Geffner
Planetary Heredity, Michel Gauquelin
Planets on the Move, Maritha Pottenger and Zipporah Dobyns, Ph.D.
Psychology of the Planets, Francoise Gauquelin
Spirit Guides, Iris Belhayes
Tables of Planetary Phenomena, Third Edition, Neil F. Michelsen
Unveiling Your Future, Maritha Pottenger and Zipporah Dobyns, Ph.D.
Yankee Doodle Discord: A Walk with Eris through USA History, Thomas Canfield
Your Magical Child, Maria Kay Simms
Your Starway to Love, Maritha Pottenger

All About Astrology Booklets

Ardor, Assertion & Anger: Mars in Your Chart   Maritha Pottenger

The Art of Chart Comparison
Maritha Pottenger

Ceres in Signs, Houses & Aspects
Simonne Murphy

Chiron in Houses, Signs & Aspects
Maritha Pottenger

Coalescent Horoscopes
Lawrence Grinnel (Dhruva) & David Dukelow

Complete Guide to Establishing a Professional Astrological Practice
Peggy Larson & Chris Rogers

The East Point & the Antivertex
Maritha Pottenger

Eris in Signs, Houses & Aspects
Thomas Canfield

History of the Planets   Robert Powell

History of the Houses   Robert Powell

Interpreting Composite & Relationship Charts   Joan Negus

Juno: Key to Marriage, Intimacy & Partnership   Maritha Pottenger

Search for the Christmas Star
Neil F. Michelsen and Maria Kay Simms

Transpluto David Dukelow and Dhruva

What are Astrolocality Maps?
Maritha Pottenger

What Astrology Can Do for You
Maritha Pottenger

What are Winning Transits? Joyce Wehrman

Wit & Wisdom: Mercury in your Chart
Maritha Pottenger

Your Love Life: Venus in Your Chart
Maritha Pottenger

The Zodiac: A Historical Survey
Robert Powell

www.astrocom.com

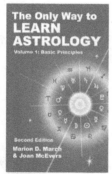
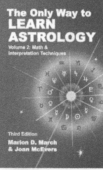
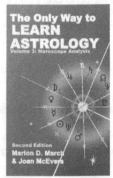

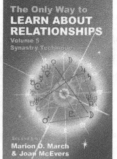
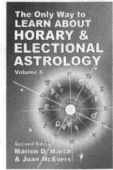

Prices subject to change without notice

Book, Report & Art   *Your Magical Child*

Magical Child astrology options for the nurturing of your children... or your inner child
Book, report and art by Maria Kay Simms

YOUR MAGICAL CHILD
Astrology for Nurturing
Your Child or Inner Child
Expanded 3rd Edition

Maria Kay Simms

Learn how each child is born with his or her own special magic in personality, style and talents. Discover how best you can assist his or her development of potential.
Your Magical Child book. **BYMC3 $19.95**

Your Magical Child Interpreted Report

It's a personalized report for any child's (or your own!) birth date, time and place. (Each of us has an "inner child" that sometimes needs nurturing and undertanding. Recently we were told by a chart services customer that she orders the report for each of her adult clients. "It's a very good natal report," she told us, and added, "We don't change that much!"
(approx. 20 pages). **AB5 $26.95**

Your Magical Child Art Options

Personalized pictures and charts include a little poem about the zodiac character. Available as print only, or in art mat, as shown. Print only 8-1/2 x 11. Matted art is 11"x14". All twelve pictures and charts can be seen on *www.astrocom.com*. Charts include a 2nd page listing of the planets in signs, houses & aspects.

Notecards can be ordered as one sign individually or in boxed sets of 12, or boxes can be one of each sign.

Your Magical Child Art Chart
based on date, time & place.**. . $9.95**
Chart or picture , matted . . $25.95

Your Magical Child notecards
One card, ... **MCC $3.50**

YMC notecard set (1 of each sign, or all 12 of one sign (state sign number). **$25.00**

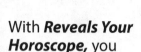

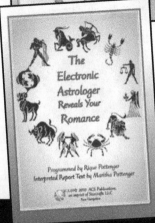

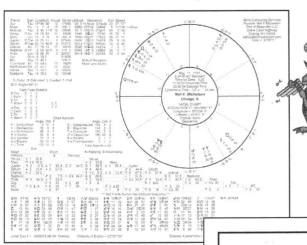

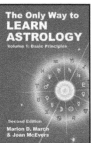

CPSIA information can be obtained
at www.ICGtesting.com
Printed in the USA
BVHW091740190919
558908BV00004B/19/P